Lavender Culture

Also edited by Karla Jay and Allen Young and published by New York University Press

OUT OF THE CLOSETS: VOICES OF GAY LIBERATION

Lavender Culture

Edited and with New Introductions by
KARLA JAY and ALLEN YOUNG

Foreword by
CINDY PATTON

NEW YORK UNIVERSITY PRESS
New York and London

NEW YORK UNIVERSITY PRESS
New York and London

Library of Congress Cataloging-in-Publication Data
Lavender culture / edited and with new introductions by Karla Jay and
Allen Young : foreword by Cindy Patton.
p.   cm.
Originally published: 1979.
Includes bibliographical references.
ISBN 0-8147-4216-5 (cloth : acid-free paper) : — ISBN
0-8147-4217-4216-5 (pbk. : acid-free paper) :
1. Homosexuality.   2. Gay liberation movement.   3. Gays in popular
culture—History—20th century.   I. Jay, Karla.   II. Young, Allen,
1941–   .
HQ76.25.L38   1994
305.9'0664—dc20   94-25988
                                   CIP

New York University Press books are printed on acid-free paper, and their
binding materials are chosen for strength and durability.

Manufactured in the United States of America

10 9 8 7 6 5 4 3 2 1

Contents

PART ELEVEN: CHANGES AND VISIONS

Foreword to the New Edition

Cindy Patton

What luck to direct attention to the republication of a senti-
nel book of essays from "gay culture"! Though I am not
quite a "gay elder" (as the book goes to press I am still shy
of forty), I approach the book from the standpoint of an
activist and, now, academic, who has witnessed and participated in several cycles of queer reinvention in a rapidly
changing political context. I must admit to a certain amount
of glee at having the last word . . . here—for now.

The republication of a fifteen-year-old collection of essays begs several questions: not only why this book and
why now, but perhaps more, how does republication exemplify and complicate the story of gay and lesbian movement
as a passage from silence and invisibility to boisterous publicity? And, how will these proudly queer voices—some of
the first available to the mass reading American audience—
sound *now?* How will *Lavender Culture* be situated historically, displaced as it is from the present by a decade so
opulently and poignantly *about* queer publicity? Popular
media accounts of people living with AIDS; ads and articles
featuring lipstick lesbians and ACT UP fashion plates; the
national marches on Washington; (and stranger yet) Larry
King Live debates about gays in the military; Queer Nation
assaults on Arsenio Hall; queer theory's assault on the halls
of the academy.

Why Now?

The obvious answer is that the twenty-fifth anniversary of
Stonewall (1969–1994) will spark an expanded interest in
lesbians' and gay men's trajectory to our present visibility.
Paradoxically, this will make some people wonder what's
the big deal while prompting others to redouble their efforts
to quash the love that once dared not speak its name.

But there is a more complex reason "why now" that will significantly affect *who* reads this new edition. The republication of *Lavender Culture* as an "academic book" means that the new edition will probably not be read by the same range of people, and those who read it before will not be reached from the same place. (We, in turn, are ourselves in different places, which is in part why a book once published as a pocket paperback can come back to life in academic drag.)

In the last five years, half a dozen academic presses have inaugurated series on sexuality, queer theory, and lesbian and gay studies, a recognition both of the interests of the lesbian and gay lay readership and of the legitimacy of the newly emerged "queer theory" and lesbian and gay studies. The first schedule of publishing included dozens of books from a range of disciplines informing us about our past and keeping our heads spinning with up-to-the-nanosecond developments in critical, psychoanalytic, and postmodern versions of queer theory. A crucial issue for historians became how to uncover and interpret a past that neither named itself as we do now, nor was able to leave a clearly legible trail. The key issue for theorists became the *status* of identity, most recently, its "performative" dimension [1]— ironically enough the sort of gesture on which the assertion of "lavender culture" failed to make good. ("Lavender is a color that has been associated with homosexuals for many decades. The color is implicitly androgynous, a combination of the male principle [blue] and the female principle [pink] which society has sanctified in its segregationist choice of baby blankets," proclaims Allen Young in his introduction, "No Longer the Court Jesters.")

It is perhaps no surprise that the second round of publishing should include reissue of historically significant works, not from hidden queer forebears "outed" in round one, but from the generation of articulate liberationist theorists who were the first homosexuals to gain a national public voice *as* a political minority.[2] Republished, these books will almost inevitably be read against the backdrop of myths about 1970s gay and lesbian culture. Our present reading should challenge our ideas about our recent past and help us reconsider the thinking that got us here. How did we posit ourselves and criticize the world in which we live before *queer* theorists won a tiny space for themselves among the Purveyors of Official Ideas?

Then and Now

Readers will be struck by how different things were *then*. A number of essays address topics which today would be presented radically differently or not at all. Several essays—now poignant monuments to the optimism engendered by the rescue of our bodies from the crushing dissociation of closet life—wax eloquent about the democratizing and antiromanticizing effects of bathhouses and back-room bars. The essays *by* gay youth remind us that we now hear more *about* suicide and the refusal to practice safe sex by teenagers than we hear life stories and political perspectives *from* them. And, the essays on aging are painful to read: our stultifying experience of deaths due to HIV-related illnesses and our growing awareness of the degree to which breast cancer affects lesbians make getting to be old a romantic challenge.

The whole concept of culture, invoked in the collection's title and developed through the essays, now operates differently. James M. Saslow contributes a detailed, liberationist essay on the subtle ways in which homosexuality and gay artists are closed out of High Culture ("Closets in the Museum: Homophobia and Art History"). In the NEA cases we had firsthand experience of much more blatant censorship of high art and its experimental kin. And the schizophrenia of gay artists introjecting queer themes into their work has changed in the context of AIDS. Gossip columns in major magazines and newspapers are virtual necrologies of gay artists; the art world now embraces its gay members, but sometimes only if they are romantically perched on their deathbed (nothing sells like the work of a dead artist). But to their credit, galleries and museums across the nation have also asked patrons to contemplate a world without art, a world of visions and dreams whose vitality has been seriously diminished by loss of life and by the perpetual depression that descends on those who cared for the sick.

The sheer body count of artists, designers, and actors sick or dead from AIDS-related illnesses has served as tragic proof of gay men's centrality to the production of High Culture.

AIDS activism produced another kind of art—closer to the notions of countercultural art proposed in the present volume, only more stridently political and desperately interventionist. The idea of developing an autonomous culture seems like a luxury now: art is best used to raise funds or consciousness. Rage and community defense fill the space occupied by exuberance and community exploration in the 1970s.

AIDS activism and its complex relationship to the gay community agencies that provide services have challenged the possibilities of cultural separatism and "androgyny" proposed by the writers here. The actual government and its medical and policy arms now seem to press down on us more immediately than the abstract ideology of heterosexism. An alternative culture is too close to official attempts to turf responsibility for care and support off onto communities that can already barely survive on their own. And there is a difficult gender asymmetry: lesbian AIDS activists are deeply affected by AIDS backlash but partially disenfranchised from directing activist politics because they aren't perceived to be affected closely enough.

The Road Not Taken

Lavender Culture sits at a crossroad, published as it was at a time when the civil rights strategy was not clearly successful; when it seemed possible to create a counterculture; when it was presumed that those in positions of power would "come out," not as a result of disclosure of their HIV serostatus or of retaliatory "outing" but voluntarily, because liberation demanded it of everyone. The myriad essays here remind us what it was like to think queer lives before a politics of marginality and a politics of publicity came into a collision course as a result of conflicting ideologies—of AIDS service provision and AIDS activism, of queer militancy, of a partially mainstreamed lesbian and gay civil rights effort. While not "queer" in the way of

xii

the recent Nation, "lavender culture" suggests both that queerness is central to the "culture" of the dominant society, but also that the possibilities for knowing this legacy are constrained by homophobia.

It would be too easy to read these voices as a half-way point between the supposed inaugural moment (Stonewall) of a new movement and the rupture of identity politics into postmodern queerdom. For example, David Holland ("The Politics of Dress") establishes the historical restrictions on and social meaning of dress on his way to dissecting the debates about "political drag" or "gender-fuck" that ensued after the Fort Hill Faggots for Freedom zapped the dress code of one of Boston's most "masculine" bars by going in drag. For the polymorphously perverse and newly feminist gay liberationists, the gender politics of dress seemed revolutionary, something to plan an entire action around. For the '90s queer nationalist, assuming confrontational attire is part of getting up in the morning.

But instead of simply marking the changes of a decade and a half, I hope readers will measure the distance of the term "culture" from both the temporal story of a riot and its results and from the assertion of a hyper-territorial Queer Nation. How and why does "culture" now mean and work differently?

I admit to trying to protect *Lavender Culture* from two strategic misreadings, one which views these writings as "authentic voices" of "essential" identity, and another which sees them only as evidence for the historical specificity of queernesses. Instead I suggest readers accept the challenge of imagining a double culture (a High Culture we have queered and an alternative culture we have created) as a way to think and be queer *now*.[3]

After a decade of academic research and fragmenting politics, we are more sanguine about the absolute value of narrativizing gay and lesbian experience. There is a tension between two ways of telling "our" story. One presses a broad claim about the pervasiveness and continuity of homosexual *culture*, while the other privileges lesbian and gay *politics* but relies completely on the meta-narratives of liberation's forward march or of liberal pluralism's capacity to muddle through.

Lesbian and gay life in the twentieth century has been marked by a war of categories: bodies that don't fit, identities that don't work. Our most intimate experiences are constantly available to the tyranny of discursive categories ("labels")—both our opponents' and our own. We feel deeply scarred by being placed under the regime of "pervert," "ego-dystonic sexuality," "queer body-to-be-ridiculed-or-bashed." But in order to say these categories don't fit, we have had first to fit ourselves into the political spaces that are the only place of legitimate speech, the only platform for queer publicity: we became a visible minority with proud, healthy, *lesbian and gay* identities. In order to make our queer bodies relatively safe, we have had to make ourselves targets (of the NEA, of right-wing politicians, of epidemiologists, of murderers) or insinuate ourselves in the very spots where dominant culture was most contradictory and queer, but has most denied that we had *always been* the ground zero of America's aesthetic (and political?[4]) sensibility.

The ironic collision of our politics and our culture is nowhere more evident than in the folklore surrounding our political genesis. The catalytic event, in the story of our political emergence that we now blithely tell, was a 1969 riot at a little bar in Greenwich Village. There, after millennia of oppression, a group of men and women (peopled by the *most* postmodern cast—Latinos, drag queens, butch dykes, hippies, depending on who's telling the story) refused to subject themselves to another evening of police harassment. This account, which I am parodying even while I am deeply moved by each variable retelling, suggests that the forms of political and cultural labor that followed were somehow natural outcomes of a more or less homogeneous, inchoate, and unspoken—dare I say prediscursive?—oppression.

Here, Stonewall divides a timeless time of oppression from the entry into the Time of History. *Before 1969:* we could only chafe and give up our fullest possibilities. *After 1969:* we could say who we are and in the unifying power of our speech, fight back. Occurring at the height of the liberationist paradigm but in the context of stabilizing civil rights structures, the riot provided the "real" event necessary to claim our first break into history's eye. There would be no retreat, no "going back into the closet." Ironically, this ragtag conflict with the police over the occupation of a bar produced civil rights activism as *the* form of publicity. But tensions persist: each year at the Boston Lesbian and Gay Pride March (never, *never* a parade), a small band of chanters could always be heard to reply to the question "what do we want?" not "Gay Rights!" but "Gay riots!"

The liberationist model informed the 1960s and 1970s concept of culture—in fact, proposed an idea of culture that may have been at odds with the lived experience of at least some of those who thought of themselves as queer. The articulate critiques of colonialism abroad and segregation of African Americans and ethnic minorities in the United States influenced the analysis of lesbian and gay men's plight. The ideas of two writers especially popular among liberationists—Franz Fanon and James Baldwin—echo in the comparisons used to support arguments in favor of developing autonomous, gay and lesbian controlled spaces:

This is our inheritance. This is where we begin: as a people neatly divided by entrepreneur-and-clientele roles fulfilling the patriarchal need for sexual segregation. We are remaindered at birth, fenced off into profitable ghettos. We are weakened by alcoholism and exploited economically. Our music, once mass produced for heterosexual audiences, is now chic. Gay bar-hopping, for straights, is fashionable. . . .

Inside we never ask: who decided on a *bar* anyway? Such a question, which seems silly here, would necessitate choices.

The refusal of politically astute gay men and women to ask this question is analogous to the self-effacing acceptance of a foreign culture by a colonialized people. And as dangerous. [Felice Newman, "Why I'm Not Dancing," 144–45]

While the colonial analogy may seem overdrawn, readers might contemplate the difference it makes to conceive queers as a "nation" intrinsic to rather than a colony under the regime of a still-heterosexist (or, as Michael Warner recently put it, "heteronormative") America that would still rather kill queers than grant us meaningful citizenship.

"Lavender culture" fuses an anthropological idea of culture with a political idea of culture. Anthropology lent credence to the idea that "minority" values and norms held by a group could form the basis of a subculture, an idea very appealing to those who wanted to parallel the successes of the 1960s black culture movement, with its more obvious claim to possession of this kind of "culture." Indeed, Jon L. Clayborne, one of the few black contributors to the volume, quietly voices concern with the growing conflict between African American politics and those of other social movements, a conflict that in part stemmed from narrowing the broad, transnational idea of culture that underwrote the unifying movement of "Third World" people to a subnational idea of minority countercultures. (See "Blacks and Gay Liberation.")

Though cognizant of global problems, liberationist theory as used by gay liberationists was anchored by a variety of Marxisms (straight Herbert Marcuse and theory pervert Wilhelm Reich make cameo appearances—Foucault and Hocquenham, whose works were only just becoming available in English, had yet to be anointed Theory Queens). The primary focus was on ways that Dominant (U.S.) Culture was the source of homosexual's false consciousness. *Counterculture,* especially political art (which, for example, viewed drag as an intrinsic challenge to sexism—*gender-fuck,* not sexist imitation), was an expression of and a means to promote revolutionary consciousness. But the final resting point still seemed far away:

So, despite these uplifting victories we have experienced recently for which we all can be grateful, we have become *more* a part of our original culture than we ever were because in seeking tolerance and acceptance from a group of anything we are really stating our desire to become one with that group. When any minority fights for recognition, the next logical step is absorption into the mainstream of that group—not a reconstruction of a

xvi

new culture. . . . Until we can honestly realize that we must dispense with the unrewarding values of a particular culture and not join it to reinforce its status quo— only then will we be able to transcend that society and create a new culture based upon the values we claim will make it a uniquely "gay" culture. [Rose Jordan, "A Question of Culture: Mirror Without Image," 451]

"Lavender Culture" attempts to weld these two ideas of culture together, suggesting both that an invading queerness is what makes mainstream culture Culture, and that the really *important* ("political") culture is the alternative one being forged under the sign of gay liberation. A "lavender culture" seemed (even to the essayists) impossible in part because of historical differences between men's and women's access to High Culture but also because of economic differences in their ability to finance an alternative one. If there were plenty of gay men poised to come out from within the dominant culture, women—lesbian or not—were excluded precisely under threat of being labeled gender-inappropriate. Class presented even more complications—working-class men might have had a better shot at queering the audience of the opera than they had at producing new ones of their own. And lesbians and gay men of color had a clearer claim on culture of the first sort through their membership in communities that were at the time often hostile to the same dominant culture which some white gay men were claiming to have queerified.

Pressing the Liberationist Claim: Identity As Cultural Development

From our late twentieth-century vantage point we can now see that there are and have been many homosexualities, a reeling matrix of class, gender (including butch, fem, sissy, clone), race, ethnicity, geographic locale which created possibilities and imposed prohibitions. A relatively small number of these now assert a commonality through "coming out," an act that takes on meaning only in the larger context which relates a *single* declaration to ever larger acts of individual and collective courage grounded by the monumental events of that hot New York summer in 1969. In this small group there are quite different and equally important relations to the nearly twenty-five-year-old narrative of fighting back:

1. Those who forged a queer life and politics before 1969—before the notion of "coming out"—and saw that life and politics mutate before their eyes;
2. Those who "came out" in the years just before and after 1969, and for whom the events of 1969 were "real," if occurring contemporaneously in another location;
3. Those who grew up in a context in which the "coming out" they experience was naturalized as the reality of "gay experience," and for whom "Stonewall" is largely a historical event, indeed, for many an event that occurred as much as a decade before they were born.

If we tell our story developmentally, we argue that successive waves of homosexual organizing made significant and cumulative gains. For example, efforts through the 1950s to emphasize the ordinariness and decency of homosexual citizens paved the way for removing homosexuality per se from lists of psychiatric pathologies in the 1970s. This, in turn, made possible openly gay and lesbian therapists with the research and clinical experience to theorize gay and lesbian identity and mental health. We could describe similar and coordinated strategies lodged at the legal system: efforts to decriminalize homosexual behavior by emphasizing its similarity (especially as "love") to heterosexual behavior made the enforcement of sodomy laws unusual.

Simultaneous with these moves to depathologize and legalize the individual homosexual were efforts to propose a common identity as a source of unity among homosexuals. There had been lobbying and social groups through the 1950s; the trick was to invent homosexual collectivities without making them seem to prove the House Committee on Un-American Activities' contention that homosexuals were an organized and treasonous force.

The emerging rhetoric of the black civil rights movement, with its concept of minority, provided an excellent device for activist homosexuals. By claiming to have always-been-here, increasingly organized homosexuals could collectively state their presence without appearing to have been hiding for the purposes of overthrowing society. The particular notion of community that emerged insisted that homosexuals had hidden in order to prevent persecution, not in order to avoid detection: we would happily claim our place if only we could be protected from violence. Thus, for example, articulating homosexuals (and gay men in particular) as a once invisible group of crime *victims* enabled the promotion of liaisons between city police and the "gay and lesbian community" and, in some places, made it possible to advocate for hiring gay and lesbian police officers as an affirmative action stance.

Once in place, this idea of gays and lesbians as a minority community with specific identities resulted in many professions and some areas of organized labor making headway toward protecting lesbians and gay men or making overt forms of harassment unacceptable. As lesbians and gay men became more acceptable as workers, *as citizens,* their acceptability as religious participants was less assured. While homosexuality lost its patina of immorality in the most liberal Protestant denominations, religious society more generally did not parallel secular society's modest accommodation to a homosexual minority, now begrudgingly depathologized and largely decriminalized. This failure to make inroads within the traditionally conservative (and largest) of the Protestant denominations was in part due to the emergence of a new right specifically opposed to the gay rights movement. Equally important, while the community rhetoric used by gay rights activists proved convincing when claiming minority status, it proved implausible, even an affront, in the face of traditional Protestant conceptions of religion as the community of Christ. Oddly enough, a conservative evangelical gay Christian group emerged (Metropolitan Community Church), and the most liberal denominations voted to include and embrace its gay and lesbian members (and sometimes ministers).

If from one view, achieving political power appears as a liberatory developmental process, from another the same events seem to be utter paradoxes: what do these people have in common? In order to achieve visibility in the 1950s, lesbians and gay men held pickets in which they dressed and groomed to look respectable. They avoided touching in public and asserted their citizenship, their *Americanness* more than their sexuality. In the 1990s, gay and lesbian visibility is achieved through Queer Nation shopping trips in which young people with weird haircuts invade the shopping malls of America, and stage kiss-ins which would be broadcast as "news" into the cozy little rumpus rooms of middle America.

If Foucault was right, the nineteenth century saw a massive buildup of institutions linked to and through discursive formations that set about codifying, surveilling, policing, and pathologizing what must have once been an extraordinarily diverse world of bodily and emotional affiliations: the description of twentieth-century resistance to those emerging categories must be one of tremendous ambivalence and contention. The procedures which consolidated a once fractious and mutually unrecognizable "us" into the category "homosexual" must have been very complex indeed. In some sense, the history of twentieth-century gay *politics* has been one of continually refiguring legal, psychiatric, and religious categories to normalize ourselves; lesbian and gay *culture* helped retain our difference to insure the continuation of the sensibility forged while chaffing against the categories.

Here, lesbian and gay life and politics is just one among a larger set of post-World War II movements organized around a new concept of minority that appears to be characterized by a set of paradoxes stemming from "visibility." The rise of mass media created an "imagined" community as a site of identity construction and debate over strategy. Ambiguity about relations between citizens and the state diminished possibilities for state campaigns to rally people around a "national identity." Techniques of social control emerged involving medical and biological intervention, often under the guise of "public health" and "social welfare." "Identity" was made possible by technologies of visibility and a political analysis of displacement and marginality.

As movements unable to enlist the power of the state (as modern representative democracy and socialist democracy suggested would be possible), the identity movements are largely reliant on rhetorical intervention into discursive practices. But in their very achievement of publicity *in* speech, the movements also produced a new form of oppression *through* speech. In "speaking," collective action becomes possible, but also in "speaking" individuals and groups come under new forms of welfare/health control.

Hate crimes legislation, for example, is painfully ironic. In order to arrest the violence against us, we have to further consolidate a definition of "gay persons," exacerbating the category tensions which may underlie the psychology that results in antigay violence to begin with.

Attempts to produce a gay and lesbian press have resulted in much greater and more effective communication among local, national, and international political efforts. The existence of an international lesbian and gay press provided crucial information and networks of resistance during the first five years of the AIDS crisis when there was a virtual mainstream media blackout.

In the midst of the AIDS crisis, we know that silence equals death, but our speech seems always to be used against us: as epidemiologic data, as fodder for the right wing. Jesse Helms and his friends read our intracommunity speech into the public record—the culturally sensitive Gay Men's Health Crisis pamphlets, or the arch *GCN* queer revenge fantasy, "The Homoerotic Order"—and successfully curtailed the means of producing the speech, which is now most essential in order to save lives.[5]

The Public Story and the Private Life

Both the developmental tale and the story of political paradoxes push the idea and resistant possibilities of "culture" aside, perhaps because its very schizophrenia continually questions each. Most importantly, the emphasis on public politics enables the construction of a powerful history or a critical assessment of our gains and losses, but it does not tell us about the aesthetic life of queers . . . not so much how we make *art,* but how we *make do* in a system that promotes some same-sex affiliations only to crush the bodies that inhabited those roles with, well, perhaps a little too much desire (two ballerinas en pointe, but never male dancers; male athletes grabbing each other's butts, but never more; women pursuing intense friendship, but "butches" mistakenly queering the sisterly bond).

Both the developmental narrative and the narrative of paradoxes flatten out the myriad ways in which people invent their gender and sexuality, invent their racial and ethnic affiliations. Dependent on the emergence of a unified homosexual consciousness, liberated from oppression, the developmental tale fails to understand the complex ways in which self-constructions of gender invent "differences" within the sameness of an apparently "homo" sexual culture. Insistent on the perpetual Catch-22 of proposing identity, the paradox narrative refuses to accept that in some places, at some times, queer bonds have been accepted, even sought after.

"Perceptive Voices"

The essays in *Lavender Culture* move between rage at the refusal to accommodate homosexualities and arch demonstrations of the ways that queerness has been able to survive. Unifying these two different kinds of criticism are particular assumptions about voice and audience. From the first glance at the original 1979 Jove pocket paperback (copyright 1978), with its black cover and strong type over a swatch of, not lavender, but pastel pink and green, the reader is encouraged to hear a special *type* of voice. The authenticity of these voices, and the authority that this authenticity is meant to convey, is doubly marked on the cover, first by the description of the editors, "Karla Jay and Allen Young, *authors of The Gay Report,*" and then by the notice that the book contains "the perceptive voices of outspoken lesbians and gay men." And consider the back cover copy written by the publisher:

Voices of Gay Culture

This is one of the first books to explore in-depth lesbian and gay creativity—language, literature, theater, graphic arts, poetry, dance, music.

It contains a wide-ranging collection of articles about the way people live: sex, bars, baths, clothing, the politics of sado-masochism, the gay male and lesbian movements, economics, aging and race.

The reader is offered a candor and comprehensiveness that make this the most fearless and far-reaching portrait of lesbian and gay male culture written to date.

The book is set in a particular genre of political speech premised on the idea of a break from silence or from false consciousness: to "speak out," to articulate experience under the conviction that "the personal is political." This genre demands that politics (or "praxis") be grounded first and foremost in the authentic voices of movement members. "Outing" had not yet been invented, but the refusal to speak what one knew—as interpreted by gay liberationists, to "come out"—was to abdicate political responsibility. The publicity of "authentic" speech was designed both to bring the marginal into the mainstream *and* to answer the mainstream's question, "What do they want?" Making ourselves heard and understood seemed easier in those first post-Stonewall days. We were just about to experience the outrage of having our first national march on Washington completely ignored by the major American media. "Read My Lips" had not been said . . . or appropriated to make T-shirt images of kissing queers.

Although many of the essays here are personal—indeed, written in the first person—they are not coming-out stories. (Rita Mae Brown's tale of going to the baths as a clone is an excellent antidote to the omnipresent apologies for the sex world of the 1970s, and Andrew Kopkind's stories of gay life in the barracks give the most sublime lie to the capacities of the don't-ask-don't-tell plan for queering the military.) Nevertheless, the voices are self-assured (nu?! we're queer!) and invoke gay and lesbian consciousness as the criterion for evaluating formal and informal culture. The essays are not a jubilant celebration: bar culture is at once a powerful preliberationists' underground subculture and an impediment to the formation of a liberated community of people across race, class, and gender. Taken at their "word," instead of in the context of the liberationist genre that underwrites their critical strategy, these essays would be easy to read as "authentic voices" and to use them as evidence either for arguments in favor of an essential sensibility or as examples of the poverty and self-delusion of essentializing identities.

But both of these readings would mistake the liberationist style for an unselfcriticalness that would underestimate gay liberation theory and would preempt the kind of aggressive reading that enables "lavender culture" to be a voice in the present. While reliant on a liberationist notion of consciousness/false consciousness, the "voice" of "lavender culture" is split, in one moment blasting the closets of High Culture and in the next staking out new ground for a utopian "lavender" community. *Lavender Culture* tries to resolve these two voices by arguing that it is not so much that in our creative impulses lesbians and gay men want the images and forms that the mainstream wants, but that the truth that we produced this culture is obliterated by discriminatory attitudes and laws. "Lavender culture" *is,* though in a deeply coded way, what the mainstream *wants.*

Reading around the contradictions about the form and history of a proposed "lavender culture," the essays as a whole suggest many ways of living in, around, and underneath a deeply queer but homo-annihilating culture. Read even more aggressively, interpreted against the right-wing assaults on the academy generally and the derision aimed toward gender and queer theory particularly, *Lavender Culture* provides a perverse suggestion about collaborative possibilities for simultaneously *being* mainstream culture and for creating an alternative to it, demanding our centrality while at the same time building a bivouac out of our widely divergent set of claims, aims, and experiences.

Readerly Orientation

But while the crisp, clear, *queer* voices are so close that they are all but "in our face," it is difficult to define *our* place as audience. In 1979 there was a presumption about "identification" that holds only partially and only with an overlay of nostalgia and utopianism today. At first, gay and lesbian books were published in tiny print runs by gay- and lesbian-supportive presses, and sometimes beleaguered gay or lesbian presses. These books presumed a kind of intimacy between writers and audience, lending credence to the idea that lesbians and gay men would be empowered by reading voices that were "authentic" and much like "our own"—quite a different experience than reading the elegant and complex theory and critical essays of queer theorists, whose queer prose stylistics and insights we admire, but who don't sound at all like the quotidian "us."

Given the small number of "out" gay and lesbian people, this early incursion into mass publishing meant that buyers would have included—indeed, may have been dominated by—prurient "straight" readers. But gay liberation theory of the time held that everyone was at least sexually polymorphous,[6] if not *actively* pansexual, so publication by a mass-market paperback publisher might have been seen as part of a recruitment plan.

Today, it is difficult to place ourselves as readers, not only because of our studied cynicism about the unity of our own gay or lesbian identity, but also because mainstream culture has already been queered by us: Liberace, certainly, but also "voguing"; the adoption by male country and western singers of k.d. lang's butch-pastiche of male country and western singers; Pee Wee Herman's playhouse and its transformation into the pee-pee-peep show; Cindy Crawford and Richard Gere's marriage (not).

Some find little value playing their exclusion. The strategy of positing our cultural marginality is now in hot contention with blatant displays of queerification. Pride marches suggested we were arriving from some distant place. "In your face" means that when straight people arrive they are forced to discover that we were already here. Like Queer Nation slogans, the "we" Lavender Culture proposes is sometimes difficult to decode precisely because both assert their own centrality to dominant culture. They propose another kind of writing, not the kind based on promoting visibility and understanding that sharpens the distinction between a minority to be understood (and self-understood) by a majority, but a *double* writing that places the "Other" not as a "hidden population," but as the very ground zero of a dominant culture that prefers not to register its own queerness.

Reading Forward

Two decades of superb historical works on the history of gay and lesbian political efforts in the twentieth century make any tale of Stonewall as the originary moment of gay political coming-out seem naively self-aggrandizing. We think we have just realized the complexity of queerness and its statement. We think we needed queer theory and queer nation to discover it. But the essays in *Lavender Culture* suggest that the tension between our need to invent ourselves and our need to express ourselves is not what have impeded queer thought, but what queer thought *is*.

Notes

1. In general, performativity means that some speech is less content than it is action in a particular context. Speech content doesn't express or describe a state of being. The act of speech itself brings something into being. Thus, in the contemporary context, such an argument suggests, statements of lesbian and gay identity ("coming out" publicly) *makes* rather than *represents* lesbian and gay people.
2. Of course, there was significant and publicly acknowledged homosexual activism at least since the early twentieth century,

but these efforts—though arguably crucial to later developments—were not reported extensively or nationally in the mainstream media, and there was not yet an extensive and publicly available lesbian and gay press, as emerged after Stonewall. Thus, to claim that the writers in the 1970s were the first to achieve a national voice is not to deny the activism that preceded them but to take seriously the role of the mainstream and mass-distributed media in community formation and in posing political issues.

3. I am invoking recent debates about "social construction" versus "essentialism," and the tendency to associate academic work with the former and activism with the latter. This way of describing a current set of impasses in gay and lesbian politics is both unuseful and inaccurate—as many of our lives attest. Lisa Duggan's excellent "Making It Perfectly Queer" (1992) describes and criticizes the way in which this association arose and notes the mutual dependence and paradoxical relation of activism and queer theory. Queer activism—which opposes the presumed "essentialism" of "gay and lesbian" identities—and queer theory, which could arise in the academy at all because of bitter battles fought by hopelessly out "lesbians and gay men," both rely on the gains of the "essentialist" politics and themselves belie the distinction between theory and politics.

4. Henry Abelove's "From Thoreau to Queer Politics" (1993) makes the compelling argument that there is a very American mode of political contemplation and populist education that has always been and been seen as "queer."

5. This was truly a surreal moment: it was not *us* making public declarations of our political position, but various senators reading gay and lesbian newspapers and safe sex literature into the public record in support of their contentions about the perversion of our lives. This public record of our words from the mouths of Jesse Helms and company (literally, their lips reading our words) would result in the ongoing prohibition against federally funded AIDS-prevention programs "promoting homosexuality or promiscuity."

6. If bisexuality goes largely unproposed in this volume it is probably because in the 1970s few people had yet had the opportunity to live in urban ghettos that were thoroughly and monosexually lesbian or gay. If my memory serves me, bisexuality was seen as a temporal fact of an individual's history (a closed chapter, hoped many—practitioners and their nervous partners alike). Though some celebrated active bisexuality,

most people viewed bisexuality as a stage prior to full commitment—"fence-sitting"—and did not envision it as a "life-style"
to be supported with clubs, political groups, and media resources of its own.

Bibliography

Abelove, Henry. 1993. "From Thoreau to Queer Politics," *Yale
Journal of Criticism,* vol. 6, no. 2.
Duggan, Lisa. 1992. "Making It Perfectly Queer," *Socialist Re-
view* (Spring 1992).
Warner, Michael. 1993. "Introduction," in M. Warner, ed., *Fear
of a Queer Planet*. Minneapolis: University of Minnesota
Press.

Introduction to the New Edition

by Karla Jay

We Are Everywhere

When we were collecting the material for inclusion in what became *Lavender Culture,* we proposed to call it *We Are Everywhere,* after a popular gay liberation slogan of the 1970s. The original title is certainly more apt in the 1990s than it was when this book was first published. Although we were invisible for much of history, surely we are not now. In the 1990s, we have become the focus of daily articles in major newspapers around the United States: the subject of gays in the military occupied much of the first year of the Clinton administration and was debated in Congress, and laws supporting or denying gay men and lesbians their civil rights have been hotly debated in several states. Even Jesse Helms got the "L-word" out of his mouth; clearly, lesbianism has emerged on the lips of even the most truly conservative. Though lesbians are historically much more invisible than gay men, a bisexual woman (Nancy) has become a regular character on "Roseanne," and feature stories on aspects of our lives have appeared on "20/20," and in *Newsweek* and *New York Magazine.*

Perhaps we're having our "fifteen minutes of fame," but I think it's more than that. Whereas gay and lesbian culture seemed new and transient in the heady days after the Stonewall uprising, in the 1990s we have become embedded in North American culture. Some of the ways are obvious, but others are less so. In terms of language, for example, most people' have accepted words like "lesbian" and "gay"—terms which routinely appear in major newspapers and phone directories across North America. But it was not always so: activists had to struggle in communities all across the continent to have us designated as anything other than "homosexuals" or "perverts." Terms originating in gay and lesbian slang, such as "out of the closet," "drag queen," "butch," "femme," and "closet" used as an adjective (as in, "she's a closet intellectual" or a "closet athlete") are routinely used by many nongay people.

Lesbians and Mainstream Culture

The mainstreaming of gay culture has most often meant "white gay male" culture, but the publishing world is an important exception where lesbians thrive. Lesbian novelists, such as Dorothy Allison, Blanche Boyd, Rita Mae Brown, Sarah Schulman, Jane DeLynn, Jennifer Levin, Carol Anshaw, and Jeanette Winterson are all published by major commercial presses. Poets like Adrienne Rich, Audre Lorde, and Marilyn Hacker are widely anthologized and nationally recognized. Lesbian nonfiction is prolific with every genre represented, from biographies to self-help, psychology, and parenting guides.

As I pointed out in an essay in *Ms Magazine* (July–August 1993), even this area has its limitations, with success in fiction primarily limited to white lesbians who write about "universal topics." Works by and about lesbians of color, experimental writing, and genre fiction (such as mysteries and romances) have been overlooked by large trade publishers.

Access to mainstream culture has been far more circumscribed in other areas because of two major factors. First, as I pointed out in my original introduction to *Lavender Culture,* entitled "No Man's Land," lesbians still lack the economic clout to produce some of the more expensive media such as films and Broadway plays. At a 1993 New York gay and lesbian film festival, there was no full-length feature film by an American woman. Most of the lesbian entries were short subjects that often lack top-notch production values and expertise. A mainstream film such as *Desert Hearts,* based on Jane Rule's *Desert of the Heart,* was many years in the making, primarily because it took so long for director Donna Deitch to raise funds. Most of the films about lesbians are made by men. They often erase lesbianism as in *Fried Green Tomatoes,* where Ruth and Idgie can be read by most viewers as "good friends," despite the semiotic clues of Idgie's Annie Hall-like attire of men's vests and ties. The erotic possibilities are downplayed by a lack of any overt physical affection and by the conflation of the novel's married Ninny with the rebel Idgie into one character at the end of the film. Conversely, lesbian eroticism in Hollywood films like *Personal Best* and *Lianna* can still be portrayed on the screen more openly than gay male sexuality because the former is still considered titillating for straight men. (Would the respected leftist John Sayles do a gay male movie as steamy as his lesbian *Lianna?* It seems unlikely.) The television movie *Portrait of a Marriage* had not only overt lesbian sexual scenes but also embroidered upon the Nigel Nicolson book on which it was based by having Vita Sackville-West rape Violet Trefusis on the latter's wedding night, despite the total improbability of such an occurrence. Harold Nicolson's homosexuality was portrayed even more negatively, especially when he announced it in conjunction with a case of venereal disease. Both *Desert Hearts* and *Claire of the Moon* contained steamy sexual scenes, whereas the American cut of the television movie *The Lost Language of Cranes* (based on the novel by David Leavitt) was a pants-on affair.

Unfortunately, lesbians are still frequently portrayed in movies and television as villains (for instance, the murderous sociopath in *Basic Instinct*), losers (Connie in *Three of Hearts,* who hired a male gigolo to get her lesbian lover back, but Joe fell for her ex-lover, too), oddities on talk shows (lesbian mothers who are frowned upon by society, as represented by the studio audience), or as social problems (for example, parents trying to deal with a daughter's possible lesbianism on "Picket Fences," which is resolved by the discovery that daughter was heterosexual all along). Shows like "Roseanne," on which the neighbor Nancy happens to be a bisexual, are still the exception. Nor do we have any exclusively lesbian shows outside of public-access stations and a "Dyke TV" on cable. (The lesbian soap opera "Two in Twenty" collapsed after a few episodes.)

When *Lavender Culture* was published in 1979,[1] AIDS had already infected many gay men, though it had not yet impacted on those who create culture or on the conscience of many caring people around the world. Now AIDS is a daily topic in many newspapers and on television news broadcasts, and one would be hard-pressed to find a gay male novel or play with a contemporary setting that does not contain a character with AIDS. Because AIDS has killed so many artists, writers, musicians, and fashion designers, it has made gay men—and then the absence of them—unmistakably obvious. The tragedy of AIDS (and it is the *major* cultural disaster in North America in this century) has given gay male art a unifying focus, though I'll leave it to the critics of the next centuries to decide whether any of it has the magnitude of works that emerged from other calamities, such as Boccaccio's *Decameron,* which was written in the wake of the bubonic plague.

Lesbians have responded to AIDS on a personal level. Many of us have loved men who have died of AIDS. We have taken care of those with AIDS, brought food to the homebound, visited those in the hospitals or hospices, walked their dogs, fed their cats, and mourned at their funerals. With the possible exception of some lesbian separatists, there are few lesbians who do not know someone who has died of AIDS. In my own case, I would estimate that at least half of the gay men I've known are dead.

AIDS, particularly as it affects affluent white gay males, has provided a thematic unity for the cultural production of gay male artists, but there has been no parallel opportunity for lesbian artists to move what are lesbian issues to the same kind of general audience that has tried to comprehend AIDS. For example, whereas several plays with AIDS themes (most notably *Angels in America* by Tony Kushner) have had Broadway productions, no play by a lesbian about any aspect of our lives has received a major production.

Equally interesting is the relatively small role AIDS plays in many aspects of lesbian culture. Characters with AIDS are included in just a few lesbian novels, including *Memory Board* by Jane Rule and *People in Trouble* by Sarah Schulman; most lesbian novels avoid the topic altogether. There are almost no songs by major lesbian recording artists about AIDS.[2] Instead, works by lesbians tend to focus on lesbian relationships, parenting, aging, addiction, recovery, women's illnesses (such as breast cancer), female sexual expression, and sex roles. Lesbians are as likely (or perhaps more likely) to try to deal with racism, anti-Semitism, ageism, militarism, ecofeminism, and spirituality as they are with AIDS. In other words, AIDS has caused many lesbians to live in two different cultural worlds, one of our own making and one of the world at large in which we are still twinned in the public imagination with gay men.

The tragedy of AIDS has made the goal of creating lesbian culture even more difficult than it was when this anthology was first published. Though money has always been scarce for lesbians, much lesbian money now goes to AIDS causes. When lives are at stake and are dramatically presented every day in the media, all else seems of little importance.

Consider, for example, the fact that in the early 1990s there is no national lesbian newspaper or magazine that is the equivalent of *The Advocate* or *The Native*. In 1993 New York City had only a slim freebie called *Sappho's Isle,* no coffeehouses, no crafts store, no art gallery, one sex shop, and one struggling women's bookstore. Consider the fact that it took the Lesbian Herstory Archives in New York years and years to raise several thousand dollars for the down payment on a building to house their collection. Then recall that predominantly gay male organizations— legal, AIDS, scholarly—have raised that amount (and often much more) in one night, and you'll get the picture. The artists we can't support wait tables or spend most of their time at some job or other, often burning out along the way.

Part of the cultural cash crunch comes from our attitudes as women. We have been conditioned to volunteer time, not money. We make less money than men anyway and try to make our discretionary income entertain and nourish us immediately. What has been an economic recession for men has been a depression for many women. But even the richer lesbians I know give to more traditional causes (such as educational institutions and established charities), for like our heterosexual sisters we have been conditioned to put our own needs last. Finally, the men I know who have died of AIDS have endowed primarily AIDS organizations and gay studies programs. One even left $5,000 to each of his writer friends so that they could take a bit of time off to create. Lesbians tend to leave money to their children, their lovers (unlike many gay male couples, in which both have AIDS, few lesbian couples die together), their siblings, their distant cousins, their alma mater.

It's clear that we're not yet a family of women, but until we are, lesbian culture will always totter precariously on the brink of financial disaster.

Lesbian Erotics

On a more positive note, *Lavender Culture* heralded the importance of what we called "culture with a small *c*." In compiling the anthology, Allen and I recognized that true culture—that which makes a people—is more than the fine arts. The cultures or subcultures that lesbians and gay men have created are as much about sex and relationships, rituals, spirituality, socializing, creating alternative families and institutions, as they are about the arts.

Lavender Culture was one of the first forums in which different aspects of sexual culture, including sadomasochism, were discussed. *The Gay Report,* a tome that Allen and I compiled on sexual practices and life-styles, followed shortly thereafter. Both books foreshadowed a preoccupation with lesbian sexuality that would explode in the early 1980s with what some coined the "sex wars."

In the 1970s, many lesbian/feminists had been concerned with "political correctness" or "being PC," which included the condemnation of butch/femme identities, sadomasochism, anonymous sex, pornography, and sometimes either monogamy or relationships, depending on who was castigating whom. But many other lesbians felt that their sexual expression was being as stifled by other lesbians as it had once been by patriarchal laws and values. As a result, by the early 1980s a defiant lesbian sexual culture emerged. Many lesbians reclaimed butch/femme identities as an inherent part of sexuality for them. S/m lesbians proudly sported their leather clothing, and brandished metal and silicone sex paraphernalia. Erotica has become a flourishing media enterprise, including award-winning books like Joan Nestle's *The Persistent Desire,* magazines like *On Our Backs* and *Bad Attitude,* and sex videos made by lesbians for lesbians. Lesbians now have the type of lesbian sex clubs that Rita Mae Brown speculates about in "Queen for a Day: A Stranger in Paradise," where she mused, "Xanadu is not a lurid dream, it's the desire of a woman to have options. Like men we should have choices: deep long-term relationships, the baths, short-term affairs. And those choices are not mutually exclusive" (p. 76). Some lesbian/feminists, however, see the new lesbian sexuality as an erosion of feminist values and as the destruction, rather than the flowering, of lesbian culture.

Lesbian Nations

For many, the lesbian spaces we have been able to carve out on a temporary or permanent basis are also of large cultural significance. Although the National Women's Music Festival is the oldest in the United States, it is the Michigan Women's Music Festival that lights up the eyes of lesbians I have encountered everywhere, including those in Europe who consider it *the* place to visit in the United States. Although these two festivals are not advertised as "lesbian," most agree that we make up the vast majority of attendees. The only startling news is how invisible these festivals remain to the culture at large. When Margot Adler did a piece on the Michigan Festival on National Public Radio in 1992, the governor of the state was apparently surprised that such an event was taking place in his bailiwick. I have to wonder what other week-long gathering of over seven thousand people could possibly go so unnoticed. Some lesbians would argue that invisibility is the best protection, and they were horrified by the national exposure of the Michigan festival and of the Northampton lesbian community on the ABC television magazine "20/20" in 1992 and in a 1993 issue of *Newsweek*.

Offended by the erasure of the lesbian majority at music festivals and in search of lesbian-only space, a group of separatists has set up two lesbian-only festivals, one on the East Coast and the other on the West Coast. Another festival, which takes place annually in Northampton, calls itself "the lesbian festival you can take your father to," and apparently he sometimes does show up. Clearly, essays like Charlotte Bunch's "Learning from Lesbian Separatism" are not about a historical moment in time. Communities of lesbian separatists are living on parcels of land and in cities across North America and England.

Lesbians of various political stripes have also populated formerly gay male enclaves like Provincetown, Massachusetts, and The Pines and Cherry Grove on Fire Island, New York. Once, women were generally made to feel unwelcome in enclaves like Cherry Grove, though, as Esther Newton points out in *Cherry Grove, Fire Island*, women have nevertheless resided in those communities for decades. With women's increased economic clout as they move toward economic parity with men and with the decline in a gay male population ravaged by AIDS, gay women have become a most noticeable group in resort towns like Provincetown, Key West, and Palm Springs. Another growing alternative is the lesbian cruise, with ships chartered by Olivia Records or Robin Tyler Productions taking women everywhere from the Caribbean to Alaska to the Galapagos Islands.[3] Lesbians have also created strong communities in cities like Northampton, Massachusetts, and in the San Francisco Bay Area and have formed land trusts in many rural areas.

Festivals across the United States and a stream of concerts and comedy performances in cities and college towns attest to the strength of lesbian culture wherever lesbians choose to reside. While the *Advocate* once purred over two 45 rpm songs cut by Madeline Davis and Maxine Feldman in 1973, the music industry has become much larger than Lynne D. Shapiro foresaw in "The Growing Business behind Women's Music." Whereas once some women's recordings sounded as if they had been produced in a do-it-yourself booth at Coney Island, several major companies, including Olivia and Redwood Records, turn out classy digital productions, which are marketed in women's and gay bookstores, by catalog companies such as Ladyslipper, and in mainstream record stores. Concerts once held in small cafés, school auditoriums, and local churches now take place in concert halls as well. Lesbian comedy, the importance of which is discussed by Sharon McDonald in "Lesbian-Feminist Comedy: Dyke Humor out of the Closet," has flourished as well. Stand-up comics like Kate Clinton, Karen Williams, Suzanne Westenhofer, and Lea Delaria tour nationally, host television shows like "In the Life," and act as mistress of ceremonies at benefits and awards ceremonies.

Lesbian Families

No matter where we choose to live or where we vacation, we want a life-style that suits and fulfills our needs, whether that means living alone, in a couple, or with children. The number of lesbians with children has been estimated by the *New York Times* and other sources as being in the tens of thousands. When *Lavender Culture* was being collected, we knew of a few isolated cases in which lesbians wanted to have children, but most of the children we knew were products of heterosexual marriages. Now most of the children we know are products of sperm donors (so-called "baster babies") or adoption. Dykes with tykes have become a formidable and inspiring force within the lesbian community and the bravest challenge to the Republican years of "family values." We have families we value!

Both lesbians and gay men are constantly battling for the benefits of domestic partnership, rights that married heterosexuals reap automatically. But until we achieve our legislative and corporate goals, we have created our own rituals to solemnize our rites of passage. These include religious and secular commitment ceremonies (and a booming business in commitment rings), alternative services for Jewish and Christian holidays like Passover and Christmas as well as wicca celebrations (goddess worship). We have also produced books for our children to read (such as Lesléa Newman's *Heather Has Two Mommies*) that present our lives fairly.

Whereas once monogamous relationships and families seemed to many radicalesbians to reek of heteropatriarchy, in the gay '90s they have become the dream of most lesbians. And this is precisely the point of *Lavender Culture:* our culture, our values, and our relationships are as historically fluid as those of heterosexuals. We are no more the lesbians of the Stonewall uprising in 1969 than we are Sappho or Gertrude Stein. We are a people becoming who we are to become.

Notes

I'd like to thank Pace University for its continuing support of my writing. I'd also like to thank Karen Kerner, Allen Young, and Niko Pfund for their help with this essay.
1. Though the copyright on *Lavender Culture* is 1978, the book was not released until the following year as Jove Books hoped to profit from the 1979 publication of *The Gay Report,* which Allen Young and I co-authored.
2. Holly Near, who has been a lesbian at times, recorded Ruben Blades's touching song, "The Letter," on her album *Sky Dances*.
3. According to an article in *10 Percent* about Olivia Cruises, the cruise business is now much larger than the record business. In 1992, Olivia took in close to $4 million from cruises, compared with $650,000 from their record business alone in 1989 (Pepper, 26).

Bibliography

Jay, Karla. 1993. "Is Lesbian Literature Going Mainstream?" *Ms Magazine,* July–August, 70–73.
Newton, Esther. 1993. *Cherry Grove, Fire Island.* Boston: Beacon.

Pepper, Rachel. "Olivia Cruises the '90s." *10 Percent* (Winter 1993): 24–28.

St. John, Martin. 1973. "Liberation Music, Angry and Proud Enters Gay Life." *Advocate*, April 3.

Introduction to the New Edition

by Allen Young

In an earlier time, not too many decades ago, life for most gay men and lesbians was relatively simple. It consisted of two main elements: desire and secrecy. Repressed by religion, pseudo-science, and government, most people whose objects of affection were of the same sex lived under a dark cloud of shame and self-revulsion. There were a significant few exceptions to this rule, but most of those who were open about their sexuality could be described as eccentric, artistic, or independently wealthy. They were the few and the brave, or the lucky. Simultaneously, a seemingly inexplicable fervor of body and mind could not be denied. Somehow, against all odds, like-minded partners were found and sexual release was obtained. Under the best of circumstances, these fortunate liaisons were accompanied by the joys of affection and even love. Rarely were such unions long-lasting. And in many cases, people lived their entire lives with no such consummation. As for artistic representations of the same-sex love or sex, the occasional picture has been unearthed, the occasional poem and essay penned, but they didn't amount to much. Of course there were great artists of homosexual persuasion in the more distant past, but to take one example, E. M. Forster, his work avoided gay themes with the exception of the love story *Maurice,* which he assiduously kept from publication until after his death.

When *Lavender Culture* was compiled in the mid-1970s, the movement that emerged from the historic 1969 rebellion at the Stonewall Inn in New York City was only beginning to have its impact on the nation and the world. This anthology offered a hint of things to come. The concerns of this book grew naturally from the political activism and cultural stirrings that were occurring at the time of the compilation and which motivated and excited us as the editors. These stirrings, it must be stressed, can best be described as a desire to get beyond the original basic facts of homosexual life: desire and secrecy. Beyond that, however, the essays in this book reflect the first efforts of gay men and lesbians to analyze in more detail the nature and contemporary expression of that desire. These writings also chart related efforts to use the arts and mass media of communication to put an end to secrecy—in essence, to create gay pride and expose the reality of gay and lesbian lives.

As this essay is being written, I am making plans to travel from my woodland home in Massachusetts to New York City in June 1994 to mark the celebration of the twenty-fifth anniversary of the Stonewall Rebellion. In so doing, I reflect on the growth of the gay liberation movement over these years; it's a case where numbers tell the tale to a great extent. I recall with chilling clarity the first anniversary of Stonewall. It was June 28, 1970, and I was among a few dozen activists from the New York Gay Liberation Front, Gay Activists Alliance, Mattachine Society, and Daughters of Bilitis who gathered somewhat fearfully on Christopher Street near the Stonewall Inn. We were totally unsure about how many people would join us, and were much relieved when about a thousand came that day to march up Fifth Avenue in the bright sunshine to rally in Central Park. In 1979, approximately 200,000 came to the first national gay and lesbian march on Washington, D.C., while in the fall of 1993 approximately one million marched in Washington and a similar number is expected in New York for "Stonewall 25."

Lavender Culture, then, explores the complexities of gay life as they began to emerge, as closet doors by the hundreds of thousands flew (or creaked) open. Courageous and thoughtful gay men and lesbians were beginning, in larger and larger numbers, to leave behind a life governed by the two simple poles of desire and secrecy. Many of us—as is reflected in my introduction, "No Longer the Court Jesters," and elsewhere in this book and other early gay liberation writings—saw the changes in gay and lesbian life, and the emerging gay community, as part of a larger struggle for social change.

Many of our cultural institutions have grown dramatically. Our impact on mainstream culture has been significant in some ways, but limited nonetheless by our continued marginalization and the continued prejudice against us. While the larger struggle continues, with gay men and lesbians an integral part of it, I am struck by the fact that change has not come as fast as expected. Especially striking is the fact that few links seem to have been solidified between gay liberation and feminism; indeed, the forging of such alliances may no longer be an explicit goal.

In my original introduction, I stated that lavender is "implicitly androgynous, a combination of the male principle (blue) and the female principle (pink) which society has sanctified." If you had asked me in the mid-1970s to peer into the future, I would have predicted the near disappearance of gay men or lesbians intent on promoting a masculine or feminine veneer. But I also would have predicted the legalization of marijuana. So much for my clairvoyance! Instead, supermodel RuPaul, a drag queen of considerable stature (both literally and figuratively), occupied center stage at the 1993 march on Washington. For a while, we saw the cloning of plaid-shirted gay men. There is an abundance of so-called lipstick lesbians who simply do not buy the feminist idea (perhaps they see it as an unwanted "party line") that the cosmetics industry is part of a woman-hating patriarchal enemy. And in both the gay male and lesbian communities there has emerged a sexual and fashion consciousness that boldly asserts the roles of butch and femme, rather than de-emphasizing them as some had anticipated.

Some more personal observations and comments, perhaps, will help illustrate the importance of gay culture in my life, and by extension, in the lives of so many gay men. In the early 1970s, I left New York City and relocated in the most rural area of Massachusetts, helping to create what might have been called a gay hippie commune. In the ensuing years, the commune gave up many of its utopian goals and especially its economic unity, and I obtained a job as a reporter for a small-town daily newspaper nearby. After ten years, I changed jobs, and for five years I have been the vice president for public relations/marketing for a small community hospital. I have participated in various town boards and local environmental groups.

Deciding how to project my identity as a gay man (while protecting my privacy as necessary) has been a major feature of my life in this community—which, it must be understood, bears little resemblance to life for a modern gay man in a major urban center. But like my urban counterparts, being open about my sexual nature is important to me as a political imperative and as a means of emotional survival. Networking with scores of other gay men and lesbians within a fifty-mile radius of my home (which includes no big cities), and building solid friendships with understanding and open-minded straight people, have been a challenge and a joy. Observing the fears and doubts of closeted homosexuals, and knowing that they are responding to the real prejudice around them, have provoked in me both sadness and frustration. About a year ago, I was a cofounder of a local diversity-awareness group that has, without precedence, raised the issue of anti-gay prejudice and made the process of education more public and more broad-based than I would have expected twenty years ago when I moved here.

I am in a long-term relationship with a man who lives fifty miles away. There are compromises in this relationship that surprise some of my friends, in part because we do not meet any of the expectations of a gay "marriage," in part because my companion has chosen to be less open to family, neighbors, and co-workers than I have. But for both of us, involvement with the gay community is vital, and we both marvel at the gay couples we occasionally observe that prefer total or near total isolation, unwilling to take any risks for the sake of their own freedom or the freedom of "our kind." For me, pursuing a relationship premised on intimacy, and working it in with the larger network of gay and straight friends, are major components of my life. This relationship—plus the books, movies, periodicals, music, plays, political groups, and other public expressions of the gay world—come together to form my own personal expression of "lavender culture."

I love the fact that I function successfully in the straight world where I work and live. I enjoy being open about my sexuality not only to my mother, but also to cousins, aunts, and uncles—relatives who have met my gay friends and lovers and often ask about them as if they have become part of our family. When straight people come to terms with me as an openly gay man, it's an important victory for me personally but it also has an important political and cultural impact. When I reflect on the national issues that appear to be important on the national political scene of the gay community, I naturally try to relate these to my own life. Some issues, such as domestic-partner legislation or the right to marry, don't concern me personally because of the reality of my relationship, but I know these are social issues of great importance to many gay men, lesbians, and bisexuals. My overall approach to life may be the assimilation that Queer Nation gay radicals decry, but I consider myself to be involved in social change while also living an ordinary life—an ideal combination, in my view. Street activism only goes so far. This does not mean I fool myself with thinking that I am accepted, nor is acceptance my goal. Every day, I am also reminded of my status as a queer (a word I have used long before it became trendy, but also one I have used sparingly). I share with all queers the powerful sense of being different and of knowing that I am held in contempt by so many. In the fall of 1993, voters in Cincinnati, Ohio, and Lewiston, Maine, voted to overturn gay rights ordinances, and the absurd "don't ask, don't tell" gays in the military policy is being enforced by a president who was supposed to be our friend and advocate. Yes, there are reminders that I live in a political climate that is generally hostile, and since nasty people live everywhere, fear lurks in the further reaches of my mind. But I don't focus on the negative, and I enjoy the broad-based social comfort that I experience on a day-to-day basis. Some may sense this as smugness, but on the other hand, I question the good sense of someone who chooses a life given over to pure rage.

While life in an urban "gay ghetto" environment where there is a lot of lesbian and gay visibility may be more exciting or comfortable for some, I would find it stifling. For some, frankly, it seems to be an escape of sorts, a decision to put down new gay roots rather than do battle with the "breeders." This is not a bad or a wrong choice for someone seeking liberation to make. It's quite a reasonable one, really, but sometimes it makes it harder for those left behind in neighborhoods and small towns where diversity is not respected. Yet at the same time, I value the accomplishments of the urban gay community, and feel very close to my friends there and to the unknown thousands who make it possible.

My connection to the urban gay community ranges broadly from the latest techno records that I dance to at parties to the issue of Boston's *Bay Windows* that arrives in my rural route mailbox weekly. I frequently read *The Advocate* and *Out*. If there's a gay play, I try to get to see it. I've been entertained by the Flirtations (the gay *a cappella* doo wop quartet). I laughed at Fred Small's clever song, "Pink Peril" (a clever spoof of tough soldiers afraid to shower with a "fairy").

As a reader of the New York *Native* and other gay periodicals in the early 1980s, I obtained crucial information about AIDS not available elsewhere early in the epidemic. Perhaps I was naive enough to believe for a time, with others, that AIDS would not touch people away from the urban centers. It didn't take long for me to change my mind, and now I find myself part of a rural AIDS awareness network. Of the eight men who cut down trees and notched pine beams in my rural commune in its first summer (1973), five are now dead of AIDS and at least one more is HIV positive. AIDS has certainly come to paradise.

In her essay accompanying this introduction, Karla Jay writes of the impact of AIDS on lesbians. The impact on gay men has been discussed by many other writers, so I won't go into great detail here. It's brought me a great deal of personal sadness, but it has also redoubled my commitment to enjoying life to the fullest and to appreciating the people around me. I think this is the mentality that has permeated gay literature and the gay male community in general. Around the time that the first of my friends died of AIDS, one of my best woman friends died of cancer. In recent years, many of my friends have had their parents die. Death is inevitable and it is horrible, no matter how much we try to visualize or imagine "a good death," but I think it has become somewhat less fear-inspiring.

The AIDS plague has thrust open more closet doors than might otherwise have occurred, and in that sense it has compelled society to grapple with homosexuality much more quickly and thoroughly than might otherwise have been the case. AIDS may have given some people one more reason to hate us, but it has also won us sympathy and understanding. The tendency of the media to divide people with AIDS into the innocent ones (hemophiliacs, babies) and the deserving ones (faggots, junkies) is a crucial indicator of the nexus between the plague and the popular prejudices of society. In the area where I live, I know of families who publicly acknowledged their sons' homosexuality because of an AIDS death (and who otherwise would have kept the secret), but I also know of families who, because homosexuality is shameful to them, tell their friends and neighbors that their sons died of "cancer."

The durability of certain broad contradictions in gay life surprises me, but I no longer expend much personal energy on taking sides or trying to resolve the contradictions. While compiling *Lavender Culture,* I chose John Mitzel's essay on sports, which appealed to me because it seemed a good analytical response to the horrible memories I have of my high school gym classes. When I first heard about the Gay Olympics, as they were then called, I was horrified and even angry, because I took them to be an attack on me and a multitude of gay men as "sissies." I felt the early writing that promoted the Gay Olympics (later renamed the Gay Games when the Olympic officials objected in court) was very defensive, as if to say that unathletic men are not representative of gay men, and those men who are unathletic should be hidden away so the athletes could show the heterosexual world that we are really "just like you." There may be some truth to my original concerns, and to Mitzel's anti-jock analysis—but over time, I revised my opinion. I've observed with wonderment and pride the accomplishments of gay and lesbian individual athletes and their organizations, and I'm sure the Gay Games must be a lot of fun for participants and spectators alike. It's really not so important what straight people think about the Gay Games, and given the way the media have buried the games so far, it's pretty much of a moot point! One point to consider about my initial criticism is this: the sense of alienation that comes from that kind of extremist political analysis is not, in the long run, very satisfying. The futility of extremism helps explain why gay people have the assimilationist values that radicals can't understand or accept.

I can appreciate popular culture (say, a movie such as *Silence of the Lambs*) even when it doesn't meet my standards as a gay liberationist. I can formulate my own criticism, and read the work of gay critics, but I don't have to buy all of it. I can support a group such as Gays and Lesbians Against Defamation, but I don't have the time to write a letter to every television or film producer every time there's a minor transgression or a "positive" representation of gay people. I do recognize we are in a war and the media play a big role in this, but coming out to family, friends, neighbors, and co-workers is still the sine qua non of gay liberation.

I love the movies, and go out of my way to enjoy gay films or films with gay aspects; these films are often burned in my memory. I remember when the late Vito Russo came to the University of Massachusetts in Amherst to present his *Celluloid Closet,* a lecture-film presentation billed as a work-in-progress. Eventually, his book *The Celluloid Closet* was released and now Vito's longtime friend Lily Tomlin is helping raise money to create a high-quality documentary based on the book. I also remember an early gay film festival—years before gay film festivals became major events in large cities. It was early in the 1970s and, again, the place was Amherst. Tom Joslin, who recently died of AIDS while making the documentary movie *Silver Lake Life,* used to teach film at Hampshire College in Amherst. When he organized a gay film festival there, I didn't know what I would see, but I remember how significant it was to see films that portrayed openly gay men. Specifically, I recall Joslin's autobiographic film *Black Star* (wherein his lover, Marc, reads from our anthology *Out of the Closets*) and I saw Jack Hazen's excellent documentary about artist David Hockney, a great film entitled *A Bigger Splash.*

Since then, I've seen Hollywood mediocrity *(Making Love)*, though even this somewhat sappy film could be considered a milestone. Considering the progress made in the film and television careers of Michael Ontkean and Harry Hamlin, who played gay men in *Making Love,* this film should be considered significant in letting actors know that playing homosexuals isn't an awful career move. I joined the boycott of *Cruising* when it was playing in theaters, but I suppose you could say I changed my mind when I rented the film on video a few years later. I question the value of boycotts, because there are always those who want to develop their own opinions, and that needs to be respected. Even though *Basic Instinct* was attacked by many because of its lesbian murderer, there were lesbians who wanted to see Sharon Stone's portrayal. Back in the early 1970s, a contingent of women picketed *The Bitter Tears of Petra Von Kant* by gay filmmaker Rainer Werner Fassbinder, but Karla Jay wrote an interesting analytical article about the movie, which she did not find offensive.

The movie *Sunday, Bloody Sunday,* directed by John Schlesinger, helped me come out to my father, and I will always remember the kiss that Murray Head and Peter Finch gave to one another. I love reading reviews and commentaries in gay magazines. I disagreed with the *Advocate* film critic David Ehrenreich when he called *JFK* the most homophobic film ever made, but he did make some good points. I agreed with the activists who denounced the portrayal of the serial killer in *Silence of the Lambs* (obviously, this man is depicted as a faggot), but I thought the intensity of the protests was a bit much. Tears flowed when I saw *Longtime Companion,* in part because it was so real and immediate. *My Own Private Idaho* was an intriguing film, but my letter to Gus Van Sant went unanswered. I asked him, among other things, why he chose to depict the young hustlers' johns in such an unfavorable light. I haven't seen Gregg Araki's *The Living End* or *Poison* by Todd Haynes, partly because I haven't had an opportunity so far. *Swoon,* a portrayal of the Leopold-Loeb famous 1920s kidnap-murder case, was an intriguing commentary on the gay relationship of the accused men. But

I'm troubled by the knowledge that so many of these movies, like so many other movies, are seen as interesting because their plots and characters focus on violence. James Ivory's *Another Country* and *Maurice* are treasures, but neither is contemporary. For me, *The Wedding Banquet,* while worth a chuckle and interesting for its portrayal of a contemporary relationship between a gay Asian-American and his lover, depended too much on its gay hero becoming a father. My point in all of this is to illustrate how stimulating gay films are to me; they enrich my life. Remembering that cinema was for decades the exclusive province of heterosexual romance, these new expressions of gay life on film are liberating not only to viewers like me but also to the artists involved in making them.

Among the friends and acquaintances of mine who have died of AIDS are many authors, including George Whitmore, Vito Russo, Robert Grumley, and Michael Ferro. I mourn these losses deeply; I have enjoyed their writing so much. I love a good gay novel, and my tastes are fairly broad as long as the quality of the writing is good. I don't judge a book by whether or not it is gay enough, by whether or not the homosexuality is raunchy or overtly sexual. The fact that the novels of David Leavitt or Michael Cunningham don't have a lot of scenes with hard-ons doesn't bother me, though some critics revile these writers for their popularity among straights. If I find the characters and situations interesting, that's enough for me—I don't think gay literature is necessarily better because it makes straight people squirm. I also like the sexual excitement in the work of Felice Picano (*Ambidextrous,* for example) and the depiction of gritty moneyless urban faggots in the work of Larry Mitchell (*My Life as a Mole*).

Good works of nonfiction with gay themes are harder to find, but they have also been a source of enjoyment for me. The late Randy Shilts has not been universally praised, but I admire his work and marvel at his career as an openly gay journalist for a major metropolitan newspaper (the *San Francisco Chronicle*), something unheard of in the mid-1970s. When I recently read Shilts's book on gays in the military, *Conduct Unbecoming,* however, I found myself irritated at the author's very unsympathetic portrayal of the Vietnam era gay anti-war activists. His compilation of facts and figures is impressive, but he seemed unable to recognize that the issue of anti-gay discrimination is not the only one to engage gay humans. Some of us will always take a principled stand against discrimination, while also feeling a profound connection between our gay identities and our quest for a world freed of armed conflict.

This is just one example. In the early days of gay liberation, we described marriage as a failed heterosexual institution. Recently, I went to a lesbian commitment ceremony that was the equivalent of a wedding, and I enjoyed myself thoroughly and wish these two friends the very best of success in their relationship. While the ceremony resembled a wedding, it was not the same thing. There was no signed contract and of course there was no license, and perhaps that's the way it should be. As for those who want the full trappings of marriage as we know it (approval of church and state), I wouldn't want to argue against it, but I'm not sure it's a wise choice. Long-term relationships can be wonderful, but I don't want to create a hierarchy where gay men and lesbians who are single, or who are interested in unusual relationships or short-term liaisons, become a source of discomfort and embarrassment for the public representatives of our movement. It seems that this potential danger exists because gay couples in monogamous long-term relationships sometimes present themselves as "the good gays," the exemplary ones.

Exploring and maintaining an array of relationships, continuing to bond with many members of my own blood family, participating in a community with strong rural and small-town traditions, and constantly nurturing the alternative family I've created occupies much of my time. All of this is colored by the fact that I am an openly gay man in a society that continues to promulgate and endorse official and unofficial prejudice. The good life, in my opinion, is one that combines an involvement with nature, art, ideas, and relationships. My consciousness as a gay person, and my connection with other gay men and lesbians, gives an added dimension to the good life I try to lead.

This essay is dedicated to the memory of Jerry Miller, Martin Roland, Tom Wirth, Steve McCarty, Bob Gravley, John Burton, and Art Platt, my "short list" of friends who died of AIDS.

I
Companion Introductions

No Longer the Court Jesters
by Allen Young

What is gay culture? When we originally conceived a collection of articles about culture, we had to confront the fact that the word "culture" is open to several interpretations. That was fine with us—hopefully this anthology reflects openness and variety. Nevertheless, as editors we have assumed two primary definitions of the term "culture"—first, culture as what is generally called "the arts," and second, culture as anthropologists use the term—that is, the patterns of behavior and institutions belonging to a particular group of people.

In this case, the particular group of people is gay people, which actually is two rather distinct groups of people—gay men on the one hand and lesbians on the other. Although the experience of being "queer" is shared by both gay males and lesbians, the broader North American culture in which we all live has rather distinct patterns of behavior for men and women, and thus the gay male and lesbian experiences are bound to be markedly different. Lesbians are generally well aware of the difference; in fact, that is one reason why many lesbians identify so strongly with the feminist movement. But in seeking out and selecting articles by gay men, I, as the male editor, have attempted to select material which shows awareness of this difference.

Perhaps the most common misunderstanding among gay men in looking at gay culture is to ignore the difference between the male and female experience, to forget everything that feminists have been saying about power relations between men and women. In combining articles by men and women in the same volume, we hope that we can accomplish a celebration of our cultural achievements and heritage while at the same time we learn about and grow from the variety of experience.

In examining gay achievements in the arts, many gay people begin with lists of famous persons, past and present. This is a rather elementary form of expressing gay pride, and indeed such "ancestors" and celebrities are a vital element in considering gay culture. However, the "famous gays" approach is also used by people who are very defensive and feel the need to name famous gays almost as a justification for their own "perversion." There are times when people name a famous gay person when I think there is no basis in fact for the comment, that mere sensationalism is at work, and there are other times when I feel like saying, "So what?" Nonetheless, unearthing and analyzing the gayness of cultural and historical figures has been an area of concern for a number of gay writers, and this material has provided some interesting articles in the gay press. This has been an important part of my own gay education, and it should not be dismissed.

The straight world's insistence on hiding gayness from young people is one pernicious aspect of its tyranny over us. In educational institutions, homosexuality is hidden from students as if to protect them, in hypocritical violation of the truth, with textbooks and teachers usually ignoring the sexuality of such famous persons as Socrates, Sappho, Alexander the Great, Julius Caesar, Michelangelo, Tchaikovsky, and Walt Whitman, as well as of more contemporary figures such as Bessie Smith, Gertrude Stein, Dag Hammarskjold, and Tennessee Williams.

It is not surprising that men dominate any list of famous gays, since the cultural and political institutions of Western civilization have been male dominated. Even today, gay men in the arts often prefer to climb the ladder of success in the established institutions of culture (the literary world, the ballet, the theater, etc.) rather than engage in the often frustrating and financially dubious struggle for an independent gay-oriented cultural expression. Such men achieve gratification from their success, yet there is often something self-destructive in the process, especially in that the art forms often display heterosexual imagery. Also, successful gay men in the arts have often advanced because the institutions are male dominated. This is one of the dilemmas for gay male culture, and it is explored in several of the essays in this book.

The Feminine and Masculine Mystiques

Since we grow up in a society that puts forth rather rigid expectations of how little boys and little girls should be, the sex role system has a major impact on our personalities and values. Most gay men grow up with a very ambivalent attitude toward the value system and behavior patterns summed up in the term "manhood." For most gay men, parts of our personalities are oriented toward achieving manhood, often embracing and cherishing it, while with other aspects of our being we despise manhood, reject it, or fail at it in varying degrees. Despite societal taboos, we gay men often find valuable characteristics that are generally reserved for women, and we absorb these. I believe there is therefore both a feminine and a masculine mystique pervading gay male culture.

One obvious manifestation of the feminine mystique is the development of emotional expression among gay men. Traditional manhood implies a detached coolness, with various physical or intellectual variations. The emotionality, intuitiveness, and warmth sometimes associated with gay men is borrowed from feminine norms. Another manifestation of the feminine mystique is the fascination with Judy Garland and other female superstars. Explored in depth by Michael Bronski elsewhere in this book, this phenomenon is at least partially based on some sense of identification between the gay males in the audience and the female personality on stage or screen. The feminine mystique also has to do with all of those things that gay men do or like which are usually associated with women, especially things involving beauty. "Beauty" is itself a feminine word—we learn at an early age that a man is "handsome," a woman is "pretty" or "beautiful." In a sense, one could say gay male culture includes interior decoration, clothing design, personal grooming and hairstyling, cosmetics, poodles and Afghans, cooking, plants and flowers, ballet, opera, poetry, and so on. In *The Boys in the Band*, Emory said it: "It takes a fairy to make something pretty."

Some would say that this is mere stereotyping. I think not, however, just reflecting on what it meant for me as an eleven-year-old to bake cakes, and what it means for me now as an adult male to pick wild flowers to put in a vase in my home. What these things mean in this culture is that I am effeminate, though, of course, I have my masculine side as well.

Nonetheless, there are those who feel the need to separate themselves from what they see as traditional and perhaps oppressive "faggot trips." In an article entitled, "The Fairy Princess Exposed," published in our first anthology, *Out of the Closets: Voices of Gay Liberation*, Craig Alfred Hanson attacked the "princess syndrome" and its "fem-identification, the fantasy imagery, the egocentricity, and the cultural conservatism of the tired old gay trip." Hanson's essay was soundly criticized as a kind of snobbery in reverse. I, for one, place a lot of importance on having a pretty home, but my tastes are rural and earthy—I like neither poodles nor crystal. Perhaps it is only a matter of taste. I think it is undeniable, however, that in American culture there is something vaguely feminine about art. Those gay men who develop artistic sensibility are nurturing a feminine side of themselves. Those who suppress or fail to develop such sensibilities, in accordance with macho norms, not only deprive themselves of a whole area of aesthetic appreciation but often set themselves up as "better" than (read more masculine than) other faggots. Sometimes, however, the "feminine" appreciation for art in its domestic form takes a uniquely competitive, masculine form—the "piss elegant queen" whose collection of art objects, glassware, or dogs is used to prove pseudoaesthetic and monetary superiority to others.

It is, of course, a largely out-of-the-closet gay male community which is capable of expressing the positive feminine side of gay culture, especially the hard-core sissies and faggots. But the masculine side, often expressed from inside the closet (as "real men"), is certainly a major part of gay culture. Often this merely constitutes efforts that gay men have made to meet the standards of manhood already preestablished—standards of success in physique, mind, business, sports, etc. When a little boy is hurt badly enough from the pain of being called a sissy, he may learn to lower the timbre of his voice or, as Bob Dobson notes in "Dance Liberation," published in this anthology, move less freely. And when he learns that a deeper voice, perhaps a moustache, and the right kind of "tough" stance make him more attractive sexually, that man is developing the masculine mystique as it relates to being gay. Some kind of acquiescence to the sex role system is involved when gay men are attracted to "butch numbers" or to "trade" (men who define themselves as primarily straight and generally won't reciprocate in sexual acts).

A special part of the masculine mystique for gay men is the interest in denim and leather, not only as fashion but as a part of sex games. It has been argued that such butch drag, along with femme drag, is an expression of oppression, and that liberation lies in abandoning role-oriented aspects of our culture. But all of this makes me uneasy. Who am I to tell someone what they should wear, or to pass moral judgment on someone's clothing? I remember when I was denounced by a so-called feminist male for wearing work boots—the accusation was that I was wearing such shoes to further a masculine image, when to me it was a question of practical footwear. Yet I have found myself with strongly negative feelings toward gay spokesmen who dress in suit and tie, which to me is the official male uniform of this patriarchy. While the formation of a right line makes me nervous, I cannot remain oblivious to the meanness and even cruelty expressed in the studded leather outfits and the facial expression and body language that often accompany such garb. I can enjoy anonymous sex, but there is often a coldness and an uncaring in such sexual contacts that hurts. I feel the need for romance and a "real relationship"—I do place the sexuality expressed romantically or in a relationship on a higher plane. On the other hand, anonymous sex and promiscuity offer valid pleasures and communications, too, and as Charley

Shively argues in "Phantasy Revolution," published in this book, "true love" may also be fantasy.

One obvious example of the masculine mystique is the gay male appreciation for the male body. There is even one gay male magazine named simply *Body*. The worship of the male body can be narcissistic (if you think your own body is fabulous) or self-hating (if your own body is in bad shape or you have a bad self-image). The worship of the male body is also illustrated by those who make pornography and those who buy it. The "manly" art photography, such as that done by Jim French, is not quite the same as pornography, but surely it qualifies as masculine erotic and creative expression. I wonder if such worship of the male form has its artistic roots partially in the Adonises sculpted in ancient Greece and in Michelangelo's "David." But where does art end and something more crass take its place? What about the physique and muscle-building magazines and the depiction in pornographic magazines of butch stereotypes such as cowboy, motorcyclist, cop, trucker, surfer, and so on?

The ideal male form—even overtly sexual depictions of it—may have aesthetic value. I have responded aesthetically and erotically to photographs of nude men. But there are complexities here that we cannot ignore, especially in a society where youth, Anglo-Saxon beauty, "manly" strength, and big cocks are worshiped along with big cars and big bombs. Too often, as in the highly stylized drawings by Tom of Finland, the male form is so exaggerated, so totally masculine, so imbued with power, so totally inaccessible as to represent for the gay man a form of self-hatred. Those male idols so worshiped cannot possibly be faggots!

The most successful makers of 8 mm. male pornographic movies for home projection, such as Brentwood and Falcon, peddle their wares by setting up situations where masculinity is portrayed, relationships are sparse or anonymous, and emotional aspects downplayed (emotion=femininity). The men in those movies supposedly aren't gay: they're just "guys who are into guys" (gay=femininity): Indeed, it seems essential in such pornography that masculinity is affirmed sometimes by having the model portrayed

28

as a real-life athlete, hard-hat construction worker, ranch hand, etc. Sometimes it is not only a masculine role, but the idea that the model is really straight—"Rick" is shown masturbating while looking at *Playboy*, or, as the advertisement explain, "Bart's wife" is out of town when "Bart makes it with Jack, the next-door neighbor."

Radical feminists have recently begun to criticize vociferously the pornography bought by heterosexual men, seeing it as a systematic portrayal of the humiliation and abuse of women. Lesbianism is portrayed exploitatively in pornography designed not for lesbians but for straight males. So far, most gay men seem wary of any attack on any kind of pornography, yet I wonder—isn't it abusive of true-to-life gay men when the pornography sold to us shows masculine fantasies as a primary erotic stimulus? Such pornography also tends to reinforce cultural prejudices around race, age, body type, and penis size. The issue is confused by the question of "freedom of the press," but *criticizing* pornography is not the same as asking state interference. There is a resistance on the part of gay men to break down or attack fantasies, perhaps because the guilt associated with these fantasies is just beginning to subside as a result of gay liberation. Generally, it would seem that gay men *like* pornography, so if the radical feminist assault on pornography gains strength, it may well cause an increase in the conflict between gay men and gay women. On the other hand, there are lesbians and gay men who make a distinction between pornography and erotica, and perhaps one could argue that at least some of the gay male sexually explicit material is indeed erotica and not pornography. Drawing such lines may be difficult or impossible.

Another element of the masculine mystique is the role of gay men in sports. How many gay men are avid sports fans? Perhaps more than is generally suspected. Like most of my gay male friends, I hated gym class and was last or next to last when sides were chosen up. Actually, I found my own niche in the sports world of my high school days by becoming team manager. I was scorekeeper, timekeeper, and towel boy. The first two roles were classier, of course, and kept the boys on the team friendly to me,

29

while being towel boy was dirty work but allowed me frequent entry to the wondrous sights in the locker room. Once in college, I abandoned this essentially forced and humiliating attachment to the world of sports. Others, consciously or not, adopt it as a permanent faggot lifestyle, and there's even a nasty term for such poeple: "jock sniffers." John Mitzel's pamphlet, "Sports and the Macho Male" (Fag Rag Books), briefly excerpted in this anthology, explores the world of sports more fully, as does the best-selling book *The David Kopay Story* (Arbor House). We know by now that not all gay men are sissies or "jock sniffers"—many are indeed accomplished athletes. No doubt, however, competitive sports and machismo are closely linked. Once I answered a personals ad in the Boston *Phoenix* and got invited to an orgy. When I got to the host's Hyde Park apartment, the crowd (mostly short-haired, conservative-appearing men in their late twenties and thirties) was watching the Boston Bruins hockey game on TV. It was part of the masculine environment that the host created to make his orgy a success. One gay writer, Konstantin Berlandt, suggested in an article a few years ago that gay liberation and jock liberation may well be the same thing! Sports are used in the culture to build masculinity and to put down "queers"; athletes use competitive sports to hide their own faggotry while they are able to enjoy the physical company of men.

The dynamic between the feminine and masculine sides of gay male cultural patterns is crucial to the future of the gay community. To the extent that masculinity—and especially its manifestation in competitiveness, violence, and uncaring relationships—threatens the human community, gay men have the choice of embracing masculinity or manhood and thus opposing the rising tide of women, or of joining with women in an attempt to recreate the world as a more harmonious place. If gay men ignore feminism, or, worse, oppose it, I think it is bound to be self-defeating, since male-dominated heterosexual society's disgust for male homosexuality is based on the notion that gay men are womanly and that women are inferior. Getting in touch with and appreciating our feminine aspects, then, is likely to be a major goal of men concerned with bringing about radical changes in society so that we may lead full, rich lives.

A Few Questions About Camp

The most expanded compilation of thoughts on camp is Susan Sontag's essay, "Notes on Camp," printed in her book *Against Interpretation* (Dell, 1966). Dedicating the notes to Oscar Wilde, she states that "the essence of Camp is its love of the unnatural: of artifice and exaggeration," adding that "Camp is esoteric—something of a private code, a badge of identity even, among small urban cliques." In his essay on Judy Garland, Barbra Streisand and other female superstars, Michael Bronski quotes from Sontag's notes, and uses them as a taking-off point for new insights.

Defining camp could take a book or two, but no one doubts that there is some connection between camp and gay culture. It might even be argued that the camp sensibility is the most significant gay contribution to contemporary culture. We have our own campy vocabulary and a book *(The Queen's Vernacular)* to document it. Camp lingo can include gender-reversal put-downs ("Oh, Mary, did you hear about Miss Thing?") and it can involve the use of gay slang such as the verb "to dish" and the expression "to read one's beads." Such slang, however, as the compiler of *The Queen's Vernacular* notes in his introduction, reflects many levels of prejudice and self-contempt.

Camp sensibility is also aesthetic and can involve an appreciation for Art Nouveau or a love for a wide variety of old movies. Sometimes there is an element of mockery or derision in the decision to conceptualize something artistically marginal as beautiful or worthy of appreciation. Who knows where lie the limits of camp! Are Gilbert and Sullivan operettas camp? What about films like *Singin' in the Rain*? The movies of Mae West?—everyone agrees they're campy! Does a gay person who is a fan of musical comedy act from a camp sensibility or is it just a matter of personal preference? Does it mean someone is "less gay" if they are *not* into camp? Surely, camp is primarily

31

a male phenomenon, for though lesbians may be familiar with camp (often from socializing with gay men), lesbians themselves are not inclined to camp it up—at least not so far as I've noticed.

Freak Culture—the Hippies and Glitter

The gay input to the so-called counterculture or freak culture has its obvious aspects. Long hair for men, the most basic hippie style, could be worn at first only by men who weren't worried about being called "faggot"—and that included a lot of faggots. The birth of the hippie, with long hair and colorful clothes and less rigid ways of thinking, took place in two places that have been established gay meccas—Greenwich Village and San Francisco. What Allen Ginsberg called in his *Gay Sunshine Interview* (Grey Fox Press) "a viable tradition of intellectual anarchism, communalism, free love" was the foundation for the hippie movement and contributors to it include such gay writers as Ginsberg himself, Paul Goodman, and Robert Duncan.

Nonetheless, the "hip scene," so to speak, quickly polarized into a world of "dudes" and "chicks," with faggots and dykes not always welcome. The finest values in what could be called "hip"—what Ginsberg termed the "panoply of tolerances and understandings and gnostic (mystic, psychedelic) awarenesses, as well as social hopes and humors"—involved a direct connection between the honesty and openness of the freak culture and the coming-out process for gay people. Also, there's a gentleness in most "hip" males that makes them less intimidating as men, and therefore, in a sense, more "gay." Gay people hear hip men say things like "Do your own thing, man," as a kind of condescending approval of homosexuality; annoying as condescension can be, I'd rather have someone respond to my gayness with condescension than with physical violence.

The rock scene and theatrical glitter/drag aspects of freak culture involve further interactions with the gay sensibility—these are discussed in this book in some detail in

32

Tommi Avicolli's article on music and David Holland's article on clothing.

The return to a masculine style by many faggots once attracted to the hippie image sometimes seems like a rejection of the androgynous aspects of the counterculture, if not a direct rebuke toward feminist women. Isn't it hypocritical for gay men to assert all of this masculinity with butch-imagery clothing—or is it merely a game, not to be taken so seriously (no straight man would wear all those studs!). The counterculture and political revolutions of the sixties have nonetheless made a permanent impact on the gay community. When I first came out, in the mid-sixties, I went to several piano bars where gay men sang "God Bless America" and felt sentimental at the sight of Old Glory draped nearby. It struck me then as an anomaly— presumably such places are harder to find nowadays.

On Creativity

One question that seems unavoidable here concerns the basic idea of creativity. Are gay people more creative? Certainly this is a common myth. In a 1976 interview with gay playwright George Whitmore, published in *Gay Sunshine*, Tennessee Williams stated that homosexuals "have more sensitivity and they are more inclined to be good artists." Asked why, he replied: "Because they have greater sensibility, and because they've *had* to develop a greater sensibility because they have been rejected. . . . They look deeper into themselves and deeper into the human heart."

Even the worst homophobes will usually agree that gay people are especially creative. A few years ago, gay people at Columbia were struggling to obtain some officially sanctioned gay space on campus—a basement lounge in a dorm building. There was considerable opposition from the administration, though the gay group finally won. Around that time a friend of mine, a straight history professor, attended a cocktail party at the dean's residence. Among those in attendance, my friend told me, was a professor of English, and a leading spokesman for the intellectual elite of New York. He expressed his views on the gay lounge controversy by saying that he thought all of this gay liberation was most unfortunate because all of that creative energy would be lost once people come out of the closet and became comfortable with their homosexuality.

In one of the pioneer works on gay men, *The Homosexual and His Society* (Citadel, 1963), Donald Webster Cory and John P. LeRoy included a whole chapter entitled "The Creative." In it, they quoted a study by psychiatrist Albert Ellis of his homosexual patients in which he concludes that homosexuals are less, not more, creative. I don't see the point to such a study (how do you measure creativity, anyway, and can a shrink's patients possibly be a legitimate sample?). As for this professor's attitude, I think it is downright cruel, saying in effect "Let *them* suffer so that *we* can have great works of beauty," and it seems to fit his infamous reactionary and snobbish temperament. I have also heard it said that gay people are more creative because we don't have children to rear, that instead of making babies we make things. Such a viewpoint is antifemale and reflects a very narrow and false view of the human capability. One could certainly argue that many gay men squelch creative impulses at an early age, when these interests are labeled "sissy," thus making a point for the idea completely opposite of Trilling's— namely, that as gay people come out of the closet they will be *more* creative.

John Rechy explores the subject of gay sensibility and creativity in his nonfiction work *The Sexual Outlaw* (Grove Press, 1977). Referring to the "unique, sensual, feeling, elegant sensibility of the sexual outlaw," Rechy explains:

To survive in a heterosexual world, the homosexual plays roles as a child. He turns to his imagination to be himself; that imagination flows easily to the arts. In touch with his sexual persona, the gay artist produces work marked and expanded by its duality—its sensitivity and strength. . . . No, the artist doesn't have to be homosexual to produce good art; and certainly not all homosexual artists are "good." But the artist who represses either the male or female aspect of his or her being produces unfulfilled work. ... If only by the nature of the acute sensibility and sensuality he has brought so abundantly to art, the homosexual should be an object of admiration, not reprobation and hatred.

Rechy's book is a personal account of his own narcissism and his participation in the "promiscuous sexhunt" of the streets, alleys, and parks of Los Angeles—and curiously he sees these pervasive aspects of his life as art, too:

The gay sensibility, obsessed with appearance, produces beautiful bodies, people. The result in males ranges widely—from ballet dancers to bodybuilders. Yes, narcissism as art form. And certainly bodybuilding as art form. Not that all bodybuilders are sexually gay, of course not, but the *form* is gay—the pursuit of the idealized grace of the "woman" and the idealized strength of the "man." ... And [also] the silently symphonic, intricate, instinctively choreographed beauty of the promiscuous sexhunt.

Personally, I don't have any answer to the question about creativity, though I know that the question makes me uncomfortable. It seems to me that some people are creative and witty while others are dull, whether they are gay or straight. In a brilliant essay on wit published in a recent issue of *Fag Rag*, John Mitzel begins by asking, "Why are straight people so dull?" a sentence which almost made me dismiss the article out-of-hand. I tend to think that one's ability to be creative is probably more a function of time and upbringing than it is of sexual orientation or gender. Nonetheless, the myth of gay creativity will probably prevail.

The Danger of Co-optation in the Mainstream

Gay people are now making incredible demands on contemporary mainstream culture. We are beginning to have an impact on the general culture of North America as open gays. Some words from gay slang ("closet," "tacky," and of course the word "gay" itself) are becoming part of standard usage. Gay characters are appearing with increasing frequency on television (though negative stereotypes still abound). Gays have a legitimate, almost daily presence in the newspapers and in the political process.

Certainly, one danger we face is that of co-optation, of losing our radical vision and becoming "like them," being incorporated into "the system." Does a meeting with "gay leaders" (well scrubbed, well dressed) in the White House do us more harm than good? Can a gay politician elected to office because of his or her ideals avoid all of the "dirty tricks" that characterize politics? When a gay organization holds a press conference for the voracious reporters, can it keep its integrity while it engages in the same manipulation and media myth-making that occur at any press conference? One middle-aged gay man, a busy movement activist, used to speak regularly to straight audiences and, in response to the charge that homosexuals "recruit" children, he made a point of talking about his own children and telling his audience how they were all straight. But it wasn't true—one of this gay man's children is a lesbian; he surrendered the truth and the beauty of his daughter's lesbianism to meet the alleged demands of straight society, all for the "good" of "the cause"!

Money can co-opt us, too. Our society is consumer oriented above all, and it is our role as consumer that makes us most acceptable to straight America. When the publishers of commercial gay male newspapers and magazines try to sell ads to straight advertisers (a major goal), one of their main arguments is that their readers have money to spend. It would presumably be a victory for such publications to have an ad from a major cigarette company—never mind cancer! Am I supposed to feel good when, one fine day, I am watching television, and lo and behold there's a pair of male lovers cooing over their shining floor or dazzling laundry?

The danger of all these various forms of co-optation is not to be belittled. The heterosexual world grants to us our bars and baths, our freedom to organize and publish, maybe even eventually our civil rights—but the assumption remains that we will think of ourselves as a distinct minority ("gay people"). There are those of us who do not want a mere current in the mainstream in which to flow, but rather we desire a part in the creation of an entirely new culture. And we rightfully remain concerned about the resurgence of establishment values in the gay subculture, even within the gay liberation movement. (Notice how many groups now speak of gay "rights," avoiding the word "liberation.") More and more gay writers, including Thomas Dotton, John Mitzel, and John Paul Hudson, have been observing with alarm that the initial impulse of gay liberation is betrayed if it has now come to mean that we are just like everyone else except we happen to have sex with people of the same gender, if, as Dotton put it, we are "merely the lavender creation of some heterosexual opposite." We should instead sing defiantly, with Ray Davies of the Kinks: "I'm not like everybody else!"

Although gay men suffer from the antihomosexual bigotry of the mainstream culture, there are frequent examples of ways in which gay male culture reflects or even contributes to the most immoral or corrupt elements of the mainstream culture. For example, gay bars that discriminate against blacks and women, often because the patrons want it that way, perpetuate racism and sexism. One cultural norm in which gay men seem to have a particularly strong hold is the youth/beauty syndrome. In their role as media workers (photographers, admen, etc.) gay men seem to play a special part in the culture as promoters of youth and beauty, even as we suffer as victims of "looksism" and the youth cult. Many faggots are made to feel "over the hill" as they hit their twenty-fifth birthdays. In addition, rigid standards of youth and beauty often promoted by gay men also contribute to the oppression of women. Gay men help in the creation and perpetuation of the "beautiful woman" in modern American fashion—as dress designers, fashion photographers, cosmetologists, hairdressers, editors of women's magazines, etc.—and it is in such areas of the culture, given the strength of the feminist interaction with the gay liberation movement, that conflicts occur. Some may argue about "aesthetics," taste, and even personal choice, but one cannot deny the powerful institutional influences over people's lives, especially when media conglomerates are publishing magazines with circulations in the hundreds of thousands.

In the Middle Ages, some gay people managed to detach themselves from the mainstream culture, an oppressive system of lords of the manor and long-toiling serfs. These gay people—mostly men, I presume—were often minstrels and troubadours. Some were court jesters, with a unique ability to say a lot of outrageous things since no one quite took them seriously and they posed no threat. Harry Hay, who helped to found the Mattachine Society in 1950, had discovered the existence of organized groups called the *sociétés joyeuses* in medieval French Renaissance society. "One was known as the Société Mattachine," Hay told interviewer Jonathan Katz *(Gay American History)* in recounting the origins of the contemporary Mattachine Society.

These societies, lifelong secret fraternities of unmarried townsmen who never performed in public unmasked, were dedicated to going out into the countryside and conducting dances and rituals during the Feast of Fools, at the Vernal Equinox. Sometimes these dance rituals, or masques, were peasant protests against oppression—with the maskers, in the people's name, receiving the brunt of a given lord's vicious retaliation. So we took the name Mattachine because we felt that we 1950s gays were also a masked people, unknown and anonymous, who might become engaged in morale building and helping ourselves and others, through struggle, to move toward *total* redress and change.

This masking tradition is alive and well today at Halloween time, at New Orleans' Mardi Gras, and various drag balls in many cities and towns, but the radical spirit behind the tradition seems nearly gone. Today, when gay people criticize mainstream American culture, it can be as harmless outsiders, as supplicants who want the proverbial piece of the pie, or as revolutionaries (is the term too dramatic?), no longer masked, who want to create something new and beautiful.

Culture and Politics: Abandoning the Dichotomy

One problem in examining culture is defining the relationship of culture to politics. Those who see culture as merely "the arts" often see no connection between culture and politics. I would argue, however, that the word culture is, in fact, widely misused and misunderstood in our society generally. To me culture is the way that a people live, the way they think and feel, involving relationships between people and to the planet. Our culture, therefore, includes religion, language, music, art, dance, government, and all human interactions, including sex. It is a matter of culture that men in our society compete on the athletic field. It is a matter of culture that women are channeled into such work as typing, teaching, and cleaning house. Thus it is of special significance when a girl wants to play Little League baseball, and it is also of special significance when a man is employed as a secretary or a nurse or keeps his own house. It is a matter of culture when people assume, often with disdain, that a male hairdresser or a male ballet dancer is a homosexual. It is a matter of culture that the words "fuck" and "cocksucker" are used to express anger and hatred. It is a matter of culture that faggots live in neighborhoods like Greenwich Village and Castro Street, or congregate in special resort areas such as Fire Island and Provincetown.

Marxists have tended to look at culture in a special way. Most contemporary writers who define themselves as Marxist examine cultural phenomena in order to determine their relationship to economic classes. Thus, a Marxist will look at a movie or a painting and try to decide whether or not it serves the "interests" of the working class (though few working people think in this manner). If the critic believes the work of art serves the interest of the working class (proletariat), it is proletarian art, or good art. Otherwise, it serves the ruling class and it is bourgeois art or bad art. Most creative artists, even those

39

genuinely concerned about the exploitation of workers, balk at this vulgar Marxist approach to criticism and to culture generally. And with good reason—for this approach to culture accepts the dichotomy of politics/culture even as it attempts to deny it, and the end result of such logic is censorious cultural commissars. In other words, the Marxist critic examines art in isolation, and when this critic states that art must serve the interests of one class or another, she or he is ultimately removing art from the overall cultural context in which it takes place.

The vulgar Marxist critic of culture, in failing to see the ultimate unity of culture and politics, refuses to see the ways in which the culture of the working class (the way working-class people live, the values they hold) often embodies the values or lifestyle of the bourgeoisie, values which may be sexist, racist, or otherwise harmful. In our society, for example, the consumption patterns of the working class serve the interest of the ruling class at the same time that they contribute to the destruction of the environment. Thus, any discussion of the "dictatorship of the proletariat" should reasonably include a discussion of these contradictions, but due to the vulgar Marxist's narrow view of culture, such discussions are avoided.

I would argue that culture and politics are completely intertwined, and that the creative process involves complex psychological and sociological processes that are hardly understood and that cannot simply be held up to a vulgar class analysis. The role of artists as rebels, as well as the role of sexual nonconformists as rebels, within any culture, needs to be examined. Culture must be looked at, furthermore, not only in terms of its relationship to labor and class, but its relationship to sex and roles. Thus, we speak of a culture as matriarchal or patriarchal, as sex positive or sex negative, as anthropologists often do, and we can analyze the politics of that culture. Analyzing the content of culture can lead to a greater sense of artistic awareness and integrity, with respect for individual expression. It is only when analysis is applied dogmatically by a given power structure that censorship and cultural fascism result.

Gay people, especially gay males, have often been said to possess their own subculture. The origins and nature of this subculture are of great interest and are only beginning to be explored. At the same time, it is widely understood that gay people play a significant role in the creation of the general popular culture in our society. In fact, gay people function in the mainstream of American culture and help to create that mainstream. But there is also a definite sense in which the mainstream culture is antigay at its core, and we know that the mainstream culture promotes the nuclear family (Mom, Dad, and the kids) as "normal," while calling homosexuality sinful, sick, criminal, and just plain dirty. Gay people are increasingly involved in rebellion against this mainstream, though at the same time we acquiesce to it because we have no choice; we live in the middle of it. (For example, we choose carefully what places we may be affectionate in public with members of the same sex. The braver among us choose less carefully.)

The subculture, too, involves some rebellion against the mainstream culture, but that very subculture is also attached to the mainstream culture. It reflects it and it belongs to it. Simultaneously, some gay people, especially lesbians, are currently involved in a high-energy effort to create a separate new culture that is defined not in terms of the mainstream but in terms of the interests and creativity and community awareness of gay people. The desire of some gay men and lesbians to go "beyond labels," furthermore, entails dealing with the dilemma of gay identity and the broader human identity. This is an important issue which I explored in the anthology *After You're Out* in an essay I called "On Gay Identity and Human Identity: A Liberationist Dilemma."

For many gay people, this new "lavender culture" has come to have increasing importance to our lives. The term "lavender" brings with it an implicit commitment to eradicating the rigid sex role system that characterizes mainstream culture. Lavender is a color that has been associated with homosexuals for many decades. The color is implicitly androgynous, a combination of the male principle (blue) and the female principle (pink) which society has sanctified in its segregationist choice of baby blankets. To examine lavender culture, therefore, is to look at the

41

many facets of gay people and our culture. The essays in this book discuss the role of gay people in the traditional arts, examine our subculture and its relationship to mainstream culture, and demonstrate that the struggle for social change that has become known as the gay liberation movement is a vital cultural and political force.

The Impact of Gay Liberation

In a gay book I read recently, the author refers to "gayness" in ancient Greece and China. Of course, homoerotic sensibility, which includes the physical and emotional attributes of gayness as we know it now, did exist in those ancient times. There were men and women in those ancient times who made love, physically, exactly as we do now, and who felt many of the same emotions that we feel now. The history of our love, what one art historian called "the other face of love," has been hidden from us as a part of the dominant heterosexual society's effort to destroy us. But gayness as we now know it assumes a kind of identifiable culture, a group of people who call themselves "gay." Perhaps there always were people who identified themselves and were identified by others as "different," but the institutionalizing of the difference as "gay" is a relatively recent phenomenon, probably dating back to the mid-1800s.

That history is now being explored for the first time and we are learning more and more about the courageous and outspoken works of Walt Whitman, Edward Carpenter, John Addington Symonds, Magnus Hirschfeld, Roger Casement, Oscar Wilde and others. References to most of these writers are made in Ian Young's essay on male poetry published in this anthology.

In his *Gay American History*, Jonathan Katz documents the existence of Paresis Hall, a special meeting place for gay men in New York City around the 1890s. Someday, perhaps, there'll be a plaque at the site of the old Paresis Hall (392 Bowery) as well as at the building on Christopher Street that once housed the old Stonewall Inn, site of the June 1969 Stonewall rebellion, which gave birth to today's gay liberation movement.

These bars have a rightful place in American history, no less so than Revolutionary War gathering places such as New York's Fraunces Tavern or the inns of Williamsburg, Virginia. I suspect that most of the people who read this book will have been to a gay bar, which is the quintessential institution of contemporary gay culture, a common denominator of sorts. There are those who don't like the bars, of course, and those who have never been to one, but there is no denying that the bar has served an essential need for sociability and communication. A whole section of this book concerns itself with gay bars, in fact.

Surely, however, our political movement has had an impact on the bars, if only because the people in them have become more aware and more self-assured. In the earliest days of gay liberation, participants expressed a great deal of ambivalence about the bars (and all of the institutions of the existing subculture). From the outset, we were not certain whether we wanted to destroy the subculture or merely have an impact on it. At the same time, our energies were directed toward the entire culture, the mainstream. All of that ambivalence, all our multifaceted efforts remain with us to this day. In "Gay Is Good," published in *Out of the Closets*, Martha Shelley describes the members of the Gay Liberation Front liberating a gay bar for the evening (who of us who was there can forget it?): "We come in. The people already there are seated quietly at the bar. Two or three couples are dancing. It's a down place. And the GLF takes over. Men dance with men, women with women, men with women, everyone in circles. No roles. You ever see that at a straight party? Not men with men—this is particularly verboten." That kind of uninhibited group spirit can be found a fair amount in gay bars today, though not as much as we might hope. But in 1970 it was unheard of.

Speaking of gay bars, I often wonder about the music in them, especially the shake-your-ass music so many of us like to dance to. If rhythm and blues, Motown, and now disco are the most popular kinds of music in gay bars, what does this have to do with gay sensibility? When I first came out, there was a tendency for men very concerned with maintaining a butch façade not to get up and dance (*that* was for the femmes, and the butch men stood around and watched). This is still true for some men, and it's a pretty obvious example of the sex role system permeating gay life. Gay liberation has certainly encouraged dancing as a form of self-expression for men. I often also wonder whether white gays and black gays experience this dance music—most of it made by blacks—in very different ways. At the risk of flirting with the old "blacks have natural rhythm" stereotype, I think it's fair to say that black men have been less uptight than white men about getting up on the dance floor and moving it. The disco as an institution of contemporary urban American culture is largely the creation of blacks, gays, and women. But what about gay freaks—us '60s people—who quickly get bored with the Motown and the disco and prefer to dance to a variety of music from hard rock to reggae—are we forsaking our "gay culture"? Hopefully, we are not dealing with rigid categories for what is proper behavior or tastes for gay people.

It is clear that the overly political explosion known as gay liberation has had an important cultural analogue. That's really what this book is all about. Articles in this book cover many aspects of gay culture, both from the perspective of post-Stonewall gay liberation and what we have called "looking at the old culture with new eyes." Explorations of the theater, literature, language, music, dance, and the visual arts are included.

It has not been possible, of course, to cover everything. Various aspects of spirituality and mass media of communication have been important in the burgeoning new gay culture, for example, but it hasn't been possible for us to include some topics in the anthology (not due to any conscious decision but simply as a factor of the process of acquisition and selection of articles).

America in the '70s has experienced a "spiritual revolution" that covers a broad spectrum of values from right-wing Christian Fundamentalism and esoteric mysticism to creative free-wheeling spiritual values sometimes summed up in the term "New Age." This has involved the gay

44

community, too. Christian churches have become the strongest gay organizations in many cities, while at the same time other gay people focus on the history of religious oppression and direct their anger toward all organized religion. When gay anarchist Charley Shively quoted Leviticus and burned a Bible at a Gay Pride rally in Boston in June 1977, he was vilified as a bookburner by gay Catholic Brian McNaught, dismissed as a fanatic by gay Unitarian and agnostic John Kyper but defended as courageous by gay Episcopalian Louie Crew, proving that the relationship of gay people to Christianity is complicated and controversial.

When religion encompasses a strong cultural heritage that may be treasured despite traditional homophobia—among gay Jews or Mormons, for example—then people have attempted to deal with the contradiction on either a private, individual basis, or in newly organized gay synagogues or Mormon gay caucuses. Those gay men who are aware of spirituality and attracted to it have also explored astrology, the Tarot, and the history of Native American shamanism, and some even strive to create contemporary faggot spirituality. Arthur Evans, one of the founders of the New York Gay Activists Alliance, has done serious research on primitive religions and sexual repression and his work is scheduled for publication by Fag Rag Books (Box 331 Kenmore Station, Boston MA 02215). Other gay people have found a comfortable spiritual home in some Buddhist groups where personal freedoms are respected and homophobic traditions are absent. Still others find agnostic or atheist thought to be most in keeping with sexual freedom, with religion seen as a source of guilt-inducing mind/body dichotomy.

Gay radio has been an important and unique form of communication. As John Zeh, the gay radio producer, told me, listeners to gay radio are often those "still struggling with their sexual identities," people who find a gay radio program—headphones (for secret listening) or not—a convenient and discreet way to make contact with the gay community. Just the names of some of the regularly scheduled shows express the lively spirit of this new movement among gay broadcasters: "Fruit Punch" and "Radio

45

Free Lesbian" in Berkeley, Calif.; "IM, RU?" in Los Angeles, Calif.; "Come Out Tonight" in New Haven, Conn.; "Gay Space" in Sarasota, Fla.; "Gaybreak" in Amherst, Mass.; "Closet Space" in Columbia, Mo.; "Stonewall Nation" and "Sappho" in Buffalo, N.Y.; "Lambda" in Pittsburgh, Pa.; "Closets are for Clothes" in Ann Arbor, Mich.; "Amazon Country" and "Sunshine Gaydream" in Philadelphia, Pa.

The production of gay videotapes and gay documentary movies has been on the increase, and the *Gayellow Pages* (Box 292, New York, N.Y. 10014) lists several groups working in these fields. Funding and access to the airwaves remain major obstacles in the area of mass communication, especially the electronic media. As Andrew Kopkind and John Scagliotti told an interviewer when they were producing the "Lavender Hour" for Boston radio station WBCN-FM, the Federal Communications Commission (FCC) is "basically a repressive institution, and it's hard to reconcile a movement of sexual liberation with an agency of repression."

The gay press has been essential for communication among gay people, and even though there are many gay people who have never been reached, the press has had an impact. Many of the articles in this book (and in our previous anthologies) were published in the gay press. A discussion of the role of the press in the oppression and liberation of gay people is included in *Out of the Closets* (Stuart Byron's "The Closet Syndrome") and in *After You're Out* (Charley Shively's "A View of Fag Rag"). As the Fag Rag collective notes in its "Second Five-Year Plan," published in this book, one concrete goal for the gay movement is the development of a network of communication. The images of gay people, or even of gay liberation, presented on network news shows, situation comedies (such as *All in the Family*), in movies such as *Norman, Is That You?*" are a mixed bag ranging from awful to tolerable. It is only in our independent gay media that we have been able to find the rich, self-aware depiction of the gay reality unencumbered by such considerations as commercialism, what-will-straights-think?, "family hour viewing," individual careers, middle-class imagery, concern about effeminacy in men and masculinity in women, defensiveness in general, and so on. The best available view of images of gays in the movies is Vito Russo's film-lecture he's been taking around the country and which eventually may make it to educational TV. Russo has an article summarizing his views in Dennis Sanders' book *Gay Source* while another helpful work is Parker Tyler's book *Screening the Sexes*.

One purpose of this book is to communicate the richness and variety of the gay experience. Another purpose is to portray that experience for what it has been in large measure—a struggle against a dominant culture that imposes strict sex roles on men and women, a culture that would prefer to deny the very existence of homosexuality. The creation of an independent, vibrant gay culture against the imposing values of heterosexual America is an impressive accomplishment. These writings add to that accomplishment as they document it.

No Man's Land

by Karla Jay

A Little Herstory

A people cannot exist without a culture—that is, a common set of values and experience passed down from person to person, from generation to generation. That is why conquering nations try either to destroy the culture of those they wish to rule, as the Christians did to the so-called heathens by forcing a new religion upon them, or by absorbing the conquered culture into their own, as the Romans absorbed the Greek gods.

Homosexuals and especially lesbians are in a unique position regarding our culture. Unlike other groups which at least have memories of having had their own culture at one time (however distant), homosexuals and lesbians (as well as all women in general, of course) have no memory of a time in which we had a separate, viable culture, of a time when we have not been subsumed into the heterosexual mainstream. Naturally, there have been cultures in which homosexuals and lesbians were accepted, and even honored (as in ancient Greece), but the homosexuality was still incorporated into the mainstream culture and the people who practiced it were not assigned a separate identity—in other words, homosexuality was an act, not a lifestyle.

More commonly, male homosexuals and lesbians were persecuted. We were burned at the stake as witches by the Inquisition, incarcerated in prison camps by Stalin and later by Hitler, and even in the United States, the "land of the free," we have been lobotomized in mental institutions, shunned as "pinkos" by the right-wingers, as "bourgeois decadent" or "illegal" by the left, and at best pitied by the liberals. Our contributions to history, to literature, to art, to education have been obliterated, whitewashed, or explained away ("in spite of . . .").

In the nineteenth century male homosexuality and lesbianism emerged from a "sexual preference," isolated as a mere sexual inclination, to become a "way of life," a culture, and places where gay people could meet one another, such as bars, were created. Lesbians and male homosexuals first began to identify themselves as living a gay life around that time.

We started to develop outward signs of a culture, such as language to define types within our community, or sexual acts, for which there was no "heterosexual equivalent." We also started to dress openly in ways which were recognizable to other gay people, for clothing is a cultural institution. When we think of certain peoples, such as native Americans or the Swiss, we immediately think of their "native costumes." We also developed meeting places imitative of those straight people had. These included private social clubs, bars, salons, etc. But because we had always been integrated (willingly or not) into the mainstream heterosexist culture, the culture we developed was borrowed, transformed at best into same-sex patterns that imitated heterosexuality. We played their roles: There was "a man and a woman" except that both were of the same gender. We danced, but it was their dances. We created some words but used their language. In short, we developed a "subculture."

As long as we hid in the darkness of bars, private clubs, or discreet salons (also bushes, baths, and tearooms for men)—as long as we didn't get so bold as to show our faces in the light of day—heterosexuals permitted our "subculture" to exist. They kept us in the darkness of the bars (usually owned by straights and later by organized crime, which manages to profit from anything "illegal") as they had kept us in the darkness of our ignorance about our past, about other lesbians and male homosexuals who had gone before us, and prevented us from knowing who else was "one of us." With the threat of ostracism or worse, heterosexuals forced us to hide our identities, to wear masks; in short, we were expected to marry to cover "it" up or at best never to reveal to them the deepest truths about our sexuality. The irony was, of course, that the masks were always on the heterosexuals, for the lesbian or male homosexual who hid never knew for certain

49

who really was aware of her/his true identity. Thus, the rulers permitted us to exist so long as we allowed them not to perceive our true feelings, and the greatest fear they left us with was one of being discovered to be what indeed we really were—different.

And if we dared to display that difference, there was always mental rape—"cleanups" at election time, bar raids, scandals, bath and tearoom raids (for men)—to keep us in our place, just as men have always used physical rape to keep women in our place. The thrust of the early homophile civil rights movement, especially in the United States and Germany, was to tone down this mental rape, to show heterosexuals that we were just like them, that we ate with forks, didn't have horns, had only one head. There was just this tiny difference. . . . For example, at the Annual Reminder, a homophile demonstration which took place every July 4th in Philadelphia during the mid-1960s, a strict dress code was enforced by the demonstrators themselves, which meant that men wore suits and ties and women wore dresses. The message was that gay people were the same, not different.

The Stonewall uprising in 1969 and the gay liberation groups that came afterward flaunted that difference. But even more importantly, we broke down the isolation and silence that had entombed us for countless centuries. We found each other *outside* the dark confines of the bars and other "social clubs." But once we gathered together in groups, rather than as couples or in fleeting sexual encounters, what was it that we had in common? Was there anything that made us a "people"?

The emerging answer is yes, and the culture that has grown since the Stonewall rebellion has been an important contribution (perhaps the most important) of the current gay and lesbian movements. Legislative gains have been minimal. We have merely chipped away at silences and at social prejudice; we have gained but a few token open representatives in prestigious positions (although thousands more lurk in the closet!). But in the almost ten years since the Stonewall uprising, we have created a culture and put fruitful energy into unearthing our heritage. That's a major achievement. Even if all the laws turn against us, if the

50

so-called backlash of heterosexuals against "permissiveness" increases (although I personally don't believe there is a backlash, since I don't believe I've ever seen a frontlash—that is, any true acceptance), we will still have our songs to sing, our books to keep with us, our herstory to treasure in our hearts, and the knowledge that there is a common core uniting us as a people. We are a people who have always survived and will always survive!

The flowering of culture in the past decade has been especially true for lesbians. I think in part this has happened because, while gay men had more of a subculture because of "camp's" acceptance in the mainstream culture (as by critics such as Susan Sontag), lesbians, since we are women, have been more subsumed and at the same time isolated in the straight culture. Therefore, theoretically, we started with a blank slate, which, though it would appear to be a disadvantage, actually made it easier to build a new and different culture. However, it remains to distinguish what is really "us" and what is the baggage of our heterosexual upbringing and endless brainwashing. So for many lesbians, separatism became the means for finding our true identities (see Charlotte Bunch's article). In self-chosen separation from straight women and all men instead of isolation within the straight man's world we can find what feels genuine and what is borrowed. We can talk with each other, expending no energy on men or straight women, and discover what we want, who we are, what our common values, goals, desires are. Gay men, due to the fact that they have for the most part held on to their male privilege (and straight institutions which give them that privilege) haven't been able to disassociate themselves as much or as often from straight culture.

Some Politics and Culture

This discovery of each other has led to a genuine flowering of culture, one which has created lesbian music, publishing houses, spirituality and religion, educational institutions, garages, restaurants, karate schools, political and social groups. That may seem like a strange mixture

51

since men, especially leftist men, have always pitted politics against culture, and posed them as two alternatives instead of as part of one whole. And wholeness, a complete circle, is a form, I believe, which is inherent to women as the phallus and phallic institutions are the archetypes of male culture. Wholeness goes back to the womb, to the mother and her mother before her, to the unbroken cycle of life (being born to a woman and giving birth to other women and to oneself). All this is, I am convinced, at the heart of women's culture. The circular form means inclusion of everyone and everything whereas phallic form and thinking with their hard, rigid structures, institutions, and rules mean divisions, exclusions. Phallic thinking also means one person rising above another, one thing or person being bigger than another—in short, the whole idea of hierarchy.

Therefore, we do not have to choose either art or politics, culture or politics, building a garage/restaurant or building a revolution. Such dichotomies indicate male, either/or exclusive thinking, the epitome of which must be the existentialist philosophers, such as Jean-Paul Sartre or Albert Camus. Thus, if we are told that we have to choose, we can answer that we do *not* have to operate within male choices or male questions, for the questions invariably set up the answers. We must and can set aside even the questions.

I keep talking about the development of women's culture and women's thinking, and this brings up two points which must be covered before I go on to discuss more specific aspects of our culture. First, I use women's culture (some would respell it *womyn's* or *wimmin's* to get rid of the root *man*) and lesbian culture interchangeably. I do this purposely because I think that women's culture and lesbian culture are basically the same. Almost all the women producing today outside of traditional home-related work—whether it be books, records, garages, restaurants, women's centers, and even abortion clinics—are lesbians. I'm even certain that if we dig far enough into herstory, we will discover that almost every woman who was doing something atypical was a lesbian. Today one has to look pretty hard to find a straight woman active in our arts. For example, in music, Holly Near was the "token straight woman," and now she too is a lesbian!

Secondly, I talk of women/lesbian culture and not gay male culture. I believe that culture is one area in which lesbians have greatly diverged from gay men, perhaps because, as I have pointed out, gay men had somewhat different roots, and after all, they *are* men. And although we do have common experiences, such as coming out, problems with the straight culture (laws, discrimination, harassment, etc.), the culture we have developed from the same sexist oppression is very different. This is true, as I've said, in part because gay men, being men, with greater stake in the ruling culture, have relied heavily on already established instititions and forms for their "new" culture. Lesbians, twice removed and thoroughly alienated, have started from scratch.

Also, we are not a people in the sense that other groups have been a people. Blacks have been black men and their women; Jews have been Jewish men and their women, and lesbians are being very careful (as Rose Jordan pointed out in a forum published in *After You're Out*) that we do not become the women of gay men. If we do become a true, united people, it will be the first union of choice, and not the domination of the male over the female of the ethnic/racial (or whatever) group. We will not allow such domination. Part of the refusal of male domination was what led many women to become lesbians in the first place!

One might argue, therefore, that this is two separate books. I have heard similar comments or criticisms about our first two anthologies, *Out of the Closets* and *After You're Out*. Certainly there are two different views as to what is culture, and the two cultures are areas in which lesbians and gay men are sometimes furthest apart. But I feel that the gay men can learn a lot from what lesbians have done, and pure separatism is a luxury enjoyed only by a few lesbians in rural communes or in large metropolitan areas (in short, you have to have enough of a group to separate!), and indeed, not all lesbians wish to separate from 45 percent of the population (the male minority).

Nor do most of us wish to totally ignore other struggles, such as racism, classism, ageism, looksism, etc.

Again, therefore (in my circular logic!) I go back to my original point about not making false choices. One does not have to belong to either the women's culture or the men's culture. One can take whatever part of each that suits one. The women can read the women's articles and the men the men's. Hopefully everyone will read some of each so that we can learn from and grow with one another. For lesbians have not been the only ones to strive toward a new society, and in all fairness we should commend the building of a new culture by some gay men, particularly the gay male press, some of which, unlike the straight press, has tried to incorporate feminist principles.

Economics and Culture

One major difference one will immediately spot between gay male and lesbian discussion of culture is that lesbians usually refer to the money involved in the art as well as the content whereas the gay men have usually discussed only the content. For example, Lynne D. Shapiro discusses the money used to put together women's music while Tommi Avicolli discusses the content of rock music. The heart of this difference again is that male homosexuals are men, and lesbians are women. That may sound simplistic, but it isn't. As women, lesbians are in the lowest income bracket in the world. And despite women's liberation, the economic gap between male and female income is increasing rather than decreasing; indeed, women now earn less percentagewise than men do than we did ten years ago, and the situation appears to be worsening. In addition, white women earn less on the average than black men. Thus, a household of any two women will probably have a gross income of under $10,000 while any two men will probably earn about $18,000—almost twice as much. (One can obtain these figures from the annual U.S. Labor Department bulletin.)

Being on the bottom of the economic ladder—and without the traditional economic support straight women have

54

gotten in return for selling their bodies to heterosexual men (marriage)—lesbians must worry constantly about money. And it takes money to start anything—the equipment to start a garage or a restaurant runs over $20,000 to begin with. As Lynne D. Shapiro points out, one concert costs thousands of dollars to produce. Even running a dance involves renting space, music, refreshments. As women, lesbians don't have access to the kind of money men have always taken for granted, and therefore when we talk about starting any sort of institution or project, we first ask: "Where can we possibly get the money for this?" As Nancy Groschwitz points out, feminist credit unions may be one of the answers.

Finally, lesbian businesses and projects are usually trying to avoid the volunteerism rut that is so much of the mentality of being a woman. If you think of volunteers—such as helpers at hospitals or low-paying professions that "serve" the public—you will think of positions which are not accidentally doled out to women. Not ironically, the gay men who are female identified often go into "volunteer" or public service professions, such as nursing.

One feminist principle is that all labor is valuable. Without free household labor, which every married woman provides so that her husband can work at his job, this country would come to a standstill. One solution to that is to pay women for household labor so that the task takes on dignity and so that the laborer acquires some independent income (not an "allowance" from the husband, controlled by him). Thus volunteerism by itself in a capitalist society is degrading in principle because the entire value code is that payment proves worth. Of course, we must in the end eradicate that entire value system, but for now most women are trying not to reinforce the volunteer mentality imbued into being "female."

Culture and Content

Nevertheless, it is not just the mechanics—money, political structure—that are different about women's culture. The content too is different. Otherwise, we would just be

55

recreating the same stories with two female heroines riding off into the sunset to live happily ever after.

It is difficult, however, to try to capsulize the content of lesbian art because there is so much variety and disparity within the different media. I'll use two—novels and music—to discuss some of the diversity. In novels, there are many different trends. On the very political end of the spectrum, there are writers like Rita Mae Brown, whose *In Her Day* is a polemic of sorts in which a dialectical struggle is set up between an older apolitical lesbian and a younger radical lesbian. Jane Rule's novels, on the other hand, could be labeled "apolitical" (although I personally don't believe that anything is without some political viewpoint, however submerged in the art form). However, her last two novels, *Against the Season* and *The Young in One Another's Arms*, have tended to have a decentralized form. In other words, there is no distinct hero or heroine, no towering phallic centrality around which the rest of the world must inevitably revolve. Lesbian novels are also sometimes "experimental," such as the works of Bertha Harris and Monique Wittig. In her novels (especially *Les Guérillières* and *The Lesbian Body*) Wittig has almost totally eliminated plot line in order to recreate the stories that affect all women (such as the myths we were all brought up with: Orpheus and Eurydice, for example) and to recreate language itself. After all, we are usually incapable of thinking without language. Thus since the root of the word *hysteria* means womb, the implication is that only women are exceedingly emotional. In Harris's latest novel, *Lover*, her characters, like the female cycles of life which I've mentioned earlier, flow together. Her characters have no beginnings, middles, or ends, and her generations of women meld (no rigid, traditional, separate character traits for each individual).

Male sexuality has a beginning (erection), middle (thrusting), and end (orgasm), and man has created all art in the image of his sexuality. However, for women the orgasm is the beginning of another cycle of pleasure, excitement and ebbing, excitement and ebbing—seemingly without beginning or end. It is fitting that we have chosen to reflect *our* sexuality in our art froms.

Kay Gardner has put this same cyclical energy into her music, which some would label "classical," since her *Mooncircles* album is mainly flute music with few sung "tunes." However, her music is not classical in the male sense of the word, for again male symphonic structure follows the pattern of the male orgasm (the erotic beginning, the thrusting middle, and the great kettledrum orgasm at the end—the climax). Gardner's music reaches a peak or climax only to gently subside and rise again to subside and rise again. Even the titles of her compositions, such as "Lunamuse," or "Moon Flow," as well as the title of the album itself, reflect the circular influence of the moon (which is traditionally female, Diana, as opposed to Apollo and other male sun gods).

Whether one prefers one's art heavily laced with politics, or whether one seeks "art for art's sake," one should keep in mind that there should be room in a matriarchal/lesbian culture to embrace both tendencies or choose some middle ground. Again, one should not have to choose at all, but I do sometimes see a demand for such choosing coming from within the women's community of music and writing. Such self-appointed critics would create a new lesbian culture with guidelines and tastes as strict as those currently endorsed by the male establishment culture, as promoted through such male-dominated institutions as *The New York Times,* the *New York Review of Books* or *Rolling Stone.*

As a writer, I suppose I especially rebel against any dictates of art. Having been told all my life to "write like a man" (and to think like one) and given instructions on how to accomplish this transsexual feat ("Get to the point," "Don't get emotional"), I raised my consciousness and rejected those doctrines: I write (and live) as I please, as I feel is good and natural for me. Therefore, I will not have a new group of fascist dictators, albeit "feminist," telling me how to write/draw/sing/make love or whatever "like a woman." Nor will I have them tell me what that means, and how to accomplish becoming a member of my own gender (now how to "think like a woman"). In short, we must be wary of new sorts of fascism, coming this time from within our movement, giving us new, unacceptable choices or demands. For feminist/lesbian artistic dictatorship would be as pernicious as male domination. Let's not exchange masters for mistresses!

Culture with a Small c

Culture, however, is not only the arts. None of us (even should we wish to) lives entirely in a world of music, novels, poetry, and art, just as we do not live (no matter how separatist some of us would like to be) in a world without men. We all face the more mundane tasks of building a culture, such as growing and preparing food to eat, creating our own schools, worshiping our own deities, having our own social settings.

The last has not changed for the majority of lesbians. For most of us the bar is still the center of social activity. Where there are enough lesbians in any given town or city, women have usually tried to build alternatives. Some of these are women's centers, coffee houses, rap groups or consciousness raising groups, women's dances (outside of bars), church groups, and so on. The advantage of all these over the bars is that one's primary purpose in the bar, however masked, is usually to cruise, and that underlying assumption reduces us to sex objects and often fills the air with tension. Also, as Felice Newman points out in her article, bars exist by selling alcohol. This leads to alcoholism at worst, and at best bars are merely a borrowed institution. In addition, bars, now as historically, are often owned by straight people or even organized crime. One advantage, therefore, of any of the lesbian-owned alternatives (women's centers, coffee houses, etc.) is that the money taken from lesbians is recycled into the community in the form of employment, better functions or centers, etc., whereas organized crime and even straight bar owners take the profits out of our communities. (In the case of the former, these profits may even be used to oppress women further, as in organized crime's role in prostitution and pornography.) As I pointed out in an article on therapists in *After You're Out,* we really need to ask where our money is going and how it is being used.

To replace bars, the church in recent times has tried to fulfill a social as well as religious function, and this has become true for gay churches as well as straight churches. A lot of lesbians, however, are discouraged by the continuation in these churches of a male God or male trinity and perpetuation of the Judeo-Christian tradition which oppresses women (Jewish men, for example, thank God in daily ritual prayer that they were not born women). Many lesbians, in response, have returned to the Dianic cult—that is, goddess worship. I myself prefer this tradition over the Judaic culture into which I was born. The goddess offers female role models, examples of genuine female power, a positive emphasis on female genitalia and bodies (Judaism used to put women away in separate tents and orthodox Jewish women still take ritual baths after menstruation because they are "unclean"), a respect for aging, a respect for all life, and herbal alternatives to the male-dominated health care system (with its emphasis on drugging women to death or tranquilizing us to keep us from "making trouble"). I see the new women's spirituality (again, most of the women in this are lesbians) as a source of energy and inspiration. I do not, however, as some lesbians do, see spirituality as an alternative to politics. I have integrated the energy I get from spirituality, vegetarianism, astrology, and so on, into my political life. In fact, I see a great danger in turning completely to religion, even women's religion, as the "answer"—that is, where religion becomes an end in itself instead of the means of bringing more energy into one's life. Religion, even women's religion, won't stop oppression. Our very lives are at stake (rape, antiabortion drives, anti-ERA drives, women-battering, and so forth,) and to drop out chanting odes to the goddess will bring no more political change than will chanting "Hare Krishna" (as a life's work). As Naomi Weisstein and Heather Booth pointed out in a perceptive, widely published article entitled "Will the Women's Movement Survive?", women who totally rely on the powers of the goddess could be as foolish as the native Americans who, in their final days of struggle against the invading white people, turned to ghost dancing and believed that dance would protect them against the slaughter-

59

ing white man. I wear a labyris to show my devotion to Diana, but it is my knowledge of karate that protects me against rape!

Religion is one of the oldest institutions. One institution which is fairly new and has become part of the women's and gay movements is conferences. Conferences are a good way of gathering together lesbians and gay men who live in a particular area or who are interested in a particular field, whether it be academia, vegetarianism, separatism, or homesteading. Everywhere one looks there are conferences, and these usually combine several aspects of women's culture, such as music and poetry, a dance, politics, consciousness raising, child care, a sharing of food, and an opportunity to meet other lesbians in a nonoppressive, nonexploitative and nonsex-laden atmosphere. The conferences offer information, entertainment, stimulation, companionship, and often result in ongoing projects and ventures, friendships, love relationships, political energy. Lesbian conferences are somewhat different from gay male conferences (for example, the male-dominated Gay Academic Union) in that male-dominated conferences usually offer "panel" discussions." That format sets up the old dichotomy of teacher/pupil. For some fields (and especially skills such as herbal healing, massage, or auto mechanics) this setup is ideal, but on a topic such as "coming out" or "lesbian sexuality," most lesbians (if we are in control of the conference) opt for an open discussion, perhaps with a moderator. After all, who is an expert on coming out?

Lesbians are also changing institutions which have historically been oppressive to us—for example, I've briefly touched on the subject of medicine. From the time Hippocrates and his followers started to turn medicine from an herbal art practiced by female witches (a word which means *wise women*) for illnesses and midwives for pregnancy into a "science" and therefore a field worthy of men (and, as we all know, a lucrative profession), women have been the particular victims of misogynist medicine. The current victimization of women by the male-dominated medical establishment (such as in the use of tranquilizers) has been documented in several recent books. One specific

60

area of mistreatment for lesbians is gynecology. I can still remember lying to gynecologists when they asked what form of birth control I used. In my mind, I would silently tell my male gynecologists that I used the safest kind, lesbianism, but I would tell them aloud that I used "foam," since when I had told gynecologists the truth about my sexual preference they had been exceedingly cruel in examining me and had used oversized cold speculums and unnecessary force. Like many lesbians I got to a fearful place where I preferred to take my chances getting cervical cancer ̈rather than to face further abuse. Other sorts of doctors were not much better. Because I was "single" and thirty, my complaints (unless accompanied by high fever) were often dismissed as depression.

Unlike the majority of lesbians, who are still entrapped in the straight male health care system, I had the luck to find a clinic in New York City which treats primarily lesbians one night a week. There no one ever asked me embarrassing and unnecessary questions about birth control techniques or how many times a week I had intercourse. The health care workers explained to me in advance everything they were going to do and why. They also used simple language instead of the jargonese straight, male physicians had used. And since the clinic took me seriously as a woman, they took my body seriously. The fee for all this was $3 a few years ago when it opened, and now it is $10 (more if you can and less if you can't, but never a hassle about the fee). The result is that my health has been better not only because of improved health care but also due to the fact that now if I'm ill I'm not as hesitant as I used to be about getting help. Finally, the clinic provides *complete* health care from gynecology to general checkups to a chiropractor to a dermatologist to a dentist (there are also referrals to other specialists who are lesbians or prolesbian in addition to referrals to a lesbian alcoholics group and to lesbian/feminist psychotherapists). That completeness is important because I've seen some clinics (particularly gay male clinics) which treat only sex-related medical problems, and that reduces us, as heterosexist society tries to, to mere sexual beings.

Obviously I'm lucky to live in a large metropolitan area

where such a clinic is available. But if more lesbian doctors would interest themselves in treating our own people (one doctor with the aid of paraprofessional health workers and/or nurses and/or a lab technician could treat a large population of lesbians), we could have these centers everywhere. I don't think such clinics are luxuries, but necessities.

Freedom of the Press Belongs to Those Who Own One

Probably much of what I've said in the previous sections of this introduction is new to you—unless you read the lesbian/feminist press. Accurate, unbiased reporting about daily realities and newsworthy events has not been part of our lives. Rather, we have been presented and portrayed almost exclusively as the heterosexist male-dominated media would have us be seen, and thus the presentations of us have been limited to sick, perverted villains (as in the lesbian rapists in *Born Innocent,* a television prison movie which blithely ignored the fact that outside of prison situations men, not women, rape women) or to the masculine cigar-smoking truck drivers (a type depicted in the play and movie, *The Killing of Sister George*). Not a very nice choice at best and gynocidal at worst.

Therefore, one of the finest achievements of the post-Stonewall lesbian culture has been the creation of our own independent and vast lesbian media network in which we present our own news with our own analyses of it, communicate with one another (without censorship) about our experiences, our feelings, our ideas, and present the world through our eyes. And, yes, there *are* cigar-smoking dyke truck drivers (and I say we need more of them to move us out of men's homes!), but we are also professors, office workers, doctors, lawyers, factory workers, grandmothers, and welfare recipients. We are as myriad as the stars, we are everywhere, and we are probably in everyone. But it has taken and will take our own media and anthologies like this one to get this message out to ourselves and to others.

As with some other aspects of our culture, the lesbian

62

media are not completely new phenomena. *The Ladder*, for example, started publishing in 1956 and continued publishing for sixteen years until it folded. How *The Ladder* survived and indeed seemed to thrive during the McCarthy era, one of whose features was a witch-hunt of lesbians and male homosexuals (who are of course un-American by virtue of the fact that we usually do not live in nuclear families), is a story which should someday be told in great length by *The Ladder's* editor Barbara Grier (known then as Gene Damon). But whatever the difficulties, the results were beautiful, and *The Ladder* contained wonderful lesbian poems, short stories, book reviews, plus news and short biographies of famous lesbians.

The proliferation of lesbian media after the Stonewall uprising led to specialization of the contents of magazines such as *The Ladder*. In other words, some feminist and/or lesbian/feminist magazines now print primarily poetry and prose (*13th Moon* and *Conditions*), essays (*Quest and Sinister Wisdom*), culture (*The Lesbian Tide*), humor (*Albatross*), health (*her-self*), rural living (*Country Women*), news and analysis (*Majority Report, Off Our Backs*), motherhood (*Momma* and *Big Mama Rag*). The lesbian newspapers and magazines vary from mimeographed (*Lesbian Connection* or *Dinah*) to slick, magazine format (*Dyke*). The circulations also vary widely, and it should be added that lesbian media are not restricted to print. Recently there was a monthly national exchange of women's news via video tape, called *Video Letters*, which women from different parts of the country shared information with one another. There are also lesbian radio shows. Radio shows have the advantage of reaching lesbians in their closets as other media cannot. For example, radio can reach lesbians who might be afraid to be spotted buying a lesbian publication or going into a lesbian meeting place. In addition, as Moira Rankin of WGTB-FM in Washington, D.C., put it: "A feminist vision of the media allows women to be trained in a technology never before available, opens the airwaves to many women whose experiences are important to understand, uses the sounds of women's cycles: our poetry, our music, our analysis, and our anger."

A culture cannot exist in a computer. Traditional heterosexist male critics sometimes think it does, and of course that they control the machine, turning it on and off when it suits them, reprogramming it to suit their needs, etc. (These critics were bred, I'm convinced, from the same idiots who preached that the world is flat.) That definition of culture goes back to patriarchal, hierarchical systems of control. The reality of lesbianism is that the culture is us; we are culture. Since there are fewer "consumers" of our culture, that culture is more directly within our control. If we do not like the food—or the politics—of a lesbian restaurant, we can refuse to eat there and soon the restaurant will close.

The power, however, is most often positive. By buying this book, for example, you are participating in lesbian culture. You are helping to support the many women who contributed to this book, and perhaps you will also contact them and give them positive feedback so that they will continue writing. Also, every time you buy a lesbian record, book, or magazine, or eat in a lesbian restaurant, or have your car tuned by a lesbian, you are giving lesbians encouragement—and the resources—to continue. You are also making a political statement that you will no longer let your culture—your very lives—be defined, controlled, owned, and operated by others, that you are the supporter, creator, and intricate component of a new lesbian society (for the distinction between the active creator and the passive consumer is again an unnecessary choice— we all create something and we all consume).

Finally, by supporting and being part of the lesbian culture, you and I will prevent ourselves from becoming co-opted into the mainstream heterosexist culture, again subsumed and eventually consumed by the so-called majority. Our goal is not to see one lesbian pursuing another across a field to advertise some product like hair coloring but to create a world in which hair coloring is not the basis for pursuit. Only by remaining outside that "acceptance" can we ever change ourselves, our gay brothers, straight sisters, and eventually the oppressive male heterosexist culture in general. Change will not happen if we are co-opted or bought by compromises. Only if we turn our double alienation (as women and lesbians) into a positive force and if we create, learn, and grow from that which is not a part of this male-dominated, non-nurturing, polluted world can we change ourselves and create change outside ourselves. For lesbians are not just another minority. If our goal becomes equal rights, we will only become the same as those who pollute, destroy, kill, rape, cherish property over life, one type of person over another. Instead, we must hold on to and practice and support our lesbian culture so that we can create a world in which we and our real and spiritual children shall be free.

II
Sex and the
Pursuit of Pleasure

Queen For a Day: A Stranger in Paradise
by Rita Mae Brown

"In Xanadu did Kubla Khan/A stately pleasure-dome decree." Don't bother booking passage, though: Xanadu is currently called The Club and rests serenely on First Avenue between First and Second Streets in New York City. No woman had ever seen this foreign place until March 21, 1975, for The Club is a "bath house" serving a gay male clientele. However, on that date I, moustache firmly in place, curiosity raging, crossed the threshold into unknown territory. The adventure attracted me, but besides that I've been raised with the constantly repeated notion that women's sexuality and men's sexuality are absolutely different. By placing myself in an all-male situation where there is no intrusion of female sensibility I hoped to learn something about that sacred cow, sexual difference.

Like Dante, I too found my Virgil—Arthur, a dear male friend as high off the fun of it all as I was. Before I could crash The Club I had to contend with the minutiae of cultural sexual differentiation. My fingernails were all wrong. Had to cut them square across. My walk, though springy, just wasn't butch enough—so I practiced a manly gait and felt like John Wayne reduced to five feet four inches. Arthur coached me in my transition, combed my hair, painted burning gum spirits under my nose, slapped on a dashing moustache, draped virile garments on my back, and took me to dinner to rev up my courage.

When the waiter looked at us and asked, "What are you fellows having?" I fought the urge to reply, "A helluva good laugh." Feigning hoarseness I whispered my order. There's no way my voice could ever be confused with a man's. The whisper worked as he didn't bat an eye. Encouraged by this success I still worried about my breasts. At dinner I kept on the short Eisenhower jacket so I passed. But how would I ever get my clothes off in the locker room without anyone noticing?

As we stood in line next to each other to get into the
baths I started sweating. Friday night is buddy night at
The Club. Two men get in for $5. At $2.50 apiece that
makes this the cheapest entertainment in town. Arthur, my
buddy, twitched a bit himself the closer we got to the entrance window. Approximately thirty men waited patiently
in line that evening. As we approached the booth, which
resembles a ticket counter in a movie house, Arthur
jumped forward, paid our money too hastily, and signed
his name on the clipboard. I signed mine "R. Brown,"
which was truthful enough. The door buzzed open and an
attendant pointed us downstairs to the lockers.

White double lockers lined the narrow room. Seven or
eight men crowded in the small space trying to get their
clothes off. I took my shoes off first. What could be safer
than feet? Then socks. Next I unzipped my pants. Wearing
what our Elizabethan ancestors called a codpiece, I felt secure about the tantalizing bulge there. As the men bluntly
stared at my family jewels I whipped off the Eisenhower
jacket. In a place like this your cock means everything. It's
unlike lesbian gatherings where your face is most important, but it does have something in common with straight
gatherings where men discuss the Mideast crisis with your
left tit. Here, in the baths, the men don't even make a pretense of looking at your face as straight men on the make
do. But how could I get my turtleneck off without my
breasts flashing like a Maidenform advertisement? Sweat
rolled off my forehead, trickling over the black moustache.
Arthur, naked in an instant, caught the moment and called
for me to come over where he was. I walked over and he
said in a forced conversational tone, "Does your arm still
hurt? Let me help you get that off." Good old Arthur!
Anxious to hit the action, all but one of the men in the
locker room left. Two new ones barged in just as I pulled
my turtleneck over my head. Arthur leapt in front of me
and threw a short little robe over my shoulders.

So that I wouldn't be the only human being among the
hundreds in a robe, Arthur put one on too. As we left the
locker room area, passing by a mosaic pool and sparkling
showers, he took my hand, for the crowd was so dense we
would have become separated.

Entering the brightly lit TV room, I was aware of being looked at. Men look at each other differently than men look at women. The leer is gone, the thinly disguised hostility of the street vanishes. Here the eyes zoom to the crotch. As I was partially covered, their glance next went directly to my eyes and since I didn't respond to the unspoken question, the eyes turned off to the side or to another person. The transaction boils down to: curiosity, no connection, disconnection.

The TV room is neutral territory, a sort of sexual DMZ. Good photographs of men cover the walls, comfortable chairs allow people to relax and compare the photographs with reality while sipping a beverage. You might find someone in the TV room but you don't begin sexual activity until you leave there. We threaded our way through as fast as we could because of the lights and because the room is next to the entrance door, so there are attendants around.

Off the TV room winds an adult puzzle called the Maze, covered with thick carpets. You have to feel your way around in its alleys, turns, and twists. The Minotaur is alive and well in this update of the ancient Greek legend of hunter and hunted. Around the corner may be the bull of your dreams or one more dead end. In choice places a small ultraviolet spotlight strikes a painted figure on the wall. Men with false teeth are careful not to smile because the ultraviolet light makes their teeth look black. Bodies in front of you, bodies in back of you, groping, pushing, trying to get to the prize at the end of the puzzle, the orgy room. Standing at strategic locations in the Maze, men waited for a partner attractive to them. If sex starts in this setting it's usually cocksucking or a hand job. A bed hid behind one turn. The two men on it attracted a small following as others watched. It isn't considered bad manners to watch others and for some men the fun is in being watched. The old taboo of sneaking away for sex doesn't have a chance in these plush surroundings. As you bump through the dim puzzle you get groped, but it's gentle compared to the kind of grabbing a woman gets on a subway.

71

At last the Maze spills into a dark and unbelievable orgy room. A large square bed, about the size of four double beds placed together, dominates the room, with about four feet of space around it so men have a place from which to observe. The silence amazed me. Seventy-five to one hundred men packed into that room, seven of them on the bed, and not one word was spoken. Heavy breathing, sucking, and a few timid moans were the only noises. Everyone watched the bed where a black man assfucked a white man while another white held his balls waiting for the surge. One couple valiantly tried to pull off sixty-nine without choking each other to death. The two other men on the bed circled each other like wrestlers trying to get the proper hold.

Inching around the bed, I felt like I was sliding by a picket fence—all the erect penises behind me were hitting me in the small of my back. People reach for your genitals as you pass. My first response was to turn around and smash the offender's face in. I had to keep reminding myself, like a mantra chant, that these men thought I was a man and being a man is much safer than being a woman.

One huge fellow with a potbelly embraced me as I nudged him to get by. Another man quickly enclosed me from behind. Fighting off my instinctive violent response, I relaxed, then hugged the man in return whispering, "Thank you but I've been here for an hour and I'm tired." He released me instantly. As we filtered through the orgy room I had to disengage every two steps. The easiness of refusal is incredible. In heterosexual life and lesbian life a first refusal never sinks in. Men and, to a lesser extent, gay women are geared to pursue you. Women, despite the "sexual revolution," demand an affirmation of your desire/affection, hence pursuit. How long this affirmation takes depends on the woman—hours, days, weeks, months. Since sex as a bargaining tool is the only thing most women control, they have to make you come to terms or they lose their market value. In the baths there was no pursuit and the reason was quite simple. Men have nothing to lose through sexual activity. If you say "no" it means "no," that's all, and that simple "no" also protects fragile egos. Sex isn't a weapon here, it's a release. There's no need to make anyone psychologically pay for your favors. Everyone pays to get in here to fuck, pure and simple.

The pressure to perform is diminished in this room because it is the ultimate anonymity. While everyone goes into the orgy room at one time or another in his sexual career, I couldn't help but think this room was the refuge for the unattractive, the insecure, and the guilty. Here you risk the least and in merging with the crowd can lose yourself in the totality of genital sex.

From the orgy room we climbed the stairs to the cubicles, small rooms where men wait for a connection. Nerves tighten here. Belying their tension, they stroll up and down the two floors of corridors brazenly checking out the men on the beds. If a man lies on his stomach, a tube of KY, sterile lubricant, beside him, it means he wants to be assfucked. If he lies on his back, legs wide apart, he wants oral sex or possibly he'll fuck you. People stare into the rooms and then move on. As I prowled the corridors looking at the display I was struck again by the silence and by the fact that everyone plays with himself, trying to get it up so it looks larger. Sex is deadly serious.

One bear of a man, probably not attractive to the other men, lay in a room desperately seeking his connection. Possibly in his mid-thirties, blue-eyed, he looked like a burly carpenter or strong dockworker. Pausing in his doorway overlong I felt his anxiety increase. Without thinking about what it meant I smiled, wanting to reassure him. He smiled back as though some awful dragon had been slain and invited me in.

"I really like the way you look," I said, "but I've had it for the night." I waited for the classic line from him, "What's a nice girl like you doing in a place like this?" Again, I didn't reckon with a man's fear of not being manly. Of course he wouldn't call attention to my voice because who knows what I'd say to rip his balls off? He nodded his head and leaned forward to shake my hand, the traditional male response of good intentions.

Since class peels off with clothing you might think a democracy of nakedness and need would develop. But here in the cubes a new hierarchy took place among these law-

73

yers, artists, grocery clerks, stockbrokers, movement activists, professors, and cab drivers. Rank now came through size of penis, condition of body, and age. The pretty young thing reigns, a sexual prima donna. Experience, intellect, talent, compassion mean nothing. Since you don't converse with your partner until after orgasm, if you talk at all, the irrationality of the flesh commands. Here the great American principle of competition and performance keep those on the make hungry, frightened, and slightly savage. If you're old or potbellied or have a tiny penis you face blatant though silent humiliation.

At the end of one corridor was another orgy room composed of bunk beds slapped against the walls. As there was more light than in the downstairs orgy room, looks were more important. I saw a guy looking over his shoulder for Prince Charming while being blown. When a more attractive man meandered by he left the man sucking him and started working on the beauty.

Amid all this one-dimensional sexual activity people still look for the "right one." It's romanticism in a mechanical setting, with a heavy load of ego. Each man wants a partner worthy of him even if it's for a hand job. Since erection is the whole show, some men will hold their come if they're being worked on in one part of the baths and go to another part to see if there's someone better to shoot for. Another reason they hold back is because if a man comes first he's got to keep working on the other guy, and that can become a colossal bore. In the orgy room you can leave someone, but in the cubicles there's more responsibility to your partner. The pressure of controlling your erection and orgasm adds to the sense of tension already existing here.

The steam bath and sauna were the only places remaining after the cubicles. Descending a narrow staircase busy with traffic, we checked into the sauna first. The heat didn't wilt intense sexual activity. The steam baths proved even busier. The hissing of the steam, the mist, and sweat provoked hot sex. My moustache drooped dangerously. By now my own frustration hit a peak, partly because I love steam baths and partly because I was tired of the deception. I wanted to take off my clothes. Under the moustache I was grand old glorious me, but whatever slender bond these men felt for me as a male would have been shattered if I revealed myself as a woman. I began to get angry that a woman would freak out some of these men. Their sexuality was their business. All I wanted to do was remove my robe, the codpiece, the moustache, and feel the sensual pleasure of heat and nakedness. But naked I would become frightening to some of these men. Their sexuality depended on my absence. Men are terrified of being women; they don't want to identify with us in any way—and gay men are no exception. We still aren't people to them.

At 1:30 A.M., after three-and-a-half hours, we left the baths. Triumph! I felt as though I had stowed away on the Queen Mary. But I still had a question: is this fuck palace the ultimate conclusion of sexist logic or is it erotic freedom? Perhaps the answer varies with each man who frequents The Club. Some men go to enjoy themselves and that's all there is to it. For other men the baths become central to their existence. Adventure, thrills, acceptance narrows down to a few inches of cock attached to strange and therefore wonderful men. In anonymity each man can be Minotaur or victim.

To a woman anonymity is currently undesirable and frightening. Rape is often anonymous. Women can't trust men sexually in an anonymous situation the way men can trust each other. Some men do need a ballet of submission or conquest for their sexual adventure, both here in the baths and out in the heterosexual world, but I don't. To those of us forced to live beneath our abilities politically, sexually, socially, artistically, and economically, sexual submission carries no hidden shudder of delight.

The men in the baths can walk out on the streets and reclaim all the privileges of maleness unless they are courageous enough to come out publicly and identify themselves as homosexuals. I walked out of the baths as I walk out anywhere, a woman. Although gay men are oppressed, they have the baths as a retreat, an outlet, a fantasy farm. I have no such sexual/social outlet.

Women build no Xanadus because we are oppressed in a different way than the homosexual male. Not only do we

75

lack the money but we lack the concept. Despite changing attitudes toward sex, we can't create our version of the baths because, for most of us, sex for the sake of sex is still wrong—whether you are a heterosexual woman or a lesbian. Cigarette manufacturers tell us we've come a long way, sociologists write books about our sexual liberation, yet we build no stately pleasure dome to enjoy this so-called liberation. Sex still calls up awesome emotions, the old tyrannies of romance. We scramble to invest sex with love and we call men dogs because they've been taught to separate the two. If a woman manages to distinguish between sex and love and her needs for both, she's "fast," as grandma used to say, whether she is straight or gay.

So I return to the question rattling in my mind ever since I peeled off my moustache. Sexism or erotic freedom depends on the person and, yes, I do want a Xanadu. I want the option of random sex with no emotional commitment when I need sheer physical relief: erotic freedom. Our Xanadu would be less competitive than the gay men's baths, more laughter would ring in the sauna, and you'd touch not only to fuck but just to touch. It is in our interest to build places where we have relief, refuge, release. Xanadu is not a lurid dream, it's the desire of a woman to have options. Like men we should have choices: deep long-term relationships, the baths, short-term affairs. And those choices are not mutually exclusive.

Going to The Club taught me more about women's sexuality than it did about men's sexuality. And it taught me about myself. Like all human growth, sexual growth is on-going. Technical sexual knowledge has limits, but sex as an integrated part of your whole life never stops unless you stop. I went to modern-day Xanadu to put myself in sexually alien territory, but I say that underneath all the posturing, the egos, and the fears, those men weren't very different from heterosexual men or from women. The need is the same: sexual release. The deeper need, human contact, love, exists also. Men simply have more ways to mask that love need than women do. The real lesson for me was that there were moments in this strangest of places when I forgot to be different.

The Bath Life Gets Respectability

by Arthur Bell

When I was seventeen years of age, I caught syphilis at
the Everard Baths. I was living with my parents in Montreal then but would come to Manhattan, my old home-
town, to see shows like *Wonderful Town* and visit my
grandparents in Brooklyn and go to the baths. Often, I'd
tell my grandmother that I was staying over with a friend
and spend the night at Everard's. It represented freedom
to me—a place where I could have sex without plodding
through the required conversation of a bar, where points
are given for social status and artistic tastes and deducted
for not knowing "Farley" and "Mabel" and for staying in
the wrong borough.

Everard's was a haven where I could stare at crotches in
dimly lit hallways, wander the steam room, which smelled
of sweat and Lysol, and screw with a cast of thousands
who, like the extras in *Quo Vadis,* were faceless and
nameless. I usually felt dirty when I headed back to
Grandma, despite the frequent showers. And I often
wanted to talk about my Everard adventures, but in those
days you spoke to your gay friends about Ethel Merman
and never discussed the dark side of your psyche. As for
parents, well, you just gave them weather reports.

My parents are decent people who never told me the
facts of life. Sex education was not taught in Montreal
high schools in 1953. A social disease, I thought, was having the whooping cough at a cotillion ball. And Gay
Liberation might well have been the name of a stripper.
Information about homosexuality came from school
chums. Through them, I learned the "dos" and "don'ts."
The height of gaydom was the bird circuit in New York
(the Blue Parrot, the Green Cockatoo) and the Oak Bar
at the Plaza. Everard's, of course, was among the "don'ts."
Like Lady Windermere behind her fan, friends whispered
about this black hole of Calcutta on West 28th Street,

where steam hissed through leaky pipes and the fat, aged, and perverted indiscriminately banged each other. Everard's, they said, was Hades. But to me it was expediency.

When syphilis entered my life, however, I thought God was telling me to "get respectable." I needed eighteen daily shots of Terramycin (I was allergic to penicillin), and there was absolutely no way of explaining my strange behavior to my parents. For weeks, I limped around in pain. When I found myself a lover—a man who was slightly older than I and somewhat prudish—we played a lot of gin rummy and talked about Gloria Grahame, but my forbidden past got nary a mention.

In the two decades that followed, other lovers have entered and exited, affairs have sizzled and gone up in smoke, armies have marched over me, and I've floated through flotillas, but when things get hairy—or horny—I know that, like the Catholic Church and the RKO Albee, there will always be an Everard's.

At present, nine gay bathhouses—including Everard's—exist in New York.* Essentially, the baths are where gay men go for sex. They are not whorehouses. No money changes hands between customers, and almost anyone can find his heart's desire if he hangs out long enough. Fantasy is part of the trip. In a dark orgy room, the man who fondles your backside could be Davy Crockett pushing you through the frontier. But not all is done in the dark. Most bathhouses have recreational rooms, locker rooms, dormitories, and private quarters. Everard's, for example, has a man-sized swimming pool, and another bath has a fully equipped gymnasium.

Baths vary in character, from the Wall Street Sauna, where businessmen get their rocks off during the lunch hour (it's called "funch"), to the Beacon, where the East Side executive pulls his socks down after cocktails. St. Mark's in the East Village is frequented by older men and Third World gays. Students prefer Man's Country, on West 15th Street. Mount Morris is an all-black bath in

*See note at end of article.—Eds.

78

Harlem. People on their way up go to the Club Baths. Those who dally in sadism and masochism prefer the New Barracks on 42nd Street (Thursdays are Dollar Dick days). And total masochists are advised to visit the Continental, only because this once-great counterculture pantheon has turned into a pit. In fact, what once conjured up Fellini's *Satyricon* now resembles *Panic in Needle Park*.

In its heyday, the Continental was a pacesetter. In 1971, Steve Ostrow, who owned the place, brought the tubs aboveground by initiating cabaret entertainment and allowing women and men of all sexual persuasions to enter its portals, catch the show, and from the sidelines ogle the odd fellows who pranced around in bath towels. Eventually, that odd fellow who had come to bathe and ball felt he had become part of the floor show, resented the fact, and, by mid-1974, stopped coming. Around that time, the Continental had a mysterious fire. Owner Ostrow discontinued the floor shows. He later tried to make the baths coed. He advertised on WBLS. Nothing worked. It had lost its chic. Still, the Continental had made its imprint. It begat Bette Midler and a play called *The Ritz*, which was made into a recently released movie by that same name—unfortunately a flat, condescending treatment of the tubs lifestyle—and a whole bath culture which is far more open now.

On a recent visit to Man's Country, I waited in line with about twenty others, paid my $8, and was given the key to a private fourth-floor cell (Man's Country is in a ten-story building, with three of those stories devoted to group grope.) There was no attendant on the floor, no light switch in the room, and the red light burned bright throughout my stay. So what if the cot in the room sagged and cigarette butts from the last customer cluttered the floor? The sound of *glug glug glug* from the cubicle next door made me forget those trivialities and almost obliterated the chatter of three men who huddled in the hallway outside my hovel commenting on the physical attributes of the passing parade.

In order to join the parade, I slipped out of my street clothes and into a white towel and waited for an elevator to take me to shower quarters. After ten minutes the elevator door finally opened, revealing a quick flash orgy. I

79

opted for the stairs since there was no room in the elevator, took a shower, and entered the steam room. The floor was treacherously slick: heads, arms, and assorted appendages were grasped as I fended my way to the rear section where I sat on a mildewed bench for a moment—but only a moment—before I was approached. The gentleman who reached for my private parts could have been King Kong for all I knew—it was so dark—but from the feel of things I'd say he wasn't. To commit a sexual act in the steam room of Man's Country, one needs strong ankles or else one will slip and fall and end up with a concussion. There are many people at Man's Country with strong ankles, but I am not one of them.

Bath sign language predates Noel Coward. The signals are the same throughout the world. Examples? If one's towel is knotted in the back, sodomy is the order of the night. Lying on one's back on a cot, legs ajar, is an open call for fellatio. And one doesn't have to be an Einstein to know what lying on one's stomach means. Sometimes the signals are introductory offers to a variety of acts. And it doesn't necessarily follow that the stallion stalks the hallway while the passive pony is holed up in a room waiting to be pounced on. Many hall walkers prefer quick feels over orgasms. Common practice is for a hand to crawl into your room, travel up your leg, hit a vital organ, rest for a moment, then, just as quickly, travel out. If, by chance, that hand feels it has hit gold, and you don't care for the arm behind it, you plead exhaustion. White lies are permissible among gentlemen.

Because verbal foreplay is rare, the accent is on genitalia. Nonverbal encounters strip away accoutrements acquired in the outside world—achievement, knowledge, worldly goods. Romance is removed from the sex-act and the act is reduced to lust. So the virile shipping clerk is a star at the tubs, while his executive boss may be a bust. Nudity is no equalizer.

Perhaps that is why the bath scene has never worked for women. About four years ago, a tiny offshoot of the Continental opened its doors to lesbians. Instead of zeroing in on each other, the women preferred to chat in the TV lounge. There was hardly any stalking, very little sex transpired. After a month, the place reverted to an all-male policy.

Straight women, too, find the bath world anathema. Feminist Betty Friedan admits she has "no concept of the Turkish-bath thing." Singer Sylvia Syms innocently volunteers that "we have wonderful places, like Elizabeth Arden, where the steam room is very therapeutic and chic and where we ladies do a lot of gabbing."

Morty Manford has a theory. Morty is a professional gay activist and his theory is that in society's eyes, homosexuals, like women, have been sexually objectified. Morty feels that the way society deals with women is inseparable from the way gay men deal with each other. We tend to emphasize the trappings of youth and beauty. Yet Morty thinks that those moments when homosexuals get together at the baths are healthy moments.

Should the society that Morty talks about dissect the bath culture, I'm sure they'd find it perverse. I can't imagine my own upper-middle-class parents approving of the tubs. But my homosexuality, per se, doesn't bother them after all these years. They think of it as political, not sexual. That I'm openly gay and that I occasionally, but with less frequency nowadays, mount the soapbox for "my people" strikes a positive note. We've never discussed "fucking." I doubt if they could visualize me at a bath in bed with another man. And frankly, I don't want them to.

Seven years ago, when the Gay Liberation Front was just a baby, I sat through countless "brave new world" seminars and consciousness-raising groups with men who called me "brother." Time and again, I was told we mustn't use each other as sex objects. The trip was touch, feel, relate, and love in a "liberated" society. Yet, after the meetings, I would bump into these same preachers sulking in their beers at backroom bars or stalking the corridors of the tubs. I didn't know whether they were being hypocritical or truly liberated.

After all, sexual liberation meant doing what felt good, without guilt or shame, even though society believed otherwise. Supposing you didn't want to touch the head of your brother but craved his body? Supposing your new consciousness was running counter to the call of your libido? Were you to holler "Jiminy Cricket"?

No wonder that the new liberationists stayed away from the singsong piano bars that catered to apolitical "queens" who related in an old-fashioned, friendly, touch-feel manner. No wonder that they flocked to the so-called unliberated places—some of them Mafia run. As the movement developed, the revolution meant quick sexual encounters in hundreds of beds with millions of extras, and all the talk was bunk. It had to be, because groin and head usually collide. You may try for a new head, but you can't teach your old groin new tricks.

In 1971, Bob Kohler, a former CORE activist, former Broadway press agent, and early member of the Gay Liberation Front ceased all formal activity in the movement. He was forty-five then and a gritty mosaic of old Alice Faye movies and new consciousness. He took a menial job at the just-opened Club Baths. Soon enough he was promoted to manager. Concurrently, the Club Baths experienced an upward swing in business. Former patrons of the Continental, disgusted with being exploited, became Club regulars. The Club blossomed into a pretty, chummy, comfortable kind of sexual Howard Johnson's.

Bill McNeeley, one of the Club's three owners, and Bob Moburg, his lover of seven years (Bob handles the Club's advertising), talked about "progress" in the study of their elegant East Sixties townhouse. "We were the first bathhouse instrumental in changing attitudes about being gay," says Bill. "We made the baths beautiful and clean and treated our customers as special human beings and made them feel good about themselves. We gave them pink spotlights and real plants and numerous facilities for anonymous sex, including a section with a Maze. For a year we operated a free venereal-disease clinic at the Club. We turn away drunks and people on drugs and customers who we know have done something wrong, like spitting or throwing cigarettes on the floor or giggling in the orgy room. We brought respectability to the baths."

That they did. Rooms at the Club are clean, with light dimmers and wood paneling. They are so attractive that they make for house calls and gabfests. On a visit last month, the man in the next room was bemoaning to his guest the closing of *Pacific Overtures*—it was the kind of conversation that softens the penis of a chipmunk. Times have changed, I thought, as I listened. These *Pacific Overtures* people are the same kids who gave me advice about the bird circuit more than twenty years ago.

Yes, times have changed. During my four-hour stay I saw more familiar faces than I'd see at a Bobby Zarem party—"respectable" people who watched *Mary Hartman, Mary Hartman* on a giant TV screen, then slipped upstairs to trick in the Maze. Years ago you'd die if you bumped into someone you knew at Everard's. Years ago you'd spend a night at the tubs while your lover was visiting his mother in Dallas. Today, the twenty-year-olds visit with their lovers and ball with their friends. (Sometimes they don't know it's their friends until the balling is over.) Occasionally, they all go home together.

Despite the burgeoning of backroom bars, the New York bath scene is more profitable than ever. According to Bill McNeeley, the Club Baths clocks about 5,000 customers each week. There are 100 rooms, 600 lockers: rooms go for $9.50, lockers for $5.50 for a twenty-four-hour stay during the week (rates are slightly higher on weekends). Statistics show that the average Club customer is white, between thirty and thirty-five, earns $12,000 a year, stays five hours, and climaxes three times. McNeeley and Moburg have shaped their empire into a cozy spot with shag carpets at $25 a yard—comfortable surroundings eradicating guilt from the impersonal sex act if, in point of fact, there was guilt to start with.

A sexual Howard Johnson's? On second thought, a naked Bloomingdales.

It's a Sunday in September. I've just swallowed a couple of tetracyclines, having just climaxed with an improper stranger, and I'm relaxing in the sauna at Everard's. Writers' block on features such as this lures me to the baths these days. Sex is the catharsis that eases me back to the typewriter.

I spot a wizened little man with great cheekbones and a

receding hairline staring at me, and I ask if he visits the baths often. He replies he's been coming to Everard's since the age of seventeen.

"How many years it that?"

"I've been coming here since 1937."

He tells me that in those days the desk clerk and room attendants pretended that nothing was going on. "Except a police guard was posted on each floor and if more than two people congregated in an area, the guard would break it up."

During the war, he says, he served in the Army and would visit Everard's when he was in town on leave.

"Things were different. If you saw someone you liked, you'd go to the room with him and say, 'Let's get out of this place, it's dirty,' and then you'd go home together. You'd probably not see him again, but you'd get to know him for the night."

Does he resent quick sex? "Yes," he answers.

Is he rejected often? "Yes," he answers.

Does the rejection bother him? Does it carry over to his job in the outside? "Sure it does," he answers. "It has for forty years." He places his towel around his middle, ties a Boy Scout knot at the back, and says, "Let's go home together."

And I reject him.

[Editors' note: On May 25, 1977, the Everard Baths was destroyed by a fire that took the lives of at least nine people and injured at least ten others. The Continental Baths, also referred to in this article, has been taken over by Plato's Retreat, a heterosexual swingers club.]

Forum on Sadomasochism

Ian Young, John Stoltenberg, Lyn Rosen, Rose Jordan

[Editors' note: Sadomasochism is a particular form of sexual expression practiced by straight people as well as gay people, both female and male. Although we have no way of knowing what percentage of gay people participate in sadomasochism, it has had a "coming out of the closet" all its own, with articles in the gay and lesbian press and the straight press, and a noticeable increase in specialized bars, the advertising and sale of equipment, and the production of pornography and erotica. It has increasingly been a topic of lively debate, with proponents and opponents of both genders. In compiling the articles for this book, we realized it would be impossible to present all viewpoints on this topic, but we felt we could not ignore it, so we decided to create a forum with the participation of four writers, two women and two men, whose views on the subject were known to us. The four people do not know each other, so far as we know, and the forum was not conducted face to face. Rather, we prepared ten questions and submitted them to each of the four, asking them to prepare written responses within given space limits. Below, we present the full responses by each of the four writers to each of our ten questions.]

1. What is sadomasochism (S&M)?

Ian Young: S&M has come to be a generic term for any inventive sexuality involving spoken or acted-out fantasy, psychodrama, domination and submission, sex toys or conscious role-playing. More narrowly, S&M is sex involving pain, either physical (such as slapping or spanking) or symbolic (such as enacted domination or restraint of one partner by another). It can be as simple as just "rough sex," with no fantasy involved at all, or the fantasy might

85

be completely verbal, not acted out but just spoken by one partner to the other, with or followed by what's commonly known as "sex"—of one variety or another.

The rules are pretty much made up by the individuals involved. Sometimes this means there is detailed planning, even what amounts to choreographing, of a sexual scene beforehand, either verbally or in writing. Or it can be very spontaneous, being made up as it unfolds. In any case, what's happening or at least what's being striven for, apart from the obvious—sexual pleasure—is an altered state of consciousness, an awareness heightened by sex drama, imaginative construction, rather than, say, by drugs. Ritual is often important. I'm very nonreligious myself, but I do feel ritual (the procedures of stylized beauty and symbolic meaning) is important in our lives, to unite the physical and the spiritual, and certainly that's what S&M does, revealing aspects of both that may have been hidden in us before.

John Stoltenberg: It is important to keep clear the distinction between sadism and masochism.

Sadism can be defined, in part, as the inability to experience an encounter with someone else as erotic except through causing that person suffering, immobility, physical pain, and/or humiliation. Sadism also denotes those behaviors—on a continuum from teasing and tickling at one end through beating and binding to torture and murder at the other—which are used to exact and effect whatever anguish, inertness, or abasement is required. Essentially, sadism in both its cultural and individual manifestations is characterized by the eroticization of violence; that is, the causing of pain, suffering, or death is experienced by persons who commit such acts as genitally stimulating and orgasmically gratifying.

Masochism is the eroticization of powerlessness; it is an erotic drive toward pain, abuse, degradation, and annihilation which are believed to be deserved because of one's powerless condition. For most women in this male-supremacist culture, sexual masochism makes sensate the cultural constructs of female inferiority and female malignity. As Andrea Dworkin has written in *Our Blood*:

86

Sexual masochism actualizes female negativity, just as sexual sadism actualizes male positivity. A woman's erotic femininity is measured by the degree to which she needs to be hurt, needs to be possessed, needs to be abused, needs to submit, needs to be beaten, needs to be humiliated, needs to be degraded.

True masochism is relatively rare in genital males. Men who pay money to women (prostitutes, wives, mistresses) in exchange for coital access, and who want women to insult or spank them first, are commonly but inaccurately cited as examples of male masochism; in fact, the sexual behavior of such men is a variant of normal phallocentric domination and economic control. In some homosexual males, there does exist an erotic drive toward pain and abuse at the hands of other men, but that drive differs significantly from female masochism. Women, who are powerless in this male-supremacist culture, are often driven to literal destruction (out- of romantic "love," out of economic necessity), but male homosexuals have the option of eroticizing their powerlessness relative to other men with quite different consequences. A male homosexual may regard another man as possessing more masculinity, which is more power in the culture, and in the course of meeting that man's sexual demands, he may imagine that that power might be incorporated into himself. The male homosexual is assumed to be masochistic when he chooses to ingest the masculinity of men who are objectively dangerous, hostile, or violent. But in this woman-hating culture, his longing is not analogous to the female drive toward destruction, because the male homosexual drive to incorporate manliness functions as a means of dissociating himself from the inferior status of the female, while the masochism of a woman functions to fix her in that state.

Lyn Rosen: S&M is a sexual act which includes the application of real or mock pain or includes the acting out of certain types of fantasies. There is always a dominant and a submissive partner, but partners may change roles.

If the reader is looking to my answers to find out why people are into S&M, stop now. Some would ask, "Why would anyone strike a loved one?" "Why would any proud gay submit to humiliation?" These questions, I believe, belong on the same scarred and dusty shelf as "Why are you gay?" I will define and explain the mechanics of S&M and some of the philosophical questions surrounding the issue. That is all.

S&M is a sexual act. Too many people confuse S&M with bad relationships in which one person dominates another or treats another badly. S&M is a sexual act in which both partners treat each other well. The S gives the M all the real or imaginary pain that the M enjoys and that turns the M on. The S can be as aggressive, domineering, or mean as he or she would like to be *as long as* it turns the M on. Since this is a sexual act and not an act of violence, the S can only be as hurting or mean as the M desires. This assumes that S&M people choose loving and caring partners. That is crucial.

The pain inflicted may be real or imaginary. Real pain in an S&M relationship actually does not harm the M. Real pain includes any bite, slap, tickle, or kick in which flesh meets flesh or any substance (like leather) meets flesh. Of course, what may be a hard slap to one may merely titillate another. Imaginary pain is the kick, bite, or slap acted out; curses, threats, or grunts may accompany the action, but no substance meets the flesh.

Fantasy S&M covers whole realms of sexual behavior such as bondage and domination/discipline, water sports and scat, and entire plays costumed, written, and acted out by two lovers just for their own pleasure. All these actions and scenarios must have a dominant and submissive partner. If lovers are pretending to be two fauns in a wooded glade taking their pleasure of each other, they are not in an S&M situation. If they are playing at teacher and pupil or slave and master, they are in an S&M situation. But there is no rule saying that the S in one game has to be the S all the time. Many people are "switchables" with different partners or with the same partner, so if your fantasies run in both directions, take heart. In S&M, you can be anything you want to be.

88

Rose Jordan: S&M, loosely defined, is a relationship that is usually, but not always, sexual in nature between two individuals, in which one accepts the role of aggressor (sadist/master/"teacher") and the other accepts the role of recipient (masochist/slave/"pupil"), which I prefer to call passive/aggressor. The concept inherent in this relationship is that the sadist will control the situation and mete out the punishment (pain, humiliation, degradation—private or public) in order to satisfy the alleged desire of the masochist to be punished for whatever offense (real or imagined) perpetrated. The guilt incurred by the so-called offense must be alleviated through personal punishment before any emotional/sexual fulfillment can occur.

There is a point, however, when it is difficult to recognize the difference between the sadist and the masochist (that's the reason I referred to them as aggressor and *passive*/aggressor) at any given moment within the S&M alliance. Consider the following illuminating definition in the *Psychiatric Dictionary* (Hinsie and Shatsky—Second edition with Supplement, Oxford Medical Publications):

Sadism, primal—a certain amount of the death-instinct always remains within the individual; it is called primal sadism and according to Freud is *identical with masochism* [italics mine]. After the chief part of it (i.e., the death-instinct) has been directed outwards toward objects, there remains as a residuum within the organism the true eroto-genic masochism, which on the other hand becomes a component of the libido and on the other still has the subject itself for an object. (Freud, S., *Collected Papers*, Vol. 2; tr. Riviere, J.; Leonard and Virginia Wolff and The Institute of Psychoanalysis, London, 1924-25).

Therefore, my idea that the "masochist" is very "sadistic" while the "sadist" is "masochistic" is also supported by Freud. After all, one has to be quite "masochistic" to be convinced to mete out punishment that someone, *wants* in order to feel *less* than human, *less* than worthy.

Another definition that is more popular and familiar is

the one offered by the Marquis de Sade (1740–1814), who wrote extensively on the subject. His name was given to that type of eroticism in which, as he stated: "sexual satisfaction depends upon the sexual object suffering pain, illtreatment and humiliation . . . ," in which ". . . sexual emotion [is] associated with the wish to inflict pain and use violence." There are many more definitions but all basically repeat the same refrain: "lust of pain" associated with masochism, and the "lust to inflict pain" associated with sadism.

So we can readily see that there is an inordinate and reversed amount of cruelty on both sides of this unique relationship; the need to control can have many disguises. Outward behavior styles are chosen from those which appeared to be acceptable within our family circles. Each person is told (nonverbally, of course) that certain personality traits and mannerisms are okay, while others are not. Thus, in our upbringing, some of us chose manipulative styles of survival, while others develop more direct, aggressive, or assertive ways to express themselves. So I don't believe that S is at all times definitely an S, nor is an M always an M!

2. What is the basis for the appeal of S&M?

Ian Young: Everyone has erotic fantasies. People into S&M are simply more aware of their erotic imaginations in this respect and have found ways to externalize their fantasies in agreeable ways, to act on them. As far as the dominance/submission aspect of S&M goes, and this is what is most upsetting to outsiders—we all have a need for aggression and a need for submission in our lives; probably each individual should try to strike the balance that's best for her or him.

One of the things S&M does is consciously to make sex part of the balance in an enjoyable and satisfying way.

One of the main bases for S&M, certainly for me, is the need for communication. Maybe I can illustrate with my own experience. I'm a communications freak, a meaning addict. That's one of the main reasons I write, of course—to get through to people, to have an effect, and at the same time to help make people be more in control themselves, more aware. But often, whether you're dealing with the effect a work of art has or your own direct effect on another person, you're not sure the connection is really being made, or that it's as deep as you'd like. You're not sure you're getting through to the degree you want to or reaching the level you want to reach. In an S&M scene, there's no doubt I'm getting through, having a profound effect on the person I'm with; and I can stand back and witness the signs of that effect on his face and body—something I find exciting.

The pain part of S&M that frightens a lot of people is really not so difficult to understand. Bites and slaps, after all, are S&M. The nervous system is put together so that pleasure and pain are very closely connected. And the "humiliation" play can be a way of stripping away the ego and its defenses and pretentions—becoming aware of different levels—again, another way to achieve what religion or drugs attempt. I think most of us have wanted at some time to "submit" to or simply passively adore a striking or beautiful person. On the other hand, we've all wanted simply to "have our way" with someone, to do with her or him what we wish, the other person enjoying it, but seeming to resist. I think an equally valid question is, "Why does S&M arouse such furious and hostile condemnation?" This is true of gays as well as straights. And much of the gay criticism parallels exactly the straight attacks on gays—often word for word and illogical connection for illogical connection!

Some people dislike S&M because it recognizes the centrality of sex to human experience and eroticizes human drives which conventionally are considered to have nothing to do with eroticism. So if you're embarrassed by sex and want to "clean it up," spiritualize it out of the realm of reality, then you'll probably be threatened by a form of sexuality that's powerfully linked to a lot of mundane interests like jockstraps, cowboy boots, blue jeans, garter belts.

Often the condemnation of S&M focuses on the role of the S, or what people conceive the role of the S to be. Partly this is because people, mistakenly connecting S&M

91

with brutality, can conceive of someone wanting to beat another person up, but can't conceive of someone wanting to be hurt. I think this is only partly because of ignorance. It's also an unconscious cover for the fact that the M role is more threatening to them—the seeming passivity, the abdication of the appearance of power or status. *That's* really threatening to a lot of people, especially men. It's threatening to some S's, I think—a problem they might benefit from by working through. The idea of "submitting" to someone sexually is as upsetting to many as the idea of being fucked in the ass. It's almost the same thing really. Cultural conditioning tells us this sort of thing is no good, expecially not for men. It's unmanly. But as someone said in a magazine article on S&M, "Men want to be submissive—that's the dirtiest secret of all!"

John Stoltenberg: The appeal of sadism and masochism is rooted in the social structure of male-over-female sexual domination.

Between a man and a woman, the conjunction of male sexual sadism and female masochism fully expresses the cultural definitions of what "real" men and women are, how they are "opposite sexes," and why they "complement" one another. For the genital male, eroticized violence against women results in male sexual identity reification; his sexual sadism is the erotic correlative of his power in the culture over half the human race. Male sexual identity is a meaningless construct apart from institutionalized and personalized sexual violence against women; the genital male reifies male sexual identity when he violates someone else's bodily integrity, when he aggresses against nonphallic flesh and treats it with contempt. For the person defined as inferior, her sexual masochism fully complements the genital male's erotic drive to actualize masculinity; constrained by culture to nonentity, she accepts obliteration of her self for his sake, which is, as Andrea Dworkin has written, the norm of actualized femininity.

It is only in this context that sadomasochism, or eroticized violence and eroticized powerlessness, is a meaningful transaction between two homosexual males. For the partner who is sadistic, his gratification consists in the fact that he fully embodies and expresses the cultural norm of male sexuality and identifies himself with male-supremacist values and behaviors. The other partner is committed to the same sexual identity, but he is emotionally obsessed with his belief that he lacks some measure of the sadist's virility. For this partner, gratification consists in the fact that he ingests the sadist's semen and/or absorbs the sadist's violence. These mythic residues of the sadist's virile presence stay in his body, and he assimilates potency like a battery getting charged. (In such transactions, urine or excrement sometimes substitutes for semen.)

Female masochism is not necessarily unlearned in women who choose erotic encounters with other women. The cultural ideal of "real femininity" is pervasive and coercive. The lesbian masochist conforms to the standard erotic definition of women in a male-supremacist society. The lesbian sadist pretends in private to have more power than she has in the culture. In her private sexual sadism, she may also act as an agent or conduit of the culture's contempt for women in general.

A male homosexual may feign powerlessness relative to another, perhaps more violent, homosexual man; a lesbian may feign power relative to another, more masochistic, woman. Neither masquerade alters the objective reality that in society at large men have more power than women, and both masquerades are erotic manifestations of that reality.

Lyn Rosen: I believe that S&M exerts an appeal because its practice allows you to be anything you want to be this time around. Many S&M people use their sexual behavior as a balancer to all the other life behavior. "I get kicked around all day on my job, but when I get home my lover will let me be boss." "I'm so tired of making decisions, but when I get home I think I'll just let my lover tie me to the bed and do whatever." I say "S&M people," because I believe that it exerts no appeal to those who are not into it, and I get a sneaking suspicion that this question is just the old "why" in a different form.

For S&M people, the desire to act out fantasies with sex

or to be tied up or to experience real or actual pain is so much a part of their feelings about their sexual selves that they do not see S&M as "appealing." It is part of their sexuality. It has been with them since their earliest fantasies. Some are lucky enough to find the right partners and circumstances in which to act out their heart's desires. Others, like the gay person who never found that partner, are destined to live out their lives with an unfulfilled longing.

Rose Jordan: A society that insists that its survival depends upon the domination of one individual over another (or one group over another) and then stereotypes each with a specific—but different—one-dimensional personality can only create situations in which sadomasochistic relationships will flourish. Furthermore, a society that instills fear and guilt into its people concerning sexuality can only expect behavior commensurate with that view. Some people, therefore, inflict pain (read punishment) upon the love subject and camouflage the fact that the sexual desire for that person is only of secondary importance; the partner in such a venture agrees to the same contract. Kate Millett put it succinctly when she alluded to the S&M quality inherent in the spanking of children (pants pulled down to expose secondary sexual object: buttocks) as a displacement of sexual desire on the part of the spanker.

Going a step further and institutionalizing S&M and making it a viable way of life (i.e., those relationships that are openly dedicated to the use of sadomasochistic devices and principles as in the man/woman ideology) can present an avenue through which one can experience a certain degree of control (false though it may be). Stress situations can create very angry and resentful people who will seek ways to alleviate their feelings of frustration at not being capable of controlling their environment. The S&M situation enables these people to believe that they are controlling their environment by consciously directing their anger toward either another person or themselves. The identical situation exists when a frustrated, angry person contemplates suicide or murder as the only two solutions to her/his problems.

94

3. Is S&M inherent in human sexuality?

Ian Young: I'm not sure that any variety of human sexual behavior is "inherent." What can one say? Only that people have a potential for S&M, for hetero- and homosexuality, for getting married and having kids, for being celibate, and so on.

S&M does seem to manifest itself more in creative and highly imaginative people than in others, even more so than homosexuality. This seems only reasonable as S&M is a pretty sophisticated and complex mode of behavior. In that sense, it's very far from the quick, functional, biologically based, breeding-connected sex that we associate with more primitive forms of life. (Though the commercial backroom bars seem to be doing their best to primitivize us again!)

Human sexuality, after all, is getting further and further away from being biologically based (heterosexual, breeding oriented, etc.) and more pleasure and communication and aesthetic based. If S&M is part of this, and I believe it is, it's a more evolved form of sexuality, higher on the human evolutionary ladder.

John Stoltenberg: Neither sadism nor masochism is inherent in human sexuality. However, they are both inherent in male-supremacist culture.

There is nothing intrinsic to genitally male anatomy which causes or produces sadistic behavior; rather, sexual sadism is an acquired compulsion which is necessary to make manifest the meaning of the phallus in culture. There is nothing intrinsic to genitally female anatomy which causes or produces masochistic behavior; rather, sexual masochism is a survival response which is necesary to propitiate the sexual sadism of men.

Homoeroticism is not intrinsically sadomasochistic either, but in a culture that grotesquely promulgates the fiction of gender polarity, most interpersonal relationships that are based on that fiction—whether homosexual or heterosexual—tend as a result toward sadomasochistic expression.

What "feels natural" about sadism to males, or what

"feels natural" about masochism to females, is that these behaviors are sensorily consonant with the cultural specifications of phallic identity and nonphallic nonidentity, respectively.

Lyn Rosen: Trying to decide if S&M is inherent in human sexuality is like trying to solve the chicken-and-egg problem. This question seems to call for the words of psychological experts, but since you can always find some source to back up any theory, I would rather call on all the experts at once. When you sift through the countless theories on human sexuality, you will find a common denominator. No expert knows why two people raised in similar ways may have different sexual expressions. A proclivity for S&M must exist in all of us if it shows up in any of us. It must be human. I would have to go along with Freud and say that it is probably present in the polymorphous-perverse state of the infant, but that it is either repressed or brought to the fore by the accidents of life that "cause" all human sexual orientation.

Rose Jordan: If by "human" you imply "conditioned," then I would say "yes." In a society where the component of aggression is encouraged in one human being (male) and discouraged in another (female), then it would follow that the creation of a sexual alliance between these two individuals (whether they are different biologically, or if the "idea" of what male and female means constitutes their way of thinking about themselves and their partner) will be one with sadomasochistic overtones. To my mind, sadism is "cultivated" aggression toward another human being and is not based on any need for self-preservation or protection—as opposed to a defense mechanism sometimes called "aggression" that is employed to ward off outside, physical danger. Masochism is "cultivated" passivity in the same sense. This sadism with all its cruelty and open desire to dominate and this masochism with all its acceptance of controlled humiliation to disguise the feeling of anger resulting from feeling out of control are synonomous with the "man/woman" relationship touted as "normal" by our society.

Even if we assume that males possess a larger amount of aggression than do females, society insists on nurturing that trait in the male with the exclusion of any other characteristic he may possess. Simultaneously, society discourages any aggressive tendencies shown by the female but encourages and develops her ability to misdirect them into passivity. Therefore, we are educated with the idea that female is "passive" (masochistic) and male is "aggressive" (sadistic) and therein lies the tale! No wonder most so-called human relations are imbued with this S&M coloration. No wonder individuals wish to conform and embrace one role or the other; they feel it's essential to their identity ... pick one.

4. What is the meaning of consent in S&M?

Ian Young: The most sophisticated discussion on the nature of consent I've heard took place at a meeting of the S&M group The Eulenspiegel Society in New York. It was certainly up to the caliber of a good philosophy seminar—and, needless to say, more grounded in reality!

I think, first of all, one has to make the absolutely essential point—and then make it over and over again for those who for one reason or another didn't grasp it the first time—that S&M is by its nature consensual. We are talking about mutually agreed upon activities. Sure, there is coercive homosexuality, just as there is coercive heterosexuality, and maybe even coercive gourmet dining for all I know. This shouldn't be held against all homosexuals, heterosexuals, or gourmet diners. There are people, some of them homosexuals, with sadistic feelings, perhaps partly repressed or misunderstood, who look for nonconsenting individuals to sexually assault, perhaps because they can't conceive of willing sex partners. I don't think such people can fairly be linked to S&M—or to gay life. Certainly they aren't representative.

People don't realize, or they forget, that in S&M, it's often the submissive partner who in effect controls and structures the scene. The S is a character in the M's created fansasy!

Jim Saslow wrote me about this—that all good sex is

psychodrama; otherwise we'd be just as satisfied beating off alone. "Role-playing" contains two concepts—the idea of roles and the idea of play, which implies volunteerism and a certain quality of abandon. If a sexual act is not consensual, it's cruelty or exploitation, which have nothing to do with S&M.

On the question of consent, there is this further point: the M may say he wants to go only so far. In fact, he wants his limits pushed a little further. A good S—that is to say, an empathetic and perceptive S—will pick up on how much further the M can in fact be taken without frightening him or freaking him out. Here the consent is bent a little, or, rather, the basic understood agreement (that the M will have enjoyed the scene) is allowed to override the secondary agreement: "only go so far." Some M's like the feeling of delivering themselves up totally to the wishes of an S, of putting themselves in a position of having to do whatever the S says. That's part of the excitement. Still, there's an underlying agreement, an unspoken understanding of what will have been consented to after the scene is over.

Both partners must rely on their perceptions of the other: the M to decide whether he trusts the S; the S to assess the M's reactions in a scene and respond accordingly.

The important thing is that both partners dominate, both submit. If the partners don't realize that, it can lead to problems. Even the terminology contains the ambiguity: masochist/master (both begin with M); sadist/slave (both begin with S).

John Stoltenberg: In an erotic encounter between two homosexual males, there really are two male sexual identities at stake. But the sexuality appropriate to male sexual identity reification is derived from a heterosexual model based on blotting out "the other." To resolve this dilemma, some homosexual males contrive a masquerade, ritualized sadomasochism, in which one partner or the other temporarily mimics powerlessness. True to their privileged status as genital males in society, the partners are at liberty to trade roles in private without jeopardizing their status in the culture in any way. Between two homosexual males, then, "consent" in sadomasochism may be meaningful, and its meaning is in their prior agreement as phallic peers to reify each other's manhood. A crucial emotional adjunct of that agreement is their mutual derision of genital females, whose actual powerlessness they are at liberty to mock.

In order to understand the meaning of "consent" in sadomasochism, it is important to understand that the very notion of meaningful and knowledgeable consent is based on the cultural model of agreement in sentiment among and between men. "Consent" presumes that both parties to an agreement are equally free to make the agreement, having the same actual freedom to agree or disagree, and having the same actual latitudes of actions, opinions, or sentiments from which to choose. "Consent" is a concept that only has meaning between two persons who are equally enfranchised by culture to act willfully and without constraint—that is, persons who are genital males.

Between a man and a woman, the structure of sadomasochistic erotic encounters is predicated on the constraint of the woman's will, as well as her body. The woman's compliance or acquiescence in sadomasochism is therefore entirely delusional and utterly meaningless. In no sense does she share in the man's privileged capacity to act. Moreover, there is no reason to presume that a masochistic woman is exercising more freedom of choice or acting more autonomously if her constrained will and body are subjected to the sadism of a lesbian.

Lyn Rosen: Consent in an S&M relationship means the same thing that it means in any sexual situation. It means that no partner is raped by the other, forced to do anything that he or she may find objectionable.

In S&M, I strongly believe, there is more consent than in any other sexual situation. Partners must discuss their needs and desires in order to enter into any sexual situation. Despite the handkerchief codes that gay men use in order to make their sexual act preferences immediately clear or key symbols that tell vaguely which side of the S or M coin a person prefers, there is an infinite variety of sexual behavior within each category. Does an M like bondage or merely verbal humiliation? Does an S prefer using leather to skin? Are both partners into fantasy but not pain, fantasy with pain? Many S&M people have only a single ritualistic scenario that turns them on. In order to enjoy a sexual encounter, S&M people must find a way to communicate their desires. If the S and the M do not match up, actually, the scene is off. That is why S&M scenes should not be entered into with someone you do not know well or trust or with whom you cannot communicate. It may happen that people jump into bed with their fantasy partner only to find themselves tied to the bedposts when all they wanted was a verbal slap or two. It may also happen that non-S&M people have bad sex because they cannot communicate with their partners. All I can say is that the practiced S&M person who wants the most out of a situation knows that he or she has to communicate with the chosen partner. Since the S&M scene may require much thought and preparation, communication becomes essential. Consent follows communication. An S&M person has a chance to say no before he or she finds himself/herself in a bad situation.

Rose Jordan: I presume that consent is the willingness on the part of each participant within a given situation to allow actions to occur within that situation which would impart pleasure to the participants, or would implement the warding off of further harm (in the case of rape). "Consent," however, doesn't necessarily mean that "choice" is exercised since "choice" suggests that the individual has a great deal of alternative information at her/his disposal and can make an intelligent decision concerning her/his welfare. For example: a rape victim, although she must "consent" to her rape for various reasons, does not do so out of choice but out of a necessity to diminish the harm done to her by the rapist. Therefore, although "consent" exists in S&M relationships, there certainly is less "choice" in the matter than we think, since the participants are conditioned to accept rigid roles and to believe such roles are "normal."

The classic example of the rat in the maze comes to

mind. Food is placed at the end of a specific corridor; the rat ultimately locates the food and eats her fill. The food is always placed in the same corridor until the rat is conditioned to expect it to be there. When that is established, an electric shock device is placed at the entranceway to the food corridor; first the rat attempts to avoid it, but hunger is too strong and the rat finally accepts the shock in order to obtain her pleasure (food). Again this situation is reinforced, and the rat continues to accept the shock. Then the food is removed and placed in another corridor, but the rat continues to return to the corridor with the shock—it is, therefore, conditioned to accept pain to arrive at pleasure. Although this is a simplified parallel, it is reminiscent of the technique of human conditioning.

5. Are S&M relationships "liberated" or "unliberated"?

Ian Young: The exploration itself is liberating. The rest will depend on the degree of awareness, sensitivity, and so on of the people involved. Blake said: "Sooner murder an infant in its cradle than nurse unacted desires." A little hyperbole there on Blake's part, but the meaning is clear. Given a basic common sense, whatever incidental harm may be done by acting on one's fantasies would be well exceeded by the harm of repression. I think a real understanding of the dynamics of S&M can be liberating in that it breaks down the conventional categorizations of sex, sex roles, and so on. It may reinforce them instead, but I think it's more likely to break them down. People who have S&M experiences have an opportunity to be more aware of the elements of domination and submission in all relationships. Being aware of the needs, they might be able to control them in more positive ways rather than pretend the needs don't exist and cause problems for themselves and others.

John Stoltenberg: It would be difficult to imagine an erotic impulse more inimical to justice, personal dignity, or reciprocal caring than sadism.

In order to believe that relationships between sadists and masochists are "liberated," one would have to believe that

101

contempt is caring, that humiliation is respect, that brutality is affection, and that bondage is freedom. The fact that many women do so believe is a measure of the extent to which men have destroyed women's consciousness.

Homosexual men make a significant contribution to that destruction by their privileged engagement in sadomasochistic sex. Their aggressive message to women is that sadomasochism is "liberating," that it "transcends" gender. Their real meaning, however, is that sadomasochism works between men because it works against women, that sadomasochism is self-actualizing only for men.

Lyn Rosen: Since those who ask these questions do not define their terms, I find myself forced to define them for the reader as I see them. I shall have to say that a "liberated" relationship is one in which the two partners have equal power in the decision-making processes that affect the two of them. Since I focus in on the sexual aspect of S&M here, I will way that S&M relationships are the most liberated and the least liberated.

They are the most liberated because each partner must fully agree to the circumstances before any sexual act is entered into. In other words, once the sexual act has begun, each partner has the power to do what both partners have already agreed upon with maybe a few embellishments along the same lines. If both partners have agreed to a bondage situation with no leather involved, they may proceed with the S making the most fantastic of knots, the most creative of tied-down positions. But the S may not use leather. The S has already relinquished that choice; therefore, once the scene begins as planned, the S and the M have equal power in making decisions as to what to do next.

However, the S is always in the M's control, so that makes an S&M situation the least liberated. Remember, it is assumed that the people involved wish to please each other sexually. Since the M is the receiver of the action, he or she really sets the guidelines. If the S wants to use *more* pain, must attach *additional* bondage, insists on *more* verbal humiliation, the M will not reach sexual satisfaction. Often it seems as if the S were the slave of the M, always careful to apply just the right amount of force, always searching for the right words, the right tone, the best positions. The S has to be careful always to keep the M titillated and turned on. Basically, the S's pleasure is vicarious—almost a watching of the M enjoying his/her position. It is a strange paradox.

My real answer to this question is that when anyone has a chance to express fully his or her sexual needs and desires, that is a liberating experience; one is setting one's sexual self free to be true to itself.

Rose Jordan: Any relationship that has as its foundation the application of rigid, inflexible behavior patterns cannot be anything but "unliberated." To restrict the partners in such a relationship to one-dimensional identities will only put the individuals in "bondage" to each other; one can never function as a free personality because each *needs* the other to complete the picture. There can be no autonomy (the capability of each person to function on her/his own). How can this be a "liberating" experience for either the S or the M? These relationships emulate the traditional heterosexual relationships—the role-playing, the avoidance of diffusing of roles, or the lack of insight that would allow each person to overlap roles. The necessity of humiliating and degrading another person in order to feel one is in control of one's own life is a rather ludicrous, male-identified way to conduct a relationship that is supposed to release the participants from the restrictions of our society. The only form of liberation noticeable is the awareness on the part of the individuals that they do indeed function in that way—that part is a good thing. However, to me it's almost as bad as saying: "Okay, sure, so I'm a person who digs inflicting pain on someone—isn't it great that I know it?" Now, what does that admission do for anyone?

6. What is the political significance of S&M?

Ian Young: I think it is significant that among the people I know in the gay movement that have been most outspoken in pro-S&M attitudes to one degree or another (I'm thinking of Pete Wilson, Charles Pitts, Fred Halsted,

Mikhail Itkin, Larry Townsend, Charley Shively, myself) all of us, with the exception of Larry, are anarchists or libertarians! Larry seems to be a middle-of-the-road Democrat. There does seem to be a close connection between our interest in dominance/submission psychodrama and our opposition to political power and injustice. I'm reminded of something Simone Weil once said—that imaginary evil is exciting while real evil is dull; imaginary good is boring while real good is exciting and invigorating. S&M involves a sort of imaginary or dramatic power—exciting where the real power in the world is tedious and squalid.

Maybe one of the most effective ways to fight political power and even render it unnecessary is to understand the impulses to power and submission in oneself and integrate them, rather than trying to extend them in political systems. Involvement in S&M tends to take away a person's "need" to oppress and be oppressed, manipulate and be manipulated socially and politically—another reason why political power-trippers tend to oppose it strongly. S&M can be part of an outright rebellion against social, structuralized oppression, which again is part of the reason anarchists and libertarians are overrepresented among S&M people.

The vulgar charge against S&M, of course, has always been that it's somehow Nazi or fascist. The same is said about homosexuality. It's true only to the extent that political power gives the person who holds it more opportunity to express his or her desires and force them on others. Political power becomes a sort of projector they can run their fantasies through, with the world as a screen. Of course, the same powerful people are usually very hostile to any private, consensual trips. They're too revealing. The politicians are right to be scared. Chuck Ortleb had a great poem, "Militerotics," in an issue of *Mouth of the Dragon* that explored this connection wonderfully.

We're dealing with a question of real power versus aesthetic power. It's as misguided to condemn S&M for being politically oppressive or what have you as it would be to condemn a work of art for its aesthetic power. But then, some of our more idiotic levelers do just that and denounce artists for manifesting undemocratic things like

104

"control" and "discipline" in their work. I despair of denting such iron-faced antilogic!

John Stoltenberg: When Kate Millett introduced the concept of "sexual politics" in 1970, she used the term "politics" to mean "power-structured relationships, arrangements whereby one group of people is controlled by another." In Millett's revolutionary analysis, sadism and masochism are revealed not only as "political" but as the very foundations of all tyranny and oppression:

> [A] disinterested examination of our system of sexual relationship must point out that the situation between the sexes now, and throughout history, is . . . a relationship of dominance and subordinance. What goes largely unexamined, often even unacknowledged (yet is institutionalized nonetheless) in our social order, is the birthright priority whereby males rule females. Through this system a most ingenious form of "interior colonization" has been achieved. It is one which tends moreover to be sturdier than any form of segregation, and more rigorous than class stratification, more uniform, certainly more enduring. However muted its present appearance may be, sexual domination obtains nevertheless as, perhaps the most pervasive ideology of our culture and provides its most fundamental concept of power.

Since the publication of Millett's *Sexual Politics*, many radical feminists have observed that there is a direct and causal connection between male sadism in intimacy and male sadism as public policy: rape, genocide, war, economic imperialism, and other assaults against human life which men have committed throughout history. It is a connection that many people reject, preferring to explain these terrors in other ways that do not detract from male sexual identity as it is and as it has been (and as they would like it to continue to be).

The political significance of sadomasochism in intimacy is that it fuels and keeps intact the cultural power structure of male sexual domination.

Lyn Rosen: Discussing the "political" significance of S&M always gets me in trouble with feminists, but I cannot figure out why. It is, after all, feminist theory that the personal is the political. We feminists, and I count myself among them, struggled for many years to convince the world that men could not take their "politics" off into smoke-filled rooms and tell women not to worry their pretty heads when it became increasingly clear to women that their simplest act, such as applying for a job, was in fact a political act. It affected everyone, especially the woman applying.

Based on this feminist principle, I believe that the person who is not sexually free is a danger politically. The person who understands himself or herself best will make the person best suited to make political decisions wisely. Such a person may not always agree with me politically; however, I trust least the person who neither knows nor wishes to explore his or her sexual self.

Taking this into a discussion of movements, and the gay movement in particular, I would have to say that the S&M people within the gay movement will probably always be an embarrassment to the movement just as the transsexuals and the transvestites are. S&M people, like the other two groups, are the least understood and the most easily mocked. When a group is trying to gain general acceptance by saying, "Gee, we are just like everyone else," it does not help to have to acknowledge that people whose sexual expression is little understood are also under your banner. I, of course, believe that until the S&M person, the transsexual, and the transvestite are free none of us is free. I think the political significance of S&M lies in our pariah role—the general gay movement should never stop to congratulate itself on its gains until these "bastard" groups have also achieved general acceptance.

Rose Jordan: At a time when women (lesbians or not) and many gay men are desperately trying to struggle toward more equitable relationships—ones in which the partners are attempting to understand and weed out behavior that would be detrimental to others—S&M thoroughly contradicts this struggle against roles in that it

106

relates strongly to the heterosexual idea that one person *must* dominate the other. Since "macho" concepts are so easily fallen back on when we are threatened in any way, we employ these methods as a form of self-protection. But to institutionalize unconscious forms of self-protection into a cult that says it's "healthy" to face your S&M tendencies and utilize them in your relationships with others reminds me of the way our society suggests that "women" should use their "unhealthy" traits as attributes to help them "get a man." Passivity is the name of *that* game and S&M is the device used to keep each person in her/his own back yard, as it were. Why would people who claim they are dedicated to wiping out the heterosexual concepts of "predators seeking prey" follow similar patterns? S&M keeps people rigidly locked into stereotypical behavior patterns that have damaged practically every individual in our society and have done nothing to liberate one single soul. I firmly believe it is not enough to call S&M apolitical; I would go further and label it a conspiracy to undermine the movement toward more freedom among individuals. It is definitely not a "liberating" element in anyone's life.

7. What is your reaction to S&M in the gay community?

Ian Young: I don't much like the exclusive connection that's made between S&M and "macho" images of men. I find the sort of hard, stone-faced, impassive exterior so cultivated by some of the leather bar regulars especially boring and unerotic. Again, this is something that's very culturally conditioned. I like something Jim Saslow said in a letter to me: "I refuse to be whipped by someone who can't himself cry." Another problem is the harm done by the popular misconceptions of the words "sadist" and "masochist." Just as gays used to become effeminate because they were told that was what it meant to be queer, if a person is told he's a sadist and therefore hard and unfeeling, he may well start to think of himself as hard and unfeeling and even behave toward people in that way, though this has nothing to do, in fact, with sexual sadism. For the same reasons, masochists sometimes come to believe they deserve or "ask for" any bad treatment they receive—being beaten up outside a leather bar by neighborhood thugs, for example. Certainly this is a problem with some people who are into S&M, though not with many I've met.

As to opposition among gays to S&M, in addition to the more serious roots of anti-S&M feeling, there's a lot of simple conventionality among gays, and of trying to reassure straights that, in essence, we're just as boring as they are.

John Stoltenberg: I do not know of a movement for liberation that has betrayed its revolutionary potential so soon after its inception as has the male-dominated movement for the liberation of "gay people." Instead of acting upon the recognition—available in feminist writings for some time—that the stigma of being queer originates in the male supremacy of culture which stigmatizes all females, most gay male activists have chosen a completely reactionary strategy: seeking enfranchisement in the culture as "really virile men," without substantially changing or challenging even their own misogyny and male-supremacist convictions.

There are many ways in which gay liberation has become a full-fledged component of the backlash against feminism: The struggle of lesbian mothers for custody of their children, for instance, has been co-opted by many gay men as a question of "gay parenting"—a self-serving obscurantism—because gay men, like other men, defend patriarchal ownership of children; and because, for gay men as for other men, the issue of child custody has become an emotional focus of their own seething misogyny against their former wives. Another instance: Notwithstanding all the evidence that queers are despised in every country where there has been a socialist revolution, many gay men have become socialists, because gay men, like other men, cannot tolerate the radical feminist analysis that posits the source of oppression in male supremacy; and because, for gay men as for other men, the ideals of socialism promise equal rank among male supremacists. Another instance: The struggle of women to combat pornography—which degrades and intimidates all women—is treated by many gay men with disinterest or ridicule, because gay men, like other men, enjoy pornography, and they mean to defend it as a privilege of their gender class. These are three examples; there are many many more.

Gay men do not simply like other men; they are like other men, as their antifeminism makes clear. Licensed by their movement which brought homoerotic sadism out of the closet (but which has not changed much else), the gay male subculture now abounds with neo-Nazi uniforms, torture toys, orgy bars, piss-and-shit shows, fist-fucking shows, films and periodicals portraying torture and mutilation—all of which is tantamount to spitting in the faces of women who are struggling to be free.

Lyn Rosen: I feel that S&M between males and S&M between females differs in quality. Men seem to be able to separate the mind and body, to make a distinction between the sexual act and the emotional reaction. For example—when I used to lecture on S&M the men always wanted to know how to carry out the act, but the women were more interested in how their relationships would be affected by adding an S&M component. I, of course, believe that an S&M component to a good relationship can only make it a better relationship. Although women are generally more frightened of the concept of S&M, once they understand it they tend to see it as an extra and fulfilling component to their relationships. Men tend to see it as kink, something to do when all else gets boring. However, many men who are closely allied with the S&M movement feel as I do that the S&M relationship is the most rewarding because it brings the partners closely in touch with each other. It is always difficult to generalize, but in this short space provided I would like to show that I have noted a difference in the two sexes' reactions to the theory of S&M when first exposed.

I also believe that a truer understanding and wider practice of S&M in the heterosexual world will bring about a better relationship between the sexes.

Rose Jordan: First, I can honestly say I am appalled by

109

the existence of S&M in the gay community. Next, I can reiterate what I stated in response to the last question. To embrace a form of behavior that ultimately destroys the "realness" of loving and/or sexual desire ("realness" in the sense of the basic fact of the feelings themselves without any displacement) can only create relationships that are false in character and intent and lacking integrity in meaning or action. To me this is the same as accepting a heterosexual way of life with all its S&M ramifications that instill an element of attack and defend as a foundation for a loving relationship (the "battle of the sexes"). How can there be reconciliation and love between a man and a woman (or even within gay relationships) if they are at war with one another? By the same token, how can there be reconciliation and love between an S and an M if one acts with contempt and brutality toward the other? The gay community has developed rhetoric concerning better ways to relate to each other, so one must ask: "Is S&M *better?*" Since S&M is no better than the relationships found in our larger society, how can the gay community blithely accept it using the philosophy that "everyone should have a choice of sexual behavior" and not see it as a threat to the idea of gayness; or, is gayness S&M in quality? One cannot claim political orientation against heterosexual values and then accept the very values we are fighting. Those who embrace S&M as a lifestyle (rather than a personal phenomenon) are supporting the basic man/woman concept. S&M, therefore, becomes apolitical; or worse yet, a part of the politics of oppression.

8. How do you feel about S&M in movies and other media?

Ian Young: Almost anything in this society is going to be commercialized on one level or another, and so trivialized and vulgarized. S&M is no exception. The current fascination with S&M among gays is partly a result of exploitation of the superficialities and cruder aspects of S&M; the interest is quite genuine, of course. Still, a certain amount of publicity and commercialization of S&M has made it easier for some people to get to know of its existence and to involve themselves in it, so it's done some good.

Almost all of the commercially produced S&M art—films, photographs, drawings, and so on—is bad. S&M is so inner, symbolic, personal that it's difficult to pictorialize effectively. Showing the mechanics just doesn't work because the mechanics are not what it's about. Drawings are usually better than photos; there is more for the viewer to do with a drawing. It's suggestive rather than explicit.

S&M is so closely connected to art—it almost *is* an art—as well as to the religious impulse that it's not easy to depict artistically. It takes a lot of skill.

What some people call S&M in the movies is actually just a lot of violence, much of it gratuitous and mindless. I don't like movies and TV shows that glorify the forces of authority and glamorize violence in doing it. But I'm getting off the topic.

I should mention the recent vogue of commercial exploitation of quasi-S&M vignettes to sell records, clothes, and various gewgaws. What is depicted is a conventionalized, reassuring image of S&M. For one thing, it's always a woman who's being tied, beaten, put down. Here, S&M is being co-opted, used to bolster sex stereotyping rather than challenge it, and to bolster power rather than examine it. For the commercial folks to go any further—in other words, to be honest—would be too threatening for them.

John Stoltenberg: The emergence of male homosexual sadism from underground has coincided with a burgeoning of overt sadism against women in all the communications media. This coincidence has not been by chance. "Creative" male homosexuals have long been influential in theatre, fashion, graphic design, photography, music, advertising, and so forth; their impact on popular culture as "style setters" has been far out of proportion to their number in the population. It is no accident that the current obsession in the gay male subculture with eroticized violence is now sweeping the country via film, print, advertising display, rock music, and live performances. While gay activists were campaigning against stereotypical images of "gay people" in the media, male homosexuals (including prominent gay liberationists) who have direct access to

111

media have been promoting with a vengeance all the stereotypes of female masochism.

What I feel I am witnessing today in the movies and other media is the convergence of what was once deemed a "gay sensibility" with what was once deemed a "heterosexual sensibility." That convergence is conspicuously a male sensibility, and it now reveals itself fully as thriving on female degradation.

Lyn Rosen: I realize that S&M, like lesbianism, has been exploited to fulfill the basest of commercial demands, but I have much hope for the future. I believe that it is through the media that an understanding of S&M will finally come about. In the past, S&M has been relegated to rather sensational articles like the *Time* article that presented the San Francisco male leather scene with no mention of S&M theory or women into S&M, or Arthur Bell's backroom bar *Village Voice* story, but the fact that major media are willing to touch it at all gives me hope that they will allow soon a more sensitive discussion by people who are really into the scene and not only by shocked observers. The fact that the editors of the gay press (and the editors of this anthology) feel that they have to give at least some space to S&M is a good sign that sensitive treatment of the subject is about to occur.

Two major movies dealing with S&M that have come out in the last few years also give me hope. *The Story of O* and *Maitresse* both have their faults, but their frank explication of the mechanics of S&M was a joy to see. I would call *Maitresse* politically incorrect since it showed that once an S is dominated by a stronger S, she will give up her S role and be happy to play M for all of the rosy future. I felt that the movie contained a sexist bias since a woman was shown to be the S who gives it all up for the man who can dominate her. Women, of course, do not have to play the M role in order to be happy. Neither does an S look for and long for a stronger S to dominate her. You can be S and happy. *The Story of O* was fantasylike and did not show the detail that made *Maitresse* so good for the S&M movement. But *O* was politically correct because it showed that the M was in control, that the M

112

position is a position of strength and nothing to be ashamed of. I kept thinking how O kept those poor men hopping and dreaming up more fantasies for her by the hour; she was a tough master. These two movies, I believe, will pave the way for all media to handle S&M sensitively in the future.

Rose Jordan: We are all aware that the media exploit people's worst ideas and feelings about themselves and others, so it is not at all surprising that they (the purveyors of films, magazines, etc.) would utilize S&M as a device for their stories and/or plays. S&M is employed lavishly, for instance, in pornographic and other violent films by portraying the love object as someone contemptuous who must be treated with disdain and subjected to inordinate amounts of degradation, using sexuality as the implement. In a society and a world that basically views sexuality merely as a necessary reproductive function and has conditioned human beings to believe that to have sex for pleasure one must pay a "price" (in this case punishment), we can expect nothing less than subtle, and not so subtle, forms of S&M within the framework of a film or play. Again, one must "spank the exposed buttocks" of the offending object; therefore, the ugly face of partriarchal concepts of power and punishment is exposed.

9. If the reader wants more information about S&M, what sources do you suggest?

Ian Young: I'm afraid there just isn't much of value on the subject I can recommend very highly. Most of the books by psychiatrists are the sheerest junk, of course, though Marie Bonaparte's *Female Sexuality* has some good things in it. Also Alan Watts's *Nature, Man and Woman*. Peter Fisher's *The Gay Mystique* and Mitch Walker's *Men Loving Men* are both sensible and helpful on the subject. One book I found to have a great deal of insight and pertinent thinking is Simone de Beauvoir's *Must We Burn de Sade?* The book *S-M: The Last Taboo* is worth reading but it's done from a straight point of view and has fairly limited value for gays. The gay and straight S&M scenes seem quite different. Larry Townsend's *The Leatherman's Handbook* (available from the author at 525 North Laurel Avenue, Los Angeles, CA 90048) gets carried away with descriptions of very far-out scenes, partly because it was published by a porno house. Larry's scene and approach are far from mine, with less psychodrama and more rough stuff. But again, it's helpful and worth reading if it's not all taken literally. There are a few good novels. I can think of some of Genet's work, Eric Jourdan's *Two*, John Glassco's *Harriet Marwood, Governess*, Jack Evans's *Biker's Boy*, and some of Larry Townsend's fiction, especially *The Long Leather Cord*. William Carney's *The Real Thing* is considered an S&M classic and it's interesting enough, but too artificial for my taste and with a gratuitous "tragic ending." Joel Hespey's *SM: Roman d'Erotism* is fine, but hasn't been translated into English. A couple of issues of *The Lesbian Tide* (November through February, 1976–77) had a feminist forum on S&M. There's a fascinating article by Glen O'Brien called "Piss, Leather, and Western Civilization" in the August 1976 issue of *High Times*. And I've gotten a lot from various articles and talks by Pete Wilson, Charles Pitts, and Jim Saslow. There's a book just published called *Hard Corps: Studies in Leather & Sadomasochism* by Michael Grumley. I haven't had a chance to read it yet.

I did a couple of articles on S&M which have been reprinted here and there. A lot of people have found them helpful. I'd be happy to send photocopies at cost to anyone who writes for them, c/o Catalyst Press, 315 Blantyre Avenue, Scarborough, Ontario, Canada.

I wish there were a really good book I could strongly recommend on gay S&M, but there isn't. Well, I might just write my own.

John Stoltenberg: There are three basic feminist texts that analyze cultural and personal sadomasochism in depth. They are: *Sexual Politics* by Kate Millett (Avon, 1970); *Woman Hating* by Andrea Dworkin (Dutton, 1974); and *Our Blood: Prophecies and Discourses on Sexual Politics* by Andrea Dworkin (Harper & Row,

1976). I do not know of any sources more informative and important than these.

Antisexist genital males might also find useful *Double F: A Magazine of Effeminism*, No. 2, Winter/Spring 1973 ($2.00; Templar Press, P.O. Box 98, F.D.R. Station, N.Y., N.Y. 10022), in which Steven Dansky, John Knoebel, and Kenneth Pitchford repudiate "sado-masculinity" and "masoch-eonism" [male transvestism] with reference to the sexism of the gay liberation movement.

Lyn Rosen: There are few good sources for the S&M person to research. I suggest: *S-M: The Last Taboo* by Gerald and Caroline Greene (Grove Press, 1974); *The Story of O* by Pauline Réage (various editions—and the movie, definitely); *The Drummer*, 1508 Crossroads of the World, # 107, Hollywood, CA 90028; a national male magazine devoted to the leather scene; *The Leatherman's Handbook* by Larry Townsend; "Sado-Masochism: The Theory and Practice" by Rosenjoy in Vol. III, No. 32 issue of *Gay Community News* (GCN), 22 Bromfield Street, Boston MA 02108.

Rose Jordan: I'm sorry, but I cannot in all good conscience direct any of your readers to any sources that would assist them in indulging in such practices.

Also, offhand, I cannot think of any *anti*-S&M sources that I might recommend.

10. Is there anything you want to add?

Ian Young: My own involvement in S&M has been primarily as an S. That's what I enjoy most of the time and most of the people I've been involved with want me to be dominant. I can enjoy the M role too. I'd had S&M fantasies since I was a little boy but my initiation into S&M activity was by a long-haired young fellow of about eighteen or nineteen whom I met in Toronto. He really liked being spanked and wanted and enjoyed it so much it was easy to get into and get turned on by. The ideologues would have it that I should refuse to do such an oppressive thing, but to my mind we both enjoyed it immensely, so why not? The ideologues from time to time claim that *any* sex other than absolutely mutual side-by-side 69, both coming at once—or better still, not coming at all and with nothing as oppressively aggressive as an erection!—anything other than that is imperialistic and so on. It's reminiscent of St. Paul, Cotton Mather, and some of the more horrifying church fathers. The terminology changes, but the puritans are always with us. My own sexual interest is strongly aesthetic and personal, and S&M gives me a feeling of deeper, more intense communication—and also lets me enjoy watching the face, body responses of the person I'm with, to watch the effect I'm having on him. And at the same time, I don't have to be "on camera" myself if I don't want to be. One of the reasons I like S&M sex is because it seems *more* personal, more intimate, more effective.

My sexual activity isn't exclusively S&M by any means, though I'd probably have S&M sex with everyone I slept with if they wanted it. It's just a lot more exciting to me, because the range of what you can do is much greater.

The great majority of people would probably never be able to understand S&M. Maybe it'll remain "the last taboo." And there's good as well as bad in that. Certainly the taboo aspect is part of the attraction. Which again brings us back not to power, but to rebellion.

John Stoltenberg: In view of the prevalence of eroticized violence (sexual sadism) among male homosexuals and male heterosexuals alike, I do not believe that it is possible for anyone seriously committed to feminist principles to maintain an alliance or affiliation with gay men as a group, except by compromising those feminist principles or except by compromising and deceiving women. I believe that the time has passed when a personal or political identification with the aggregate of male homosexuals had moral or revolutionary integrity (and that time passed very quickly, within a few years of the beginning of the gay liberation movement).

All males who are fully men got that way, gay or straight, by committing crimes against women; they *are* therefore obstacles to women's freedom and dignity. Any

116

genital male who decides not to live as such an impediment would not equivocate about that fact—he would instead take a stand against male sexual identity itself. He would work conscientiously toward a world in which eroticized violence and powerlessness would both be destroyed, and someday, perhaps, eroticized justice could supplant them.

Lyn Rosen: [No response was given to this question.]

Rose Jordan: I can't think of anything else except to say that I am extremely disappointed with the lesbians who profess to be "political" or "feminist," or whatever, who are either accepting this form of sexuality for themselves (and thereby reinforcing the male concept of domination over others as decent and rewarding behavior) or disregarding the importance of S&M, not seeing its antipathetic position to radical change in behavior patterns. It seems clear to me that we as political people dedicated to the change in patriarchal culture should be investigating ways to dispense with S&M just as we are trying to alter the false images of women by understanding and rejecting the butch/femme concept. I see a glaring parallel in both ideas—the phenomena of S&M, butch and femme, man and woman. All are connected with the principle that one person must dominate and control another in order to create a relationship of any kind, but especially one in which sexuality plays a major role. It should be our aim to destroy all that is male identified instead of becoming a party to its ideals through the use of S&M in our human relations with one another. This is one of the many ways in which we can effect changes in our world and, if we consider ourselves revolutionary at all, we should get down to the business of conscious-raising on this particular issue.

Phantasy Revolution

by Charley Shively

I have explored cocksucking as an act of revolution (in a series of articles in *Fag Rag*) in search of ways to break down sexploitation, discrimination, and private property. Against theory and good wishes, I have noticed that my body responds more warmly to some potential lovers than to others. On a basic level, the signal of this discrimination is sexual arousal (for faggots a "hard-on"). "Hard-ons" involve much more than a simple physical response. Water always boils or freezes at precisely the same temperature and pressure, but unlike water, the body never responds in exactly the same way to the same sexual circumstances. The "hard-on" represents only the tip of our sexual iceberg that would frustrate any personal, sexual, social, or political change. Faggot phantasies provide a direct road through the social structure, and they open possible avenues of change.

I want here to explore (1) What Are Phantasies, (2) Where Do Phantasies Come From, (3) A Link Between Class and Sex, and (4) Possibilities of Change ("What Does Not Change/Is the Will to Change"). As usual I explore my own experience hoping that this will help others. If you have a response, please write, c/o Fag Rag, Box 331, Kenmore Station, Boston, MA 02215.

Faggots have cultivated phantastic delights, eaten where others have only licked, deep-dived where they gingerly test the water. Just dressing, walking into the street, or answering the telephone actualizes phantasies both of one's own design and of others' dreams. Bars, baths, cruising places, lovers, and quarrels—we weave them all out of one web of phantasy. The Ritch Street Bath in San Francisco needs only three words to advertise: "Actualize Your Phantasies."

118

What Are Phantasies?

In discussing phantasy, I want to set aside notions of its being only illusion, delusion, hallucination, whimsy, or caprice. I spell the word "phantasy" to relate it more closely to "phenomenon" than to "fiction." I follow psychoanalyst Susan Isaacs, who writes that "There is no impulse, no institutional urge or response which is not experienced as unconscious phantasy." Phantasy is not only the image of desire, want, and love; it is also the process by which impulses, instincts, and feelings are experienced. Operationally, phantasy expresses, forms, and directs everything we are.

Phantasies for faggots clearly represent something valued or wanted, a particular image, type, form. Types include (here I quote from advertisements): "Rugged and handsome hunky, hairy Italian, endowed"; "Tall, slim, well-hung, boyish"; "Nature-lover/Desert hiker"; "Tough young ex-marine"; "Fair, blond, blue eyes, well-defined surfer's body"; "Teddy Bear"; "executives, teachers, doctors, lawyers, horse ranchers, actors—people in the public eye"; "Gorgeous nineteen-year-old black"; and many, many more.

My favorite phantasy/person/faggot enriched my understanding of the medium. For years I had admired him on the Fenway and Esplanade, more or less at some distance. He was thin, wiry, moved very fast—seemed totally oblivious to everyone. Once I did him in an orgy. I had waited and not said a word/"finally it wasn't necessary/was he so stoned he couldn't tell/it was me?/or had I changed/during these years/of being ready/only one person/could answer/and he wasn't talking/as he zippered up" and left. Those qualities of mystery and noncommunication—the specter of a person, pants, cap, sweater, tight face, body continue to intrigue me: "blind Orpheus/cool cruel/lonely tonight/he looks neither way/knit cap/silk shirt/tap hands/rose grows/cold here/he doesn't see us/a stalk garden/brown plants/our oval hotel. . . ." Once he came up to me just after I had finished fucking someone; I was limp and slightly anxious to finally be so close to him. After trying awhile to excite me, he wandered off—aloof and untouchable as ever.

Just this summer, though, my triumph came. He was pissing by a tree; I came over eager to engage him—not sure whether I should drink the piss or not. We started kissing, holding each other. He was as excited as I was; my ripped and patched Levis turned him on. We went further into the bushes behind a big oak tree. He just stood me there for about an hour while I danced, did deep-knee bends, bent, twisted, and turned my ass near his face. Slowly he would run fingers into me (never quite the whole hand or fist), examining over and over again the back of my body—pants up, pants down, halfway up, buttoned up, unbuttoned. Suddenly I was a sex god in this past-midnight temple as he kneeled to worship my every vibration—never daring to look me in the eye, even sneaking behind the tree at times and peeking out, searching constantly for new directions, new vantage points, new angles for looking up my legs into the rose of my anus. Never in my life have I been so totally beautiful; I would have done anything he asked; I was his slave; I wanted to be a spectral projection of everything in the world he had ever looked for. For those few moments we became one phenomenon, one phantasy—both of us absorbed in the image of each other. Finally, winding down, we both lied and said we didn't have anyplace to go, split. And that was that.

Phantasy is a process as well as a particular image, a filmscript as well as a slide. Sergio of San Francisco promises in an advertisement: "FANTASY FULFILLMENT SPECIALIST. Handsome, aggressive, leather man . . . dominates all scenes in full leather, chaps, smelly jockstraps, or uniforms." Another seeks "Fidelity, sincerity, stability, integrity" with interests in "music, theater, books, traveling, fishing, hiking." A MAN FOR ALL SEASONS calls out: "share with me excitement of football, country drives, visits to historical sites. Saturday auctions, concerts, operas, films in fall; cross-country skiing, basketball, hard sweaty workouts with weights. Sundays at museums, curling up next to cozy fire listening to records in winter; jog in park, whipping up gourmet meals (occasionally splurge at superb restaurant, or maybe Big Mac), exploring byways of Europe and Hawaii, strolls in city and country to enjoy exhilaration of spring; lazy summer days on beach." The search for the perfect actor never ends. "PRAYING FOR A MIRACLE to find that one special very masculine, ruggedly good-looking, white/Christian, 58–68, athletically muscular, well-built yet warm and caring—a man's man with whom to make a home and share the last miles in a one-to-one, loyal, stable friendship."

Where Do Phantasies Come From?

To paraphrase a great poet/philosopher: Where do phantasies come from? Do they drop from the skies? No. Are they innate in the mind? No. They come from social practice and from it alone. Most people would think phantasies had to do with magazines like *Stud, Colt, Big Load, Well Hung,* or movies in the shadows of what's called "The Combat Zone" in Boston. But these phantasylands are only part of a system that extends into every part of everyone's life; they are formed out of social practice and in a dialectical way continuously challenge and rebuild the existing social structure. Let me illustrate with my own life.

I suppose my very earliest phantasy comes from when I was only five, sucking off a twelve-year-old. The erect cock and the gooey cream come which dried sticky and dark on my hand still glistens in the mind; Virgil Jeffrey standing in the weeds between the corn crib and barn in Ohio. The difference between age, height, power, penis, pubic hair as well as social position (he was a minister's son) all became incorporated in my psyche as a master-charged beauty.

Likewise when I came to puberty myself, I came to dream on a wonder boy. In sixth grade, we moved out and I changed schools at mid-year. Queer, poor, and strange, I found one friendly face in Bill Schul—who was the son of a banker/school board member, circumcised, friendly, and athletic. He wore Levi's, T-shirts, short hair, and was always smiling. I remember him forever in ninth-grade gym class in the shower; I was fat, dumpy—deathly afraid of being seen naked. He was like a perfect god with the water running down his well-formed, well-endowed body. Later he played varsity basketball; I can remember the wonderful nylon uniforms and my watching as he went to make a shot to see if the jockstrap would show. And on our senior trip I almost choked when we got to share a room (with another student); I can still see his tan lean ass stretched across the bed—corn-fed Ohio basketball boy. I was almost shocked later to learn his left elbow was slightly deformed; I couldn't believe my god has a single imperfection.

Because of the taboo on sex in Western society, many would divide phantasies into the clean and the unclean; they would not recognize that all phantasy comes out of sexual yearning. Greg Lehne in his article "Gay Male Fantasies" (*Body Politic*, No. 14) reports that among his fifty respondents only fifteen report a specific sexual phantasy, but thirty report dreams of a warm, loving relationship. I would maintain that "a warm, loving relationship" is itself a sexual phantasy and (like all the others) involves a master/servant, dominance/submission component. At the very least every holder of a phantasy has some dream of having other people fit in (or submit to) their own dreams.

My own love phantasy does not involve a particular body type or any specific sexual activity. I have a dream—not really so very impossible—of being abandoned, separated, lost, left behind—and then crying my brokenhearted memories. One particular image I can still relive: I had visited a lover in the army at Fort Knox and was returning home with his womanfriend and a brother/lover, who were asleep. Driving between Louisville and Cincinnati at night, I saw eight of him standing in a line down the highway. Anguish and sorrow were in his eyes; I could taste the salt of his body in my desperation of having left, lost him. Swerving to the shoulder and braking, I stopped the car. Did he wake me up at the wheel or put me to sleep?

Another time with the same lover, traveling from Cincinnati to Wisconsin, we stopped in Chicago and camped overnight on Lake Michigan near the University of Chicago. Wayne and I slept best we could on the rocks. I dreamed a deep snow and holding him in my hands limp, dead, weeping at the loss. The crystals of snow were soft and beautiful, dry, dusty, as I lifted him in the wind corridors of Lake Michigan, bearing witness to my love, my loss. I always dream of my lovers being lost, buried, stolen, or best of all: running away and leaving me to suffer. My better poetry seems to come from being left, separated, or away from some lover/lovers. A quarrel and estrangement seems more exciting than the quiet steady flow of being together. It's all part of the wonderful joy of being in love—a subject I want to turn to later; here it is sufficient to urge that love itself is the phantasy of phantasies.

Wayne was such a powerful phantasy/person because he filled so well the high school basketball star as well as a James Dean/Dean Moriarty/Neal Cassidy image of rough wildness. He was both an outlaw and a representation of the sexual dominance system of my Ohio environment. In adoring him I was turning away from my gayness, sacrificing it totally to those powers that be.

A Link Between Sex and Class

A person may often not see how phantasies link sex with class, how "love" is a euphemism for some power relation, or how social practice both creates and is created by phantasies. Yet this process often can become suddenly obvious as one's social status changes. The grand craftsperson of phantasy, Jean Genêt, in *Miracle of the Rose*, describes in himself how he dreamed of the more powerful when he was lacking in power:

I longed at the time—and often went so far as to imagine my body twisting about the firm, vigorous body of a male—to be embraced by the calm, splendid stature of a man of stone with sharp angles. And I was not completely at ease unless I could completely take his place, take on his qualities, his virtues;

123

when I imagined I was he, making his gestures, uttering his words: When I WAS he.

Genet suggests that his worship of the other's mystery comes from his own weakness, inadequacies, and subordination. Once he reached a level of equality, once he became a peer with those he had worshiped, all changed:

> If my sense of wonder, the joy that suspended me from boughs of pure air, sprang chiefly from my identifying myself with the handsome thugs who haunted the prison, as soon as I achieved total virility—or, to be more exact, as soon as I became a male—the thugs lost their glamour.

Myself, I can remember changes in my phantasies and self-image after I received my Ph.D.—a graduation analogous to Genet's becoming a master burglar. I had considered education from the first as a way of rising out of my class. Learning was a way of escaping dirty people, messy lives, and poverty. I cultivated classical music to separate me from country music yokels; I learned to sneer at anyone less educated than myself; I came to consider literature as something precious and elevating. The sexual dimension of such a phantasy/dream rests in the symbolism of "higher," "advanced," and "universal"—all involve elevators, flying, the wings of the mind—symbols of sexual arousal. And they all designate dominance, power, authority, and prestige.

In receiving my degree these phantasies collapsed. The academy appeared as a sham, filled with place seekers, C.I.A. contractors. "The thugs lost their glamour." At the same time my father died, I tripped on LSD for the first time, became involved with SDS, and ceased being monogamous with my lover of several years. As I became a part of Boston's Gay Liberation Front, I lost my admiration for straight trade, learned to enjoy my own orgasms, body, and self more. I no longer took pride in keeping a neat household, always having dinner ready on time, and generally wanted to be more than just a shadow of my man.

Our phantasies incorporate the power system, the social hierarchy into our own individual pysches. They link sex with class. They specifically internalize economic relationships. This is the ultimate means of social control—far stronger than any marines, police, or other symbol of external power. A few recognize the bondage and discipline qualities of their phantasies, but most consider S&M to be a special taste of a small minority. In fact, all phantasies directly express the social structure from which they are formed; every phantasy has some element of either ruling or submitting.

Generally I would guess that the amount and degree of phantasy one entertains relates directly to one's social position; they are indistinguish-position. (Indeed, as I argue again and again, one's phantasy is one's social position; they are indistinguishable.) Freud said on this subject of phantasy (he repeated the observation some three or four times without elaboration):

> The contents of the clearly conscious phantasies of perverts (which in favourable circumstances can be transformed into manifest behavior), of the delusional fears of paranoiacs (which are projected in a hostile sense on to other people), and of the unconscious phantasies of hysterics (which psychoanalysis reveals behind their symptoms)—all these coincide with one another even down to their details.

Freud was absolutely right here: the three kinds of phantasies are the same. I would add that they reflect social position, not some alleged insanity; in fact, they represent a revolt against an intolerable society. Women are generally considered hysterical; schizophrenic paranoid delusions are almost exclusively the property of the poor (Paul Roman and Harrison Trice, *Schizophrenia and the Poor;* cf. John Wieners, "Children of the Working Class.")

Those in power or with relatively more power have less to repress. Phantasies of those "in the know" pass as "reality"—something of which outsiders get only fleeting glimpses. Anxiety, guilt, and fear haunt the powerless much more than the powerful. If we do not voluntarily hide our phantasies, the authorities with the pornography laws, family pressures, arrests, and social pressure will suppress what dreams we might have of making it. Generally, in every way in which we are confined, either by age, class, gender, sexual preference or other hierarchical categories—that category becomes encapsulated inside us and is expressed through phantasy.

An individual's phantasies reflect one's repression, suppression, and oppression. For instance, the photographs accompanying this article [portraying a smooth-skinned white boy of about sixteen posing naked on the shore of an idyllic pond or stream—Eds.] startled me when I saw them: I was immediately uncomfortable because they aroused me. My first *feeling* was one of repression: "This feeling I have is wrong, must be put down, out." It was not a conscious thought, it was a spontaneous impulse implanted in me by a homophobic society. My second thought was one of suppression: a notion that these were not gay liberation images—they denied my own age, body shape, image. Perhaps a jealousy at not being so attractive, of never being able to arouse such interest in the cameraman or the reader. My third thought was of the printer, post office, authorities—although here my dream of martyrdom, court trials, dramatic appeals, testimony from luminaries in our favor, etc., offsets worry about oppression.

Possibilities of Change ("What Does Not Change/Is the Will to Change").

Phantasies thus link our private/sexual lives with our public/social position. Pushing faggot phantasies (however imperfect they might be) is a really threatening gesture to existing power relations. I think we have a destiny and duty to explore fully and actualize as many details as possible for our phantasies. Freud was worried that "in favorable circumstances [pervert phantasies] can be transformed into manifest behavior." His worry is now actuality in the faggot movie houses, publications, baths, bars, and lives. As one gay pride poster declared, "We are your worst fears." We should all applaud the idea of everyone coming out and actualizing their gay phantasies.

The censorious will raise the question of rape and maybe even murder: you can't let people *do their thing;* you must have police/restraint unless you want to be destroyed. In fact, those holding power in their police/restraint functions commit almost all of the rape and murder, both in their phantasies and in fact—check out all deaths in war and auto "accidents," or in marriage, romance, or sowing wild oats. Their phantasies include "crime" statistics purporting to prove that *we* need them to protect us as well as their phantasies themselves. The latter as expressed in the Boston Strangler or Charles Manson are always cited as dangers of what happens when phantasy is let loose. These *men* have been turned into woman haters because they cannot accept and enjoy their own sexuality, sensuality, homosexual phantasies. They project their hatred for their own gay self onto women, whom they attempt to hurt or destroy. Certainly an expansion of gay love among men would cut down both rape and murder.

Rather against my wishes, I also have to consider the phantasy around Dean Allen Corll. I would ignore the question myself, but Kenneth in typing this article rightly pointed out that in urging people to follow their phantasies most people would think of Corll, who in league with teenagers Henley and Brooks had sex with and then murdered several Texan males. First, let me *repeat* the *Fag Rag* "Open Letter to *The Advocate*":

Why doesn't the *Advocate* expose the *causes* of mass murder and sexual exploitation in America? Among these, we see the preoccupation of Americans with violence that stems from an economy of overconsumption and a politics of war; inequality and injustice in an "affluent" nation that keeps 20% of its people in poverty and many of its teenagers in prostitution to get the "things" the society says are important; the continuing oppression of gays, especially in school; and the packaging and temporary fad of "campy" homosexuality, rather than an honest

127

treatment of it. Why haven't you mentioned that mass murders and sexual violence are especially peculiar to the U.S. and are seldom heard of in socialist, sexually-liberated societies like Scandinavia? [*Fag Rag*, No. 6, Fall/Winter, 1973].

To that I might now add that the murders so titillated the *Advocate* because they demonstrated that gays might be just like other men: effective rapists. While straight men dwelt on the story because it fed their fears of homosexuality, the *Advocate* provided sensational coverage because it encouraged antilibertarian attitudes toward sexuality within the gay community. I suspect that Corll developed his sexuality not out of gay consciousness but out of a hatred for gayness itself. And his violence came from Texas and his straight life not from his gayness. The *Advocate* quoted a comment that "He was in the army when, you know, he turned into a fag, and ever since then it got worse and worse." The army is designed to cultivate killers of men; perhaps in the training some wires got crossed and Corll in becoming a lover of men failed to shake the ideal of being a killer of men. Of course, murder is dreadful, but the further question must be raised of whether some men—perhaps all "men"—should be killed. Valerie Solanas in her *SCUM* (Society for Cutting Up Men) *Manifesto* addresses the "man" problem and Franz Fanon in *The Wretched of the Earth* writes about revenge as a necessary step in decolonization. Although a believer in nonviolence, I don't think faggots need further lessons in being attractive victims. And ultimately, all faggots someday will have to kill their love of straight men before they can love themselves.

I am not the only faggot who has phantasies about straight or straight-looking men. William J. Slatter's *The Erotic Imagination, Sexual Fantasies of the Adult Male* (1975) includes a straight-man phantasy. The faggot explains that sucking off someone makes him feel strong and masculine; he says, "sucking off a straight guy is twice as good as blowing a gay. . . . It's like an injection of rocket power or something. When you can get that kind of come, the come of a real man, you become a real man yourself."

128

Many gay liberationists would protest that such a phantasy represents the false consciousness of the unliberated. But I notice that some of the most liberated rush headlong after the same dream-phantasy as their less liberated compeers. Whatever the problems of relating rhetoric and practice, phantasies of straight men internalize society's value system and deny us ourselves as faggots.

Unquestionably every change in power will carry with it a change in phantasy structure. Susan Brownmiller discusses the question of phantasy for women and raises problems that apply as well to faggots:

> Because men control the definitions of sex, women are allotted a poor assortment of options. Either we attempt to find enjoyment and sexual stimulation in the kind of passive/masochistic fantasies that men have prepared us to have, or we reject these packaged fantasies as unhealthy and either remain fantasyless or cast about for a private, more original, less harmful daydream. Fantasies ARE important to the enjoyment of sex, I think, but it is a rare woman who can successfully fight the culture and come up with her own non-exploitative, non-sado-masochistic, non-power-driven imaginative thrust. For this reason, I believe most women who reject the masochistic fantasy role reject the temptation of all sexual fantasies to our sexual loss. [*Against Our Will: Men, Women and Rape*, pp. 323–24]

Even with masturbation one links into the power system; even in abstinence one becomes a victim of the power system. And asserting a self-fulfilling phantasy/pleasure/sensuality/sexuality life for one's self brings one intimately into the power nexus—in particular with other people. A primary problem arises in understanding how one's phantasies can be achieved without essentially curbing the dreams of others. Presently too many just assume that other people have the same phantasy system as themselves. That is rare indeed. Usually "warm and loving relationships" quickly run amuck as lovers discover that their phantasies do not lock. Perhaps Gore Vidal's joke might hold a key to more than domestic harmony: after having sex with another man, he says, "You tell me your phantasy and I'll tell you mine." Certainly a relationship cannot get very far if the people involved are not able to share *and shape* their phantasies.

In the power nexus of phantasy relationships, the problem arises of how to understand one's own phantasies as power desires and essentially curb the dream of having every other person have exactly the same phantasy as oneself. Phantasy imperialism, as it were. Most so-called "warm and loving relationships" quickly run amuck here because phantasies seldom click together. People readily see the needs of others as "phantasy" while their own wildest phantasies often seem like commonsense "reality."

The question of secrecy is itself a form of phantasy that I as a let-it-all-hang-out freak violate. According to authorities, my own detailed (and I hope honest) account of my phantasies is a classic illustration of the masochist personality. Dr. Peter Dally says, "It is much easier for the masochist, with his fantasy desire for self-humiliation and suffering, to expose himself if need be to others, in contrast to the sadist, who is horrified by the idea of anyone discovering the nature of his fantasies." (*The Fantasy Game*, 1975). Larry Townsend also points out in *The Leatherman's Handbook* that an S would "seldom condescend to reveal himself so completely" as an M. Thus, in the phantasy game I am not only revealing myself but implicitly chipping away at those who would keep their silence.

In fact, many thoughts of revolution tend toward what authorities would call masochistic phantasies. Ideas of openness, vulnerability, mutuality, softness, tenderness, expression of one's feelings, kindness—they all add up to values antithetical to mastery and power. What would all the masochists do if all the sadists were shipped beyond the sea? If there were no state, no police, no bullies, of what freedom then could we who are anarchists dream? In other words, what would become of phantasies once the present hateful oppression was ended? Would they pass

130

away entirely? Or would they take on new dimension and richness?

A partial answer to this question can be found within gay oppression. As we achieve more freedom to live our phantasies, they do change. Returning to Boston from San Francisco, an early *Fag Rag*ger brought the alarming news that in that golden land every phantasy was realized. Whatever you dreamed of in men you found. One poet from San Francisco, Tom Kennedy, addressed the topic:

the fantasies have expired
&
i have had all men
in all ways—
have had all cockshapes
and the most centerfold men
and as much at once and
as little at once and
all the firm and
solid and so on and on and on
and the men thrusting
and the men passive
and the men caring
and the men cold and . . .

o but now
i want
a river home
in redwoods
far removed
from alcohol
baths
& disco—
far
far away
from
you
city wasteland—
i will not perish
like the others

Fag Rag rejected this poem in part because its conclusion was contradictory! As though contradictions are not the stuff out of which revolutions are made. Revolution and change may itself be a phantasy. If so, I say let's live it and see what happens. The alternative is to accept authority, the status quo, the rule of straight white men. In revolting against such "reality" we still have to find how to proceed effectively so that we not just modify "reality" but destroy the very thing of "reality" itself. That would be revolution.

III
Watering Holes—
Today and Yesterday

Sexual Anarchy

by Brandon Judell

I climb the narrow flight of stairs to find myself being inspected by a black body-beautiful bouncer in matching leather. His job is to make sure the clientele is wearing the necessary denims and/or leathers. He sniffs me. If I were wearing Aramis, I'd be out in the street again. No colognes allowed. If I were wearing a Pierre Cardin suit, I'd either have to take it off or leave the premises. What am I and the twenty or so people behind me trying to get into? It's called the Mine Shaft and at the moment it's the most popular fuck bar (backroom bar) in New York City.

The fuck bar seems to be reaching its high noon of popularity and notoriety. The straight presses are running weekly articles on the happenings going on in them, the jet set gets chauffeured to them, and some law officials are rumored to be making a profit from them.

What goes on in such a place? It might be easier to say what does not go on. But to get to actualities, one can witness and experience cocksucking, regular and fist fucking, water sports, gang bangs, sadomasochism, beer slurping, gum chewing, masturbation, group sex, and even two people unaware of the rest of the world kissing because they love each other. Not a bad way to spend the night, especially if you find out at the last minute that the David Susskind show is a repeat. Also these bars tend to stay open to the wee hours of dawn, which is a godbless for insomniacs.

History

When did these bars start? And where? No one seems quite sure. The battle seems to be between San Francisco and New York City. Warhol star and chanteuse Tally Brown swears by San Francisco. Alan the bartender made a blood oath that the Big Apple had the first backroom bar. Was the year 1967 or 1968? Was it called the Barn or the Zoo? The correct answer depends on whom you ask. How and why they got started is much easier to answer.

The answer is good old capitalism. Before backroom bars, men were being erotic with each other in trucks and alleys, on deserted hills, and in warehouses. Amidst all these glorious, sweaty entwinings, there was always the possibility of being hurt by someone or something. A loose floorboard. A lonesome nail. A screwy sailor. So why not open up a place with loose floorboards, lonesome nails, and screwy sailors? Serve beer. Have a jukebox. It will take very low overhead to supply all that dangerous eroticism of the old hangouts, and the profit will be huge and quickly gathered.

Well, one bar opened after the other, and all of a sudden Mother Nature no longer controlled sleazy sex. Gays no longer listened to the weather report with their fingers crossed. Snow. Rain. Who cared? The fuck bars had heat most of the time, and most of them had no mud to stain knees, and no rocks to scuff Gucci loafers. They were a big sexual step forward for America under Lyndon Johnson. Thank you, Lyndon.

Why Do People Go to Backroom Bars?

The answer I received most often was impersonal sex. For some it is sex at its purest, while to others it is sex at its most valueless. Whatever, impersonal sex is reaching or approaching orgasm with one or more strangers without having any personal responsibility for them. It is intimate physical contact with someone whose political, cultural, and hereditary backgrounds are hidden from you, and in most cases will remain that way out of choice. And maybe that's what's so exhilarating about backrooms. In how many other places can one see staunch Republicans rimming Mao-quoting Marxists? Where else can opera aficionados be seen going down on Blue Oyster Cult freakies? "Only in heaven," my grandmother told me, "will lions walk alongside lambs discussing the merits of Shaw."

Putting Grandmother aside, most everyday prejudices are tossed away once the participants enter the darkened rooms of lust. Only what turns one on is important. A slightly elongated nipple, a nine-inch shaft, or a bearded face. Fulfill your fantasies while you are unconsciously, simultaneously realizing your partner's dreams. Men who find themselves climaxing only once or twice with a mate at home find themselves spurting four or five times in a backroom bar evening.

Of course, if you are lonely and horny, impersonal sex will quench your horniness, but will probably inflate your loneliness. In a lonely state, one tends to perceive the hundreds of bodies swarming past each other as ants on a mound of a sugar. No time to reach out and hold on to somebody for any length of time. Especially the time-honored code of not kissing what you are groping will reinforce your distastefulness for the situation. So check out your state of mind before taxiing over to a backroom, because the possibility of your having a good time depends on what mood you are in, what you have had for dinner, and how long it's been since you have awakened in the morning to find an unfamiliar shape in the bathroom using your toothbrush. If you *come* contented, you'll *come* contented.

The next favorite reply to "Why are you here with your pants down?" was group sex. Group sex is when you are having all of your orifices plugged, some nice genitalia in each of your hands, a mouth on your own organ, and somone licking your toes. This type of sex can be labeled impersonal at times, but usually one does not have time to think about labeling it.

Then there is voyeurism, the art of looking, the act which Jean Cocteau had endorsed in his anonymously written *The White Paper* (Macaulay, 1958). So closet your qualms if you are a voyeur and speed off to the closest backroom, where you will discover paradise. Get into a comfortable position and watch the leathered devils handcuff the wrists of the overly muscled shirtless angels, and then shove them to their knees and slap their asses. Watch the angels gasp as very long shafts are pushed down their throats. Watch the angels' eyes water as the devils

137

shudder and explode with passion. (Watch as Satan's servants search and search for the key to open up locked wrists of God's helpers as the helpers curse them out.) Or just mosey over to the endless maze of oral/anal Olympic contenders. Judge yourself what is the most unique couplement of the night. Who has been entered the most? Who has swallowed the largest quantities of the liquid of life? You do not care? Not perverse enough you say. Then walk over to the bathrooms and see the human urinals. Fuck bars are like kaleidescopes for voyeurs. They never get a glimpse of the same thing twice.

Some Psychology

C. A. Tripp, author of the controversial *Homosexual Matrix*, feels that backroom bars will reach their peak of popularity around 1980 and then quickly subside. Why? Because the people attending these places for the most part are ones who were brought up in a sexually repressed society. In the fifties, college students were being asked questions such as whether they've "petted a girl's breast area from outside her clothing." Lily Tomlin says, "The fifties were ten years of foreplay." So people born in the era of repression of the late forties through late fifties, when faced with the freedom of the sixties, tended to practice sex enthusiastically but with a sense of guilt. And then in the late sixties, they stopped masturbating with liver in the bathroom, and began sucking, fucking, and doing what they considered dirty in a special dirty room, a fuck bar. When they leave a fuck bar, what they've done is done and left behind. Corroborating Tripp's theory is the fact that most of the people in the fuck bars today are between the ages of twenty-five and thirty-five.

Another interesting theory from Tripp applies to why all that leather and denim is worn in bars. Tripp states that one of the "sought-after rewards" of coupling is "the symbolic possession of those attributes of a partner which, when added to one's own, fill out the illusion of completeness." Men born in the above-mentioned era were constantly imbued with the idea that to be homosexual

138

was to be less than a man. Macho was being a cowboy, a construction worker, or a Marlon Brando. So by mixing your juices with someone attired in a flannel shirt, carrying a drill, or clad in a leather jacket, their manliness is rubbing off on you and in you.

In Conclusion

In the out-of-print book *The Ultimate Solution*, Eric Norden writes:

> Business sounded good by the grunts and screams and whipcracks echoing from the curtained alcoves lining the room, but the place stank of stale beer and semen, and I didn't plan to hang around. When an aged three-piece orchestra groaned into life and the curtain opened on the crucifixion of a nude Slav with stringy blonde hair and saggy tits, I slid the change from my first drink across the bar and got up. . . . As I walked out a reeling sailor was driving the first nail through the blonde's palm . . .

Hopefully, Mr. Norden's imaginary bar will never be. But fuck bars will be around in 1980 and 1990 and as long as there are hot-blooded gays because there should be a "public place" where people can go to suck and fuck without restrictions. There should always be a place to act out sexual fantasies. And most important, there should always be a place to go when the David Susskind show is a repeat.

Why I'm Not Dancing

by Felice Newman

> We pack it in at Shawn's. Two
> dollars gets you past the door, a
> quarter for a game of pool, booze
> runs through our pockets. That in-
> scrutable maze of legs and faces is
> its own entertainment. The dancing
> is free.

Written accounts of first encounters with gay bars are
numerous, appearing in new novels, in books on lesbianism and male homosexuality, and in "coming out" essays
in feminist magazines. In these a theme occurs and repeats
itself, becoming a predictable script. There is a woman,
new to her own identity as a lesbian. She comes to the
bar, with varying degrees of self-knowledge and varying
degrees of sophistication as to what she expects the bar to
offer her. She comes here, having pushed aside her fears,
her sense of degradation at having to assume outcast status
in order to pursue a preference for her own sex. Inside,
she may pause, searching for a face that promises to be
more open, more receptive than some others. What she is
looking for is an image: the proven fact of her existence
mirrored in the face of another who is "like" herself. Before the evening is over, she may find that her expectations—the casting off of masks, the discovery of an
accepting community—were sadly naïve. But for this
moment, she is firmly planted by the bar, drink in hand,
swaying imperceptibly to music that ricochets off the walls.
Once arrived, she will stay. There is simply nowhere else
to go.

The bars are not a gay community, but a substitute for
a gay community. In some large cities, lesbians and gay
men are fortunate to have satisfying alternatives. In other
areas, small collectives formed to organize centers of

community activity (both social and political) have been frustrated by a lack of support. Thus, for the majority of us, the gay life still revolves around the bars.

Most simply stated, the function of the gay bar is threefold: to provide a place of relative anonymity and safety where gays can meet members of their own sex (as most gays cannot afford the danger of assuming "likeness" in others outside explicitly homosexual or feminist settings); to provide an atmosphere in which the tensions of a potentially schizophrenic existence may be released; and to simply provide a setting for social enjoyment. These are stopgap measures set against the atrocities of heterosexist America. At best, and with luck, gays may develop a circle of friends—or one friend and a life of bell jar monogamy—whose support will be the deciding factor in personal survival. But personal survival is not enough. And the bars are not simple places.

The illusion of the public ("out for the evening," "a night on the town") and the private (the semidarkness of anonymity) are carefully balanced. Patrons must be able to flow freely within an aura of protection. The casual socializing of public life must mix well with the intimacies that would be impossible elsewhere. This careful balance is not without its effects. I first went to the bar with a strong desire to meet new friends, to cut loose, to move easily through knots of people at the bar and on the dance floor. Yet I felt frozen, inhibited.

My understanding of my own sexuality first stirred as I was becoming increasingly angry with the highly competitive sexual manipulation—"game playing"—I observed as a high school student. I went to the bar looking for relief from heterosexuality. Instead I found a parody.

Although physical imitations of heterosexuality (butch and femme role-playing) were already waning due to the healthy influence of feminist ideology, game playing was still very much accepted. Among lesbians, often the temptation was to accept this surface improvement as evidence of a new mode of human relating, and as Adrienne Rich writes, to "lie down with the sherds we have painfully unearthed and be satisfied with those" (*Women and Honor: Some Notes on Lying*). The lessening of extreme

141

role-playing was long awaited and genuinely welcomed among so many of us, but taken as the deliverance of our lesbian culture, it was misleading.

I walked into the bar unaware that beneath the excitement of women being together "in their own place" was an arena of sexual competition. The rituals of visual language—to be learned for dancing, sexual innuendo, and courtesy—were unknown to me then. I had to learn "rules" to help me navigate the maze of protective lovers, regulars, and newcomers. To approach another woman became frightfully complicated. I was sure that any effort to strike up a conversation would be construed as a rude come-on and rejected; since that is what the bar is for, that is how I imagined my actions would be understood.

Because it is difficult, if not impossible, to develop much of a conversation in a bar setting, the projections of age, class, race, clothes, hair length, bodily proportions, and dexterity replace language. I did not feel that I could be known by anyone. Physical projections—how I walked or danced, smiled, and held my drink—were my only voice.

It did not occur to me then that I was also responding to women on the basis of limited information.

This was to be my community, and I felt excluded from the start. Having no other comfortable space, I retreated within the body: the private and tentative feeling of alienation. *I do not know why I am like this,* I thought. *No one else was ever like this. . . .*

The sound of my own voice addressing a stranger was strained and distant. The feel of my body in a chair was suddenly foreign. It was as if I had never bent to find my place in a seat, as if my limbs were brittle, my joints like old hinges. I was more self-conscious and more tense here than in the company of heterosexuals whose presumptions about my sexuality were insulting. How odd to feel so oddly out of place.

I remember my shock at finding out that women who "crossed" the bar owner—by feeling attraction for someone she also liked, by not responding to her attractions, or for some who angered her by being black or Jewish—were banned. Cut off.

I remember my shock at hearing stories of bar violence—the night the bar owner, angered by a "slow" employee, hurled a bottle at the woman's head; the employee who chose pride—never looking up, but methodically picking the glass slivers from the floor; the lover's quarrels; the acts or words that are so senseless among women.

And, yes, many women enjoy the bars, and are unaffected by the alienation and violence. Often they bring their own community with them, having developed friendships through the feminist and gay communities. They are looking for a place to enjoy what they already have. Others do well in the bar because they are adept at playing a game of sincere superficiality. They are on a flash high, floating among the people, delighting all with their energy and outgoing personalities. Early on, in trying to emulate these good spirits, I found I was more comfortable responding to a stranger with a brash and carefree hug than with the quality of my full presence. While knowing myself to be overly sensitive then, I remember trying to seem sure of it all, and was flip, cocky. At such times the shelter of social pleasantry was a burst bubble, a short-lived joke. As gay activist Kevin McGirr has written in *After You're Out,* "One perhaps has questioned, 'Are you having a good time?' and a not an unusual response [is], 'Are you kidding!' "

The bars are more than imperfect, more than unfortunate. They represent lives spent in complicit and habitual superficiality. Superficiality is a breed of silence, and silence has a long history in us: most of us have spent the larger portion of our lives denying the fact of our existence. My lesbianism is more than a matter of how I am sexual. If there is no room for self-revelation, for encounters beyond the tired script, then my community does not serve me.

In silence we have lost connections. As single threads we lack the strength of bonds. We come to expect little from one another. Entertainment becomes a reasonable replacement for growth. Survival becomes a reasonable replacement for political change. The possibility of working together, of sharing our deeply felt observations, is too much to ask for. Reality is neatly divided: "politics" and "real life" are something happening outside us.

Inside we forget to notice how much the images of patriarchal sexuality—the economy of commodity dominance—have crept through the woodwork. We forget our bars are a borrowed theme, the altars of masculinity transformed for gay purposes. For women, this means our borrowed culture is *twice* removed, and the remnants of the masculinity cult resurface in us as self-hate. Sexual manipulation among women is not lesbian love, and certainly posters depicting women in traditionally alluring poses (found in a male-owned establishment, placed in a "women's section" to make us feel at home) are not evidence of high feminist consciousness. For gay men, acceptance of the patriarchal view of sexuality produces extreme woman-hating. David Loovis (*Gay Spirit: A Guide to Becoming a Sensuous Homosexual*) personifies this sensibility, witnessed in the bars, baths, tearooms, and on the cruising route:

> We as gay people do *not* have to contend with bloody menstrual periods, opening car doors, fingering the clitoris, protecting the honor of a partner from gossip . . . virginity, diaphragms, condoms, black or white gloves one of which is forgotten and for which one must go back, frigidity, lacy nighties, vaginas, vaginal jellies, dried-up vaginal fluids . . . breasts (pendulous or small), the belief that the world revolves around the vagina . . . pussy, little print sun dresses, cunt, toplessness . . . remembering to put down toilet seat, cunnilingus, and lovely hands.

Gay, of course, meaning male. The contradiction is clear: for gay men antifeminism is suicidal. For in America, gayness in men is always viewed along with womanliness: "You're a faggot," . . . "You're effeminate," . . . "You're nothing better than a woman. . . ."

This is our inheritance. This is where we begin: as a people neatly divided by entrepreneur-and-clientele roles fulfilling the patriarchal need for sexual segregation. We are remaindered at birth, fenced off into profitable ghettos. We are weakened by alcoholism and exploited economically. Our music, once mass produced for heterosexual au-

144

diences, is now chic. Gay bar-hopping, for straights, is fashionable. We dance the latest dances, which straight men emulate to manipulate straight women throughout the single bars of America. We dress to please. We don't talk much. Inside we forget to remind ourselves that prisons are antithetical to cultural growth, that social asylum must assume alternatives—freedom to move about, try different things, change, and grow.

Inside we never ask: who decided on a *bar* anyway? Such a question, which seems silly here, would necessitate choices.

The refusal of politically astute gay men and women to ask this question is analogous to the self-effacing acceptence of a foreign culture by a colonialized people. And as dangerous.

The point is that our communities must be consciously created, not adapted from a sexist mold. Alternatives come to mind easily—coffee houses, organizations working to bring concerts and films to communities, settings which allow for more than a come-on or a game of pool, collectivization of the existing centers of community activity on a nonprofit basis. In one city I know of there is a combination women's restaurant–bar, collectively owned and run by committees that include volunteers. The result is a more relaxing atmosphere.

We must understand our collective potential for growth, and create settings which will help us unravel and discard the heterosexism that now pollutes our communities. The possibility of a feminist gay community is the potential of relationships without sex roles, of social affairs free from dominant–submissive models.

Our sexuality is not a pretty coat worn on the surface of the body. Our importance to each other cannot be measured in a commodity market. When our bodily expression is more than an energy release or a sexual ritual, when I can feel the body's emotional voice joyously refusing to be censored, when our communal goals challenge and delight us, then we will really dance.

The Cleveland Bar Scene in the Forties

by John Kelsey

There was, of course, nothing spectacular about Cleveland's gay male bars in the forties, but the point is simply this: they existed. Gay men had places to meet, not only in San Francisco and New York, but in a city easily scoffed at or ignored by sophisticates on either coast. These meeting places existed not so much because we wanted them, of course, but because bar owners knew that we needed them and that they could make high profits selling us liquor. In those days, no one would think of protesting or boycotting a bar because it excluded certain people or because the drinks were watered down or the prices too high. There was, in fact, gratitude at just having the space where one could relax and be with one's own kind. That curious combination of exploitation and liberation helped define the mood in gay bars then as it does now, though perhaps both elements were more extreme in those days.

The bar scene in the late 1940s was small. Only three or four gay bars for men would be in business at the same time, although there were quite a number of such drink spots in the years of economic boom which followed the end of World War II.

A new bar would open, and everyone would flock to it, only to tire of it; and a few months later it would close its doors. Most gay bars were owned by straights and were adjoined to a straight bar or nightclub. And almost all were dark and cheaply furnished, some being little more than cleared-out storerooms.

An exception was the Cadillac Bar, located on East Ninth Street, a door south of Euclid Avenue and opposite the Cleveland Trust Co. The Cadillac was clean, well lit and comparatively well furnished. It was a long, narrow room with the bar on your right as you entered and a banquette with tables to your left. I recall much blond

146

leatherette and woodwork and also some rather good murals of tropical scenes.

Almost every night, seated around the curve at the far end of the bar, and nursing a drink while talking to her brother or some old friend, was Mrs. Gloria Lenahan, the owner. Mrs. Lenahan, a handsome woman with a pleasant drawl, was a little aloof from her customers. She ran the most strict liquor spot—gay or straight—in Cleveland and probably in the entire Midwest. Trouble was turned away at the door. Too loud a laugh or coarse talk put you on the street. And the slightest hint of backtalk to the management meant banishment from the premises for months or even years.

A jacket-and-tie code of dress was required of customers except on Sunday nights, when Mrs. Lenahan was absent.

Another popular bar was located in the basement of a restaurant near the Cleveland Public Library. Here things were more informal; almost anyone was let into this large, dark room, and there was no dress code. Yet you had to watch yourself there; sometimes rather shady characters, such as shakedown artists, would turn up in the weekend crowd.

Foolhardy gays in search of rough trade would sometimes drop in on Mac & Jerry's, not a gay bar, but a hangout of spot-laborer workers and minor hoods. At least two murders and countless near fatal beatings of gays have been traced to pickups at M & J's, which was on Superior Ave, opposite the Cleveland Hotel.

Probably the most famous customer to enter M & J's was U.S. Undersecretary of State Sumner Welles, who gained considerable praise during World War II by his negotiating of reciprical trade agreements between the U.S. and South American nations. Perhaps Welles was negotiating some such agreement when Cleveland detectives found him in this notorious bar and escorted him across the street and up to his suite in the Hotel Cleveland. An hour later, back he was at M & J's; and Cleveland's finest had to launch another rescue operation.

Most of the other gay bars were run ostensibly as private clubs (sometimes you needed to produce a membership card at the door; sometimes not). Most had female impersonators as entertainers. I have not checked on the current bevy, but thirty years ago impersonators were a dreary lot indeed; most were overmade-up and undertalented, while their stage talk was invariably silly and foul mouthed.

Mr. Lynn Carter, however, had a clean act. I first saw Carter in the backroom of the Musical Bar on Huron, where Publix Book Mart now is. Today Lynn Carter imitates Channing and Diller; but thirty years ago he was a grande chanteuse in the style of Hildegarde and Dietrich. Fresh out of Cleveland Heights High School and dressed in an expensive gown donated to him by Billie Holiday, Mr. Carter would sweep onstage, genteelly wave a gloved hand at the audience, and launch into "April in Paris" or "I'll Be Seeing You."

Another impersonator I recall was Mr. Kit Russell, who was billed as "the world's most beautiful impersonator," and what a good-looking woman he appeared! Yet any glamour was quickly dispelled in an effusion of one-and-a-half entendre jokes; he also had a dismal habit of going into fits of tittering.

The most famous impersonator of thirty years ago was undoubtedly the legendary Titanic, who often would play the East Coast, but sometimes would return to Cleveland, his native city. His songs were the standard impersonator fare ("You've Got the Right Key, Baby, but the Wrong Keyhole," and something about the artwork on a circus tatooed woman), but he was really famous for his murderous sense of ridicule from which no person in the room was safe. Between sets, he would preside at a ringside table, unleashing barbs at the other occupants. Only an extreme masochist would ever heckle a Titanic performance.

Titanic, in men's attire, was quite good fun, with a rather sly, but not hurtful, wit. When not working he was a great customer of gay bars, sometimes taking his mother along. I was saddened last year to hear of his death. I first saw Titanic in 1947 at the Viking Club, which was on East Fourth Street, I believe.

If the professional entertainment was bad, the amateurs

148

were unbelievably awful. Sunday afternoon was amateur time at the Hide-Out Club, an upstairs bar on Walnut Street. Here male typists in Grandma's cast-off finery would take the stage, forget lyrics, and flee in tears. And stockroom boys would take absolutely dreadful spills during their ballet–tap routines. One I much enjoyed was a short, middle-aged man who would sing "Indian Love Call"—part of it in the voice of Nelson Eddy, and part in the voice of Jeannette MacDonald.

There were other gay bars in the downtown area during the late 1940s, but most were desperation moves. As the postwar boom faded and the straights got married and moved to the suburbs, downtown bars would "go gay" for a month or two before finally being forced to close.

The real difference between the 1940s and the 1970s is that thirty years ago most of us were in some sort of closet or other. The bars were really mere hunting grounds, not places you would go into to relax, enjoy a drink, and talk with friends.

Missing the Ports O Call

by Jim Jackman

Everybody knows where Worcester is. It looks like a part of Brooklyn stuck in the middle of Massachusetts. It's too big to ignore altogether, but up around Park Square the word is that it's "very fuckin' tired." No apologies. It's true if you're a fag with money, but for the rest of us— the stockboys, the dishwashers, and the hairdressers—Worcester is like most other towns on earth where you have to take it any way you can get it.

The Ports O Call was *the* gay bar here for almost a quarter of a century. When I first came out, fifteen years ago, I had to adopt the customs that prevailed there if I wanted the affair I dreamed about.

It was around 1951 that the vice squad closed down the Coronado Cocktail Lounge on Salem Square. The Coronado's missionaries banded together on the common and marched to the New Yorker. In towns like Worcester, where most of the population didn't even make it to the middle class, this was how gay bars were made: by naïve faggot suffrage.

The New Yorker, later on known as the Ports O Call, was owned by two elderly Irish sisters who were horrified at the idea of doing business with such repulsive sinners. They didn't like the winos they were serving either, but at least they understood them. They were men who failed at this late stage in life and seldom had the energy to do much more than swear or simply sit there and look dirty. Queers, however, never even tried in their eyes, let alone failed. To add to that, they were outrageously voluptuous. Straights had visions of declines and falls when fairies went too far.

This initial attitude was undermined, of course, by their account books at closing time, bending the scales to tolerance. A new policy of smiles and nods insured the new wealth pouring in on them. They wore neat black

150

dresses and they waited on their pagan clientele as if it were an Irish wake. Betty's contempt for these creeps softened as the profits put her son through Holy Cross.

Other critics of gay life did not agree with the cash register. These were the days of crackdowns, witch hunts, John Wayne movies. Popular songs about marines left over from the forties and the Loretta Young shows carried on about manhood as if it were a sort of mysticism. Heroes were made overnight as moral warriors from other neighborhoods would visit this new den of deviates to start riots. Many of them ended with an ambulance carrying a bunch of bloody fairies off. They were not sure what a real man was back then, but after a few beers they definitely knew what he wasn't.

The sisters didn't worry too much about the chronic rumbles that all this new business brought with it. There really wasn't anything in there to destroy except the bottles neatly lined behind the bar. The New Yorker's walls and tables looked left over from another era. I heard an old auntie say that it was once a pre-Depression ballroom featuring the big names in Dixieland. By the fifties, it was dirty. Even when it was swept, it looked unswept.

Like most working people, gay or straight, I thought that all fags were French-Canadian because they were the only ones I knew in there. All the other homosexuals were well off and they went somewhere else for their fun, so that Worcester's gay community was made up mainly of machinists, textile workers, kitchen helpers, hairdressers, and, on weekends, farmhands. Lack of education forced us to accept society's opinion of us: that we were immoral, trashy, and repulsive.

Within a year after its revivification, the New Yorker was the synonym for gay life throughout Worcester County. With it went that legendary myth you hear about when you're fourteen: this bar, appropriately resembling the inside of an outhouse that has since been turned into a zoo, is loaded with these creatures, not unlike a cheap sideshow, that will suck off anything in pants, and you don't even have to wink.

To help this pubic fable along, the gay crowd carried on

like cheerleaders at a football rally, screaming over how they loved to suck cock, nothing else, just that.

Today, I hear that there's a label for this phenomenon. It's called "conditioning." To me, however, this was gay life, take it or leave it: witty one-liners, quickies, and contempt. It was a tremendous down. I couldn't take it. I began associating with a strange straight crowd that let their hair grow, sang folk songs, read T.S. Eliot, and smoked pot. I felt at home with them, although I masturbated regularly to keep their buns out of my mind.

Through the sixties, when the young revolted to the point where it was almost necessary socially to adopt this revolutionary set of tastes—work clothes, long hair, guitars, pot, poetry, Oriental music, rock—the faggots with their brushcuts were still stepping to the "Alley Cat" in the New Yorker's jukebox. It wasn't just a gay bar anymore, it was an institution, an established form that people, straight and gay alike, did not want to change.

But change it had to, because young faggots from the working neighborhoods no longer daydreamed over Judy Garland shows or Bette Davis or the other goddesses that Hollywood created, and business for the sisters went downhill. They willed their exhausted gold mine to one of their old customers. He formed a committee that re-designed the rickety New Yorker, converting it into a discotheque with strobe lights, psychedelic walls, new chairs and tables, and, of course, a men's room that resembled Oz. This became the Ports O Call.

It was noisy there, but it drowned out the acid sarcasm that I associated with gay life. I didn't have to join the camping competitions or go "fishing" or bring fag hags with me to protect myself. I loved it. Gay life in Worcester was finally updating itself. That distant ideal of mutual consent, as foreign as it is to us, finally seemed a possibility within the Ports O Call.

Today, Worcester's working class is shrinking. The barbed wire and bullets that this town is famous for producing has since been replaced by banks, banks, and more banks. The new class of people that works in the skyscrapers that have gone up now has its own gay crowd and this, at first, meant competition for the Ports O Call.

152

The middle-class gay world, however, is removed from the working-class gay world. Appearance was much more important when the Exit II opened. Some of the Ports O Callers visited the Exit II and were amazed. There were at least three times as many faggots here as they thought there were. Where did they all come from? What did they do in bed?

The new Exit II was elegant. Wall-to-wall carpeting, Victorian design, a disco, little café tables. This original delight turned into disappointment when they found out that they had to learn a new approach. Nobody cruised. This new crowd of gay bank tellers and actuary clerks was dressed to kill. They stood around and chuckled, sipping cocktails, flapping wrists, ignoring even Warren Beatty if they didn't know him.

The Exit II changed hands to an ambitious owner who renamed it the Mailbox, but the story was the same. It wasn't the gay world that Worcester County talked about in whispers—it was as if an expensive Boston bar had been transplanted here and all the wealthy closet cases were finally admitting it by being seen within.

It was the end for the Ports O Call. A third gay bar, the Mauai Kauai, opened its doors. It emptied out the Ports O Call. It wasn't until after it was gone that I found out how unfortunate it was. All that working-class folklore that had been invented through the years during Worcester's otherwise monotonous coffee breaks will end. As factory workers migrate west and are replaced by secretaries, agents, and executives with their neckties and white shirts, all that spicy gossip that has been traditionally associated with gay life will die. What's worse, the fatties and the homely faggots with loud nicknames and the aging aunties will have to rely completely on the tearoom from now on. The club with which they've identified is gone. With the middle class, everyone is strictly beautiful with a clear line. A weeknight in the Mailbox reminds you of the illustrations in the *Watchtower*. That's a difficult adaptation if you're a dishwasher.

Since the closing of the Ports O Call and Worcester's gradually resembling Hartford, Connecticut, I've seriously thought of moving on to Boston. Unfortunately, the rent there is the highest on earth.

So that's why I miss the Ports O Call. The ideal of equality which the middle class is always screaming about does not mean that they will consider me an equal—it means that I'll have to become a bank teller. Well . . . I hate numbers. Anybody got any suggestions?

IV
Dance and
Music

Toeing the Line:
In Search of the Gay Male Image in Contemporary Classical Ballet*

by Graham Jackson

The Ballet *Monument for a Dead Boy* was first performed in Amsterdam on June 19, 1965. Produced by the Dutch National Ballet, *Monument* was the work of Rudi Van Dantzig, co-artistic director of the company.

Monument was one of the first ballets to deal with homosexual love. On a stage, empty but for some impressionistic, Noguchi-like set pieces, a young man, the title character, alternately stabs the air with his arms in what seems like a futile attempt to break free of his past, and doubles up in total position while a flock of black-draped furies hover near. This balletic agony is supposed to represent "homosexual conflict," to borrow a phrase from one of the less enlightened reviewers.

The boy, it seems, has been traumatized by a brutal display of parental coitus. He can't make it with a shaky seductress in blue; he feels dirty just thinking about it. He wants to go back to the days when he kissed a little girl among the hollyhocks, but his innocence is irretrievable and he turns to a young man for comfort. For this, the boy is taunted and gang-raped by a pack of schoolchums. With insult heaped upon injury, the boy kills himself—of course.

Van Dantzig's use of symbolic gesture in *Monument* is vague enough to allow of several interpretations, but the above is the most popular one with the critics and, all benefits of the doubt aside, the most logical.

In 1965, *Monument* was bold and daring. While it didn't garner rave reviews, the public and the critics

---

*I have not attempted to analyze the female image in contemporary ballet in this article. I feel that a woman should do that. There is certainly enough material to make such an analysis worthwhile.

treated it seriously. In early 1966, ballet critic Peter Williams interviewed Van Dantzig in the British journal *Dance and Dancers,* and reviewed *Monument* as "one of the most distinguished works to emerge from the mainland of Europe in many a long year." Typical of the seriousness with which critics felt compelled to discuss *Monument,* Williams wrote:

> It would be a grave mistake to dismiss *Monument* for *a Dead Boy* as something merely with a homosexual label. Admittedly homosexuality is touched on; it would be hard to create an honest work about adolescent mental confusion which didn't, but such suggestion is only a small part of the buildup of forces which can lead youth to a violent crossroads—leading possibly to suicide. Where the depth of this document lies is in its honest approach to the lack of care which can lead to the bruising of a tender and unformed mind—possibly beyond redemption.

After its first presentation in New York by the Harkness Ballet on November 2, 1967, Doris Hering, reviewer for *Dance Magazine,* didn't mince her words: she knew what *Monument* was all about. "*Monument* is, quite simply, about how a homosexual gets that way," she wrote in her inimitable journalese.

Although not as pussyfooting or sententious as the British press, Hering and the New York critics tended on the whole to admire *Monument* more than their overseas colleagues. *Monument* had the gutsiness and, yes, the vulgarity that American dance critics eat up. The subject matter not only shocked them, it also titillated many of them. Men touching one another in a sensual way! How different from all those pretty girls in white tulle! The serious young men who had sat through countless *Giselles* and *Swan Lakes,* more interested in the boys in white tights than the prima's pirouettes, look to championing *Monument* as the beginning of a new era in dance.

Pretty soon, *Monument* was in the repertoire of two or three dance companies, and choreographers in the States and Britain were vying with one another to produce a ballet on a homosexual theme. But this was the era of *The Boys in the Band*, when the sentiment, "Show me a happy homosexual and I'll show you a gay corpse," was a popular one and most of the offspring of *Monument* were, as a result, lurid and bleak.

In 1973, *Monument* was revived by the prestigious American Ballet Theatre. This time, however, the critics were not impressed. In fact, they reacted with a yawn. Even those serious young men who had made such a fuss on its first appearance now sniggered—after the polemics and the parades, who wouldn't? Van Dantzig's psychologizing seemed threadbare and often downright silly to them.

One of the most eloquent dance critics writing in the States today, Jack Anderson, summed up what he thought had happened to *Monument* in the eight years since its world premiere in these words:

> What has caused *Monument* to crumble is a shift in social attitudes. In 1967, its presentation of homosexuality startled us. Since then, thanks to the sexual liberationists, we have become slightly less self-conscious in our discussion of sexual matters. *Monument* . . . survives from a period in which, possibly to mollify the prudes, an artistic representation of homosexuality had to have a slightly whining tone and an obligatory unhappy ending.

What then can the National Ballet of Canada have been thinking of when, in 1976, it added *Monument* to its repertoire? It has often been said that we are culturally a few years behind the U.S., but *this* is ridiculous.

The acid-penned critic for *The Globe and Mail*, Lawrence O'Toole, praised the National's production, but called the ballet "a slow ache." William Littler of *The Star* also drubbed *Monument* for being clichéd and boring.

Who decided to include *Monument* in the repertoire? Is the decision a significant comment on the direction classical ballet is taking in this country? Is this as daring as the National wants to get in its balletic treatment of homosexual love?

To try to understand the thinking that prompted yet another production of *Monument,* I talked to Peter, one of the major dancers in Van Dantzig's work here. Although I didn't get answers to all the questions, I learned a lot.

Graham: Why *Monument?*
Peter: The company wanted a work by Rudi Van Dantzig. *Monument* was the obvious ballet. It really didn't have anything to do with the subject matter.
G: Whose decision was it?
P: David Haber [former artistic director] was responsible for getting the work.
G: How would you describe *Monument?*
P: It's about a young man who's on the verge of deciding whether to go on or whether not to go on. In the ballet he basically goes over his past life. I won't go into specifics about each of the relationships he has, but in order to go on he has to leave his youth behind him, he has to break away from, say, the girl in blue, the girl in white, and his youth completely. As far as I'm concerned, the boy does break away.
G: Then you don't think the ballet is really about homosexuality?
P: I never saw it as being a homosexual ballet. Originally I did, then I found out that it really wasn't about that. The relationship with the boy is an important aspect of his life, but whether there was actually any homosexual relationship isn't clear in the ballet. He [Van Dantzig] didn't want to make any points.
G: Do you think the ballet is dated?
P: I don't think it's dated. Ten years ago the thing that stuck out about *Monument* was the fact that there was a homosexual relationship in it. What people termed a homosexual relationship. There actually is a homosexual relationship, I will admit that. One out of three relationships is gay.

What puzzled me the most was Peter's initial refusal to recognize the obvious, i.e., the homosexual content of the ballet. Was this a personal evasion, I wondered, or was he merely toeing the party line? If he were straight, then his interpretation of *Monument* would be understandable if not acceptable. But Peter is gay, as he confessed to me later on.

We had been talking about the possibility of trying out a gay ballet at the National's annual workshop in Toronto, a forum for the choreographic talent of the company's dancers, when he opened up:

G: Would you be interested in doing a gay ballet?

P: I'm really leaving it open now. [Pause.] When I do ballets about sex that involve something between a man and a woman, I really don't know what I'm talking about and I can only do it as something between two men as I know it. So it's always there if you know me.

My obvious rejoinder would have been, "Well, why don't you do a *pas de deux* for men?" but Peter seemed so awed by the notion of presenting a gay ballet, fearful of repercussions from the almighty board of directors, which might affect his career as dancer and choreographer, that I forbore saying anything. In fact, I already knew the answer to my unspoken question.

When, at the end of the interview, he requested that I not use his real name, I realized that there was something more rotten in the state of ballet than *Monument for a Dead Boy,* that the latter was just a symptom of a much larger problem.

Classical ballet is conservative and tradition-bound. Its language is very formal. Only choreographers with the stature and genius of George Balanchine can tamper with the language without undue censure.

At the 1974 Gala Opening of the Harkness Ballet in its new home near Lincoln Center in New York, the company gave a work by Vincente Nebrada called *Percussion for Six Men* which allowed some of the company's best male dancers to display their versatility. In one segment, a dancer performs on 3/4 pointe. This apparently shocked the critics for, as everyone knows, pointe work belongs in the realm of the female dancer. A man never dances on pointe unless he's playing a special character role as Anton Dolin did in 1926 when he created a mild sensation dancing on pointe as the dandy in Nijinsky's balletic adaption of Molière's *Les Facheux.* But for a hale

161

dancer to perform on pointe in an abstract ballet where there's no story to excuse it—that's unforgivable!

A typical reaction to Nebrada's *Percussion for Six Men* was supplied by the resident dance critic for *Time* magazine, John T. Elson:

> One soloist performs a legato variation delicately poised on tippy-toe. The display might have been aesthetically more attractive had he been a girl, or had the performance taken place at the Continental Baths.

This type of smug reportage is not unique in ballet criticism. I think it is the highly physical, often erotic nature of the art that brings out a critic's defensiveness.

Ballet is all about bodies, bodies in motion, about line and curve and bulge, about arms and legs and backsides, as much as it is about princes and swans. There's no escaping it, although many hotly insist that to talk of ballet as physical and erotic is to demean the art. What is at work here is obviously the age-old dilemma of integration: is sexuality something one keeps carefully apart from the other activities one engages in like eating, bathing, thinking, dancing, or even appreciating dance; or should it be integrated naturally into the fabric of human experience? Obviously critics like Elson subscribe to the former *modus operandi* and as a result are offended when ballet is too explicitly sexual or erotic.

The classical dance aesthetic is obviously also a straight aesthetic. It is for the most part about the interaction of man and woman, most of the time in sexual or erotic terms. Men are allowed to dance together only in certain stereotyped relationships—as rivals for the same woman, for example, or in athletic displays of one-upmanship. If, as some people in dance have objected, the dance aesthetic has to do with bodies as instruments and not with socially defined gender roles, then why, I ask, is there still a hesitancy to juxtapose male bodies on stage in certain attitudes?

The answer, irrational as it is, is that the contrast between a male and a female form is more interesting in terms of line, etc., than that of two male forms. It is noteworthy that these dance aestheticians don't make the same remarks about two female forms. They know that Balanchine has proved time and again, in ballets like *Serenade* and *Concerto Barocco*, that women dancing a *pas de deux* can create a very beautiful rapport. In a society accustomed to see women as innately prissy and fey, this is not offensive. The same society does not recognize gentleness, either in movement or feeling, as being masculine qualities, let alone the basis of male interaction; and it is this unspoken dictum that dance critics and aestheticians are unconsciously observing.

The result of all this is that a ballet featuring a man dancing on pointe, or, what is infintely more daring, two men dancing together in a lyrical or erotic manner, unless backed by big money and an audacious artistic administration, is bound to be short-lived.

One of the most conservative views of ballet and the role of the male dancer comes from Joseph H. Mazo, dance critic for *Women's Wear Daily*, in his book *Dance Is a Contact Sport*. Mazo spent a season (1973–74) absorbing all aspects of the New York City Ballet (NYCB). Some of his discoveries are interesting and nearly always amusing. For example, he decides that "ballet is about sex," but not just any sex—ballet is about the penis–vagina variety. He doesn't have much more than that to say about ballet as an art form. He prefers to concentrate on backstage ballet, on the personal lives of choreographers and dancers: what they drink, how they dress, who they ball, areas of activity which are very important to a public still somewhat suspicious of the art.

If anyone had doubts about the masculinity of male dancers, Mazo lays them all to rest, or at least most of them. Calculating the number of gay dancers compared to the number of straight, he arrives at a reassuring figure: six of the eight principal male dancers in the NYCB and about half the soloists are "practicing (and, one assumes, believing) heterosexuals." The boys in the corps, however, are another story: "overwhelming gay," Mazo proclaims. He has his theories about the discrepancy between principals and corps, and they're dandies:

163

The principals are a good deal older than the boys in the corps and less often in residence at the theatre. As they matured, as dancers and as men, they very well may have put away youthful attachments—if they ever had them—and gone on to make their peace with women and enjoy it. Another explanation for the smaller number of gay men in the higher echelons of the company is that a homosexual dancer, if effeminate, who allows his homosexuality to dominate his dancing is unlikely to become a superior performer. A homosexual dancer, effeminate or virile, who allows his homosexuality to dominate his life also is unlikely to become great.

While we grant Mazo his point that an effeminate dancer will not make a very convincing Siegfried or Albrecht, he should realize that there is more to male dancing than *danseur noble* roles—as the repertoire of the NYCB itself testifies.

There is room for both macho dancer and the dainty dancer as well as for something in between, something little appreciated in North America—the androgyne. The Royal Ballet in England abounds with androgynous dancers; in fact, one of the best male classical dancers performing today, Anthony Dowell, is androgynous in both appearance and technique. When Mazo throws this term "effeminate" around, he means this intersexual quality—one he obviously can't come to grips with.

Another interesting point in Mazo's explanation is that homosexual dancers must repress their homosexuality if they are to become great and, more specifically, successful dancers. What about heterosexuality? Doesn't it interfere with the progress of the dancer? Apparently not. Mazo doesn't ask Edward Villella to cut down on his butch act—in fact, Villella has made a career out of it—but he chastises the kids in the corps for camping it up! This is just the sort of sanctimonious double standardizing that paralyzes talented dancers like Peter from developing a personal dancing style reflective of their characters, limits the range of male dancing severely, and successfully keeps people thinking of artistic endeavor and sexual expression as totally alien, incompatible facets of human experience. Bravo, J.H.!

Another dance critic, the omnipresent John Gruen, who has probably fawned over everyone worth fawning over in his time from dancers to poets, presents a picture complementary to Mazo's in his book *The Private World of Ballet*. The book is a compendium of interviews starring the legends, new and old, would-be and has-been, of the ballet world.

With the exception of a joint interview with dancers Anton Dolin and John Gilpin, who have been "friends" for years, most of the interviews turn out to be a paean of straight marriage and "normalcy." Reading Gruen's book, one wonders how the stereotype of the faggot dancer ever arose—you can just see them all stewing about the mortgage and the baseball pennant—and that's probably just what Gruen and his interviewees wanted. Gruen's presentation of dancers as just plain folks has serious implications for ballet as an art form.

What Gruen and Mazo are doing, whether they realize it or not, is selling ballet like a commodity to a public tired of violence and "depravity" in plays and movies, a public eager for escape into a fantasy world. They don't sell ballet as it might be, they don't chart the future of ballet as a road leading somewhere; they flog *Coppelia* and *Swan Lake* instead. Concomitant with this sort of entertainment is a wholesome, "normal" image for the dancer.

An intelligent critic like Oleg Kerensky (grandson of *the* Kerensky) who writes for *The New Statesman, The Daily Mail*, and occasionally *Gay News* is, sad to say, in the minority. Although a trifle finicky in his approach to the question of male sexuality in ballet, his views are far more rational than those of his American counterparts.

Although sex is now openly discussed and portrayed in the theatre, cinema, and literature, there still lingers a relic of the idea that it is in some way improper for a man to flaunt his sexuality. A woman making herself as glamorous and appealing as possible is regarded as normal; a man doing the same thing is not. Just as some people still object to men

165

using perfume or wearing jewellery, so they find it difficult to accept the idea of men in tights, displaying their figures for the admiration of an audience. Many great male dancers have been bisexual or entirely heterosexual, married and fathers of families. But it is equally true that many male dancers, including Nijinsky, have been bisexual or homosexual.

(Ballet Scene, London, Hamish-Hamilton, 1970)

What is more important in Kerensky's comments is the purpose behind them—which I see as an educative one—rather than the comments themselves—which are true, certainly, but not deep.

Kerensky has few allies in thought but a handful of concerned, intelligent ballet-goers. Gruen and Mazo not only have public prejudices working for them, or rather with them, they also have a large number of male dancers whose aim in life seems to be convincing the masses—and possibly themselves—that ballet dancing is a masculine activity.

Foremost among these dancers is Edward Villella of the NYCB, who has taken his act into the high school gym to show the boys that anything they can do in free-form gymnastics, he, as a ballet dancer, can do with more control, precision, and style. This routine, which has lately been preserved on film, ostensibly proves that ballet isn't sissy. Needless to say, the boys run right out and buy ballet slippers.

Six years ago in an issue of *Dance Perspectives* (#40) devoted to an examination of the male image in ballet, Igor Youskevitch, former principal dancer with the American Ballet Theatre and celebrated partner of the Cuban ballerina, Alicia Alonso, described what he thought male dancing was all about:

When man lifted his first stone he knew *why* he was doing it. Reason has always been the basis of his dance innovation. He did not dance for dance's sake. He danced for the gods, for success in war and hunting, for a mate. There was always a purpose in his dance, reflecting his masculine inclinations to lead, to

166

go forward, to achieve. Civilization does not change basic masculine nature; it develops progressive images of the man-hero. A man must keep in his dance the seeds of this heroic nature.

... For the female, a dance does not need to have a meaning. As long as she feels herself a woman she can use her inborn qualities to give life and excitement to her movements. But as long as a man has no reason for his dancing he tends to drift into feminine interpretation.

Four other dancers were asked to contribute their impressions about the male dancer's image. Bruce Marks thought masculinity was a question of "weight," of keeping close to the earth, of aggressiveness. Villella thought it was a question of muscle. Of the lot, only Luis Fuente, formerly of the City Center Joffrey Ballet, offered the only sensible and nonsexist opinion:

We don't need to get a headache thinking about how to look masculine. A man always is a man, and you don't have to build muscle to show it. When you dance you show what is true of you as a person. It comes very easily. You just do the movements, very freely. When I am dancing I am not thinking how to show I am a man: I am dancing to show the audience how a dancer dances.

Is it any wonder that amid all this silly talk about masculinity, many serious dance lovers switched their allegiance from classical ballet to modern, avant-garde, and experimental forms of dance? To many, it seemed that choreographers working in a modern idiom—like Paul Taylor, Louis Falco, Lar Lubovitch, and Twyla Tharp—were comparatively unconcerned with questions of male–female polarization. Most of them preferred a more androgynous dancer. (Tharp in fact often creates movement that can be danced by male or female interchangeably without any alteration in the steps.) And yet for all this, there have been few dead-on confrontations with homosexual themes.

167

In Canada, where classical ballet is fairly traditional, modern dance troupes like the Toronto Dance Theatre, Entre-Six, and Le Groupe de la Place Royale have proved more adventuresome. They have each briefly exploited the dance possibilities of homoeroticism.

Jean-Pierre Perrault, co-artistic director of Le Groupe, is, like Louis Falco, self-avowedly gay. But whereas Falco subscribes to a cooler, bisexual lifestyle, Perrault is unabashedly militant. It is all the more unfortunate that his militancy hasn't touched his work in a more significant way.

What interests Perrault is not "content" or "message," but production technique, a term which here means a mélange of bizarre lighting effects, slide projections, and electronic sound as well as an abstruse experimentation with space that passes for "content." But Perrault is not alone; his interests are reflected in the repertoire of several modern dance companies, with the result that the dancer as performer becomes an entirely mechanical, sexless object.

Right now the public and, to some extent, the media are clamoring for a return to "normalcy" in all the arts. The theatre queues in New York and London are for revivals, *My Fair Lady*, Feber and Kaufmann's *The Royal Family*, Ben Travers's farces, and musical revues. At the same time, ballet is beating a hasty retreat over territory just recently won, territory which is just a scrap when you look at it.

In order to be able to expand the accompanying list,* we would have to have a revolution challenging the very aesthetic on which dance and arts like painting, sculpture, photography—arts which focus largely on the human body—are founded. This revolution is not likely to come from the "straight" dance-makers. It's possible that women might start it, but so far classical choreography has been a male-dominated field.

A sizable number of these men are gay—if the exact

* "The Homoerotic in Ballet: A Partial List" appeared with this article when originally published in *The Body Politic*, August 1976; back issues are available from *The Body Politic*, Box 7289, Station A, Toronto, Ontario, Canada M5W 1X9—Eds.

number were known, I'm sure it would be staggering. They were initially attracted to ballet because of its ambivalence, its latent homoerotic potential, and yes, its reputation for being a sanctuary for "faggots." Once "in" however, they become very self-protective, very conservative; they are careful not to jeopardize their position with critics, public, or management by being too blatant, an old-boy network is established to ensure the status quo. It's a fairly familiar pattern, one that happens in most of the arts at some time or another; but in classical ballet, which has a history of conservatism, the result is quite simply stagnation. The very men who should be at the head of this "cultural revolution" are busy making pretty dances for girls in tutus claiming all the while that one's personal and creative lives must be kept separate—for the sake of the art!

When Peter described to me how he went about choreographing a male–female *pas de deux*, I wondered if he realized the dishonesty of such an approach:

G: Is the reason you choose to present a man and a woman rather than a man and a man because of your audience?

P: Yes, usually.

G: Is that a true expression of yourself, do you think?

P: Yes. If you try something between a man and a man, you're saying a whole other thing and audiences aren't ready for that yet. It's the audience that tells us what to do.

Attractive, articulate, and very talented, Peter is also— like the men mentioned above—somewhat of an opportunist. His opportunism must be seen, though, as part of his fear of coming out in creative terms. In the end, he will only cut his own throat: he has abundant choreographic talent but a deliberately limited vision—the combination is not a healthy one.

On such men as Pete rest the mettlesome task of realizing a new facet of the dance aesthetic only sketchily or covertly explored heretofore.

The ballet audience, a great bulk of which is gay, is no

help to them. Gay balletgoers consent to support countless repetitions of the grand old classics without complaint. They don't demand anything more daring than Les Ballets Trockadero de Monte Carlo, a drag ballet with a lethal gift for satirizing romantic, classical, and neoclassical styles of dance.

One might suspect that for many gay balletomanes, ballet is a retreat into a fantasy world too—one in which they can covertly ogle the boys and at the same time live in a pretty world they think they always wanted to inhabit, but from which they are banned by virtue of their sexual proclivities. This might seem to some an unflattering, exaggerated picture, but it is one that is too often true.

Gay people have never been too vocal about what they want to see in the theater or on the movie screen. To make a "revolution" possible, they would have to be willing to sponsor, finance, and support—in terms of their attendance—companies that dare to challenge the established dance aesthetic and produce "gay" ballets—ballets that feature men doing beautiful, delicate, lyrical, sensual, erotic things—together! Only then will other companies realize the importance of the gay balletgoer and the gay choreographer. Until that time, we're stuck with the sylph, the swan, the doll with the china-blue eyes, and pseudoexpressionist dreck like *Monument for a Dead Boy.*

Dance Liberation

by Rob Dobson

When people ask me what I do I sometimes tell them (reluctantly) that I dance. And if they respond to that at all it's usually with "Oh, what company are you with?" And then I shift around a little and mumble something about not being performance oriented. Or they'll ask "Who do you study with?" and I'll make some attempt to explain about a couple of my friends who teach dance classes that I go to. Or they'll ask what I "plan to do" with my dancing or if I'll ever be able to make any money at it, and I'm reminded one more time of how much our culture values the product over the process and how loaded the word dance is with countless connotations and associations. I wish I didn't have to use the word at all. Sometimes I don't use it. Sometimes I call what I do movement improvisation, but even that has many different meanings among dancers. Or I call it creative movement, which always sounds somewhat lame or pretentious.

How can I describe this thing that has been so central in my life for several years now? There's really no way, of course, because its very essence is radically opposed to language and rational thought and the perceptions that language creates. ("The finger pointing to the moon is not the moon.") For me, dance is one of the tools for "stopping the world," for helping me to enter the eternal present, letting each moment be fresh and new, exploring the infinite universe, making endless discoveries, untainted by anything I've ever been told about the nature of things. It's like what Walt Whitman says about trusting nothing but your own experience. It's my favorite kind of play and also my favorite kind of work. Both. Nothing more enjoyable, nothing more serious for me. It's immeasurably therapeutic, of course, but I don't like to focus on the benefits only. They just seem to come about as by-products

171

of the creative efforts. And therapy is another loaded word anyway.

So I still haven't told you what I do or what I feel when I dance. The only way you'll ever really know is if you do it yourself. And I'd love to see that, because, besides dancing myself, one of my greatest joys is helping other people find enjoyment in their own movement. I won't really be satisfied until I see everyone in the world dancing. But I might settle for just a few other faggots to share it all with.

Etc., etc., and so on and so forth *blah blah blah.* Anyway, a few days ago I went outside in the morning and walked back behind the barn, through the gate, onto the old grass-grown road that runs across the hillside. It felt like a spot I might like to spend some time moving in. So I started stretching and bending and twisting and flopping around a little to "wake up some movement feeling," as one of my most admired teachers, Barbara Mettler, would say, and then I started listening to the air flow past my ears as I was swinging up and down and around, swooping down to touch the grass. And I played with making some shapes with my body in space, then spending some time listening for a movement impulse to begin in one part of me and letting it travel through the rest of me, and then experimenting with leaping down the long tire tracks of the road, and then standing out of breath for a moment with my arms crossed over my chest and feeling my heart pounding, and rocking gently from side to side with that rhythm as I watched the trees swaying against the windy gray sky.

Rain began spitting down a bit, and I found my hands dragging down across my face, and when they came off there was a new expression on it—my face muscles were in a different place. So I held them there and let my body move in a way that seemed to match my face. I wiped it off and left a new one and moved again. And I did that for quite a while, making masks to dance with, until the rain came harder and I ran to the barn and continued dancing there, watching the rainy forest hills through the open door, noticing how I felt about moving on that wooden floor, how this new environment influenced my

movements—more playful now, more stamping and fling-
ing and turning. And when I got tired I rested and watched
the rain a while longer and then went into the house.
And that was fairly typical of the way I like to work.
Sometimes it's much more frivolous and lighthearted, and
sometimes it's very deep, carrying me into worlds beyond
description. But it's always full of surprises.

So what was I doing that morning? What good was it?
What did it communicate? What did my dancing express?
If someone pressed me for answers I guess I'd have to say
basically that the morning's dance as a whole had something to do with expressing celebration of the spot in the
road and celebration of me being alive that morning in the
country. But I wasn't trying to communicate anything to
anyone else. I dance because I like the way it makes me
feel. I don't do it for someone else's benefit. Oh, there are
times and places for honing skills and performing in the
presence of other people. But how interesting would it be
to watch, how convincing would it look if I didn't know
how to enjoy it myself? My favorite way of thinking about
performance is as a kind of sharing, especially among
other people who like to dance. (Who else can even begin
to appreciate what I'm sensing as I move?) Dance in the
Western world has degenerated into a primarily visual art,
something for us to watch professionals do on a two-di-
mensional proscenium arch stage. No longer is it a felt experience in which all people can participate. One more
spectator sport.

Dance is the language of awareness. Human bodies,
their movements, and their shapes and postures (which are
formed by their movements) are more immediately,
potently expressive than words or any symbols or
representations could ever be. Dance is not an interpretation or a translation of life; it's the experience of life itself.
People who understand this can share the experience together. They can speak to each other with movement, exchange energy with each other, and celebrate life in and
through their bodies. I wonder if faggots will ever grasp
that for themselves, touch that magic and power with each
other.

I see only two places where dance and male homosexuality intersect at the present time: gay bars (interestingly, always considered the best dance bars in town) and professional dance companies. Almost universally, bars provide gay men's only dance experience. I'm thankful we at least have that, and yet after having tasted the unbounded possibilities of movement improvisation, the dancing in bars seems like such a pitifully narrow band in the spectrum of dance. The range of movement experience is severely controlled and codified, very strictly limited by small space, certain kinds of loud music, and a highly charged social atmosphere. I can enjoy it once in a while. When I find myself becoming bored with it I challenge myself to find more ways of moving in that situation, more things to do with that kind of music and the people around me. Limitations often help produce a lot of growth, but strobe lights and mirrors usually create irritation rather than ecstasy for me. Loud music hurts my ears, and I hate the smell of cigarette smoke and amyl nitrite, and it all seems more desperate and destructive than joyful and creative. As for professional dance companies, a great percentage of the men in them are gay, but most of them don't consider their sexuality as a central, deeply influential factor in their lives. And almost all professional dance, as well as dance in bars, takes place in cities and reflects urban life.

I find it impossible to separate my dance involvement from my self-identification as a faggot. It's revolutionary for anyone to devote a major portion of his time to dance in this culture. Perhaps for women it's not quite such a radical activity, because they have always been allowed more emotional and expressive use of their bodies, possibly stemming from the assumption that biologically women are more inextricably bound to their bodies. Until the very recent days of more widespread birth control and abortion and ideas about feminist/lesbian separatism, women's roles have been biologically defined. But men's dance is even more revolutionary, because men are expected to be the workers, the breadwinners (ignoring the validity and value of all the hard *work* women have always done in this culture). It is more threatening somehow to see men enjoying their bodies through movement for its

174

own sake, rather than serving some respectable utilitarian purpose, innocently enjoying the body, producer of feelings and emotions themselves, such unmanly things to exhibit. Men dancing together form an even greater threat, and men dancing together with any kind of affection or eroticism create the greatest threat of all.

What about the prominent male dancers in our culture? It seems that we can support only a very small number both economically and psychologically. We have token dancers in the same way that smaller groups within the society have token blacks, women, and faggots. Let Fred Astaire and Gene Kelly and Rudolf Nureyev do our dancing for us. We can tolerate them, let them amuse us, provide us with some kind of vicarious release. And, of course, their dancing is almost always heavily tempered by plenty of female partners to help keep the homosexual ghosts at bay and holy heterosexuality intact.

When I began dancing at the University of Arizona, I connected very luckily with a wise teacher, Sue Pfaffl. Within an hour in her first class she had managed to lead me into an astonishing revelation-filled movement experience. I was stoned for days. This was it. Why hadn't I been doing this all my life? I realized in a flash that dance could be the means of going beyond self-consciousness tied to my body. I had always thought that dance would only enhance nervousness about my body (one-two-three, point your toe, and does it look pretty, am I doing it right?). But through improvising, focusing on letting the impulses come from inside somewhere (how much of that first year did I spend dancing with my eyes closed?) I felt good about my body for the first time in my life. I was the kind of skinny kid who got C+'s in gym class and nearly died there in the competitive macho jockworld. No one ever told me that there were ways for me to enjoy my body without straining and exercising and fighting and comparing myself to everyone else. No one ever told me that coordination and sensitivity and expressiveness counted for much of anything. Consequently, when I began to dance I suddenly felt strong, empowered. Here was something I could do, and I could do it well, simply because that meant doing it in my own way, meeting no one else's standards.

I felt almost guilty for a while for perpetuating a stereotype, that all male dancers are gay. But I see it quite differently now. What man is readier than a faggot to break the shackles placed upon his body? Who more willing to enter forbidden territory? Who more able to explore a traditionally female activity? For a long time I was virtually the only male in any class or dance session I attended. When more men at the university finally started to dance I was somewhat relieved, since I no longer felt the burden of often being expected by female dancers to move in male ways (whatever *those* are) and having to put up with comments like, "It sure would be nice to have more men to provide more yang energy." (As if the women couldn't provide it themselves.)

Socially produced movement inhibitions begin forming immediately after birth, and they are inextricably involved with rigid sex role definitions. A friend of ours told us that one day in the park when he was little his mother turned to him with a bewildered look and said, "You know, you're just like a little girl." What do you suppose he had been doing that prompted her to say that? I imagine that he was walking on tiptoe or skipping or playing around with some kind of soft gentle movements. Entire chunks of our movement range get chopped off right and left like that during childhood. Parents and peers insure that socially unacceptable behavior in the form of body movement is strictly controlled. Don't use your body in any way that feels good or interests you. Make sure it expresses something meaningful. Make sure it leads to a useful product. Don't make a face like that. Don't move your hands in such a weird way. Don't walk like that— you look like a sissy. Don't experience your body. Don't experiment with it. Don't let your movement awareness (your kinesthetic sense and your sense of balance) help you explore and deal with objects and people just as your other five senses do, although surely they too have been culturally stunted.

As a result of this kind of conditioning, most of which is so subtly pervasive that we don't even realize that it happened, our adult bodies move awkwardly and have the capacity to sense only a certain repertoire of movements. Almost all of us, including the most radical faggots and the most dedicated dancers, have chronically contracted muscles in our lower backs, at least partly for the reason that movements of the pelvis, so closely connected to genitals, have been grossly inhibited. (Try having a totally satisying orgasm while arching your back.) And that's only the most blatant of examples. The same kinds of things exist throughout our bodies. Fortunately it's never too late to begin to reverse the process through various kinds of body work and a creative approach to dance.

What about cultures which are more vitally connected with the earth? In these "primitive" cultures it is much more common for men to dance. Not very surprisingly, these same cultures often respect homosexuality as a valuable form of human experience. In martriarchal cultures, such as the Hopis, the men even have the major responsibility for performing most dance rituals, although it is questionable whether or not they hold this control, associated as it is with the men's directing of the Hopi spiritual life, as some kind of compensation for the fact that the women hold the property. It's always risky to try to peer into another culture and sense the meaning in its participants' lives. It's difficult to avoid projecting romantic fantasies onto another group of people somewhere else. I really don't know anything about Hopi sexuality in particular. Homosexuality may not be a viable part of Hopi culture, as it is with many other primitive peoples, but in many ways Hopi men do seem like wonderful sissies. (They are notoriously nonviolent, and they do all the weaving too.) Unfortunately it's very difficult to get a clear picture of the true extent of feminism and homosexuality in other cultures since almost all history and anthropology has been written by straight men, who have very little empathy for the forms of human expression which mean so much to us as faggots. I do know that when I'm in the Arizona desert I feel close to mystery and power. And I identify with the Hopis' sense of gentle reverence for the earth. Often I feel compelled to move in some ritual way, dancing for joy when the rains come, dancing

177

solemn watchful patterns as the desert awakens at dawn, dancing in honor of simple miracles—plants growing, days passing, water running.

It's also very interesting to me to think about male shamans. In cultures in which this role exists, the shaman is healer, artist, and religious figure all in one. He is the person most in touch with honored states of consciousness and the powers associated with them. He deals with the true nature of reality, expressing it through art, reminding people of it to help heal them, leading the worship of it. How do shamans get in touch with what it is they know? Interestingly enough, shamans are quite often gay. Almost by definition, that gives them one foot out the door, a way to step outside of their cultures' values and perceptions (often loaded with sexism) and enter into other visions, other worlds. Dance is essential as a means of attaining these perceptions, sometimes allowing the shaman to transcend his personality and reach a trance, in which the shaman may realize truths about the nature of reality, and sometimes his dancing is powerful enough to break up the binding perceptual framework normally used by the shaman's patients/observers. In the language of astrology the planet Uranus has traditionally been linked not only to homosexuality, but also to revolution, spontaneity, creative genius, and healing powers.

Is there any historical precedent for gay men dancing together? There is some evidence. Arthur Evans, in his series of articles on witchcraft as gay counterculture, published in *Fag Rag*,* has brilliantly indicated the importance of gayness in the pagan nature religion of ancient Europe, continuing into the Middle Ages. Dance was most certainly a major part of the rites of this religion, just as it was in the Dionysian celebrations earlier in ancient Greece. In fact, it seems that the Christian church spent as much energy trying to suppress dance, "this evil, this lascivious madness in man called dance which is the devil's business," as it did trying to suppress gayness itself. (For information on dance in the Middle Ages, see Chapter 3,

* Available in book form from Fag Rag Books, Box 331, Kenmore Station, Boston, MA 02215.

"Body and Soul" in Walter Sorrell's *Dance Through the Ages*.) We know that men danced together in "lewd" dances called the *kordax* and the *sikinnis* in Greek comedies. In the pagan "witches' " rituals men who enjoyed their gayness danced and feasted and sang along with the rest of their community. As for other instances in which we find that men danced together, we can only dream about the homosexuality involved. Morris dance in England, for instance, was a vigorous but formal fertility dance performed by six men. Or consider the Egyptian picture of two men performing a kind of greeting dance. *(Dance Through the Ages*, pp. 24–25.) How many such men shared love that we'll never know about? How much secret communion has thrived throughout history despite the severest cultural oppression?

When I'm feeling the most ineffectual and overwhelmed by the world, if I manage to get up and start moving I feel better instantly. For me, every time I dance from my own inner impulses, it becomes an affirmation, not only of my own worth, but of life itself. The introspection, the self-criticism, the endless mind games fade as the movement gently dissolves my self-consciousness. It seems that faggots especially could find value in this experience, being so burdened as we all seem to be with the "I'm ugly and worthless" syndrome caused by so much internalized oppression. More than any other activity, dance makes me feel good, makes me feel whole, makes me feel like a living thing, like a healthy member of the world community of beings. Dance reminds us. The Zuñis say, "We dance both for pleasure and for the good of the city."

In the country the experience is further intensified. In the country I feel support, protection, comfort. When I'm in the country I find that I'm much more likely to move as I want to, rather than as someone else wishes. A great amount of my energy is freed because I don't need to expend so much of it protecting myself (often unconsciously) from real and/or imagined threats in the city. My reality is no longer defined by other human beings. Plants and animals accept me as I am. And everywhere I look I see movement, rather than concrete immobility and rigidity. I see that life is movement. Even on the cellular, molecular, and atomic levels everything in the world moves.

When I dance in the country I hear my breathing as a very basic element of the dance. Not as something interesting to concentrate on and use, but as a prominent inevitable feature of the movement of all organisms. The wind is blowing across the field and the air is going in and out of me. I'm an animal. I'm alive. It's quite enough to hear my heartbeat too, and it's easy to use that rhythm as part of the dancing going on.

Dancing in the country has many other attractive characteristics for me. I often sense myself as the steward or caretaker in my environment, not only by attending to physical needs (watering gardens, pruning trees, cleaning up trash) but also by simply caring about everything, enjoying it. Dance works as a way for me to express my appreciation. There's something magical about a dancer in his environment, something about setting everything right. There can be a powerful exchange of energy. In return for my love of the space and its inhabitants, my environment provides me with infinite influences on my movement. And without four walls to stop me I enter more completely into flow. I'm reminded that dance can happen anywhere at any time. I don't have to go to a studio or gay bar to do it. As my movement awareness increases I find that the sensitivity and efficiency can be applied to everything I do, and everything becomes a dance. Movement is essential in everything that human beings do. Improvisation becomes a way of life, and I try to approach every act in the most creative way possible with the elements at hand.

Dance is found throughout the world as a road to ecstasy. Ecstasy as a word can be thought of as meaning beyond stasis or stillness. Entering into the vibrating, pulsating, flowing, changing universe. Joining the cosmic dance. Joining Shiva in the never-ending creation and destruction of forms.

There are glimmers of hope for men dancing together again in our time. During the earlier days of gay liberation people danced in circles in the bars and shared rebellious exhilaration. In a bar in Portland now there is folk dancing in the early evenings. And on a farm in Oregon men do Scottish dance with each other as partners, looking each other in the eyes as they pass and turn and fly feeling joyful. In San Francisco this spring I've been teaching an improvisation class for gay men through Lavender U., and of course it's a great delight for me to see these men catching on to the things I have to share.

In the same way that women have begun to reclaim their bodies from the heterosexist male machine that demands that they shut up and make babies (which most men think is the only thing they can't do yet by themselves), I wish for faggots to take ownership of their bodies, to wake up to the psychophysical torture we've allowed. I think we should reserve the right to be silly sometimes, to giggle, to do what feels good, not only erotically in bed, but in everything we do with our movements. And I hope we can dare to try out body movements that may seem undirected, maybe even threatening, even to us (maybe especially to us) with no goal in sight. Unless we let this kind of dance help us to explore the unknown, we will probably remain inside our gray shells, moving along the prescribed track, never to emerge, never to come out into ever brighter worlds.

May we reclaim our bodies from the culture which has tried to possess them for so long. May the deformations and disfigurements which result from the tension and stress of trying to be what we aren't be erased. May we restore to ourselves our beauty. May our lifelong movement inhibitions dissolve. May we have strong, resilient bodies that move with ease and fluidity. May we see each other as this happens and rejoice.

Images of Gays in Rock Music
by Tommi Avicolli

For years now gays have been portrayed in rock music, often, I've discovered, without our knowledge. Many of these portrayals have been, surprisingly, positive. Most people, for instance, do not know that Janis Ian in 1967 recorded a pro-gay song—"Queen Merka and Me" (on the album *For All the Seasons of Your Mind*)—which contained a verse about two male lovers—or that an unknown singer named Judi Pulver in 1973 released an album (MGM; *Pulver Rising*) with a lesbian song entitled "Part-Time Woman."

Part of the problem has always been that major record companies don't push gay or gay-related music. Steven Grossman's openly gay LP—(Mercury; *Caravan Tonight*)—failed to gain the widespread recognition it deserved. True, the record company wasn't totally at fault here; the gay community also failed to support Grossman's effort. But then gays shouldn't necessarily endorse all attempts by gay artists to create an openly gay art form; it is obvious, though, that the majority of gays are unaware of Grossman's LP. Ours is still (despite the almost nine-year lifespan of the gay liberation movement) an uninformed community—our diverse parts have yet to come together, and our attempts at creating a culture of pride often go unnoticed by those who don't read gay papers or attend gay community center functions. The gay publications and recordings that have come out of the movement are yet relatively unknown. Most gays still identify "gay" music as the recordings of Bette Midler or Judy Garland. How many gays know of "Stonewall Nation" by Madeline Davis?

Olivia Records—a national women's recording company—has released many important feminist and lesbian songs by artists, such as Meg Christian and Teresa Trull, some of whom are beginning to gain airplay on the

182

"straight" radio stations. Anthony Louis, a Philadelphia-based gay folksinger, released "Fantasy" last year; it even appeared on jukeboxes in some of the gay bars in the city. However, Mr. Louis's record and the work of gay performers in general have still not gained the widespread support of the gay community. The greater number of nonmovement gays don't care if there ever is a distinctly "gay" music. And surely one can argue the merits of having an exclusively "gay" music.

But the image of gays in rock music needs to be examined—if only to make us aware of what was and is being written about us. Rock music—as an institution and as a piece of contemporary culture—must not be taken lightly. Its influence on our mores has increased over the years. It's no longer the voice of a few so-called malcontents. It's a multimillion-dollar industry with all of the muscle that goes along with possessing money, a large captive audience, and performers whose godlike statures endow them with invitations to the White House and the power to influence politics (for example, Dylan's campaign for the release of Hurricane Carter). When and if gay issues are included in the myriad causes promoted by rock musicians, then the public's consciousness will finally have a chance to absorb gay liberation the way it absorbed hippiedom many years ago.

Prior to the Beatles' invasion of America (with their inane invitation to "hold your hand"), folk music had laid a solid trail of strong protest against the imperialistic and inhumane values of the rulers of this country. Songwriters like Bob Dylan, Joan Baez, and Peter, Paul, and Mary were the voice of a generation dissatisfied with the conditions of the world. It is said that Dylan expressed the passion of an entire generation when he wrote "Blowing in the Wind." Yet Donovan, another young folksinger, expressed more to the point the feelings of a lot of gay men when he wrote and sang, "To Try for the Sun," probably the first (and one of the most beautiful) male/male love songs ever written.

The song shows the gentle sensitivity of Donovan, and its chorus demonstrates his impatience with intolerance for his lifestyle.

There is not another reference to gays in rock music until around 1967 when a daring young performer (only fifteen at the time!) recorded "Society's Child," a record which was banned in parts of the country. In fact, due to its theme—interracial romance—disc jockeys in the South were beaten up for playing it. The performer was, of course, Janis Ian. In her song "Queen Merka and Me," she described two men who walk through the park holding hands and declaring quite boldly, "Our love is not wrong."

About a year later, Neil Young—along with the Buffalo Springfield—recorded "I Am a Child," which even to many straight rock critics had homosexual overtones. Of course, to many others the song was about the relationship of a father and son. Yet the homosexual theme is evident whether it's father/son incest or male/male lovers.

"Lola," by the Kinks, was released just before the onslaught of that period of rock I shall unflatteringly dub the "bisexual chic." The Kinks, from the beginning of their career, symbolized the new generation's rejection of the establishment's values. They were always more political than the other rock groups. They sang of the triteness of overly romanticized heterosexual relationships, and they ridiculed the absurd shallow value system of the "well-respected" men, even while the Beatles were still in their adolescent love stage. The Kinks never suffered from acne, that's for sure. They were unacceptable for American Bandstand, showed contempt for the British government even before John Lennon did his antigovernment number in 1969. So it was no wonder the Kinks created "Lola," about an outrageous transvestite who confuses the hell out of a straight man in a bar.

This is definitely not your typical teeny-bopper unrequited love song, epitomized by the early exploits of such bubble-gummers as Donny Osmond. Instead it is ultimately a song about the sexual politics of being a man (or a nonman!)

The persona in the song is perplexed because Lola does not fit into either a strict male or female role. He concludes, he's glad he's a man, ["I thank thee, Lord, that I was not born a woman," as the prayer goes] and so

184

is Lola." Now is Lola glad that he (the singer) is a man, or that "she herself" is a man?

The Kinks' political ideology is a strange blend of longing for a utopia and realizing the inadequacies of any human social structure. In Ray Davies' cynical lyrics, utopia is quite impossible. Yet from time to time he still dreams of a "Village Green" where war, poverty, and hatred don't exist. Perhaps, like all of us, he needs those moments of release.

From the beginning, the Kinks identified with the plight of the worker, the outcast, and the persecuted. They never endorsed any political system, and always found reason to mistrust church and state. In *Preservation Acts I and II* (their second rock opera) the Kinks explored those forces which are shaping modern society. Among these are the political wheelers and dealers, the voices of the different classes, and such notables as the Vicar. In *Preservation*, as in Greek tragedy, the chorus expresses the feelings of the people. Their despair over corruption and crooked politicians lures them into the clutches of Mr. Black, who makes familiar promises.

The sentiments of this song are familiar ones. In their first rock opera, *Arthur*, the protagonist is lured to Australia, another of Davies' utopias, by visions of a society, where there is no poverty or class distinction.

But the forces of the right also plot to build a better world in *Preservation*. Their plan is to eradicate the so-called works of the devil. Among the immoral practices leading to the destruction of society, in their view, is, of course, homosexuality.

The Bonzo Dog Band was another politically conscious group who often commented on the sexual politics of manhood. In the song "Sport, the Odd Boy" they satirized the mentality which says: "It's an odd sort who doesn't like sports." In "Mr. Atlas" they spoofed body building and the male obsession with physical prowess.

Around this same time, the Who released their famous rock opera (later to become a movie) *Tommy*, which contains a song about Uncle Ernie, who, with the aid of a lot of booze and in the absence of Tommy's parents, performs a sexual act upon the boy. Tommy's reaction is

185

neither positive nor negative. For him it's just another experience in the vast deaf, dumb, and blind abyss in which he lives. However, the image of Uncle Ernie is another reinforcement of the old "child molester" myth. Too many straights already have the notion that gay men are child molesters; we don't need The Who to reinforce that stereotype. To add to the antigay message of the song, in the movie version Uncle Ernie is seen reading London's leading gay liberation journal, *Gay News*.

With the coming of the 1970s, we have an increase in the number of gay images both in rock music and in the image of rock stars. People like David Bowie, Alice Cooper, Marc Bolan, and others donned various degrees of drag to elevate their stage acts to theatre performances. Along with the drag came the safe pronouncements of bisexuality. For the men, at least, bisexuality quickly gained a new status. The women, like Janis Ian and Joan Baez, were met with hostility when they came out. But the boys were allowed their diversions, since "boys will be boys."

I guess David Bowie started the "bisexual chic" phase of rock music with his *Ziggy Stardust* LP—a concept piece about the rise and fall of a bisexual rock star, and the disintegration of our overly technocratic and inhumane society (a theme more fully developed in *Diamond Dogs*, an album that is stark and intense).

The songs on *Ziggy Stardust* do not present a positive view of homosexuality; rather they treat it as a symptom of Ziggy's decadence (and the chic crowd loved decadence!), with references to "darkness" and "disgrace."

Ziggy is ultimately murdered on stage by his fans because "with god-given ass" he went too far. Obviously, what he took too far was his homosexuality.

In his stage show, Bowie, in the finest tradition of Alice Cooper and the New York Dolls (later exploiters of the drag-rock phenonema), would go down on his lead guitarist, Mick Ronson, in a mock blow-job. Ronson would shove his guitar near Bowie's ass while the latter was lying on the floor on his stomach still singing. These antics gained him the title "Queen of Rock" in some circles.

In "Cracked Actor," a song on the *Aladdin Sane* LP,

Bowie expresses nothing less than contempt for an elderly gay actor who resorts to paying hustlers along Sunset and Vine in Hollywood. For someone who has made his reputation by exploiting gay sex acts (and images) on stage, he has very little good to say about homosexuality in his lyrics. Yet the homosexual communities in both Europe and America looked upon Bowie as some sort of idol, the androgynous and liberated nonman.

Similarly, Lou Reed, lead singer of the Velvet Underground of sixties fame, was elevated to the position of a cult figure—especially with the release of his *Transformer* LP. Three "gay" songs were featured on this endeavor, packaged as sensationalistically as Bowie and others of his school of hype had packaged other "bisexual chic" products. "Walk on the Wild Side," the hit single from the album, was an invitation to take a walk on the gay side of life, while it portrayed three of Andy Warhol's transvestite superstars—Holly Woodlawn, Jackie Curtis, and Candy Darling. As a statement on sexual politics, it said nothing; as a "gay" song it was, to use a popular Bette Midler line, "the pits." The melody was uninspired, and the lyrics inane. The only interesting part of the song was the sax solo toward the end.

The other two gay songs on the album—"Makeup" (about a tranvestite getting into drag) and "Goodnight Ladies" (about closing time in a gay bar, ho hum)—are boring, trite, and fail to inspire any kind of gay pride. The lyrics of "Makeup" are a lackluster attempt at such pride, merely paraphrasing the slogan "Out of the closets, into the streets!"

Jobriath, a latecomer to the glitter scene, released two LPs which presented some gay images. "I'm a Man," from the first album, is a cute commentary on sex roles, while the naughty "Blow Away" on the second is somewhat coy in its praise of cocksucking.

Mott the Hoople, an English group with moderate success in the sixties, really cashed in on the "bisexual chic" trend of the seventies with a Bowie song called "All the Young Dudes." The song included a verse about Marc, who wears feminine clothing but can kick hard.

Elton John, glitter's most extravagant spender (he's

been reputed to spend thousands on a single pair of glasses!), did two songs of interest to gays. An admitted bisexual, Elton John confessed his love for Daniel in the song of the same title. Though the lyric also lends itself to the interpretation that Daniel might be his brother, the sentiments expressed in the song are nonetheless homoerotic. The "confession" of bisexuality came long after Elton John had recorded "Daniel."

In contrast, Elton John's song "All the Girls Love Alice" on the album *Yellow Brick Road* is strikingly antilesbian. Alice, a sixteen-year-old lesbian, is portrayed in the song as simpleminded, confused, and very pathetic. I guess we are supposed to feel sorry for her. There is a nasty reference to "middle-aged dykes."

The emergence of "cock rock"* was fated from the beginning of rock 'n' roll itself. The punk attitude of rock stars from Elvis to Jagger had developed on its own as an ideology, a driving force. While the early lyrical antics of rock writers trivialized heterosexual relationships, women in general were victims of songs that characterized them as inane (for example, "She Wore an Itsy Bitsy Teeny Weeny Yellow Polka Dot Bikini," and "She Can't Find Her Keys").

The progression from depicting women as sexy but dumb to depicting abused women on album covers was a sudden one. Years were spent idolizing women in hopelessly unrequited and juvenile fashion. The change occurred when rock music merged with the flower children and acid rock was born. Acid rock had no holds barred, it was "tell it like it is," or rather like the boys in the band wanted it to be told. The teen madonna—idolized for her sweet smile— now became the "bitch" (as the Stones term her in the song of the same title) who is castrating, arrogant, and merciless in her manipulations. She is also a groupie, a mixed-up tough dyke (like Alice in Elton John's song), and, when she is tamed, becomes a hippie communal housewife, who scrubs floors, bakes "fresh bread" as her

* The term was coined in an article published in 1970 in the women-controlled underground paper *Rat* (New York), reprinted in *Counter Culture and Revolution*, edited by David Horowitz, et al.

188

grandmother did, and is at the disposal of the hippie male's sexual whims.

Acid rock defined for women what the literature of D.H. Lawrence, Henry Miller, and Norman Mailer had done years before—that is, an unbridled sexuality. One could consider this almost liberating, except that in the above-mentioned literary works, as in acid rock, the woman served the male's fantasies—to the hilt. She never pursued her own pleasures and seldom experienced orgasm. She was the "bitch in heat" who existed only as an appendage to the male's sexual whim. In acid rock, women received similar treatment, and for the first time in a popular music form, men were free to glorify the oversexed (but totally servile) female.

Acid rock gave the flower child his maschismo back—a machismo robbed from him by the "effeminate" folk-rock stars like Donovan. Acid rock was, in my opinion, a reaction to an art form that was becoming too "sensitive."

Acid rock tended to ignore gays, with rare exceptions. The Jefferson Airplane (before they became Jefferson Starship), one of several acid rock bands to come out of the San Francisco Haight–Ashbury scene, gave us "Triad," a song sung by Grace Slick which is about either two men and a woman, two women and a man, or perhaps even three women.

The term "cock rock" was born out of the feminist movement. Its analysis of rock attacks the machismo, the insensitive portrayal of women, and the glorification of rape and the sexual submission of women. In "Under My Thumb," the Stones boast of subduing "the girl who just had me down." The Stones' sexuality, and Jagger's in particular, is rough, dominating, and insensitive. In "Satisfaction," Jagger tries to impregnate a woman. But by far the most blatant example of the Stones' lyrical chauvinism is in "Midnight Rambler," a song about the Boston Strangler, a song that blends sex, violence, and misogyny—all the prime ingredients of male fantasy. The Stones have never made any gripes about the violence of their art form—Altamont is a prime example of the violence invoked by lyrics that depict rapists, murderers, and sadists (for example, "You Can't Always Get What You

Want," "Street Fighting Man," "Jumping Jack Flash," "Gimme Shelter," "Sympathy for the Devil" and "Brown Sugar"). In "Brown Sugar," the slaver beats the women in the nighttime. Are these also black women as the title suggests? "Black and Blue," their latest, was promoted with a billboard in Los Angeles depicting a woman tied to a chair. She is saying, "I'm Black and Blue over the Stones and I love it."

A group called Women Against Violence Against Women was formed to deface the billboards and then to organize a boycott of record companies selling their wares with album covers that show women as blissful victims of sadistic male sexuality.

Yet there is another side to the Stones, a side sensationalized by both the "straight" (establishment) press and the rock journalists: Jagger as a swishy androgynous bisexual. Partly due to hype and partly due to Jagger's onstage antics, he has obtained the reputation of being a sexually "liberated" individual. Nothing could be further from the truth. Sure, Jagger swishes on stage; he even takes the microphone between his legs or makes like he's fellating its phalliclike form. But the image of the swashbuckling "Midnight Rambler" is more dominant, more convincing somehow. The swish is mockery, mere entertainment, a release for the violence accumulated through a fusion of loud chordy music and raunchy sadistic lyrics. The androgynous act is just that—an act. There is little consciousness in a Stones concert, for consciousness dwells on the other side of where the Boston Strangler and Jumping Jack Flash live.

One cannot, on the other hand, discard the few sensitive songs—"As Tears Go By," "Angie," "Time Waits for No One" (in my opinion, their best!), and, of course, the hypnotic "Wild Horses."

The glorification of violence and machismo and the use of so-called "gay" images to gain national attention are even more evident in the antics of rock drag extraordinaire Alice Cooper. From the start Alice claimed to be a wholesome sort, with a monogamous heterosexual relationship, and a propensity toward good old American leisure sports like golf. On stage, however, the bizarre side of this

190

typical American boy is projected—with makeup, tight leather pants, and live snakes wrapped around him. He gained national attention by throwing live chickens out into his audience and chopping off dolls' heads; his most popular antic was to use trick lighting and effects to simulate his head being guillotined. Alice knew what American rock audiences wanted, and he gave it to them.

The violence implicit in the loudness of the music was not enough: it didn't sell as well as the more explicit on-stage violent theatrics. And the drag identification—the long hair, the makeup, the female nomenclature—were all good gimmicks. Musically, Alice Cooper was sadly lacking or downright unbearable. The punk idol plays at master of ceremonies in the person of Alice much the same as the M.C. in *Cabaret* watches the Nazi takeover with a bemused smile.

Rod Stewart was always something of an outcast in the rock world. He was too poppish to be considered in the same genre as serious hard rock musicians like Eric Clapton, and yet he was raunchy and loud and macho. At least to all appearances he was. Rising to fame with a voice like Dylan and a sound like Joe Cocker, Stewart took years before he did what has to be one of the more revolutionary gay lyrics in the hard rock genre: "The Killing of Georgie," Parts I and II.

Part I is based on a chord progression that Dylan often used, and its sound is Dylanesque, but Dylan was never so daring in his lyrics. Georgie, who is rejected by his parents after he informs them that he's gay, goes to New York where he becomes the toast of Broadway. Life is good to Georgie and he makes lots of friends until one night he runs into a gang of young hoodlums. Though the story of Georgie is tragic, the haunting sentiment of Part II is not. The melody of this part of the song is similar to the Beatles' "Don't Let Me Down," yet the lyrics mark a breakthrough in their bold display of male/male affection. Who would ever have thought that Rod Stewart would be the one to violate the sacred macho code of hard rock? But then, I guess it's easier for someone who isn't held in line by the genre to violate its tenets. "The Killing of Georgie" is a new image for rock

191

'n' rollers, an image of caring and feeling: "The Killing of Georgie" is a song that will remain unrecognized for years, but like Janis Ian's "Society's Child," it, too, will return someday when attitudes toward homosexuality become more liberal.

In the realm of folk music, some extremely innovative and sensitive material emerged in the seventies. Laura Nyro, whose music rose to fame in the hands of groups like the Fifth Dimension, recorded "Emmie," easily identifiable as a song with heavy lesbian overtones.

"Stephanie's Room" (from the *Gulf Winds* LP) by Joan Baez is the song of a lover left wondering if her beloved will remember their relationship. It poses the age old (gay) question: Can ex-lovers still be friends? Or do they always disappear from each other's lives, like Stephanie seems to have done, leaving only memories?

"The Altar Boy and the Thief," on the other hand, is a song about a gay bar with a portrait of the various people Baez observed there one night. In concert recently, she introduced this song (from *Blowing Away,* her latest LP) as her answer to Anita Bryant. There are various characters in this song—the Latin drag queen, a tall, bejewelled, black man, a trucker who has a wife and kids, and, of course, the couple on the dance floor, the altar boy and the thief. The essence of the song lies in the fact that, for her, the inhabitants of this bar are seeking "a little relief" from the world outside.

Joan Baez's songwriting has matured in "The Altar Boy and the Thief." From the heavily political to the quietly persuasive poetry of lyrics free from rhetoric, Baez has finally reached a zenith.

Dory Previn—rising to fame after her husband, Andre Previn, ran off with Mia Farrow (her first big hit was about that episode: "Beware of Young Girls")—has more references to gays in her songs than any other nongay performer. Her first LP, *On My Way to Where* (Mediarts), contained "Michael, Michael," about a hippie-type gay man who sells LSD and "makes it best with men."

Previn's characters are often bizarre; yet her vision of the universe is through the eyes of an absurdist. In the finest tradition of writers like Jean Genet, she presents Esther, who lusts after Jesus, and the midget who wishes she were black.

An ardent feminist, she extols the virtues of androgyny (*Mary C. Brown and the Hollywood Sign* LP) and comments on political issues in some of the most delightfully satirical styles on record. In "Midget's Lament," she sums up the way people stereotype: "I mean, y'seen one midget, y'seen 'em all, oh yeah, midget, oh yeah *small*." One could substitute any minority for midgets and the equation fits. In the song, Previn even reminds us that there are gay midgets.

Of course, there are many, many more gay images; to do them all justice would take far too much space. A closer examination of gay images would include the questionable "Ballad of the Sad Young Men" by Roberta Flack, or the much debated "Just Like a Woman," the Dylan song I do not believe is about a transvestite/transsexual as some gays insist.

Then there are the more recent examples, such as the lesbian songs of Patti Smith, a somewhat androgynous woman who has often disassociated herself from both the gay and feminist communities. Patti Smith sang at the New York City Gay Pride rally in June 1977, but she seemed hostile to the idea behind the gathering, and, in her comments, merely thanked the crowd for the opportunity to sing in Central Park, where she had been unable to sing recently (though she didn't explain why).

So what do we make of all of this? Though there have been both positive and negative treatments of homosexuals in rock, the overall picture is still not very pleasant. There is surely a lot of consciousness-raising to be done. And even the positive material presents some problems; for instance, while "Lola" is a brilliant commentary, it also plays into the hands of those homophobes who believe that all gay men are transvestites. And while Janis Ian's "Queen Merka and Me" is strong and militant, it is also part of an album which is out of print! Bowie, on the other hand, has sold millions of copies of his dreary images of gays.

Bowie was once asked by a London gay group to write

a gay pride song. He refused. Why? Is it still that risky to be openly associated with gays? It certainly hasn't hurt Bette Midler's career any. But then, she isn't gay.

Rock music—like the subculture that spurned it—is in dire need of consciousness-raising. We need more gay rock stars coming out, as Elton John did, but in their songs and not just in interviews. We need more positive gay role models for young gays to look up to; We need songs like "I'm Gay" (from *Let My People Come*, a landmark musical)—songs which assert what we already know—that homosexuality is not decadent or degrading. We need also more gays to support people like Meg Christian and Steven Grossman and others who are recording positive gay music. Without our support these people may as well be singing in the middle of the Sahara Desert.

The Growing Business Behind Women's Music
by Lynne D. Shapiro

In the growing independent women's culture (of which many lesbians are an integral part), there has been a proliferation of professional women musician-songwriters who speak either directly to the lesbian experience or to the more encompassing woman-identified lifestyle.

The music these accomplished women present is rich and varied: it covers the gamut of musical styles—rock, country, blues, jazz, disco, pop, classical, and ritual music—and includes lyrics about the many aspects of being a woman, the ins and outs of being a lesbian, and love situations from friendship to crushes. What characterizes all the music, however, is the strong sense of positive energy, growth, and selfhood shown in both lyrics and style.

In 1972, it was rare to hear such music. But since then women such as Meg Christian, Casse Culver, Alix Dobkin, Holly Near, Maxine Feldman, Kay Gardner, Sally Piano, Linda Shear, Teresa Trull, Chris Williamson, and Willie Tyson, and such groups as the Berkeley Women's Music Collective, Be Be K'Roche, Jade and Sarsaparilla, and Medusa Music have made frequent appearances around the country. And more women are recording; almost all of the above-mentioned have records out, with some working on their second or even third albums.

But to make one's music go, it takes more than being a right-on woman and a good musician. The details of live performances, record production, and record distribution have to be handled. Concert production requires scheduling, acoustics and lighting, publicity, selling tickets, etc. Record production involves, among other things, drawing up contracts, bringing in and arranging for backup musicians, engineering, mixing, designing the album cover, and pressing. And among the tasks in record distribution are shipping, sales, publicity, advertising, and getting airplay.

Musicians involved with corporate record companies usually have these details handled by the companies' publicists, producers, etc. But with some exceptions, the musicians generally considered part of the independent women's culture have rejected that world which pressures women to be more male-identified—to fit some man's image of his "ideal woman." So in response to these independent women musicians working outside corporate record companies, a network of other women (and some men) involved in concert arranging, record production, and record distribution has developed.

One company in this network that has grown considerably since its founding in 1974 is Wise Women Enterprises, Inc. (WWE), which at this writing had produced two records—Kay Gardner's *Mooncircles* and Casse Culver's *Three Gypsies**, and was producing and distributing *Debutante* by Willie Tyson.

In the spring of 1977, I interviewed the WWE members who work in New York City—Marilyn Ries, business administrator, production manager, and chief engineer; and Betsy Rodgers, New York office coordinator and business administrator.

All three of us marveled at the growth of the circuit supporting women's music since 1973. As Marilyn reflected, "Going back a little in history, many things were only dreams and hopes and plans at the First Women's Music Festival in Champaign, Illinois. There wasn't a production company like Artemis in Boston that puts on regularly sold-out three-day events; there weren't women working as Olivia distributors as well as setting up concert gigs in Syracuse, New York, New Orleans, and Florida; there weren't the number of women's conferences, festivals, and coffee houses. All this was a fantasy!"

But now close to seventy independent businesswomen across the country work actively with Olivia Records as distributors, delivering records to their local stores and selling records at concerts, conferences, and festivals. Over

* Both distributed by Olivia Records, a similar women's record company in Los Angeles.

196

twenty-five companies handle concert productions. Large numbers of women work on record productions as musicians, arrangers, recording and mixing engineers, production assistants, album designers, etc. And working with the companies are accountants, lawyers, business managers, fund-raisers, publicists, advertising people, printers, etc.

How do these people meet to form this circuit? Many are basically committed to working in the women's community and know the music workers in the community. Another connecting place is the music festival, like the ones held annually in Champaign, Illinois, where some of the women involved in WWE met. Or a touring performer might jam after a gig with local musicians; that's how a New Orleans trombonist came to work on Willie Tyson's *Debutante*.

For many, women's music provides an income source, if not a means of making a living. Indeed, providing jobs for women is an objective of WWE (as well as Olivia Records in Los Angeles). In line with this, WWE pays everyone involved in the production of their records. However, as Marilyn puts it, "In terms of energy and skills, what we're paying is not commensurate to what the record industry pays for the same job." And while Marilyn and Betsy felt the pay was "more than a pittance and a definite step in the right direction," from my own observations, no one makes an easy living from women's music. Even the more well known performers have several things going to make ends meet.

However much anyone gets paid, financing is a big problem. Concert production in New York City costs $1,200 to $1,500. Record production is much more; Betsy quoted a top budget of $25,000 (including promotion) for Willie Tyson's album. While funds come in from sales, up-front money is needed, especially for records which can take up to a year to recover production costs. In the case of WWE, much of their upfront money has been provided by interest-free and then 7 percent loans from women who have invested in the company through personal contact with WWE members and/or individual performers. About

197

thirty to thirty-five women have thus provided WWE with loan capital with loans ranging from $50 to $10,000.

Although WWE is a business involved with money, interest, etc., like other women's music companies, the company adheres to the feminist principles of nonauthoritarian, nonhierarchical structures in which each woman has considerable say over her work. The WWE structure reflects these principles. As Betsy explained, "There are seven women who spend a lot of time thinking, meeting, and talking about what we do and what will be our projects. Some of us are on full-time salary, some on half-time salary, and some on no salary, but we all have equal say regardless of how much we make. We all have our own territories and responsibilities. We all answer to each other."

These principles also apply to relationships with record production workers. Much of this is worked out through written contracts, the basic purpose of which, according to Marilyn, is to "clearly lay out on paper what you agree to do and what we're going to do so we're both clear about our joint responsibilities." The contract WWE signs with its performers is, of course, then entirely different from the standard artist contract which says the company owns you body and soul. Instead, considerable back-and-forth discussions between the various parties and their lawyers take place to arrive at a contract that will work in the court system yet give enough political space so that responsibilities and commitments are mutual.

Once areas of responsibility are defined, decisions about almost everything involve all people doing the work. For example, Casse Culver and Kay Gardner worked out the instruments for the songs on *Three Gypsies*. Then during rehearsal, the backup musicians discussed their parts with Casse involving them too in decisions about the sound of the music. On Willie's album, the guitar player was able to decide the type of amplification that would best suit each piece according to her judgment about how the music should sound.

Developing nonauthoritarian work environments is only part of WWE's political concerns. Another is outreach. The WWE members are not dyke-separatists. As Marilyn

198

explains, "In terms of company, our idea is to garner money for the women's community to make more women independent of the structure and the establishment, using their skills professionally and with impact to make a statement to society. . . . We know exactly where we want to put it to make women stronger, independent, useful, more aware of things. Just like some of the songs on our albums, they have to raise consciousness. If we sell them only in the lesbian community, what about the woman who doesn't necessarily want to become a lesbian, but all of a sudden has a real different feeling about herself as a woman and how she's going to relate to all the pressures—her family pressures, her role? How's she going to hear that other women feel the same way?" And Betsy agreed: "It's a way to bring money back to the women's community and to provide outreach to those women who cannot go directly to the women's community or lesbian community at this point and can be touched through music."

To obtain exposure for women's music for this outreach, WWE does considerable advertising and public relations work, advertising in *Billboard, Ms.* and community publications, and obtaining interviews in electronic and print media on radio stations in the South and in Maine as well as feature articles. So far they have had coverage in the New Orleans major daily newspaper *Seven Days*, and in *Billboard*, and in radio programs in the South and in Maine. This publicity, as well as that of Olivia Records, distributors of their first two albums, has had impact. After only four months, 5,000 copies of *Three Gypsies* were sold; over 10,000 of the classically oriented *Mooncircles* sold in a year's time. But still, Betsy's community work in New York's Lesbian Feminist Liberation has shown that many women don't know the extent and variety of women's music and hence don't buy it.

What will help this situation is airplay, but so far that of independent women's music on major commercial radio stations has been limited. So WWE and others must spend considerable time obtaining airplay by calling DJs to request women's music and by approaching program directors with our music. So far they have had some success in

New Orleans, Maine, San Francisco, and Seattle, among other places.

So through the hard work of WWE and the hundreds of others in the women's/lesbian music network, this part of our culture, with its enormous powers to raise consciousness and nurture independent women/lesbians, will keep growing. And who can say how many more records will be out and how many more will work in women's music by the time you read this book?

Judy Garland and Others:
Notes on Idolization and Derision

by Michael Bronski

The most expanded compilation of thoughts on camp is Susan Sontag's essay, "Notes on 'Camp,'" printed in her book *Against Interpretation*. Dedicating the notes to Oscar Wilde, she states that "the essence of Camp is its love of the unnatural: of artifice and exaggeration," adding that "Camp is esoteric—something of a private code, a badge of identity even, among small urban cliques." In his essay on Judy Garland and others, Michael Bronski quotes from Sontag's notes and uses them as a taking-off point for new insights.

Toward the end of her Carnegie Hall concert Judy Garland gives in to the crowd's demands and says, "We'll stay the whole night, we'll sing them all tonight." The crowd screams, "We love you. We love you, Judy." The uninitiated may not realize it but this screaming, wildly adulating audience is made up mostly of gay men. They are here to celebrate one of the first in a long series of comebacks by their idol. She is in rare form, perhaps the best she's ever been; but it doesn't matter. They've come to see her and even if she wasn't well, had had too many pills, too much booze, could hardly get on stage, never mind sing, they would still love her.

For many gay men, Garland transcended whoever and whatever she was and became almost goddesslike. But this worship was not confined to Garland alone. Barbra Streisand got her start in two New York gay bars, *Bon Soir* and *The Lion;* Bette Midler started in the baths. Bette Davis and Greta Garbo are also gay favorites; Davis' staccato delivery is now almost mandatory in any drag show, while Garbo's name is usually spoken reverently and knowingly.

These are women that many gay men have idolized and worshipped. They can be said to have been placed in a sort

201

of pantheon of gay culture and sensibility. But there are others who have also been singled out by this same group of gay men. These performers are not idolized, but are held in some form of dubious esteem that comes from the fact that they are somewhat peculiar, not talented at all, or possess bizarrely idiosyncratic gifts. This group includes performers like Eartha Kitt, Carmen Miranda, Tallulah Bankhead, and Maria Montez.

What is it about these women that has attracted gay men over the years? It is hard to say, for the complexity of the relationship between performer and audience does not lend itself easily to analysis. The following are offered as a series of notes and thoughts on the nature of this phenomenon.

Susan Sontag in her essay "Notes on 'Camp'" (*Against Interpretation*, Dell Publishing, 1966) wrote insightfully on what must be considered an overlapping issue. This essay is both an application and a continuation of what she has already mapped out. The quotes included are from her essay.

1.

The two pioneering forces of modern sensibility are Jewish moral seriousness and homosexual aestheticism and irony.

Judy Garland led a remarkably uncharmed life that began with constant touring of the vaudeville circuit and ended with an overdose of barbiturates. That her theme song was "Over the Rainbow" should come as no surprise; her life was a series of tragedies which she bore then overcame, almost miraculously, the next almost always worse than the last. It has been said the gay men were drawn to this ability to spring back into action, to make so many comebacks against such great odds. This may be true but it is only part of her appeal. Her stamina was amazing, and she probably should have been dead several years before she actually was. But it was precisely the quality that was the cause of all that pain that was also appealing to her audiences. When she sang she was vulnerable. There was a hurt in her voice that most other singers don't have—Joplin did, Nina Simone does—and an immediacy that gave the impression that it was *her* hurt, not merely the hurt in the song or in the persona of the singer. She became her song and as a result the songs themselves became a lot more powerful and commanding.

Unlike someone like Frank Sinatra, who is an amazing stylist but not at all emotional, Garland related to her audience on an almost personal/emotional basis. When she was hurt you hurt with her and wanted to help her. When she was happy—as in "The Trolley Song"—she could carry you with her. Most of all, when she was on stage, she was pleading with the audience to love her. She projected her vulnerability as an attempt to gain love and friendship.

The lack of any overtly gay art has always been a severe problem for gay audiences. It is not only the heterosexuality of most art that gets in the way, but also a certain amount of indirectness. Possibly the fact that gay people were already hiding within the culture made them unwilling to relate to a song that was filtered through the persona of a singer. Garland sang directly to her audience and, what is more, she needed them probably as much as they needed her.

The homosexual sense of irony that Sontag talks about is present in a great deal of gay sensibility, humor, and culture. It can be seen as a defense mechanism to avoid being hurt. Garland avoided all of that by almost reveling in being hurt. That was what she was up there for—she sang her hurt/their hurt, and the two became one. She made a solid identification with the audience and they loved her as much as she loved them.

If Garland's stamina was appealing to her audience, then Streisand's nerve, *chutzpah*, and determination not to be hurt were much the same, only before the fact. It wasn't that Barbra couldn't be hurt; she was as vulnerable as Garland, only she wasn't going to wallow in it. It made her angry. When she sings "Cry Me a River" you know that she is out for blood, not sympathy. In some ways Streisand was a post-Stonewall Garland. She was tougher, sensitive, and capable of anger and self-defense. Most times this self-defense was humorous, and self-deprecating. A great deal of Streisand's early jokes were self-acknowledged put-downs of her features: she was determined to make it as a big star in spite of how she looked. In a sort of Horatio Alger story she did make it; she proved that you can overcome your state in life. But in this case it was not by becoming acceptable to them (the typical Alger story) but by making them accept you. Streisand was Jewish, and looked and talked Jewish. That may be all right on the Borscht Circuit but such ethnicity does not go over big in Middle America. Streisand's triumph is not only that of the ugly duckling made good but that she overcame a great deal of prejudice to get where she is.

Streisand's drive to be accepted, her ready wit, and her strength of character makes her an easy role model. You can be sensitive, outcast, and alone, and still make it.

As a taste in persons, Camp responds particularly to the markedly attenuated and strongly exaggerated.

Bette Davis's most famous bit may well be from *Beyond the Forest*, although it was popularized by Liz Taylor in *Who's Afraid of Virginia Woolf:* "What a dump!" The image of Liz with her hand and cigarette going a mile a minute en-nun-ci-a-ting that line is a vivid one, although most of its power comes from the fact that it is *such* a Bette Davis line. That, of course, was the secret of Davis's acting—she almost immediately claimed the part/the lines and they were hers. It is amazing that so much of her material worked for her. She is so stylized, so mannered at times that it is hard to imagine how Davis could create a character. They almost all seem like extensions of her.

It was rumored years ago that there was a clique of queens who would go to all of the showings of *All About Eve* in New York and chant Davis's lines along with her. (The thought of thirty men chanting ". . . nice speech, Eve. But I wouldn't worry too much about your heart. You can always put that award where your heart ought to be . . ." is staggering.) The existence of such a story, whether true or not, is indicative of a devotion that eclipses a mere recognition of talent; it borders on the fanatical.

Camp is the consistently aesthetic experience of the world. It incarnates a victory of "style" over "content," "aesthetics" over "morality," of irony over tragedy.

The sheer theatricality of Davis, her style as it were, raises her above the rest of the world—either in real or screen life. Her mannerisms, speech, the arched eyebrow, the gesturing hand with a cigarette all made her larger than life, without ever losing the emotional context of the film.

She also played strong-willed determined, uppity women. Her Jezebel broke every moral and social taboo of the old South as she insisted on wearing scarlet red to the cotillion; in *Marked Woman* she screams from the witness stand: "I'll get you if I have to come back from the grave to do it!" Movies have always tended to bring out the worst in sex stereotyping. It is easy to see how gay men would be attracted to Davis—the other options are dismal: the woodenness of a George Brent, the gross vulgarity of an Errol Flynn. The actresses of the time were as vanilla as Davis was strong, Joan Fontaine, Olivia de Havilland, were Hollywood's concept of what women should be. Davis, by sheer strength of will, was who she wanted to be.

The androgyne is certainly one of the great images of Camp sensibility. Here, Camp taste draws on a mostly unacknowledged truth of taste: The most refined form of sexual attractiveness (as well as the most refined form of sexual pleasure) consists of going against the grain of one's sex. What is most beautiful in virile men is something feminine; what is most beautiful in feminine women is something masculine. . . .

It is not surprising that in a society which places so much emphasis upon gender roles gay men should be drawn to personalities that blur such distinctions. Greta Garbo, Marlene Dietrich, and Mae West, each in her own way, manifest a merging of femaleness and maleness. In the cases of Dietrich and West, their early gay appeal in some ways shaped their later image, and they were not only appreciated by gay men, but to some degree have played to them.

Film critic Molly Haskell has said of Garbo that "she understood instinctively the trick of being actively passive, of being all things to all people." She is the embodiment of the purity and *passion* of love, transcendent of the social situation and circumstance, and as a result had to be punished for her moral transgressions.

While Garbo was *love eternal,* Dietrich was *love incarnate.* She was mysterious, exotic, and very sexual. While Garbo's trademark was her full-faced fragile beauty, Dietrich's was the knowingly arched eyebrow, the not-quite-believing tone in her voice when accepting protestations of love. She accepted her sexuality and expected to be respected for it. Even when she became the "tarnished woman" she took full responsibility for all of her actions: "It took more than one man to make me Shanghai Lily," she tells stuffy Clive Brook in *Shanghai Express.* She also played with the idea of bisexuality both in her films and in her public image. In both *Morocco* and *Blonde Venus* she dressed in men's clothing and made playful sexual advances to other women. One of the first women to wear pants in public (along with Garbo and Hepburn), her name has been associated with lesbianism since her early film career in Germany.

The institution of Mae West over the years has given rise to many rumors. Said by some not to be a woman at all but a drag queen, she has always displayed both a healthy attitude toward sex and disdain for the hypocrisy and repressiveness of sexual morality. In *Gay American History* Jonathan Katz traces the difficulty that she had getting her 1927 play *The Drag* produced in New York. If Dietrich showed her lack of naïveté with the arched eyebrow, West showed her anger with the cutting one-liner, the biting comeback: "Showing contempt for this court?" she says to the judge in *My Little Chickadee*—"I'm doin' my best to hide it." Her dress, deportment, and flagrant sexuality made her a parody of what men viewed as sexually desirable in women; her subtext however showed her to be nobody's fool and in complete control of the situation. While Garbo and Dietrich became victims of the sexual/political war between the sexes, West was in some ways a double agent: dressed and holding her body to please men, she secretly hated them and found every opportunity to expose their sexual vanity and the hyprocrisy behind their values. West's knowledgeability of sexual power games put her in the same league as an Errol Flynn —a carnal, not romantic hero (Garbo was the ultimate romantic)—but with the advantage of also having been a victim and knowing the game from both sides. Still not having the privileges of maleness, she is forced to combat with verbal wit, using the put-down and the innuendo rather than outright attack.

In naïve, or pure, Camp, the essential element is seriousness, a seriousness that fails. Of course not all seriousness that fails can be redeemed as Camp. Only that which has the proper mixture of the exaggerated, the fantastic, the passionate, and the naïve.

Garland, Davis, Streisand are women who are taken seriously. In the case of Garland and Streisand it is their directness that is prized, Davis's directness comes from her exaggerated status as a person; she was larger than life; therefore, anything that she did was super-lifelike. There are other women who are favorites of gay men, but are not idolized. They are prized for what Sontag would call their personification of pure Camp.

Carmen Miranda is a perfect example. Also known as The Brazilian Bombshell, she specialized in Latin-American songs and dances. She wore elaborate costumes that seemed to consist mainly of a gold lamé skirt with a lot of flowers and fruit over the rest of her (she was also called the lady with the tutti-frutti hat). She was used as a speciality number by the studios; there was really not very much else she could do. It would be unfair to say that she was talentless—she did what she did very well. But gay men prized her not because she could sing and dance well but because she was fairly ridiculous. It would be difficult not to appear so wearing fruit on your head, at least in the U.S. (In Carmen Miranda's native state in northeastern Brazil, however, women shopping in street fairs carry fruits and vegetables home in large baskets on their heads, and this fruit-hat motif is common to this day for women—and drag queens—dancing in carnival pageants.)

In her own absurdity, Maria Montez is similar to Carmen Miranda. However, in her case there was little or no talent involved. Usually cast in semi-Oriental and jungle movies, she spoke dialogue badly and emoted even worse. To be very fair it is hard to say lines like "Give me the Cobra jewels" and make it work. But Montez, like Miranda, is loved because she is so terrible; she is so completely awful that she has to be good.

There is really not much to be said for women in this category. The list is long and could comprise such diverse people as Eartha Kitt and Jane Withers. Kitt, a fine dancer, singer, and actress, has built her career upon an exaggerated sophistication, a feigned world weariness that would seem out of place in *La Dolce Vita*. It was a persona that allowed her, as a black performer, to work more than she ever would have been allowed otherwise. But at the same time it limited her; she became an oddity—the extreme feline vision of black womanhood—and only recently has she made some fine jazz recordings that show the true range of her talent. Withers, a child star of the thirties, was always cast as the less pretty, mischievous type pitted against the more pretty, American ideal-type, Deanna Durbin. In the past ten years she has become Josephine the Plumber on TV. As with Montez it is impossible for Withers not to appear ridiculous with her material. (Advertising appeals to the lowest common denominator and there is no way to elevate the peddling of capitalism to art.) But it is exactly for this reason that she is liked. Whatever their intentions, their talents, or their abilities, they strike attitudes or are in positions that show them to be faintly ludicrous, somewhat ridiculous.

2.

Camp rests on innocence. That means Camp discloses innocence, but also when it can, corrupts it. Objects being objects, don't change when they are singled out by the Camp vision. Persons however respond to their audiences.

The life of Tallulah Bankhead was not a happy one. There is no need to go into the details of it here except in so far as she was, to a large degree, the personification of an assumed camp sensibility. A great deal of her career was founded upon being a personality—she was clever, witty, vulgar, and generally thought of as being a "real camp." There are probably more "Tallulah" stores floating around the gay world than about any other single person (and almost all of them are untrue).

Bankhead was an actress of apparently varying talent, but worked hard at it when she wanted to and had several stage and film successes. Throughout her entire career she had cultivated a strong male homosexual following and played much of her public life to them. In 1956 she decided to try serious acting again and was going to appear in Tennessee Williams's *A Streetcar Named Desire*. She worked hard for the part, gave up booze and cigarettes (major sacrifices), and was generally thought to be very good. On opening night the audience was filled with her usual following. Throughout the whole performance they hooted and cackled every time she did anything. It was a nervewracking experience and she later told someone that she "wanted to stop the performance and beg them to give me a chance." She did receive some good notices, but on the whole the experience was appalling, and destroyed whatever faith she had left in her abilities as a professional actress.

There is no easy moral to be drawn from the story. Lee Israel in her biography of Bankhead simply says that "Tallulah had used her life as art for too long." And, for sure, a great deal of the fault lay in the way that she chose to manage and package her life. But there is also some responsibility that has to be met by her following. There is something very wrong with adulation and praise that is allowed to turn into destructiveness and what seems to be barely concealed hate.

The case of Tallulah Bankhead is a specialized one because she consciously created herself as a gay figure. (She herself was bisexual.) It is generally agreed upon that she had a huge dislike for women, and would only tolerate particular women if they praised her excessively. She liked gay men because they thought that she was funny, but they may have been laughing at things other than her jokes. One of her friends has said: "She was doing on stage what they did when they played. Hers was *their* kind of talk, *their* gestures. She was a highly identifiable creature. They identified." One of the cruelest Tallulah stories that is told is that she was once seen walking down Fifth Avenue by two gay men. As she walked past them one turned to the other and said, "Really, how tired. Tallulah drag."

There is an ugly misogyny that is present in a lot of the Tallulah stories. To be sure, Tallulah herself was probably very misogynistic, and no doubt she and her following fed upon this in one another. But it is the same misogyny that is somewhat present in the fawning over the Carmen Miranda group. It would be absurd to want to pretend that any of these women had a great talent, but what does it mean for a large group of gay men to like a female performer expressly because of the fact that she is terrible? It is interesting to note that in all of Sontag's notes on camp, and hundreds of examples that she produces, there are very few male personalities. Garbo, Dietrich, Mae West are all there, but they are all women.

Bette Midler is a strange combination of pieces from gay culture. She has the self-promoted gay mascot appeal of Bankhead. Her jokes are aimed at a gay audience—she has probably introduced a great deal of gay slang to the straight world ("It's the pits"; "tacky"; "I'm sick"). If that all weren't enough, she got her start at the Continental Baths in New York. She has the early Streisand energy and force behind her singing; in her ballads there are even hints of a bluesy Garland.

Her attitude toward her audience seems mixed: "You mean how do I like playing for faggots? Well, they're just people really. And as far as being categorized, I don't think that anyone could categorize me at all—because I'm beginning to get all kinds of people now. I love those boys at the baths because they were the first to encourage me." (*Rolling Stone*, No. 128)

She is vulgar and misogynistic on stage: "This is my backup. They're called the Harlettes. They're real sluts."

"You like these tits? Well, you don't get 'em for the six-buck ticket. This ain't no cheap meat." On some level Bette Midler has mined gay culture (or at least what gay men like to see on stage) and has come up with an act that is sure to please. She is the fast, dirty-talking heterosexual woman who plays to faggots. The novelist Rosalyn Drexler has praised Midler and has said that "She's given camp back to women." I'm not exactly sure what that means, or if it means what it seems to, if it is true. Misogyny is misogyny and when it is aimed at getting laughs from men I'm not sure that camp has been given back to women. If it has, I don't think that is any better than it was before.

3.

Judy Garland's fans have always been faithful and kind to her. When female impressionist Craig Russell does his show most of the impressions are witty, edged though not malicious portraits of people like Carol Channing, Peggy Lee, Bankhead, and Ethel Merman. When he does his Garland number it is dead serious, almost reverent. The pain, the vulnerability, the hurt is there, but so is the strength and power to go on in the face of almost anything.

There is little chance of what happened to Bankhead ever happening to Streisand, or even Bette Midler—the first is too much of a professional to ever let it happen, the second too much of a hustler not to make it work for her if it did. To a large degree the gay male audience of these people live off of the performer's strength. They recognize the emotional capabilities in the performer and respond to them—capabilities and expressions that are found in few female performers and almost no males. While a Carmen Miranda is to be laughed at, a Garland is to be listened to, sympathized with, loved, and loved back by.

In a recent issue of *People* magazine Paul Lynde (gay culture's gift to *Hollywood Squares*) said that he did not want a gay following because gays killed Judy Garland— a remark that made a few people wish that they had killed Paul Lynde too. While it is obnoxious coming from Lynde, the remark raises some interesting questions. As with Bankhead, was Garland's relationship with her audience a particularly healthy one? She did not pander to them as Bankhead did—they accepted one another as equals on mutual territory. If anything, they idolized her, sincerely idolized her, and had no ill intentions whatsoever.

Several years ago the MGM lot was auctioning off some of the props from the old films. An unknown millionaire paid $15,000 for the ruby slippers that Garland wore in *The Wizard of Oz*. There is an article in the *Los Angeles Times* of April 13, 1963, that details the obsession a Wayne Martin has about Garland. For twenty-seven years he has been collecting Garland memorabilia. His collection includes everything from bits of her costumes, to 100 tapes of her radio shows, and every item he could find in gossip columns.

It would be difficult to say that these people constitute a fan club—they are religious fanatics who have made Judy Garland their religion. The term idolization is now taken literally.

What does all this mean? If there is something suspicious about the gay male love for Maria Montez, there is something equally strange about the carrying of admiration to such an extreme. Garland and Streisand are loved because they are strong, emotional beings in a world where emotion (especially for men) is downplayed or ignored. It is a sign of respect for them as people and as performers to respond to that emotional output. But it is imprisoning, and damaging—just as damaging as it was to Bankhead—to enshrine them and place them beyond reach.

V
The Visual Arts
and the Theatre

Closets in the Museum: Homophobia and Art History

by James M. Saslow

Perched on a rocky bluff at the edge of downtown, the stately colonnades of the Philadelphia Museum are surrounded by high stone walls, elaborate fountains, and cascading staircases. This overpowering monumentality could be looked upon as symbolizing either of two ideas: the dignity of art's function, or the power of the institution itself.

One glance at the surrounding landscape makes clear which connection is intended. The vista down the imposing boulevard from the museum's front plaza leads the visitor's eye directly to the great tower of City Hall. The rear façade overlooks the historic palaces of the 1876 Centennial Exhibition. Art lies on axis with temporal power and national glory.

A coincidence of urban planning, perhaps—but a revealing one. Over the last several years, as a student, writer, and lecturer on art, I have been investigating our gay heritage in the visual arts, and find that it is richer than many of us are yet aware of. I have also found that the powerful complex of institutions that are the custodians of our artistic heritage—museums, galleries, universities—tends to overlook or suppress the historical evidence of gay artists and gay themes. Based on my own experience, I will attempt here to provide a brief overview of the art world's present attitudes toward homosexuality and homoerotic art, and of some progress that has been made toward breaking the hold of tradition on our past.

The art world has declared gay people and their emotions "obscene"—which derives from the Latin *obscaenus*, literally "offstage." As one element of society's existing structure, the art world has good reason to curtail the subversive power of gay images. To allow visual expression of gay themes would have two effects: it would show that the

215

existing order is incomplete, and thus illegitimate; and it might lead to a threatening sense of solidarity among those who share a sense of beauty in the same "forbidden" images.

Tennessee Williams eloquently evoked this power of images in his poem "The Dangerous Painters":

> I told him about the galleries upstairs, the gilt and velour insulation of dangerous painters. I said, if they let these plunging creations remain where they sprung from easels, in rooms accessible to the subjects of them . . .
> they would be stored fuel for a massive indignation. The fingers of misshapen bodies would point them out, and there would be always the goatlike cry of "Brother!"
> The cry of "Brother!" is worse than the shouting of "Fire!", contains more danger. For centuries now it has been struck out of our language.

Museums are our culture's most visible art institution—often the only setting in which most people come into contact with "fine art," especially art of the past. A surprising number of our "dangerous" gay brothers—and sisters—are represented on museum walls. Often, however, their art "sneaks through" because it is barely recognized as such, even by the curators. And if *they* don't recognize it, you probably won't either; the average viewer lacks the specialized knowledge needed to catch the gay references. On the other hand, trust your eyes: the gay viewer is usually far more open to suggestions of gay emotion than the art "experts." This is one field where the old taunt is meaningful: it takes one to know one.

"Gay art" really includes several different aspects. First, gay artists and gay subject matter are separate, though related, issues. Second, within gay subject matter it is necessary to consider separately the twin categories of male eroticism and female eroticism.

When confronted with the first issue—secrecy regarding artists who were themselves gay—museum staffs could well argue that it is not the museum's role to explicate the private lives of the artists whose work it displays. This argument might hold true, unless that private life has some relevance to the meaning or intention of the individual's work. Unfortunately, it is precisely that relevance which the art world is unwilling or unable to perceive.

If a heterosexual male artist paints a portrait of his wife, or even his mistress, for example, that relationship is usually evident from the title or conveniently noted on the frame or nearby wall plaque. This information calls our attention to a potential layer of meaning in the work. Yet in 1975 Francis Bacon, a highly respected painter from Britain, exhibited several dramatic canvases depicting the death of his lover of many years, George Dyer; New York's Metropolitan Museum coyly identified Dyer as a "close friend and model."

Such sins of omission are especially unfortunate in the modern period, where the subject matter of a work is often intimately bound up with the artist's personal concerns. Knowing that the great Baroque painter Caravaggio was suspected of sodomy may have only tangential bearing on his seventeenth-century depictions of Madonnas. But it is essential to our understanding of Marsden Hartley's 1915 "Painting #47, Berlin" that we be informed the initials "KvF" on an army helmet stands for Kurt von Freibourg, and that Hartley lost his young German lover in the Great War.

Sometimes even admitted facts are misleadingly interpreted to fit established values. I once heard a Metropolitan tour guide's commentary on "The Horse Fair," the major work by the French artist Rosa Bonheur (1822–1899). Bonheur lived with another woman for forty years, and had a government permit to wear men's clothes—a preference the guide excused as somehow necessitated by outdoor sketching, even though Bonheur also wore trousers to sit in her garden, and wore her hair so short she at times passed as a man. While we can't know precisely what she and fellow artist Nathalie Micas "did in bed," it comes as a shock to anyone familiar with available nineteenth-century options for gay expression to hear the guide airily assume that "Rosa had some problems in that she never married." The guide simply could not see Bonheur's unorthodox life as anything but the one thing it was not—unfulfilled.

Naturally, we want to learn about past gay artists and take pride in their achievements. More important than these "guessing games," however, is exposing the gay content of works of art. In this sphere the uncomfortable curator has a distinct advantage: interpretation of the past often requires information that was commonplace to original viewers but is now unfamiliar.

Neo-classic subjects of the late eighteenth and early nineteenth centuries, for example, are particularly rich in gay imagery—at least partly because the artists sought inspiration in ancient Greece, the last Western culture to depict homosexuality freely and positively in literature and on vases and other paintings. But Benjamin West's "Death of Hyacinthus" (on extended loan to the Philadelphia Museum), which portrays the stricken boy expiring in the arms of Apollo, would probably strike an unknowing observer as a sort of 1770s colonial Red Cross poster. To appreciate the real pathos of the scene, you have to know that the two men were lovers—a bit of mythology not likely to have come out in grade school. Thomas Sully's "Orestes and Pylades" (1809; Brooklyn Museum) illustrates one of the most famous loving male couples of antiquity—but come prepared with a copy of Bulfinch's *Mythology*.

Similarly, the suggestiveness of Pierre Mignard's delicately boyish "Ganymede" (seventeenth century), in San Francisco's Palace of the Legion of Honor, will elude the visitor who doesn't know that Ganymede was "cupbearer" to Zeus, who swooped to earth as an eagle to carry him off. It might be possible to infer the full interpretation from the details within the picture itself—if you know that the pitcher in his hand used to symbolize, for young girls, virginity about to be broken. However, that interpretation is hardly, as straight people are fond of requesting, "pushed in our faces": given the total lack of explanatory material about the painting, the museum staff could be accused of shirking its educational duty.

One small but noteworthy exception to this "benign

neglect" was the treatment accorded the French painters known as Les Barbus (the bearded ones) in the mammoth exhibit, "Age of Revolution: French Painting 1774–1830" (Louvre and Detroit Institute of Arts, 1975). The wall plaques for two paintings by Barbu artists, including another "Apollo and Hyacinthus" by Jean Broc (1801), noted matter-of-factly that "homoerotic" themes were frequent in their work.

Intimacy between women has been permitted in Western art more frequently than male eroticism for several reasons. As in much contemporary pornography, the close physical contact between women in Ingres' Turkish bath scenes, Degas' prints of brothels, or Courbet's "Sleep" titillates straight men. The deeper implications of such scenes are overlooked, thanks to the traditional notion that women cannot really be sexual by themselves. This conception of women as passive, "decorative" objects may effectively prevent even the historian from imagining any emotional interaction between them. Hence the Hellenistic Greek statuettes of women seated together in intimate poses are usually assumed to represent trivial scenes entitled something like "Women Gossiping."

In the enthusiasm of revisionism, we must be careful not to impute to every depiction of women a conscious intent on the artist's part to portray lesbianism. Nevertheless, we today are more sensitized to the broad range of possible meanings inherent in a portrayal of women alone together. One of the most complex examples of lesbian portrayal-*cum*-avoidance is the frequently painted myth of Diana and Callisto. François Boucher's eighteenth-century French version (now in San Francisco) shows us two women lying together in the woods, one slyly tickling the other's face with a straw. Viewers are supposed to disallow this obvious lesbian eroticism because (*if* you know the plot) the tickler isn't "really" a woman. It's actually Zeus again, this time disguised as a woman to gain the affection of Callisto, a chaste devotee of the virgin goddess Diana. That explanation used to both titillate and pacify more innocent observers; today, we would probably make a case for how such inversions actually heighten the picture's eroticism. (There is more than a hint of "women-identified women," by the way, in pictures of Diana's Amazon cortège, who destroy men who intrude on their rituals.)

(Although I am concentrating here on Western art, it should be pointed out that most of the major non-Western cultures have long, valued traditions of erotic art, more extensive and more explicit than our own—and usually including gay subjects on a more equal footing. From mass-produced woodblock prints in Japan to illustrations of Chinese lesbian novels, or the manuscript illuminations of India, depiction of gay love—more frequently female than male—is widespread and accepted.)

Despite a general rise in the social consciousness of museums over the last decade and a half, increased visibility for gay artists and subjects will probably come first through the exhibits of individual contemporary artists who happen to be gay and feel comfortable about letting that be known. We must, therefore, touch briefly on the role of the commercial art gallery; fortunately, the news in this sphere is somewhat encouraging.

The gallery world, like the museum world, is notoriously gay, at least by reputation; for familiar reasons, it too used to be discreetly closeted. A few gay artists, like Paul Cadmus in New York and David Hockney in England, have been able to show somewhat erotic works for as long as the last thirty years, but these artists are a tiny minority.

However, the first stimulus a commercial venture responds to is money. As gay people, primarily men, begin to constitute a visible market, with its own channels of publicity, galleries have begun to react favorably. New York artist John Button recalls how his gallery panicked when he proposed a show of his male nudes; the management was won over when every work on display sold out on opening day.

Gallery owners now tend to be glad to see me coming to review a show for *The Advocate*. Some owners even seek out the gay clientele: last year New York's Fabian Gallery invited the gay press to an opening of works (some with gay content) by Brazilian constructionist Hely Lima, and calmly pinned up favorable reviews from other gay magazines—including semi-beefcake photos of the artist. On the other hand, a group of lesbian artists met with so much hostility from established New York outlets that in 1976 they formed their own collective to provide exhibit space. The majority of the galleries the women approached expressed the opinion that it was commercially acceptable to be feminist, but not *lesbian* feminist. This attitude, too, has some economic stimulus: lesbians are perceived to be a small market, and, like women as a class, to have less expendable income.

For truly significant signals of a "push" for new information and interpretations in art, we must look to the academic community. The history of art is primarily preserved, researched, and disseminated in the university. Art history is, therefore, subject to the same conservative tendencies as most academic disciplines—plus a few added problems of its own.

In the very recent past, a few cracks have appeared in the formerly monolithic silence of the academic world on gay matters; there are hopeful, even exciting, signs. It is at least possible to indicate on a graduate school application that you are gay—as I did—and not be summarily rejected. But in assessing present gay awareness in the academic world, I am still reminded of the Red Queen's remark to Alice in Wonderland, "I've seen gardens, compared to which this would be a wilderness."

It is oversimplified to suspect conscious prejudice and deliberate suppression behind every professor's door. Academia is a gerontocracy: a student who entered college the year of Stonewall is finishing the Ph.D. just this year—with luck. Most of today's academics, lacking exposure to a coherent philosophy of sexual politics, are (with significant exceptions) unprepared to grasp the importance of gay art or its broader ramifications. When I informed an adviser, now nearing retirement age, that I wanted to write a psychological study of images of women in the work of Sandro Botticelli (the Renaissance master whose life contains more than a hint of homosexuality), he looked bemusedly startled, then shrugged that he couldn't see "any reason why you *can't* do it."

Of course, such topics have been all too easy to avoid until recently. Homosexuality is only now entering art his-

221

tory as an issue to be openly confronted, because the first generation of modern Western artists that could be openly gay—around World War I—has only recently receded far enough into the past to become the province of historians.

Among the juicier anecdotes art historians now have to cope with, my personal favorites involve the artists who served Serge Diaghilev's Ballets Russes. Léon Bakst created the scenery and costumes for *Jeux* and *Afternoon of a Faun* (1912), including a famous watercolor of Nijinsky as the Faun. Nijinsky's autobiography frankly recounts his five-year affair with Diaghilev, commenting significantly, "The Faun is me, and *Jeux* is the life of which Diaghilev dreamed." Nijinsky's revelations also shed light on the paintings by Picasso for the 1917 production of *La Parade;* Picasso's backdrop contains portraits alluding to the relationships among some of the same personalities.

Such inside information is, unfortunately, rare. Especially in researching earlier periods, art historians (those who are trying) share with other disciplines the enormous obstacles to uncovering gay people's private lives. Until very recently, artists would seldom commit such revelations to paper. Even in contemporary times, surviving friends and relatives are notoriously the worst source: they often think they are helping the artist's memory by covering up "embarrassing" information.

What little we know of the private life of painter Florine Stettheimer (1871–1944), for example (designer of the innovative cellophane sets for Gertrude Stein and Virgil Thomson's opera, *Four Saints in Three Acts),* strongly suggests at least a woman-identified woman: she never married, living all her life with two also unmarried sisters and their mother. But this information may remain a permanent riddle. After her death, Stettheimer's sisters physically cut from her diaries all entries they said "pertained only to family matters."

Despite the difficulties of "de-closeting" artists of the past, once homoeroticism can be proved scholars do accept the new information. Whether such discoveries will be absorbed in a professor's total outlook is another matter: they are still considered at best irrelevant, at worst shameful.

While the scholarly literature has long acknowledged the unavoidable documentation of gay leanings in such figures as Michelangelo and Leonardo da Vinci, the tendency persists to try to explain away prima facie evidence of homosexuality. Botticelli's arrest for sodomy in 1502 has always been considered insufficient reason to pursue possible gay content, on the grounds that "in those days, *everyone* was accused of it." The obvious suspicion is never seriously entertained: that perhaps everyone was accused of it because everyone was *doing* it (Raymond deBecker alleges precisely this interpretation in his full-length study of homosexuality in art and society, *The Other Face of Love*).

Even where an artist's sexuality was clearly known to his or her contemporaries, and relevant to the work, this information is usually discreetly ignored in lectures and publications. The most infamous example is the Italian Renaissance artist Giovanni Bazzi, whose sexual proclivities earned him the nickname *Il Sodoma*, "because he always mixed and lived with beardless boys, and answered willingly enough to that name," as the chronicler Giorgio Vasari recounts. Bazzi is listed in encyclopedias under "Sodoma," but mention is seldom made of the origin of his sobriquet, or of what connection this knowledge might have to his work. His portrayal of the baby Jesus fingering an arrow proffered by an androgynous nude Saint Sebastian, for example, takes on new suggested overtones if we recall Vasari's report that "most of the young men of Siena followed Sodoma."

This silence is self-perpetuating. Art historians trained in such a milieu can enjoy the false luxury of treating Michelangelo and Leonardo as great exceptions, "excused" by genius. Thence the pathetic, and infuriating, ignorance of a professor to whom I once revealed my desire to investigate gay art history. After inching his chair back two strides from mine, he replied blandly, "That's fine, but don't you think you'll run out of material pretty quickly?"

This professor's pointed withdrawal brings up a second, more personal reason for avoiding gay topics—a reason which remains virtually unspoken among art historians, yet subtly influences their behavior even today. Few male professors in that past have been willing to broach homoeroticism in the classroom for fear of bringing suspicion on their own heads. As much victims as perpetrators of current stereotypes, they still suffer from the ancient specter of effeminacy that haunts men engaged in any way with "the arts."

In part because of homophobic stereotypes, the field of art history is, in fact, dominated by women students (though women are still not proportionally represented on many faculties; sex discimination suits have been filed at such colleges as Tufts University). The predominance of women has helped art history become a pioneering field in feminist scholarship; the impact of the women's movement has provided at least the beginnings of a similar openness to gay scholarship for two reasons.

At the most basic level, any serious research into creative women was bound to turn up a percentage of them who loved other women. The clearest case in point is the legendary "Paris in the Twenties," where the literary and artistic community included, besides Stein and Toklas, the American painter Romaine Brooks, who painted portraits of her lover, author Natalie Clifford Barney, as well as pictures of the dancer Ida Rubinstein (with whom Brooks was infatuated) and of Una, Lady Troubridge.

On a more philosophical level, the issues raised by feminist art historians have begun to "clear the ground" for a more sympathetic understanding of concepts important to developing a theoretical justification for gay art. Prominent critics like Linda Nochlin of Vassar and Lucy Lippard bring to their analyses a concern for gender roles and androgyny as well as a psychological and sociological understanding of oppression, both of which clearly overlap with gay concerns.

The greatly increased attention given to women's issues in recent scholarship is heartening evidence of the flexibility of academia. There are some snags, however, to extrapolating a parallel future for gay studies. While oppression of the two groups shares a clear relation, resistance to admitting the reality of homosexuality is even more deeply ingrained than resistance to the value of women. More practically, women are a much bigger presence in art than gay people, particularly since, unlike women, gays can choose to remain closeted.

The obstacles to gay acceptance make the events of the 1977 College Art Association Conference all the more striking and encouraging. The venerable professional association for artists and teachers issued a call for its first panel session ever on "Homosexuality and Art: Classical to Modern Times" and, according to the committee chairperson, was deluged with forty-two requests to submit papers. Nine studies were eventually presented at the Los Angeles colloquium, on topics ranging from male/male courtship scenes on Greek vases to the lesbian vision of Romaine Brooks, who died in 1970. The panel was well attended, and caused little overt outcry from conferees.

Two of the topics discussed at the session illustrate the kinds of essential work just now beginning to "rehabilitate" neglected aspects of art history. Both deal with bisexual figures whose gay sides have often been bowdlerized. Wayne Dynes, well known in New York as an openly gay art scholar, recounted the adventures of Orpheus after he lost his beloved Eurydice. Greek art often depicted his subsequent activity, the introduction of pederasty to Thrace (for which the city's angry maidens decapitated him). Similarly, Judith Stein of the Tyler School of Art discussed depictions of Sappho, who most often appealed to later painters not in her documented role as the greatest creative lesbian of antiquity, but for the supposed drama of her suicide after rejection by a legendary male lover.

Such openness is to be lauded, but it is still a novelty in "official" circles. Within the gay community itself, however, the Gay Academic Union has consistently provided a forum for gay-related research at its annual conferences, each of which has included some discussion of the visual arts. Topics have ranged from Michael Lynch's research on Hartley, to silent films by Eisenstein and Genet, and the visual imagery in contemporary gay publications.

Art historians rely on a number of scholarly and general publications to disseminate new findings such as these. Here again, while an occasional article surfaces dealing with topics like homoerotic imagery in Caravaggio, the number of such studies to see print does not yet seem

225

commensurate with the potential material for study. Fortunately magazines, unlike museums, are already within the gay community's own capabilities. A number of respected publications such as *Gay Sunshine* and *Body Politic* already devote space to scholarship and criticism in art. Also, the newly formed Gay Academic Union Journal *Gai Saber* will cover art among many gay-related scholarly topics.

In summation, we have seen that museums are storehouses—and, like most storehouses, they are full of closets.

But what is shut up in the basements of great classical temples across the land is more than musty canvas and crackled varnish: it is the visible record of human consciousness.

Part of that consciousness, in virtually all times and all places, has been gay. And, contrary to what most of us have been led to believe, that gay consciousness has found innumerable, sometimes truly beautiful ways to break through to artistic expression. But for the most part, access to these expressions is still effectively denied to us—indeed, to the entire culture.

The history of America—if you will, of Western civilization since the decline of feudalism—has been a struggle for gradual extension of pride and power to an increasing number of individuals. In this struggle, art has been utilized by ruling elites as well as by the insurgents.

For their part, the powers that control society are well aware of the usefulness of structured uniformity. The Soviet Union sponsors "Socialist Realism," an official state vision of industrialized optimism; dissident artists made headlines a few years ago when their impromptu outdoor show of abstract works was obliterated by government bulldozers. In America intervention is less obvious; nevertheless, one need only look at the crazy-quilt of restrictions imposed on "obscenity" to see that our society, too, acknolwedges and fears the power of art to encourage nonconforming thoughts and behavior.

For art is also the first and ideal weapon of those groups who seek to establish *new* cosmologies that will legitimize that group's particular values. From Eugène Delacroix's 1830 "Liberty Leading the People" to the explicit illustrations for *Fag Rag*'s "Cocksucking as an Act of Revolution," as well as in myriad less polemical ways, art has served as midwife to new social values. Once visualized, ideas and images which were formerly only the property of a few scattered minds can be shared, can serve as the basis for a more complete imagining of shared consciousness.

In *Counterrevolution and Revolt*, Herbert Marcuse clearly defines the role of art in social change:

> *Cultural revolution*: the phrase, in the West, first suggests that ideological developments are ahead of development at the *base* of society: cultural but *not* [yet] political and economic revolution. . . . The strong emphasis on the political potential of the arts . . . is the effort to find forms of communication that may break the oppressive rule of the established language and images over the mind and body of man— language and images which have long since become a means of domination, indoctrination, and deception.

Art is a major battleground in the struggle for self-determination—for gay people even more than for others, because, unique among subgroups, we are not born into our own culture. We discover its relevance only later in life, and it is then we desperately need models and images that are too seldom available.

By continuing to ferret out these images, hitherto ignored or suppressed, that prove gay people are a continuous presence in human culture, art historians will be adding to the "stored fuel" needed to establish gay people as an intrinsic and beautiful part of the larger universe. Marcuse envisioned this role of art in sociological terms. Tennessee Williams, later in "The Dangerous Painters," phrased the same thought more poetically: "Revolutions only need good dreamers."

Weaving a Whole Life

by Gerard Brender à Brandis

As someone who has chosen the visual arts as a career and means of expression, I am unsure of my ability to express myself verbally, although I have dabbled at writing some poems and short stories and bits of music.

A number of years ago my first and only loving relationship collapsed and left me feeling so much a failure as an emotional-sexual being that I decided to put all that aside and make my work the only important thing in my life. After all, how many people had told me that "to be an artist must be *so* satisfying!" Surely I needed nothing else?

The following years were very productive as far as the quantity of my work was concerned; several exhibitions each year and at least one edition of handmade books, not to mention the many sketches and drawings required as preparation for block prints. What I had not foreseen, however, was that I would begin to move in very narrow and repetitive circles. "I haven't done an old barn for quite a while: I must do another barn." There was no creative impulse to do another print of a barn, just the need to keep busy.

What I had failed to realize was that, by closing off my channels of emotional expression, I had seriously constricted my channels of artistic expression as well. I had made the common mistake of believing that I could separate the various levels of my life, that one could flourish while the other died. I now realize that when I am sketching a landscape or a flower I am functioning on several levels, including the sexual, just as when I am in bed with someone I am being an artist as well as a lover, that these facets of my life cannot be strictly separated although one may play a more important role than another during certain activities.

This realization has brought me to the inescapable

228

conclusion that as a gay person I must express my gayness in my artistic efforts. How to do this is a problem I have just begun to gnaw at because my work has always been primarily concerned with a fairly realistic representation of the rural scene. The obvious solution of including two people of the same sex in intimate contact in each composition is not artistically valid, though I have begun to explore the possible relationships of human and botanical forms. For the time being I have to be content to feel that while botanical illustrations and engravings of rural buildings do not necessarily affirm my sexual orientation, they don't deny it either, and that certain forms such as iris buds or silos may carry in their phallic forms something of my sexual responses. After all, flowers are not, as so many people think, merely "pretty things for old ladies to look and sniff at while strolling through a garden": they are the sexual organs of living beings. What is more important is to realize that the presence in my life of interpersonal relationships nourish my entire being and spill over into my creative processes, just as my creative vitality makes me more capable of contributing to another man's life.

The difficulty has been to make a new start, to dare once again to be open to the joys and hurts of interacting with people. Whether I will be able to enter into a loving relationship depends both on myself and on the people I may meet. What is important now is to participate in the gay community, to be a member of it in the giving and receiving sense. The only concrete proof of this effort I can show so far is the recently completed anthology of poetry for gay men, *Larkspur and Lad's Love* [Brandstead Press, Carlisle, Ontario, Canada—Eds.]. I hope that participation in other gay cultural events will make me able to participate fully as a gay creative person.

Theatre:
Gays in the Marketplace vs. Gays for Themselves

by Don Shewey

LAURA: [hardly daring to suggest it] But, Bill . . . you
don't think Tom is. . . . [She stops. Bill looks at her a
moment, his answer is in his silence.] Oh, Bill!
　　—from *Tea and Sympathy*, by Robert Anderson, 1953

FRANK: *Are* you a homosexual?
JAY: I'm *the* homosexual!
　　—from *The Haunted Host*, by Robert Patrick, 1972

What is gay theatre? How do you define it? What are
its parameters? What is its audience? Does a definition of
gay theatre involve value judgments about literary merit
and attitudes toward gay life? And what does gay have to
do with theatre?

Try conducting a survey asking those questions to any
group of people—large or small, random or handpicked,
gay or straight—and the chances are the consensus will be
no consensus at all. Yet, despite its lack of a concrete definition, the term "gay theatre" is far from meaningless. I
for one have no qualms about talking about gay theatre,
even though I freely admit, when pressed for a precise
definition, that the more I examine the term, the less sure
I am exactly what it means, how it should be applied, and
even if gay theatre constitutes an identifiable genre within
the realm of drama.

Still, I have a good idea of what I mean when I say gay
theatre. I mean any work for the stage in which gay
characters and gay lifestyles have some kind of visibility,
and I like to make that a firm rule. An argument could be
made that anything written by an open or acknowledged
gay playwright is, per se, gay theatre. But a close study of
the collected works of gay playwrights such as Oscar
Wilde and Tennessee Williams turns up very few plays (if

230

any at all) that deal specifically with gay characters or homosexuality. A corollary to this is the temptation to read into plays homosexual interpretations that are not apparently provided by the author; this is often done with the plays of Shakespeare, as well as modern classics like Samuel Beckett's *Waiting for Godot,* and even contemporary plays like Peter Shaffer's *Equus.* Sometimes gay interpretations of these plays contain illuminating insights, but just as often they reek of overstrain and projection. If you want badly enough to believe that *Snow White and the Seven Dwarfs* is a gay allegory, I have no doubt that you can eventually succeed, but really, who cares?

I do care about plays in which homosexuality and gay characters are out in the open, which means that some of these portrayals are bound to be distorted, unrealistic, oversimplified visions of gay life. But visibility in the media, as in society at large, is, I think, a positive goal for gay people. Visibility is the best tool we have to get rid of fears, myths, and misconceptions about homosexuality. And an unsympathetic or unrepresentative portrait of gay people can often be as beneficial as the most sensitive one if it succeeds in opening up a dialogue. The best example of this is Mart Crowley's *The Boys in the Band.*

For all intents and purposes, gay theatre began as a result of *The Boys in the Band,* much the same way the gay liberation movement began with Stonewall. In both cases, gays were extant and visible before, but the event was the catalyst for a sudden eruption of activity. But while *The Boys in the Band* is undeniably a turning point in the evolution of gay theatre, its influence must be documented through two entirely different histories. One, the history of the mass-audience image of gays, is rather simple because plays about gays in commercial theatre have gotten a lot of attention. The other, the history of contemporary theatre that has been informed and influenced by the creative input of gays, is more complex because creative visions are more slippery, more complicated, more dangerous to talk about than specific, finite dramatic characterizations, and also because they are manifest in the

231

work of small theatre companies in New York familiar to few outside the city.

Before I begin, a couple of prefatory remarks are in order. In putting together this article, I have tried to mention and deal with, however briefly, almost all the plays I've ever heard of that feature gay characters or gay concerns. I have seen and/or read perhaps half of these plays; the other half is composed of plays I have only learned about through secondhand sources. Therefore, unless otherwise noted, the inclusion of a play in this survey does not indicate that the play is well written or sympathetic to gays. In fact, I have included plays that I have every reason to believe are terrible and other plays which I have very little information about. But because I was intrigued in researching the article to find a surprising quantity of plays with gay content, I thought it would be of interest to the reader to get a sense of this quantity.

Also, I wish I could say that the use of the word "gay" in this article refers to both men and women. Unfortunately, this is not the case. For reasons attributable partly to the society we live in and partly to the peculiar traditions of the theatre, there has been very little theatre written/created from a lesbian perspective. Gay theatre is as male-dominated as straight theatre. One reason is simply the sexism that is handed down from generation to generation in our patriarchal society; another is that those men who may be inclined to write about gay women often feel incapable of supplying the requisite sensitivity to lesbian/feminist politics; and another is that, although a great many women are employed in powerful (if unglamorous) technical and administrative threatre jobs, women playwrights are sadly scarce. In her introduction to *The New Women's Theatre,* poet/playwright Honor Moore perceptively points out, "One appeal of the theatre to writers has been the relative camaraderie it provides; the playwright puts words on paper alone, but the work is brought to fruition in company, with the help of actors and directors. Male exclusion of women from this camaraderie, perhaps more than any other single factor, has been responsible for the lack of a female tradition in playwriting similar to that which exists in both fiction and poetry." What is needed, obviously, is a proliferation of women writers; more importantly, it is necessary for male theatre artists not only to support but to actively solicit creative participation in the theatre by women. But as it stands now, please bear in mind that in most instances references in this article to "gay theatre" means "gay male theatre."

The Simple History

The history that leads up to *The Boys in the Band* and goes further to *A Chorus Line* and *Streamers* begins in the days when homosexuality was not allowed on the stage under any circumstances. *Sappho,* a play by Alphonse Daudet and Adolph Belot about the lesbian poet, was first performed in the U.S. in 1895, but when revived in 1900 it caused a great scandal and was banned. In 1926, *The Captive* by Edouard Bourdet and *Sex* by Jane Mast (better known as Mae West) met similar fates. West's *The Drag* (1927) and *Pleasure Man* (1928) were also banned because of their gay content. And as late as 1944, theatres refused to rent to the producers of Dorothy and Howard Baker's *Trio* because the play dealt with an older woman's "unnatural" feelings for a girl.

When homosexuality did begin to whisper its name onstage, it was usually in melodramatic treatment of false accusation (Robert Anderson's *Tea and Sympathy,* Lillian Hellman's *The Children's Hour,* briefly in Arthur Miller's *View from the Bridge* and Allen Drury's *Advise and Consent*), vice (William Inge's *The Boy in the Basement*), or violence (Inge's *Natural Affection* and *The Cell,* Frank Marcus's *The Killing of Sister George,* LeRoi Jones's *The Toilet*).

By the 1950s and 60s, somewhat more noble attempts to portray homosexuals had begun to appear, although the gay content was still largely between the lines and often as not gays were ultimately seen as unhappy and pathetic. This group would include famous plays such as Noel Coward's *Song at Twilight,* Shelagh Delaney's *A Taste of Honey,* Peter Shaffer's *Five Finger Exercise,* and Edward Albee's *Malcolm* (adapted from James Purdy's novel) and

233

Tiny Alice, as well as lesser-known works like *The Immoralist* adapted from André Gide's novel by Ruth and Augustus Goetz, Terence Rattigan's *Man and Boy*, Arthur Laurents's *The Enclave*, Robert Gelbert's *Quaint Honour*.

In the late 60s, James Goldman's *The Lion in Winter*, Charles Dyer's *Staircase*, and *Fortune and Men's Eyes* by John Herbert made breakthroughs in the honest treatment of gays, particularly the last, a frank examination of homosexuality in a Canadian prison.

In addition, mention should be made of three playwrights from this pre-*Boys in the Band* era whose open homosexuality informed their innovative and successful theatrical works. Although Jean Genet's plays (*Deathwatch, The Maids, The Balcony*, etc.) contain much less homosexual content than his novels, his visionary perceptions of sex and power obsessions in human behavior are clearly influenced by his homosexuality and his prison experiences. And the late Joe Orton (whose works include *What the Butler Saw, Lost* and *Entertaining Mr. Sloane*) perfected a dramatic style that was as much concerned with demolishing traditional sex role expectations as with combining classic farce and absurdist theatre into a topsy-turvy reflection of the chaotic modern world.

Tennessee Williams, who was forthright about his sexuality long before it was anywhere near acceptable, touches on gay themes rarely and, except for his latest play, *Vieux Carré*, only in passing (*Streetcar Named Desire, Cat on a Hot Tin Roof, Suddenly Last Summer*), but there is a very important association between his homosexuality and the female roles which he includes in his sweeping emotional dramas. Actresses often claim that Williams is one of the few modern playwrights who has created rich, complex roles for them to act in; on the other hand many feminists feel that Williams's women conform to our society's stereotypes of women as weak, neurotic, and masochistic creatures. Behind the paradoxical truth in both statements must stand the perception that Williams's female characters, while they're certainly not models of healthy womanhood, serve as a gallery of the masks which women—and gay men—have been forced to wear by our male-dominated society. In effect, that society has responded to the otherness of women by defining them in an idealized, nonhuman way as highly emotional, physically weak, dependent, virginal—i.e., all the things that men "should not be." Likewise, straight male society has assigned to gay males many of these "feminine" qualities, with the implication that they are inferior when attached to men. In addition, gay men have been assigned the qualities straight men dislike about real (nonidealized) women—bitchiness, vulgarity, sexual promiscuity, vanity. Williams has made the link between straight male fantasies of women and gay men and exaggerates them in his female characters (*Streetcar*'s Stella and Blanche, Amanda and Laura in *The Glass Menagerie*, Maxine and Hannah in *Night of the Iguana*, to name a few) to the point of puncturing the credibility of those images. By making the exterior larger than life, even unbelievable, he exposed the interior reality more frankly than straight men would dare to. Williams may be totally unaware that he has done so, but his personal identification with his women as fellow victims of straight male oppression is unmistakable.

In this field of theatre I've been talking about—the mass-audience, commercial-based theatre, the straight theatre if you will—the appearance of *The Boys in the Band* signaled another step in the increasing boldness (or tastelessness, to the easily shocked) of stage productions. Its four-letter words made it racy, and its setting in the homosexual milieu gave it a sort of freak show attraction. The play's roaring success seemed to indicate that homosexuality was no longer a taboo subject—in fact, that it was commercially viable. This realization proved to be both a step forward and a step backward in the stage image of gays. On the one hand, it enabled writers to deal with homosexuality on a more honest, open level without suffering instant doom; but on the other hand it opened the doors to a flood of sensationalized plays using homosexuality as a kinky novelty. The dichotomy exists to this day. Since 1968, the growing acceptance of gay characters in the theatre has brought about sensitive, well-written (though not necessarily positive) plays recognizing gay lifestyles. A sample of these (with brief synopses to

235

indicate the range covered) would include: Simon Gray's *Butley* (professor is deserted by both his wife and his boyfriend), Christopher Hampton's *Total Eclipse* (about the love affair between French poets Verlaine and Rimbaud), John Hopkins's *Find Your Way Home* (man must choose between his wife and male lover), Charles Lawrence's *My Fat Friend* (comedy about single woman and her gay neighbor), Miguel Pinero's *Short Eyes* (prison drama), James Kirkwood's *P.S. Your Cat is Dead* (down-and-out actor matches wits with bisexual burglar), Kirkwood and Nicholas Dante's *A Chorus Line* (major character recounts his early career as drag performer), David Rabe's *Streamers* (playful flirtation between two soldiers turns to violence), John Guare's *Rich and Famous* and *Marco Polo Sings a Solo* (each includes a minor character who has one great monologue about his/her unusual sexual history), Neil Simon's *California Suite* (gay actor maintains marriage for appearance's sake), David Rudkin's *Ashes* (husband briefly discusses with wife his past gay activity), Michael Cristofer's *The Shadow Box* (dying man confronts both wife and male lover), and Albert Innaurato's *Gemini* (young man discovers his attraction to his girlfriend's brother). Two arguable additions to this list are Richard O'Brien's *The Rocky Horror Show*, which features a bisexual transvestite in the lead role, and Terence McNally's *The Ritz*, a farce set in a gay bathhouse. But the liberalized atmosphere has also inspired playwrights to produce works, however well meaning, that exploit gay characters and gay themes for sensationalism or cheap comedy, often with no understanding at all: Ron Clark's *Norman, Is That You?*, Gerry Raad's *Circle in the Water*, Ed Jacobs's *The Evil That Men Do*, Robert Lane's *Foreplay*, Richard Johnson and Daniel Hollywood's *All the Girls Came Out to Play*, Michael Sawyer's *Naomi Court* and *Best Friend*, Earl Wilson, Jr.'s *Let My People Come*, Christopher Durang's *Titanic* and *The Nature and Purpose of the Universe*, Enid Bagnold's *A Matter of Gravity*, Bob Barry's *Murder Among Friends*, Neil Cuthbert's *The Soft Touch*, Bruce J. Friedman's *Steambath*, and so on. As this history progresses, only one thing is certain: theatre audiences can hardly avoid seeing gay characters on the stage today, and even if they are incomplete portraits or reworked stereotypes, the visibility is still a plus.

The Complex History

The simple history above covers the presentation of gays in theatre created ostensibly by heterosexuals for an audience composed primarily of heterosexuals to many of whom homosexuality is a foreign, often distasteful subject. But the history of what could more accurately be called gay theatre, as opposed to an easily exploited genre within traditional theatre, is more complex, bound up as it is in the burgeoning Off-Off-Broadway theatre and the politics of the gay movement. In this perspective, *The Boys in the Band* was a more influential turning point, but let's start at the beginning.

By the late 1950s the New York theatre had reached an appalling economic state. Broadway was going the route of the big Hollywood studios. It was producing fewer plays and each production was more expensive. The goal was superproductions with star-studded casts, equaling *safety*. Off Broadway, traditionally the home of the experimental, was finding itself in the same position. By 1960 it cost between twelve and fifteen thousand dollars to produce a straight (non-musical) play off Broadway. The audience that Off Broadway had developed, the intelligentsia, were interested in revivals: O'Neill, Ibsen, Chekhov, and the avant garde (Genet, Pinter, Beckett, Ionesco)—but they were not interested in unestablished new American playwrights.
—from the introduction to *The Off-Off Broadway Book*, edited by Albert Poland and Bruce Mailman

The accidental birth of Off-Off-Broadway is generally attributed to Joe Cino, whose Caffé Cino started out in 1958 as a bohemian hangout. The regulars began putting together poetry readings and scenes from plays, and before long the Cino had become a real theatre, an anarchic, un-

237

pretentious, amazingly prolific collective of actors and writers, and from the very beginning most—if not all—of the Cino core were gay.

Plays by established gay writers were frequently performed—Wilde, Inge, Coward, Genet, Gide, Williams, Capote, Cocteau, etc. But more important, the Cino attracted, inspired, and nurtured a number of young, untried playwrights—Doric Wilson, H. M. Koutoukas, Lanford Wilson, Robert Patrick—whose gayness was an essential part of a new, freewheeling, often whimsical, often campy type of theatre. Among the significant gay plays that came out of the Cino are Patrick's *The Haunted Host*, in which a rather zany New York writer exorcises the ghost of an unhappy love affair; Lanford Wilson's *The Madness of Lady Bright*, in which a lonely, aging drag queen goes to pieces and slowly puts himself back together; and Doric Wilson's *Now She Dances!*, a surrealistic farce combining Oscar Wilde's sodomy trial and his play *Salomé*, the teatime chatter of *The Importance of Being Earnest*, and a lively discourse on contemporary gay liberation. When the Cino closed shortly after its founder's death in 1967, many of the Cino regulars moved over to the Old Reliable, a seedy bar with a backroom theatre presided over by playwright-in-residence Robert Patrick and owner Norman "Speedy" Hartman. Again, an anything-goes style flourished.

After the Caffé Cino was born, a number of other OOB theatres sprang up, among the first the Judson Poets' Theater run by Al Carmines. The Judson attracted the vanguard of new playwrights, many of them gay, and among its most noted productions were Carmines's adaptations of the plays of Gertrude Stein. With the founding of Ellen Stewart's La Mama Theatre, the Off-Off-Broadway movement was off and running, and the percentage of gay input was high.

In 1966, a group of flamboyant gay actors and writers put together a theatre devoted to total outrageousness called the Play-House of the Ridiculous under the direction of Ronald Tavel and John Vaccaro (and known as the Ridiculous Theatrical Company, under Charles Ludlam's direction). Vaccaro was quoted in a recent *New*

Yorker profile of the Theatre of the Ridiculous as saying, "Maria Montez was the particular idol of our theatre. She was perfectly awful. Jack Smith [avant-garde filmmaker] used to say she was the only fit object for worship, and she was. When I was growing up in Steubenville, Ohio, she transported me into a world I wanted to be in." Montez, who was a Hollywood film star in the forties often known as the Queen of Technicolor, represented an ability to imbue preposterous material with a total artistic commitment that the Ridiculous Theatre sought to emulate. But a dispute developed between Vaccaro and Ludlam (then only a featured actor in the company) which came to a head over Ronald Tavel's play *Gorilla Queen*. In the same *New Yorker* article, Ludlam recalled, "We'd all heard that title, *Gorilla Queen*, which suggested many things—jungle movies, Montez films, the camp idea of a monster gorilla that's gay, that's a queen. Everybody was expecting something lighthearted and campy, and then it turned out to be heavy, very word-heavy. John is not confident with dialogue, and he hated the play." Besides, said Ludlam, "I felt John was too conservative. He didn't want homosexuality and he didn't want nudity onstage, because he was afraid of being arrested. I wanted to commit an outrage. For me, nothing was too far out." As it turned out, *Gorilla Queen* was done at the Judson, Vaccaro started his own company, and Ludlam took over the Ridiculous Theatre as star/writer/actor/director. The theatre acquired a large gay audience, and gay camp and monstrous excesses were its specialties in plays like *When Queens Collide* and *Turds in Hell*.

The importance of the early Off-Off-Broadway movement is that it instigated a renaissance in new American playwriting that eschewed the rules of traditional commercial theatre both in style and in substance. And just as Off-Off-Broadway incorporated the voice of the emerging black theatre, it gave gay artists a forum for the unself-conscious exploration in the theatre of their own lifestyles. It also built up a high consciousness among gay audiences and gay theatre people who were sorely offended by *The Boys in the Band*. Many felt that Mart Crowley's play was well written and accurately represented a certain part of the gay world, but objected to its pretense of representing all gays and confirming all the old stereotypes about gays being pathetic, neurotic, effeminate, incomplete people. Most of the critics, and presumably the Broadway audience, fell for this misrepresentation.

Time magazine's reviewer wrote, "Beneath the bitchy, lancing wit of the verbal byplay, playwright Mart Crowley keeps a dead-level eye on the desolating aspects of homosexual life. He records the loveless, brief encounters, the guilt-ridden, blackout reliance on alcohol, the endless courtship rat race of the gay bars with its inevitable quota of rejection, humiliation and loneliness. Crowley underscores the fact that while the homosexual may pose as a bacchanal of nonconformist pagan delights, he frequently drinks a hemlock-bitter cup of despair." Walter Kerr in the Sunday *New York Times* explained that the play's impact "is that of permitting us to inhabit and understand a world in which anguish cannot spend itself because it is condemned to seeing itself as antic, as not real, as not discussible, as something to be tied up with a tidy bow and then flung . . . in someone else's face." Gay people knew there was more to their lives than *Boys in the Band* led theatregoers to believe, and so this resentment, combined with the genesis of the gay liberation movement as a result of the Stonewall riots in 1969, provided the impetus for a theatrical backlash to *Boys in the Band*.

One person who made the connection between the Off-Off-Broadway movement and the gay movement was playwright/director Doric Wilson. "I was always into Off-Off-Broadway, and I was always planning to start my own theatre. I got into the bar business to get the money, as a bartender, to support a theatre. About the time when Stonewall happened, I was helping to start the Circle Repertory Theatre. There were a lot of gays up at Circle, and finally there was a viable, visible gay movement starting, and I got involved in it. I would run back and forth from the Circle to GLF and then GAA, and I began to realize I didn't like the schizophrenia that was going down. No, we didn't like *Boys in the Band*, but on the other hand those of us who were creative did not like the idea of censorship, particularly in a society that is as essentially free as this one. The more I thought about the problem of *Boys in the Band,* and the more I wondered, 'Why aren't gays who are creative making some gay statement?,' then I thought that there should be a place where authors and artists who want to deal with their gayness can have their work done, and done well, and done away from the marketplace where sensationalism is the rule of the day." Accordingly, Wilson established in February 1974 The Other Side Of Silence (TOSOS) with the opening statement: "TOSOS, Inc., is a nonprofit workshop of the performing and visual arts committed to an open and honest exploration of the many expressions of the gay life style; the purpose of TOSOS is a pursuit of self-identity and respect, and a broadening of gay and straight attitudes through the creative process."

TOSOS opened with a very successful production of the original musical *Lovers* by Peter del Valle and Steve Sterner and went on to present new plays (Sandra Scoppetone's *Home Again, Home Again, Jiggety Jig,* Martin Sherman's *Passing By,* Charles Jurrist's *Michael's House*), plays by the Caffé Cino writers (Lanford Wilson's *The Madness of Lady Bright* and *Great Nebula in Orion,* Robert Patrick's *The Haunted Host,* Terence McNally's *Noon,* Doric Wilson's *Now She Dances!*), and revivals of older plays by established gay writers (Noel Coward's *Design for Living* and *Hay Fever,* Joe Orton's *What the Butler Saw,* Brendan Behan's *The Hostage*). Beset by financial difficulties, TOSOS suspended its regular activities in early 1977, and for the time being it exists only as a production company. (For instance, in June of 1977 TOSOS co-produced the premiere at the Spike, a West Village leather bar, of Doric Wilson's *The West Street Gang,* a polemical satire concerning the punk gangs that prey on gay men and women in some areas of New York City.) But during its three years of steady operation, TOSOS broke ground for an ongoing theatre run by and for gays.

John Glines, an actor/director/writer with a background in theatre, films, and television, was associated with TOSOS for a short time before he left to form his own theatre, the Glines, in 1976. The concept of the Glines was very close to that of TOSOS—"to explore the gay ex-

241

perience, to create a space where it could be examined: what it means to be gay"—but its basic distinction grew out of Glines's dissatisfaction with what he felt was Doric Wilson's dependence on plays not specifically related to the gay experience. "I am more interested in doing the flawed play that is daring, that really confronts some aspect of what it is to be gay, than I am in doing something fairly well made and easy." Consequently, the Glines has presented almost exclusively new plays (*The Soft Core Kid* by Frank Hogan and Walter Proczak, Paul Vanase's *A Drop in the Pudding*, Richard Hall's *The Love Match*, Ramon Delgado's *Once Below a Lighthouse*, Sidney Morris's *Last Chance at the Brass Ring*) and musicals (*Something Hopeful* conceived by Loretta Lotman, *Women on Mars* by Cortnie Lowe and Nita Sell, *Fascination* by Michael Bottari, Quitman Fludd, III, and Michael J. Green, *Gulp* by J. B. Hamilton, Stephen Creco, Scott Kingman, and Robin Jones).

The idea of a working gay theatre was by no means universally embraced by gay artists, however. Both TOSOS and the Glines encountered resistance from gays uncomfortable with contributing to an openly gay company. Doric Wilson described to me the apprehension of gay actors about playing in gay roles and the irony of homophobia in the theatre business. "Most of Broadway is gay-produced gay theatre. For instance, *A Chorus Line* is basically the work of a number of gay people. Those same gay people treat other gay people, "our own tendency to means second-rate, because somehow gay is second-rate. When I first started the theatre, the first response from people was, 'Gay has nothing to do with my art, gay is what I do when I get to bed.' It seems to me as long as we defined ourselves only sexually, then we are also going to have a slight puritanism about sex and so a slight dismissal of any public statement of our gayness." The reluctance to associate themselves with gay artistic enterprises, Wilson posited, reflects an oppressive attitude with which some gay people treat other gay people, "our own tendency to deal with people from a purely sexual point of view. That is, 'You interest me because I'm also slightly turned on to you'/'You don't interest me because I'm not turned on to you.' Or the reverse of that: 'Uh-oh, are you turned on to me? Therefore I'm going to be defensive.' "

Similarly, John Glines commented, "We don't ask when somebody comes here how they swing, only that they commit themselves to the principle of the theatre: that it's a forum for the gay experience. That was an immediate problem with a director that I had to fire—he did not want on the flyer for the show 'a forum for the gay experience,' because he thought it would be somehow detrimental and not bring in as many people. That was, like, blasphemy. That's the worst thing you can do here—try to straighten the place out. Because then that brings out a tackiness, like something dirty. For instance, the musical *Fascination*—almost everyone involved with that was gay—was straight-out campy, a light, fluffy musical, boys bumping their crotches at the audience, and, my God, it was filled with couples from New Jersey! They loved it, because that's what they come to Off-Off-Broadway for. But there was nothing in the show that tried to tame it down, somehow make it more sellable. That would make it somehow dirty." Both theatres found that by accepting the responsibility of finding an expression of gay art, they also had to deal with the resistance of artists to identifying themselves and their work as gay.

TOSOS and the Glines were not the only outlets pursuing a theatre indigenous to gay culture, however. The nascent gay activist movement and an increasingly public gay populace brought about theatrical endeavors as diverse as Jonathan Katz's stage documentary *Coming Out* and semiporno gay celebrations like David Gaard's *And Puppy Dog Tails*, A. J. Kronengold's *Tubstrip*, and Gus Weill's *Geese*. The early Off-Off-Broadway playwrights continued to explore gay themes in such works as Al Carmines's *The Faggot* and Charles Ludlam's *Camille* (in which Ludlam performed the title role).

In the last few years, the increasing activity in gay theatre at all levels—on and off Broadway, regional theatre, gay-oriented theatres—has brought playwrights out of the woodwork. Robert Patrick's *Kennedy's Children*, which included a character based on the author's own Off-Off-Broadway experiences, made it to Broadway;

Eve Merriam's *The Club,* a musical in which female actors portrayed the members of a turn-of-the-century gentlemen's lodge, was an Off-Broadway hit. Gay output of varying quality and success has included the musicals *Gay Company* by Fred Silver and *Boy Meets Boy* by Bill Solly and Donald Ward, as well as dramas like Lee Barton's *Nightride,* George Whitmore's *The Caseworker,* and Martin Duberman's plays (including *Payments, Electric Map,* and *Visions of Kerouac).* Canada has several active gay playwrights such as Robert Wallace (*'67, No Deposit, No Return*), Michel Tremblay (*Hosanna, La Duchesse de Langlais*), and Ken Cass (*The Boy Bishop*). Productions of Genet's *Deathwatch,* Patrick's *The Haunted Host,* and Kirkwood's *P. S. Your Cat Is Dead* have enjoyed long runs in Boston, and homegrown offerings have included *Masques,* a pansexual erotic fantasy conceived and performed by the local troupe the Stage One Theatre Ensemble, and *The Marlowe Show* by John Adams and William Kromm, a fascinating stage biography of fifteenth-century playwright Christopher Marlowe (whose collected works feature a history of homosexual British monarch Edward II). In Providence, Rhode Island, the Trinity Square Repertory Company under the direction of Adrian Hall has mounted gay works such as a stage adaptation of James Purdy's *Eustace Chisholm and the Works,* San Francisco has hosted productions of *P. S. Your Cat Is Dead* and *Boy Meets Boy* along with its locally produced camp musical *Beach Blanket Bingo Goes Bananas,* and in Los Angeles, the small theatres have produced works with gay themes like George Birimisa's *Pogey Bait,* Lonnie Burr's *Over the Hill,* Diana Frolov's *Mirror, Mirror. . . ,* and Donald Driver's *Special Delivery.* In 1976, gay activists Loretta Lotman and Owen Wilson compiled *Lesbian and Gay Male Theater Resources,* which lists plays, playwrights, and theatre groups from all parts of the country devoted to gay-oriented theatre.

As I write this in early summer of 1977, it seems that there are more gay playwrights, plays with gay characters and themes, and theatre groups exploring gay and straight identities all the time. The conditions which thirty years ago prevented the honest presentation of gay life onstage—authorial timidity, fear of censorship, society's lack of understanding—have lessened, if not disappeared, and gays are beginning to be represented and to represent themselves in theatre with the frequency and diversity with which they appear in "real life."

It's true, of course, that most of the quality gay theatre—the innovative stage works that function both as good theatre and as reflections of contemporary gay life and thought—are accessible mainly to those who are able to take advantage of New York's Off-Off-Broadway movement. The theatre that reaches the mass audience, even if a good deal of it is created and performed by gay people, is far from the forefront of gay theatre; it is still subject to sensationalism, still bound to old theatrical forms. For those with limited access to the experimental gay theatre in New York, gay theatre seems to be growing only slowly, and progress seems to be coming play by play.

Gay Theatre in the "Real World"

by George Whitmore

In 1972 I wrote a play which was finally produced almost exactly four years later as *The Caseworker* at Playwrights Horizons, Off-Off Broadway, in New York.

It wasn't my intention to write "a gay play." On the contrary, I wanted to write a play with gay characters that would reach beyond what I felt was a very limiting genre, judging from most of what had come before. I wanted to write a play that didn't sag under the label of homosexuality—in other words, a gay play that wasn't about homosexuality per se.

At that time there wasn't a gay theatre in New York, a place you could go to to see gay plays. There were plays about homosexuality or with a stray gay character here or there; there were plays (for example, *The Madness of Lady Bright*) by Lanford Wilson and other writers that exemplified the gay sensibility; there had been *The Boys in the Band*; Charles Ludlam's Theatre of the Ridiculous was already playing variations on high camp to a faithful following. But gay theatre remained largely an abstraction, and still does, in spite of the efforts of TOSOS, John Glines's theatre, and others, to work through the theory of what gay theatre should be.

When I wrote *The Caseworker*, I didn't write with an exclusively gay audience in mind; nor did I write for a straight or "general" audience. I wrote a naturalistic drama quite like anything you ever saw on "Playhouse 90." But I wasn't ignorant about the political ramifications of presenting gay characters. I made an effort to short-circuit the sideshow atmosphere that so often results when gay characters appear on the stage. My characters were nothing if not antistereotypes. They were also antiheroic, "little people" (as in Odets) who I hoped could assert their humanity strongly enough on their own terms without my editorializing. If so, I thought, the play would make a

246

political point sufficient to the limitations of the form. Jonathan Katz's *Coming Out* was (and still is) the best example extant of political gay theatre, but that kind of theatre simply wasn't my style.

So *The Caseworker* was tricky—a gay play, actually, masquerading in a well-worn straight form. There was no indication to the uninitiated that the characters were homosexual until well into the first act. By that time, I hoped, the spring of the play would be tightly enough wound to hold the audience in its coils.

What followed for me, during the next four years and into the production of the play, was to a large extent what any playwright selling a first play in New York might expect. At first I kept track of the number of copies I made and sent out. After a while I stopped keeping count. I got some good criticism from some playreaders, silence from many more. My scripts had an unusual propensity for disappearing from file cabinets for months at a time. Generally, I felt as if I were throwing them into a deep, black pit.

A few years into this, I had two experiences that gave me my only reading on what people thought about the gay content of the play. The first was with one of the producers of a gay theatre (there *was* one by then) who rejected *The Caseworker* on the grounds that the play was too depressing. The characters weren't "happy" enough to make the risk of producing the play politically feasible. I had been reading notice after notice in the gay papers from this theatre, begging for scripts, money, support. So I was confused when he told me my play was the best they'd received that year, but that they couldn't produce it.

The second experience wasn't as amusing. One of the more established Off-Off Broadway (OOB) theatres expressed an interest in doing the play, then lost the script, then lost the second copy. When I called them months after that, the woman who had taken over the script department promised to read yet a third copy if I would send it. I did, she did, and she called me, saying she'd like to talk to me even if they didn't want to do *The Caseworker*.

I went to see her on my lunch hour. She told me she was anxious to see another play and liked my writing very much. I told her there wasn't another play yet because I was busy with other things but that I was flattered. What about *The Caseworker?*

"Oh," she said, "we've seen so many plays like that this year." Plays like what? "Oh, boy meets boy, boy loses boy, boy gets boy. You know." I didn't know. *The Caseworker* is about a repressed, middle-aged welfare worker who may or may not have a crush on a drifter he's taken into his dingy West Side apartment. What she was describing seemed infinitely more light and gay than *The Caseworker.*

"It's hardly a romance," I said.

"Well," she said, "what *is* it about, then?"

"Death. Paternity."

"Oh."

After half an hour we came to the principal point of objection. "I don't know how I would rewrite it," she finally said. "Maybe you could make him a woman." With a crush on a young man. "Yeah." But that wouldn't be the same play. "No, it wouldn't. But I don't think our audience is ready for a play like yours." The Off-Off Broadway audience wasn't ready?

"What you're telling me," I said, "is that the play is perfectly fine but doesn't qualify as a human drama because the characters are gay."

There was a pause. "Yeah," she said.

Both of these reactions to my play gave me some idea of what theatre people might (or might not) be thinking about it around town.

Late in 1975 I met a director who liked *The Caseworker* and often worked at Playwrights Horizons, one of the more prolific showcase theatres in Manhattan. The production was scheduled for May 1976 and we started working together in January.

We agreed on necessary rewrites and on other things. Since we were both gay and both fairly political, we wanted a gay cast if possible. We had gay designers and, as it turned out, a gay stage manager. We wanted it to be a gay enterprise and we wanted a gay audience. We were sure we could get one through our own various connections and through publicity.

The roles were unusually difficult to cast as we had to

248

cast according to unusual types. The most difficult was our main character, the caseworker. It's hard to find middle-aged male actors who are willing to do a showcase for no pay, however large the role, even if you can find middle-aged male actors who are still working.

I put a code on my casting sheets during the grueling weeks it took to cast the play: "G" for Gay, "S" for Straight, "?" for Can't Tell. I realize I might be accused of practicing reverse discrimination, even though there's no law protecting actors from discrimination according to sexual preference in the first place.

Some of the actors who auditioned for us sat down, opened the script, began reading a scene, and then realized their characters were gay. Some of them hotfooted it out of the place. Others were intrigued. Some of the straight types were visibly offended. Many gay actors, especially the older men, had obvious difficulties with the idea of playing a gay character. All in all, we got some interesting interpretations of what a gay male is like.

Finally, after auditioning at least fifty actors for the main role, we found our caseworker. It was a good thing. He was the last to read. He looked perfect, sounded perfect—and we were pretty sure he could do it. We cast the other characters around him.

As it turned out, none of our actors was gay.

With *The Caseworker*, our job was to build a credible, very particular stage reality, not to educate our actors on the ins and outs of the gay world. We had to explain certain references to gay life. We even took a field trip to the bars with a couple of them, one who played a bartender and another who had a speech set in a gay bar. Both of them were comfortable with the scene. We all came away with some insights into what we were dealing with on stage.

Our caseworker seemed to have some problems with the gay content of the play. They surfaced now and then in the form of stage fright. Often he would reveal to us that he was translating straight experiences whole cloth into gay ones, even though the director would explain how they varied.

In the final weeks of rehearsal, those of us not involved

in the play leafleted the bars and sent out announcements to gay groups, friends, and our mailing lists of gay acquaintances (many of them in the arts). There was other publicity, too, and we got very little response, finally, from gay people. Perhaps that's in the nature of showcase productions, but my feeling was that the gay audience is so well integrated into the general audience that the play had no special appeal to them. We were disappointed that so few of our gay friends and acquaintances came to see *The Caseworker*, yet we didn't want to use the gay "issue" as a crutch or excuse.

It was only after the play opened, when the second stage of my own work—listening to the audience—came about, that I was able to assess *The Caseworker* as a gay play.

Generally, on the nights when there was a good proportion of gay people in the audience, the play came alive. When there wasn't, it was often dead. I could always tell what sort of an audience we had at the turning point when the characters' gay identity becomes clear. With gay people in the audience, the reactions to this scene or that didn't seem to diminish from the first. With a more general audience, there were fewer laughs, more chairs scraping, coughing, or an uncomfortable silence. Sometimes this threw the actors off. It certainly made my own judgments as to what was working and what wasn't more difficult. On some evenings an almost tangible veil seemed to separate the stage from the house. Yet the play worked well enough often enough for me to see that the gay content was an obstacle.

Perhaps the audience reaction can be explained if you think about what theatre usually is—a compact between a community of actors, spectators, and playwright. Even the most political or agitprop theatre doesn't violate that sense of community. Eric Bentley points out that propaganda plays don't often seek to convert the unconverted, merely to affirm, and perhaps strengthen, convictions (or prejudices) that already exist. When an audience is free to laugh at a gay character or cry over his/her situation, the compact remains intact. By taking a naturalistic, cool, and ambiguous approach to the gay content in *The*

Caseworker, I subverted that interaction. Rather than being drawn into the characters' lives and real concerns and sticking with them through the play, the audience seemed drawn in and then somehow betrayed by me and its own ideas of what gay people are like. Without a clear point of view or message to guide them, they were puzzled.

After the run of the play was over, I came to several conclusions about gay theatre and my work in it. The first is a personal modus operandi. I've started writing plays with two distinct audiences in mind. Out of the handful that I've written since *The Caseworker*, half are "general" plays with one or more gay characters and half are "gay" plays for an exclusively gay audience. I hope this doesn't sound too rudimentary, but it's been a liberating decision. I don't think gay playwrights have an obligation to fail commercially, just to be honest. To me, none of my plays are actually gay or straight. The political questions raised for me before and after *The Caseworker* seem very distinct from the questions of character and style I have to deal with when I write. But I'm sure my plays will always have a gay profile to one extent or another because they couldn't be honest expressions without being gay as well.

This conclusion has opened up into some others for me. One is that even the most sophisticated audience expects a gay play to proselytize for gayness, even if that isn't the author's intention. And no matter what, the audience gets uptight about it. Of course, you can't very well proselytize and entertain at the same time unless you're a genius. But I recognize that certain kinds of subject matter are more difficult to present in a theatrical framework than others are. Sexual identity seems to be one of those, even now. I'm sure that if *The Caseworker* had been less realistic, perhaps more sentimental than it was, or conversely more political in its approach, the audience would have been just that much more comfortable with it. The gay "issue" is still very much an issue.

Another conclusion of mine is that gay theatre is, indeed, a separate entity and should be fostered as such. The simple fact of gay characters removes a play to a certain distance from the audience, as I've implied—even a gay audience. I think this means that gay theatre must have a primarily didactic point of view right now. In plays like Tennessee Williams's where the gay sensibility comes through strongly even though there might not be any gay characters, this isn't necessarily the case. But in plays where we intend to treat aspects of gay life and identity in a direct manner, it's almost always bound to be so. I'm not exactly sure what that didactic gay theatre should be like or where it should fall on the spectrum between radical/confrontational theatre and camp/illusionary theatre, but I'm heartened by the literary and cultural gay antecedents we have for it.

Another conclusion: If gay theatre can best suit our needs right now as a minority form, as I believe it can, and perhaps only peripherally enrich the general culture (setting aside the disproportionate contributions gay people already make to theatre), many other complications set in that will have to be worked out in practice. One of them is the conflict between aesthetic and political demands. We feel a sense of affirmation and community as gay people when we see a play like *Coming Out*. But often we have to operate on a whole new set of assumptions about theatre that differ tremendously from our usual expectations. For one thing, that's *us* up there for a change. We've all grown up in the general culture. Except for any particular affinity any of us might have with the avant garde, the general culture has shaped the way we perceive a theatre piece, let alone the way we interact with mass entertainment. If straight people are uncomfortable with gay characters on the stage, we have to admit that many of us are as well. We've all felt that stiffening of the spine that accompanies the entrance of a gay character— what next? In spite of our qualms about the treatment of gay characters in shows like *A Chorus Line*, where an attempt has been made to integrate them into the story line and the milieu, I suspect we're usually more comfortable and, ultimately, more satisfied with those productions than we are with a purely gay theatrical event. Box office figures alone would bear this out. I think we can look forward to some time in the near future when gay theatre establishes itself as a coherent and sophisticated form in its own right, but it will establish itself as a minority theatre first. For now, the audience/stage dynamics of gay theatre are nothing if not more complicated than those I witnessed during the run of *The Caseworker*.

Perhaps an example from Genet will show what I mean. Although *The Balcony* isn't generally considered a gay play per se, it's certainly gay theatre. The central image of the play is the mirror in the whorehouse, which reflects the characters' fantasies and the audience's perceptions of them at the same time. This concentration on fantasy and identity is a very gay concern. In a sense, the audience is looking *through* the mirror and *into* the mirror at the same time when it watches *The Balcony*. How much more complex, then, would our reactions be if another layer were applied to this, as it is in a play with gay characters, where the basis of the stage illusion is also the fundamental question of gay identity. No wonder, then, that we tend to think of gay theatre in political terms before we consider the vagaries of its aesthetics. Politics is the glue that binds the gay population together—or the lever that pries it apart. Aesthetics seem almost beside the point. Perhaps these questions express an even more basic conflict between individual and mass identity, a conflict all minorities experience. Certainly they tend to militate against art as we customarily view it.

It's a commonplace that for writers, directors, actors, and other theatre people limitations equal liberation; it's only by working within a set of limitations that we discover the style appropriate to what we want to express. The "legitimate" theatre suffers as much from an excess of means as it does from a lack of imagination. This is true for any art form that becomes bloated and, paradoxically, diminished by commercial demands. The legitimate theatre, such as it is, may not be didactic in intent, but its overall message is clearly didactic. The classics are revived and staged at a safe remove, quite a distance from the remove of even the most rudimentary gay play. The musical comedy is most often a celebration of bourgeois values (even as it expresses the confusion and discontent of the middle class). As the greatest theatrical event of our time, Monday night football is a celebration of violence and masculinism. This is why I've come to the conclusion that gay theatre as an avowedly limited and minority form is liberating and productive.

Generally, I feel after my experience in the "real world" with *The Caseworker* that, while I've scaled down my expectations about the reach of gay theatre, I've also come to a greater understanding of what it can be and what theatre in general is in danger of becoming. What gay theatre needs most at this time is what all of us gay humans need—a community to accept and nurture it. Working out its identity is a lot like working out our own. Gay theatre should reflect that process accurately and truthfully and remain art at the same time. It can evolve as we evolve, affirm, even question, what we discover for ourselves. If it does, it's mainstream theatre anyway.

VI
Purple Prose and Violet Verse

The X-Rated Bibliographer:
A Spy in the House of Sex

by Karla Jay

As lesbians, like other oppressed groups before us, reach out to claim the herstory long denied to us by predominately male, heterosexual historians, one woman—Dr. Jeannette H. Foster—comes to most minds as our unchallenged foremother in this field. For in 1956, in the twilight of the McCarthy era, Jeannette Foster published *Sex Variant Women in Literature* with $2,000 of her own money, a year's salary.

Aficionados of the work, which up until now was available only to those able to pay up to $30 per copy from rare book dealers or those near one of the few libraries in the country containing a copy, will tell you with absolute reverence of the monumental significance of *Sex Variant Women in Literature*. The opus catalogs with great accuracy almost every work dealing with lesbians from Biblical and ancient Greek literature through the first half of the twentieth century. The book is full of fascinating bibliographical information (most people are startled that famous authors—for example, Mary Wollstonecraft—wrote lesbian works), careful plot analysis, and even brief biographical sketches of some lesbian writers. And the work is not confined merely to works in English or to better known foreign works, such as the poems of Sappho, but it also lists barely known works in English, French, and German among other languages. In short, the real marvel of this work is not the fact that Dr. Foster gathered material on such well-known lesbian writers as Radclyffe Hall *(The Well of Loneliness)*, but that she discovered such obscure American writers living and writing in France. For example, she discovered Natalie Barney (known as the "wild girl from Cincinnati"), who wrote scathingly funny and irreverent accounts of some of her contemporaries, and Renée Vivien (Pauline Tarn), who

257

was considered to be one of the best French poets of her time. Or rather, Dr. Foster rediscovered them, as they had almost been completely forgotten, despite the fact that several of them, including Natalie Barney and her lover Romaine Brooks (an American portrait painter and also a member of this circle of lesbians living in France) were very much alive in 1956.

But what even the aficionados of the book don't know is that this seemingly modest book is the work of a lifetime, of approximately forty years of research, much of which was not easy and which culminated in a struggle to publish the completed material. It all started when Jeannette Foster read Volume Two of Havelock Ellis's *Studies of the Psychology of Sex* while she was an undergraduate at Rockford College near her native Chicago. In this book she discovered the subject of homosexuality. "Then," she told me, when I visited her, "I began a bibliography of various sources, but I didn't get a chance to do anything about it until I moved to the East Coast [Philadelphia] in 1937."

The path to information, however, was not always as simple as going to libraries in the Philadelphia area. For example, there were only four copies of Catulle Mendés's *Méphistophéla* in the United States. One was in the Rittenhouse Club in Philadelphia, which wouldn't admit women—for any reason. As Dr. Foster told me, "I went down there one Saturday morning and asked, 'Please, might I be admitted merely to the library (which was a front room—I wouldn't even have had to meet any of the pious members)?' No, I couldn't enter its pious walls. So I went back out, and I talked to the assistant librarian of the University of Pennsylvania, who was a nice guy, and he grinned and said: 'Well, you know, I'm a member of the Rittenhouse Club. I'll get that book out if you promise to read it *here in my office*.' So I read *Méphistophéla*—it was about three hundred ninety-two pages long in French—in his office at a distant desk, sort of the secretary of his secretary's desk. And lots of funny things happened like that."

Perhaps it was Jeannette Foster's good humor which kept her implacably on the trail of any material which

258

might contain information on sex-variant women (which to the author means "differing from a chosen standard," without necessarily the sexual implications associated with the word lesbian). On another occasion, she learned that there was a copy of *Mary, a Fiction* by Mary Wollstonecraft at Yale. "I had to take a library school class from Drexel on a tour of the New York area," she told me, "and after I had gotten as far as Columbia, I sent them home—they were all graduate students, and they didn't need a chaperone. I took a northbound train to New Haven. I got there at night, and I was at Yale's doors when the university opened the library at eight the next morning, and I read *all day* Mary Wollstonecraft's *Mary, a Fiction*. So that's how that got into my bibliography. I'm sure that was the only copy in this country."

Obviously, the largest library of sexual material in the United States was definitely not at the Drexel Institute nor in the Philadelphia area but at the Kinsey Institute at Bloomington, Indiana, so off Jeannette Foster went to work as the librarian of Dr. Alfred C. Kinsey from 1948 until 1952. The position paid her more than she could make at that time as a professor of library science, but it was clearly not the money that interested her. She was a spy in the house of sexuality, and when she had got the information she wanted, she left the Kinsey Institute and took a position at the University of Missouri at Kansas City (then the University of Kansas City) for two-fifths of what Kinsey was paying her. And I believe that her dedication was so great that had the only sexual library been the Pope's (which Dr. Foster claims is larger than Kinsey's), she would have become a nun to gain access to it (or perhaps disguised herself as a monk since it is doubtful whether nuns are admitted to this collection)!

After over thirty years of research, what started out as a bibliography turned into a book of over 400 pages of densely packed information. "As it grew, I began to see the pattern for a book, and I worked awfully hard to find a title for it which would begin with the word sex. As I had learned from searching bibliographies, a title beginning with the word sex couldn't be ignored!"

But a catchy title and the completion of the book itself

were only the beginning of Dr. Foster's struggle, for she had to find a publisher for her work. She was told and also realized that this was not the sort of material a regular trade publisher would handle, so she took her book to over a dozen university presses, but they weren't willing to publish it either, and it was obvious from one or two rejection letters that some presses wouldn't even read a manuscript on sex-variant women. Finally, Dr. Foster sent it to Rutgers University Press. "Rutgers kept it seven months because a woman, whose name I have fortunately forgotten—the manager was out of town, . . . took it home, and let all her friends read it. During those seven months, the editor of the press, darn him, died, and his successor agreed that it was well written but he didn't want it to be the first title which came out under the Rutgers imprint when he was the editor. So that finished it with Rutgers. That was the point at which I decided to come into subsidy publishing. I had just read *The Rogue of Publishers' Row* by Edward Uhlan. It's the story of subsidy publishing, and the only reason I never even sent my manuscript to Exposition Press (Uhlan's press), which was the first of the subsidy presses, was he spends his first chapter saying that the minute he advertised he was in the subsidy publishing business—why, of course, the first mass of material he got was from perverts who wanted at last to get their stuff published. . . . I located it with Vantage. I wanted to locate it with Pageant, but the Pageant job was more expensive by quite a lot. . . . Actually they wouldn't have been had I known what a mess the one that they printed me was going to make. They gave it to absolutely illiterate readers who altered my script. If there's one thing I'm proud of, it's my ability to write decent English. I taught college English for ten years, and I know I can write legible English. And the editors and the readers messed it up, and I sent it back the way I had written it, and I said: 'That *stands* or else.' And they charged me for author's alterations!"

And so her $2,000 investment was applied against royalties when Dr. Foster refused to send them any further money, Vantage kept her royalties against what she owed them. Vantage then sold the British rights to Frederick

Muller Ltd., who published the book in 1958, but Dr. Foster learned of the sale only from reading about it in *Publishers Weekly* (a trade publication), and, of course, she never received anything from that sale. In fact, she finally received a sum of $240 when a secondhand dealer bought the 2,400 remaining unbound, unfolded sheets of the book (from an original printing of 3,500) at ten cents per copy.

Thus a book which had taken a lifetime of preparation seemingly slipped quietly into oblivion. It had never even been reviewed, except for one very negative review in a psychology publication and a brief mention in the Kansas City *Star*. The author received no publicity, no money, no fame, and probably, as a consequence, no harassment. Yet the proverbial grapevine (with the help of *The Ladder*, a lesbian publication which raved about the book for years) accomplished what the publishing industry couldn't and/or wouldn't: Word of the book's quality spread apparently by word of mouth and also by later lesbian scholars (and other researchers) who mentioned the pioneering work in footnotes or other references. And ironically, by the time Dr. Foster was over eighty, partially paralyzed, and living in a nursing home in Arkansas when most of the world assumed she must be long dead, the demand for her book had reached such proportions that Diana Press of Baltimore agreed to reprint it in the spring of 1976.

And so, Dr. Foster's lifelong work, her faith in that work, and her determination to have it published were not vain or vague dreams but were representative of the dreams and aspirations of many women. As a result, Jeannette Foster's struggle against closeted knowledge and an obstinate publishing industry has been won—not only for her but also for the many lesbians and feminist herstorians who have picked up and carried on the torch she so bravely lit for us.

Some Pulp Sappho

Fran Koski and Maida Tilchen

What am I then, some pulp Sappho? The library of cheap paperback Lesbian affairs full of sentiment I hoarded once because they were the only books where one woman kissed another, touched her, transported to read finally in a book what had been the dearest part of my experience recognized at last in print. Kept them hidden in a drawer so visitors would never spy me out. Afraid the sublet might find them, I burned them. . . . Really I was ashamed of them as writing, the treacle of their fantasy, the cliché of their predicament, heartbroken butch murders her dog, etc. The only blooms in the desert, they were also books about grotesques. [Kate Millett, *Flying*, New York: Ballantine Books, 1974, p. 202]

We collect dyke books. No, we don't mean the new lesbian-feminist ones fresh off today's woman's presses. Until just recently, writers on lesbian subjects had no alternative—like Daughters, Inc.—to the male-dominated publishing houses. During the 1950s and 60s, hundreds of lesbian novels were published—many as paperback originals—by companies like Fawcett-Crest, Midwood Tower, Beacon-Signal, and Macfadden-Bartell. Their packaging included lurid covers of pornographic appeal, bearing blurbs like "A Twilight Sin: Toni hid the truth of her physical craving under the surface of an attractive marriage and a successful career. It took a totally immoral and oversexed young actress to bring the truth into the open. . . ." (Rhoda Peterson, *A Twilight Sin*, [New York: Midwood Tower, 1965] back cover.) It is this exploitive packaging (which may or may not have anything to do with the contents of the book) that seems to be the reason many lesbians avert their eyes from our collection, for puritanical or political reasons. They don't know what they are missing. We've acquired and read over 200 pulp novels in the past year and feel like we've unearthed a fascinating heritage—a recent heritage which, in this era of Gay Liberation, is already being forgotten or deliberately buried.

It's true that there is much for today's lesbian feminist to object to in these books. You have to wade through stereotypes (seductive bitch,' violent butch) for the rare and memorable strong woman. Then there are the unimaginative plots whose narrow scope restricts the lesbian to an ingrown isolated society: as likely as not, it's gay Greenwich Village in the 1950s, or the bored suburbs of the same era.

There's also the issue of *male* authorship, editing, and control. Though many of the authors' names are unisex pseudonyms, it's not hard to guess when a pulp novel was probably written by a man for the titillation of men. Valerie Taylor, a (female) writer of several famous lesbian "pulps," tells of a man named Paul Little who claims to have written over 500 such novels under the name of Sylvia Sharon. A publisher's machismo, Ms. Taylor says, was often satisfied by "happy" (i.e., heterosexual) endings; hence the proliferation of the dilettante-dyke-returns-to-her-husband plot. It also seems to us that some of the novels intended by the author to end in fulfillment for the lesbian protagonist have been changed by the (male) editor to "punish" lesbians and teach that perversity doesn't pay. And we suspect that some basically fine novels of lesbian love have been routinely injected with voyeuristic sex scenes for salability; e.g., *Chris* seems to have sex scenes written in two different styles (Randy Salem, *Chris*, New York: Universal Publishing and Distributing, 1959)—though Gene Damon (Barbara Grier), an expert on this subject, maintains that it's usually poor writers, and not the editors, that make a trashy lesbian novel trashy.

Most disturbing, the lesbians in many of the pulps hate themselves, or think they should. They've internalized the homosexuality-as-sickness attitude of their time, and are forever coming up with explanations, such as "Daddy always wanted a boy" (in *Beebo Brinker*, by Ann Bannon), and, alas, sometimes even cures, like "a *real* man to love" (as in *The Strange Young Wife* by Kel Holland).

In *After School,* by Donna Powell (Detroit: Satan Press, 1966, pp. 81–2) a teenager who's just had her first sexual experience with a woman feels guiltless until her actions are labeled "lesbian." Suddenly society's stigma overcomes her own natural reaction of pleasure:

> We'd enjoyed ourselves and that was that—it was over and done with. No regrets. No shame. No guilt. It had been a natural thing, occurring because of natural desires, and now it was natural to be talking and laughing and drinking together like three natural human beings.
>
> And then Doris sort of dropped a word—"lesbian" —and in a flash my brain completely convoluted. I looked down at my hands and they looked all ugly and yellow. I smelled one hand and nearly retched. I wiped my mouth hard on my arm.
>
> I undressed, got in the shower. . . . Then I scrubbed myself. Everywhere. Even my mouth I washed with soap.
>
> "Lesbian! Lesbian! Lesbian!" I repeated, beginning to cry. And then I got sick and threw up all over my legs and feet. . . .

In the fifties the enemy was one's own "abnormality" and the recourse was self-destruction; alcoholism, suicide, and violence are rife in these books. Because their creators had no political vision, the lesbian characters are given none. The fact that lesbians are oppressed, that lesbians have the right to be themselves, that they deserve—as much as any other group—the rewards of this society or the chance to build a better one are beyond the imagination of a character who says, "I'm a genuine lesbian, truly twisted, and I know it . . . oh God, why am I a lesbian?" (Ann Herbert, *Summer Camp* [New York: Softcover Library, 1966,] p. 102). By the 1970s, lesbians have exchanged armchair psychology for political analysis; the enemy is now located *outside* the self, located in the oppressive society, and the recourse is positive political action. In *Small Changes*, Beth, a lesbian, says,

> What's best for us is not to let them use the courts to terrorize us. I believe in a separate women's movement so we can be in control of our own destiny and our own struggle. [Marge Piercy, *Small Changes* (Greenwich, Conn.: Fawcett-Crest, 1972), p. 493].

In books like *The Cook and the Carpenter* by June Arnold and *Riverfinger Women* by Eleana Nachman (published by the feminist-owned Daughters, Inc., press) lesbian-feminist characters create alternative societies or fight the existing one. These books are far more incisive and visionary than the fifties and sixties "pulps." They orient us toward structuralist critiques of the society that keeps us down, and they show us what we can be. But the pulps show us where we were, at least as far as literature reflects life. The historical accuracy and objective presentation of past lifestyles are always uncertain in fiction. We've unsuccessfully searched for, and someday hope to see, an opinion by a lesbian who lived in the era and milieu on the accuracy of the pulp presentation of gay life. Lacking confirmation, we try not to take the books at their literal word about the past, though they contain enough common elements and descriptions (of gay Greenwich village in the fifties, for instance) for us to consider them fairly accurate. But we don't expect them to be more accurate than any other fiction.

Within their narrow scope, these books have much to offer. We like the strong lesbian characters in some of them. Trapped though they may be in closety roles or preposterous plots, some nevertheless emerge as colorful, admirable, woman-identified women. The milieux, often the big city butch-femme bar scene of the fifties and sixties, revive for us—through the filter of fiction—a culture we've never experienced, we who came out in the seventies. Universal lesbian rites of passage like coming out or connecting with your first lesbian crowd are often told in sensitive ways. Finally, we turn to to the "pulps" for pure escape. Lesbian characters may live on a houseboat, have an affair with a movie star, or inhabit the hermetically sealed world of an all girls' school.

The Bars and the Butches

Differences in style aside, we as history-seekers feel that there are no "bad" as opposed to "good" lesbian pulp novels of the fifties and sixties; though we have our favorites, all are revealing or interesting in some way. Even the trashiest ones—not necessarily the ones with the most graphic sex but the ones that present lesbians as disgusting or unnatural creatures (not always written by men: see Sheila Donisthorpe or Ann Aldrich)—are fascinating documents for a lesbian truly interested in our history.

For lesbians coming out in the seventies, the old gay bar scene and the butch-femme role scene may be totally alien. If in the 1970s we want to forget the bars and the butches, then we are whitewashing our history as oppressively as the straights have rewritten it for us. We were curious about the recent past, and we found only the books of the fifties and sixties to explain it to us. When more lesbians see the importance of unearthing and examining our entire lesbian heritage, this heritage will become more readily available to today's lesbian.

Often the setting of fifties and sixties books includes a gay bar. The author's description of the bar can be part of the plot and theme of the book. In *Beebo Brinker* Ann Bannon lets Beebo find gay life a valid lifestyle for herself, so the bar scene is presented positively.

It was almost one in the morning when they left the co-ed bar and Jack asked if she was game for one more. "This one is just for lesbians," he said. She nodded, and a few minutes later they were being admitted to a basement bar saturated with pink light, panelled with mirrors, and filled with girls, more girls, more sizes, types, and ages than Beebo had ever seen collected in one place. The place was called the Colophon and it was decorated with the emblems of various famous publishing houses. [Ann Bannon,

266

Beebo Brinker (Greenwich, Connecticut; Gold Medal Books, 1962), p. 40]

In Valerie Taylor's *Whisper Their Love*, the protagonist decides to go back to men after seeing the ugliness of a gay bar:

The place, Club Marie, was a let-down. It looked like a dozen cheap joints she'd walked past, quickening her step, and turning her face away from the smell of stale beer, the bursts of laughter, the seamy-faced little old man who always seemed to be sitting on the doorstep. Only this one was brightly lighted. There were thin fluorescent tubes in the ceiling, parallel rows of them picking out glitters on the bottles and showing up the spills and dirt on the bartender's apron and the gummy places on the tables. [Valerie Taylor, *Whisper Their Love* (Greenwich, Connecticut: Gold Medal Books, 1957), p. 123].

In another Valerie Taylor novel, *Stranger on Lesbos* [Greenwich, Connecticut: Fawcett, 1960,] pp. 66–7) a bar is the scene of the alcoholism and violence often found in the pulps:

"Dance?"

She turned. A tall, thin woman of her own age stood beside her, dangling a cigarette from her veined hand. Frances said uncertainly, "I don't think so, thanks."

"She doesn't want to dance with you," Bake said.

. . . The thin woman looked Bake up and down, her eyebrows raised. "Are you married to the girl or something? I only asked her to dance."

Bake said between her teeth, "Will you go away?" She moved closer to the woman, who took an uncertain step backward and stood swaying a little on high heels. Oh, God, Frances thought, she's loaded too.

Mickey said, "Break it up, kids. Let's be friends."

"Friends; hell," Bake said. "Get out of here, you bitch." She laid her hand against the woman's flat chest and pushed. The other customer, caught off balance, went down gradually, like someone in a slow-motion film. There was a sickening thud as her head struck the edge of the bar. . . .

Fixtures in all bar scenes include the bar butch. In *Whisper Their Love* one bar butch explains herself:

She was nineteen, Bobbie said, and had lived on a farm in southeastern Missouri until her folks died, a couple of years ago. "I always liked to work in the fields, and fool around with animals and stuff. Pa always said I was the best hired man he had." She had never had a date when she was in school, never thought about boys much. . . .

It was while she was living with Karla that she decided to change over to men's clothes. She went to a man's barber shop and got her hair cut. "Real short, you know, he like to scalped me. Now I like this here D.A. better, it's got more style, I always wanted to be a boy from the time I was little. Boys get all the breaks. . . ."

Anitra asked, "Didn't you ever go to bed with a man?"

"Sure, I'll try anything once. Didn't mean a thing to me," Bobbie said proudly. "If you're a real butch you don't get hot for men. Only sometimes they're okay to have around for buddies, like Doc here. I could go for him in a strictly platonic way. Not for lovin' though—uh-huh . . ." [Valerie Taylor, *Whisper Their Love*, Greenwich, Connecticut: Fawcett, 1957, pp. 125–127]

Femmes also are found on the bar stools of the pulps. They are invariably slender and sad, as in *Strange Are the Ways of Love* by Lesley Evans:

She was beautiful. She was tall with silky red-brown hair that fell to her shoulders and framed her face. There was a deep, haunting sadness in her eyes and a constrained beauty in her face that . . . could

268

only accompany unhappiness. She sat at a table near the dance floor . . . her body was a good one, slender but with full curves.

. . . Her name was Laura Dean. She was twenty-three years old, and she had spent four of those years at a girl's prep school and four more at a girls' college. . . .

Her father was the only man she ever really knew. She lived with him in a big stone house in upper Westchester county ever since he divorced her mother for infidelity. . . . She cried a great deal when he died. . . . She fell in love with her French teacher and spent many hours talking with her and more hours thinking of her in secret.

The following year she danced with her roommate at the school dances and kissed her several times in their room with the door shut.

The year after that she began sleeping with another girl, a senior.

Since then she had gone with many girls, too many to remember. After she graduated from college she moved immediately to the Village. [Lesley Evans, *Strange Are the Ways of Love*, (Greenwich, Connecticut: Fawcett, 1959), pp. 31–34.]

Strong Lesbian Characters

Perhaps the greatest attraction these books hold for us is the lesbian character. Vicki Lennox in Dallas Mayo's *Silky* (New York: Midwood Tower, 1961) is one of many such women. A professional photographer on the staff of *Glimpse* magazine, Vicki is self-made and successful. ("*Glimpse*'s circulation increased with every picture layout she did, and within recent years the judges of various contests had paid her full measure of tribute," p. 32). Almost entirely independent of men, strong and seasoned, Vicki is nevertheless not a stereotypical butch.

For all her masculine adaptation to hard work and her customary attire of tailored slacks, in appearance she was not an unfeminine female. . . . There was a

slim shapeliness to Vicki that was extremely fetching.
[pp. 33.34]

Vicki initiates Silky into lesbianism in a kind and loving way, after Silky has thrown herself at her. By the end of the novel Vicki has a fulfilling and stable relationship with Julie, a nightclub singer who, though she is Vicki's femme ("Julie [was] completely feminine, while Vicki emphasized . . . mannish ways", p. 134) is also her equal as a self-supporting career woman. Vicki Lennox is a good example of the independent, positively drawn lesbian character leading a rewarding life. It is interesting to note that such good lesbian role models can be found in the works of authors like Dallas Mayo, whose generally lewd novels one might be inclined to dismiss wholesale.

A notable paperback fictional lesbian is Leo (Leonora) Lane in Mary Renault's exquisite novel *The Middle Mist* (New York: Avon Books, 1945). Leo leaves the sterile respectability of her parent's home for life on a houseboat with her lover, Helen. Quiet, capable, analytical, lanky, and androgynous, Leo supports herself by writing cowboy novels. A complex and delicately drawn character, Leo is strong not only in her independence but also in that she is brave enough to question herself, face her own fears, and ultimately change her life at the cost of great pain. If the ending of *The Middle Mist* is ambiguous at best and anti-lesbian at worst, Leo nevertheless emerges as a marvelous and unforgettable lesbian character.

Rites of Passage

Art is supposed to be about recognizing one's self in a universal experience. There are experiences which, by their very nature, all lesbians share and only lesbians can experience. These include a woman's making lesbian love with a woman for the first time, admitting and seeing one's self as gay, and fitting in with a dyke crowd. In the novels of the fifties and sixties we have found many beautiful descriptions of these universally shared events. In the straight world, shared events are often validated and ritualized by ceremonies like weddings or club initiations. For

270

lesbians, there are no ceremonies. Only through art can we share our experiences.

> Her smooth belly rounded when she inhaled, hollowed as she exhaled. Her thighs looked sleek as marble and at the same time soft as a cloud. There was a small vein in her creamy throat which beat with the rhythm of her heart.
>
> I slid onto the bed next to her. My hands touched her belly, then came seeking upward toward a breast.
>
> "Penny."
>
> My hands stopped. "What, Bernice?"
>
> "Mark," she said. "He called you a lesbian."
>
> I said nothing.
>
> "Penny—isn't a lesbian a girl who likes other girls?"
>
> "Yes," I said. . . .
>
> "So—" I could feel her body breathing beneath my palm—"if she wants to have sex, she must have it with another woman. Is that correct?"
>
> "Yes."
>
> "And if she wants to love somebody—wants somebody to love her—" the breathing became more rapid—"then that somebody must also be a woman. Is that what a lesbian is?"
>
> "Yes," I said.
>
> She shifted her shoulders, inched her body down the sheets, and suddenly a warm, soft breast had been delivered into my hand.
>
> "Then I'm a lesbian," she said simply.
>
> We fell together and spent the rest of the night proving it. [Jesse Dumont, *I Prefer Girls* (Derby, Connecticut: Monarch Books, 1963), p. 95.]

The first venture into a lesbian bar is an experience often described in the pulps as exhilarating:

> The other bars had been all male or mixed. In this one, Jack Mann and the two bartenders . . . were the only men in a big room solidly packed with women. It excited Beebo intensely—all that femininity. She

was silent, studying the girls at the table. . . . For the first time in her life she was proud of her size, proud of her strength, even proud of her oddly boyish face. She could see interest, even admiration on the faces of many of the girls. She was not used to that kind of reaction in people, and it exhilarated her. But she didn't talk much, only answering direct questions when she had to; smiling at them when they smiled at her; looking away in confusion when one or another tried to stare her down. . . .

. . . The floor was jammed with a mass of couples, a mass of girls dancing. . . . There was no shame, no shock, no self-consciousness about it at all. They were enjoying themselves. They were having fun in the most natural way imaginable. They were all in love, or so it seemed. They were—what had Jack called it?—gay.

Beebo watched them for less than a minute, all told; but a minute that was transfixed like a living picture in her mind for the rest of her life. She was startled by it, afraid of it. She was obsessed momentarily by the desire to grab the girl nearest her and kiss her. [Ann Bannon, *Beebo Brinker*, pp. 41–42]

Jean looked about them. A group of girls had entered, most of them in pairs. They seemed to be tourists—but tourists with a difference. They were all women, and obviously Lesbians. Several of them were very attractive. One blonde girl had the face of an eagle, with an aquiline nose and high cheekbones, her curly hair short-cropped against her head. Joan's arms and legs grew cold with desire. She did not understand her feelings, but they were so intense she wanted to faint. She felt, somehow, that she should be honest, that she shouldn't hide anymore, that she should somehow try to join the women who were to her so compellingly beautiful—the Lesbians. [Artemis Smith, *The Third Sex* (New York: Softcover Library, 1969), p. 13]

These scenes and the many more they exemplify feel good to us. They record rites, necessary "firsts" we've all been through, validating and enriching our common and individual experience. We feel, as Kate Millett wrote, "transported to read finally in a book what had been the dearest part of [our] experience." That these passages predate the existence of women's presses and are often found between unprepossessing or lurid paperback covers makes them all the more precious to us. They are found passages about fictional lost women.

How We Get the Books

We've collected about 200 of these books this year. Almost none of them is still in print. We got our copies at used paperback bookstores. Finding books is like finding treasure, which is why it's fun. You look through thousands of books and find maybe ten you'll buy—but then you can have a great time reading those ten. We found all our books in central Indiana, so it's not necessary to look only in cities, although you'll find more used bookstores in a city. Prices are low, too—our collection cost an average of $ .50 per book.

For collecting, we recommend the fantastic bibliography *The Lesbian in Literature* by Gene Damon and Lee Stuart. With it you can know quickly if you have a relevant book or not—very few books have the word "lesbian" in the title. Also, in the last few years many essentially straight novels have had lesbian subplots or characters—for example, Jacqueline Susann's *Once is Not Enough*. The inclusion of lesbian subplots or characters is often not indicated by the title or cover blurbs, so this incredibly complete bibliography is very useful.

The 1967 edition of *The Lesbian in Literature* includes all lesbian books—known to the authors—that were copyrighted before 1967. A brand new 1975 edition, by Gene Damon, Jan Watson, and Robin Jordan, runs to January 15, 1975. It can be purchased for $10 from Naiad Press, 7800 Westside Drive, Weatherby Lake, Missouri 64152.

The 1967 bibliography is a full-bloomed version of earlier efforts. It contains some 5,000 entries. It is not annotated, but uses a rating system. Books are rated A: major lesbian characters or action; B: minor lesbian characters or action; C: latent, repressed lesbian characters (often called "variant" by writers on this subject); and T: trashy quality books. In the 1975 edition the books rated "T" were dropped for the most part, and many nonfiction titles were added. Since we believe that art and value are wherever you find them, we're sorry to see the "T" category dropped. Frankly, if we came across a copy of *Strange Nurse* by Arthur Adlon or *Darkroom Dyke* by Les Cooper (both T's) we wouldn't kick them out of bed. As we've noted in this article, you can find passages worth reading if you look for them. Although we regret the disappearance of the "T" category, we've found *The Lesbian in Literature* bibliography invaluable and we use both the 1967 and 1975 editions when we go book hunting.

There's very little written about this genre of pulp lesbian literature. The Jeannette Foster book, *Sex Variant Women in Literature,* includes some discussion of paperback originals. (Foster's unique book was reissued by Diana Press in 1976.) In Betty Wysor's *The Lesbian Myth* there is a brief mention of the genre.

The availability of many excellent feminist press lesbian novels means no one need seek major lesbian characters and plots only in the often grotesque and rarely feminist pulps. Still, these books shaped and also reflect the 1950s and 1960s societal stereotypes of the lesbian, many of which survive today. If to become a revolution a movement must change *everyone's* consciousness, then it is important for political- and change-oriented dykes to be aware of the progression, or lack thereof, in public attitudes towards lesbianism. Familiarity with the "pulps" can enrich such a study.

The Poetry of Male Love

by Ian Young

"A gay poem is one that's sexually attracted to other poems"—William Barber

There is a gay cultural, and specifically a gay literary, tradition which informs and is an important part of the cultural history of the West (and of the East as well). Although this tradition is neither unworthy nor insignificant, it has been routinely neglected, dismissed, or ridiculed by straight critics and cultural historians (and even by gays themselves), with only a few exceptions.

The need of gays to know and draw on and identify with their past is still being brushed aside as "the 'all-great-men-*were*' (gay) syndrome," as something defensive and ridiculous. But gays' ignorance of and amputation from their past is merely another facet of the general isolation that straight Judeo-Christian society (including its secularized modern forms such as Marxism) imposes on those whose selfhood is self-defined and whose sexuality, by its very nature, leads them toward values other than the prescribed preoccupation with hierarchy, work, production, and maximum security.

It is a particularly numbing part of the societal attempt to anesthetize gay sensibilities to replace them with implanted, synthetic organs, with more "moral" (i.e., orthodox, controllable, and immediately practical) motivations.

Psychological oppression relies on the lack of self-confidence, and even self-knowledge, by the oppressed group. A person who feels guilty and ashamed of what he or she is—whether black, gypsy, heretic, or homosexual—is far easier to control than one who feels the support and solidarity of past ages, and who is therefore more able to surmise and construct his own future possibilities.

A sense of the past, of its own past, is infinitely valuable to any group that feels the need to define itself and to

275

create or develop a sense of community. A knowledge of gay history and culture, and especially of gay literature, is worthwhile not only to put the larger questions of cultural development in their right perspective, but to help individuals now to realize themselves, to see, and to act.

The gay tradition in poetry is a substantial one, more so in cultures other than the Western. The Greek, Persian, Arabic, and Japanese cultures all produced openly homoerotic verse, whereas in Europe the fervid morbidities of Christianity led to the suppression of gay writing, or at best its concealment by the alteration of gender—a sort of literary sex change.

Many of Byron's poems are typical examples of this dissimulation. Some of his love poems, such as "The Cornelian," are obviously addressed to males; in many the gender of the beloved has been changed. Still others, including the "Thyrza" poems lamenting the early death of the Trinity College chorister John Edelston, are ambiguous:

> Without a stone to mark the spot
>> And say what Truth might well have said,
> By all, save one, perchance forgot,
>> Ah! wherefore art thou lowly laid?
>
> By many a shore and many a sea
>> Divided, yet beloved in vain:
> The past, the future fled to thee
>> To bid us meet—no—ne'er again!
> . . .
>
>> But when no more
> 'Twas thine to reck of human woe,
> Affection's heart-drops, gushing o'er,
>> Had flow'd as fast—as now they flow.
>
> Shall they not flow, when many a day
>> In these, to me, deserted towers,
> Ere call'd but for a time away,
>> Affection's mingling tears were ours?

Ours too the glance none saw beside,
　The smile none else might understand;
The whisper'd thought of hearts allied,
　The pressure of the thrilling hand:

The kiss, so guiltless and refined
　That Love each warmer wish forbore;
Those eyes proclaim'd so pure a mind,
　Each passion blush'd to plead for more.

The tone, that taught me to rejoice,
　When prone, unlike thee, to repine;
　The song, celestial from thy voice,
　But sweet to me from none but thine;
　. . .

Teach me—too early taught by thee!
　To bear, forgiving and forgiven:
On earth thy love was such to me,
　It fain would form my hope in heaven!

It has been a conundrum for many writers, before Byron's time and after, whether to equivocate or falsify gay
sentiments in a work and thereby perhaps reach and affect
more people, or to be honest and make a truer, stronger
statement, knowing that many will block on the homosexuality and reject the work for that reason.

Critics, although they have addressed themselves to the
most minute and recondite points of style and interpretation, have rarely examined this question and almost never
given it the attention it deserves. The gay element in
poetry, when not denied outright or explained away, is
seen as trivial or trivializing (though heterosexuality is
never viewed that way). As homosexuality is considered
rare, freakish, pathological, and bad, to mention a poet's
homosexuality or to say that a poem is a "gay poem" is to
damage it, to diminish its value as art. Art lovers become
incensed. Yet if *Wuthering Heights* or *Doctor Zhivago* can
be considered, among other things, great "love stories"
(read: heterosexual love stories), why should Tennyson's
In Memoriam for Arthur Hallam or Hart Crane's "Voy-

ages," for his sailor lover, not be considered, among other things, "gay poems"?

"In the world of poetry," Charley Shively wrote in the Boston gay journal *Fag Rag*, "no 'gay' poem can be 'serious' unless it applies to the world of straight white men; otherwise it is supposedly less than universal. . . . One poetry magazine," he added, "rejected my 'License to Innocence' by saying that 'gay' love is not accurate enough for one who attends to words. I guess everyone knows what the 'accurate kind of love' is. . . ."

The unorthodox vision of homosexuality is connected to the kind of fresh and individual perception that is at the core of all good poetry; yet even today, the poet is pressured by publishers, editors, critics, readers, and his or her own internalized stigmata of guilt to deny the gay emotions that are often the heart, body, and breath of the poetic experience.

In spite of this, gay poetry has managed to flower in the West, especially during two periods of the past century: from the 1860s until the 1910s or early 1920s, and from the late 1960s (after the rise of gay liberation) to the present. The early pioneers of the tradition, unlike many of their successors, were unconnected with any literary groups or circles of similar interests. They include Tennyson in England and Walt Whitman and Bayard Taylor in America. Taylor, popular in his day but now for the most part forgotten, was a great traveler, and his many poems with strong underlying motifs of male love include many imitations or pseudoimitations of Persian and Arabic poems: a good excuse, or disguise, for otherwise taboo sentiments.

But it was Whitman who provided the strongest influence (though more thematic than stylistic) on the many English homosexual poets of the last part of the nineteenth century. His "ideal of democracy" based on homoerotic affections was seen to supplement and update the Socratic vision, and his outspokenness gave others courage. His most notable devotees in Britain were his avowed (and more self-aware) disciple Edward Carpenter, and the Renaissance scholar and biographer of Michelangelo, John Addington Symonds.

Symonds frowned on the "decadence" of Oscar Wilde and his circle, who were influenced by Swinburne, Baudelaire, and the French symbolists, and whose sensuous aestheticism and flirtations with death, danger, evil, and "sin" he considered unhealthy. He felt about Wilde as Winston Churchill quipped about an unpopular Labour Member of Parliament, that he was "the sort of man who gives sodomy a bad name!" The bombastically robust Whitman was more to the taste of the serious, tubercular Symonds.

A passage in Symonds's poem in homage to Whitman, quoted in Brian Reade's *Sexual Heretics*, shows not only Symonds's Whitmanism but his use of what Reade calls "Greco-Medieval chivalrous fantasy" as well:

There shall be comrades thick as flowers that crown
Valdarno's gardens in the morn of May;
On every upland and in every town
Their dauntless imperturbable array,
Serried like links of living adamant
By the sole law of love their wills obey,
Shall make the world one fellowship, and plant
New Paradise for nations yet to be.
O nobler peerage than that ancient vaunt
Of Arthur or of Roland! Chivalry
Long sought, last found! Knights of the Holy Ghost!
Phalanx Immortal! True Freemasonry,
Building your temples on no earthly coast,
But with star-fire on souls and hearts of man
Stirred from their graves to greet your Sacred Host
The Theban lovers, rising very wan,
By death made holy, wave dim palms, and cry:
"Hail, Brothers! who achieve what we began!"
Thou dost establish—and our hearts receive—
New laws of Love to link and intertwine
Majestic peoples; Love to weld and weave
Comrade to comrade, man to bearded man,
Whereby indissoluble hosts shall cleave
Unto the primal truths republican.

"All that is very well," Reade comments, "but knowing, as we do, about John Addington Symonds, it is difficult not to repress a smile at the thought of clashing beards and tinkling watch-chains as the comrades become more and more republican. Symonds was not without a sense of humour; yet here he shared with the French generals of fifty years back a solemn innocence of the English Eye.

"The idea of chivalry between men, and between men and youths or boys, or even between boys, survived a whole half-century, to emerge again in [Charles] Kains-Jackson's article 'The New Chivalry', published in 1894. . . ." Edward Fitzgerald's *Euphranor: A Dialogue on Youth* (1851) had also set forth ethical notions of chivalry as applied to male friendships.

Both Symonds and Whitman's other great champion in Britain, Edward Carpenter, wrote books explaining and defending gay love: see Symonds's *A Problem in Greek Ethics* and *A Problem in Modern Ethics*, and Carpenter's *The Intermediate Sex* and *Intermediate Types among Primitive Folk*. Carpenter was a refugee from the nonconformist clergy who, along with his writing and lecturing, applied himself to market-gardening, sandal-making, and the preaching of anarchist socialism—sustained by a private income. In many ways he was ahead of his time, though his kind-hearted enthusiasms sometimes carried him into dubious territory. *Love's Coming of Age* and other books reflected many of the concerns (and fads) of "progressive intellectuals" in his day and now ours: socialism, feminism, "natural foods," interest in Oriental philosophy, and, of course, the "intermediate sex." Carpenter's book of poems, *Towards Democracy*, gave voice to these issues, sometimes eloquently, in a style heavily influenced by Whitman.

Other poets of homosexual love in England at this time (some more overt than others) included William Johnson Cory, Digby Mackworth Dolben, Gerard Manley Hopkins, Roden Noel, Edward Cracroft Lefroy, John Gambril Nicholson, and the loosely connected group of writers who sometimes referred to themselves as "Calamites" or "Uranians." Quite a few printed their homosexual poems themselves, for private distribution to friends; the work of others was suppressed and not published until years later.

Many of these poets (and poetasters) were schoolmasters or clergymen. And the works of at least two prominent churchmen of the time, John Henry Newman and Frederick William Faber, reveal strong underlying homosexual preoccupations. In many writers, and especially in many of the Victorian writers, the religious impulse and the homosexual impulse were deeply meshed. The spiritual struggles of such men as Newman, Hopkins, Faber, and Dolben, their idealistic striving and yearning for beauty and love, remained enmeshed in Christian injunctions, restrained by social convention, and channeled into acceptably orthodox (and celibate) pursuits. Dolben died young; the others became pillars of the Roman Catholic Church.

Other poets, like Stenbock, Raffalovich, and Crowley, with no deep interest in religion, still found the exigencies of Victorian society deeply frustrating and hurtful, and took refuge in the self-consciously sinister. The seemingly uncomplicated idealism of such writers as Lefroy and Symonds appeared here in frustrated or repressed form, as morbidity and longing for death. The trappings and rituals of religion were often used either to appease God or to flout him; often, as in the case of the occult and pagan preoccupations of Father Montague Summers, it is difficult to tell which.

Paganism (often closer to Satanism) and idealized versions of Classical Greece, the Middle Ages, and the ritual and code of Christianity often provided the homosexual poets of the time with the vehicles to justify the ways of man to God, and to other men. All these influences combined and found expression in the work of Oscar Wilde, with such poems as The "Sphinx," "Hélas," "Santa Decca," "Wasted Days," "In the Forest," "Désespoir," and "Charmides." Though stylistically derivative, Wilde's poetry was, in spite of that, highly personal and distinctive, and illuminated the concerns of many (especially homosexual) poets of the time, perhaps more than that of any other single writer.

The attitude of these poets to the boys and men who attracted them was generally one of concern and love—sometimes earnest, sometimes playful, occasionally maudlin, but almost never cynical. As a group, they displayed the repression, religiosity, sentimentality, and "high ideals" of the Victorian period, yet also the incipient breakup of those conventions by deeply individualistic and erotic forces behind the dangerous desire for greater freedom.

Victorian society's reaction to all of this varied from embarrassment and shock (as seen by contemporary responses to Tennyson's *In Memoriam*, including *The Time*'s stuffy harrumphing), to simple censorship, to naïveté (the same newspaper's benign approbation of the Rev. E. E. Bradford's series of sunny pederastic narrative fantasies), to . . . the sentencing of Oscar Wilde to two years' hard labor.

The Wilde scandal put a brake on the rise of gay literature and was part of a generally philistine climate that frightened such men as Henry James, Thomas Hardy, and A. E. Housman, and made all but the most blatantly "hearty" writing suspect.

One of the few not to be intimidated (along with Edward Carpenter) was Aleister Crowley, who published his book of exuberantly erotic poems, *White Stains*, in 1898, only a year after Wilde's release from prison. (Most of the copies were later destroyed by Her Majesty's Customs and the book was not reprinted until 1973, again in a limited edition.) Crowley loathed the pious grundyism of the time and took a childish delight in shocking the respectable. He could also display romanticism and (a characteristic of Crowley's often forgotten today) a genuine tenderness.

AT KIEL

Oh, the white flame of limbs in dusky air,
　　The furnace of thy great gray eyes on me,
　　Turned till I shudder. Darkness on the sea,
And wan ghost-lights are flickering everywhere
So that the world is ghastly. But within
　　Where we two cling together, and hot kisses
　　Stray to and fro amid the wildernesses
Of swart curled locks! I deem it a sweet sin,
So sweet that fires of hell have no more power
　　On body and soul to quench the lustrous flame
　　Of that desire that burns between us twain.

What is Eternity, seeing we hold this hour
    For all the lusts and luxuries of shame?*
    Heaven is well lost for this surpassing gain.

Crowley's "Go into the highways and Hedges and compel them to *come in*" strikes a different note, but is equally defiant:

Let my fond lips but drink thy golden wine,
    My bright-eyed Arab, only let me eat
    The rich brown globes of sacramental meat
Steaming and firm, hot from their home divine,
And let me linger with thy hands in mine,
    And lick the sweat from dainty dirty feet
    Fresh with the loose aroma of the street,
And then anon I'll glue my mouth to thine.
This is the height of joy, to lie and feel
    Thy spicéd spittle trickle down my throat;
This is more pleasant than at dawn to steal
    Towards lawns and sunny brooklets, and to gloat
    Over earth's peace, and hear in ether float
Songs of soft spirits into rapture peal.

Crowley was obviously one of the most shockingly uninhibited poets of his time, but in the main the English and

* The word "shame" used here and in a number of gay poems of the time was a code indicating male love. It appears in two poems by Lord Alfred Douglas which were quoted at Wilde's first "trial" (the trial for libel of Lord Queensbury). "Two Loves" features a conversation between two youthful spirits in a garden, each claiming to be "Love." The figure representing heterosexual love accuses the other of being an impostor:

'He lieth, for his name is Shame,
But I am Love, and I was wont to be
Alone in this fair garden, till he came
Unasked by night; I am true Love, I fill
The hearts of boy and girl with mutual flame.'
Then sighing, said the other, 'Have thy will,
I am the love that dare not speak its name.'

The second poem, "In Praise of Shame," has as its last line, "Of all sweet passions Shame is loveliest." There is, interestingly, the suggestion of masochism as well as social stigma.

American poets have been more timid than the Europeans in expressing homosexual sentiments. Cavafy, Stefan George, Kuzmin, Anatoly Steiger, Fernando Pessoa, Cocteau, Sandro Penna, Genet were all relatively outspoken in a time when poets in England were still hiding and hinting. In large measure the Victorian legacy, the Wilde trial, and its aftermath of philistinism were responsible.

One of the very few English poets who refused to equivocate or conceal was Ralph Chubb (1892-1960), a visionary poet-painter who lived as a semirecluse and aspired to be a gay twentieth-century William Blake, a prophet of a spiritual, pederastic future age. His books were self-published in large, handsome, extremely limited editions which he handprinted and illustrated.

Another isolated figure (and strongly gay poetry in English was for forty or fifty years largely the province of a few isolated figures) was Frank Oliver Call, a professor of modern languages at the University of Bishop's College, Quebec. His chapbook *Sonnets for Youth* (1944), a small collection of delicate and charming poems to one of his students, harks back to the Calamite poets of the 1890s and (stylistically) to the Georgians of 1910-20.

From the 1930s through the 1950s, it was the novelists rather than the poets who pioneered in their treatment of homosexual themes. The few American exceptions such as Allen Ginsberg and John Wieners employed, in those years, a tormented if not apologetic tone. Of the better known poets, only Paul Goodman was able to write on gay themes in a positive and matter-of-fact way.

As the "agonized" stage began to be left behind and some poets began to be more open and accepting about their own gayness, the charge of "sentimentality" was often leveled at them (as it was at gay novelists—and even composers and choreographers!). It is still a favorite term of opprobrium for straight critics attacking gay artists; to treat of homosexuality without handwringing or cynicism is to be "sentimental." Dancer Edward Androse, in an interview with *Gay Sunshine,* talked about this. When asked about American ballet's tendency to play it safe (and straight), "expand the appeal," and avoid exploring taboos, he said, "No one wants to deal with specifics. If you deal with specifics, they call it 'obvious,' 'blatant,' or 'sentimental.' I want to do it anyway. Really *say* what I want to say. . . . You've got to remember who's reviewing you. They're closet cases and straights, writing for a predominantely mass-market, straight audience who are still unliberated in sexual and artistic terms."

To quote James Baldwin, "People do not take the relations between men and boys seriously, you know that. . . . They do not believe there can be tears between men. They think we are only playing at a game and that we do it to shock them."

One gay poet, Robert Duncan, has written:

"Sentimentality" is often the accusation brought by the critic when he would refuse some experience or ideal arising in the poem that does not satisfy or support his personal world of values but would threaten, if it were allowed, to undo that world. The word *sentimental* means "supposed" experience, I suppose. "You do not really feel that" or "you are letting your feelings get away with you" is the reproof often where we would not like to allow the feeling detected to advance, lest we feel what the advancing feeling brings with it. Much of modern criticism of poetry is not to raise a crisis in our consideration of the content or to deepen our apprehension of the content, but to dismiss the content. When such critics would bring the flight of imagination down to earth, they mean not the earth men revered and worked with love and awe, the imagined earth, but the real estate modern man has made of earth for his own uses.

In a time when "black" or bland emotions have come to dominate poetry, in understandable rejection of the popularly "poetic" and conventionally reassuring, gay poets are coming out in the open with something positive; they want to celebrate with words their gayness, their insights, and their humanity. Defeatism, always on the defensive, feels threatened, sexually and artistically, by what it is unable to believe in, and coupled with homophobia and ordinary philistinism condemns any positive expression of gayness as false sentiment, "sentimentality."

Sidney Abbott and Barbara Love in their book *Sappho Was a Right-On Woman* recall:

Isabel Miller, author of *Patience and Sarah,* a positive book about two lesbians who lived in the nineteenth century, said that for years she found publishers unwilling to accept the plot, even though they gave her otherwise favorable comments. . . . She says publishers wouldn't touch her novel because there was not enough tension, not enough conflict. In her own words, "What they really wanted to know was when does the horrible stuff start? They wanted misery."

It took the gay liberation and women's liberation movements of the late sixties and the seventies to draw a large number of (mostly young) poets out. And several poets who had already published openly gay work were active in starting gay liberation groups: Perry Brass in New York, Jim Eggeling in Texas, Ian Young and Paul Maurice in Canada. These younger, openly gay writers are in the main more interested in life-oriented poetry than in academism, technical "experimentation" for its own sake, or purely literary concerns. They tend to identify more with the gay community than with the literary community, and their personal, experience-oriented approach is reaching far more readers than most other poetry.

Here is Gavin Dillard's "may we place down our arrows":

may we place down our arrows?
i am a bow before you
my back arched, not unlike a halloween cat

i am placed before you my hands outstretched for
    yours
your palms downward

touch my forehead and cover my eyes
adding dignity to your reply

soft beneath you, putty
angels soft inside your hands
my teeth force me to be as a trapped wasp or
    hornet
but my tongue to sooth the sting
the pain it will bring as calming as your breath in
    my head

Perry Brass's "The heart does not care":

The heart does not care.
It breaks and leaves.
Like a door opened
to the evening breeze
rushing through and then gone;

as a moment
of intense movement,
heartlessly, artlessly
caring and then leaving,

breaking. Then silence
once more resumes, until dishes,
car horns, clatter back
in the wake, but the heart

does not care; it breaks
and leaves the broken moment
for the whole body
to bear.

Lee Harwood's "For John in the Mountains":

In a mountain sun
pursued by my own phantoms
monsters lurking in the forest
in my head

an innocent forest out there
mountain flowers and meadows
the swirl of grass and pines hissing

at each open bush a terror
behind me a dark snow
darker than your eyes'
dark snow
in which some flowers
can grow into me
a night when your river
could have left its bed
a desert awakening
a maniac pyramid
settle into a newness

your kiss holds such towns

and a poem from the gay anthology *The Male Muse,*
"Honi Soit Qui Mal y Pense":

A boy of fifteen,
he wore a jacket, dark shirt, wool tie,
his bright eyes studying earnestly
Androcles and the Lion
in the Shavian alphabet . . .
His friend, a few years older,
blond and bundled in overcoat and scarf,
carried a flute
as they sat at the next table
of a café in Toronto.
My friend knew the younger boy
and I asked her who they were.
"He used to be a nice, ordinary kid,"
she said; "Then he met *him*—Brett.
Brett took him to Montreal,
did things to him . . . I don't know . . .
they're fags . . . you know . . . Music Room types."
When they left, they were laughing.
planning how to spend Brett's paypacket.

288

I noticed they'd written Shavian
all over the serviettes.
That's what corruption does for you.

A process of personal struggle, growth, and change is
reflected in much of the new gay poetry, not only by
younger writers, but by more established poets like Robert
Peters, Kenneth Pitchford, and John Wieners.

Irving Layton has written,

> It seems to me that blacks, women and "the dear love
> of comrades" are creating some of the best, some of
> the most moving and powerful poems of our era. I
> suppose it has something to do with having something
> urgent to say. . . . I must add, however, that humor
> and the feeling of confidence that one is supported by
> a long and venerable tradition give the gays the edge
> over the two, too embattled as they are for the poise
> or detachment that good poetry demands. Or might it
> be something else which puts them out in front—the
> grand theme of love? Though one can write weakly or
> sentimentally about love one can never when writing
> about it disown common humanity as so many of the
> black writers and the sisterhood do. . . .

There are a few rare writers (the late Joe Ackerley was
one) whose each work is a masterpiece, a unique book,
and, among the younger gay poets, Tom Meyer is
certainly in that category. He has published four books to
date: *The Bang Book*, witty, exuberant cowboy fantasies;
Poikilos, a handful of exquisite small sensual impressions;
O Nathan ("excerpts from the book of Jonathan"), funny
erotic fragments of devotion; and a complete issue of a
magazine called *Aggie Weston's* devoted to a sequence of
lush and tactile nature poems. Meyer's work blends heart
and craft beautifully into rare heart-craft that can exhila-
rate and transform even a casual reader.
Another unique creation is Kirby Congdon's *Dream-
Work*, a collection of hallucinatory motorcycle fantasies
which is becoming something of an underground classic:

THE CROWD GATHERED ON THE MEMORIAL HOLIDAY

The crowd gathered on the memorial holiday at different vantage points around the sharp turn on the cliff's edge as the motorcyclists, every now and then, came roaring down the steep hill, turned off the shoulder at the curve and spun out into space. Some clung to their machines as an almost sexual unit, and others flung their arms in the air and separated from their bikes like high-divers, arching out over the tree tops and down out of sight to the rocks below.

Some of the performers let out a last minute cry of terror, or sucked in a sob caught in their throats. But this natural and human response only prompted the shy ones to accept their private election and soon followed their heroes to a similar fulfillment.

Through all this, the women spectators wept, but most of them men displayed crotches that were soaked, and were hardly ever seen with their hands out of their pockets.

. . .

JOY RIDE

All eight of us, shaved, scrubbed, our best uniforms on, jammed ourselves into the car, dressed fit to kill.

We didn't crash. The car ran into a comparatively shallow canal and wasn't even dented. We drowned, one by one, clutching at each other. It was great.

Meyer and Congdon, like many of the new gay poets, have been published exclusively by small presses. The commercial publishing houses, not very enthusiastic about any kind of poetry, even the most respectable, have largely shunned gay poets.

A commercially published anthology of openly gay

poetry by established writers was not possible until 1973, four years after the New York Stonewall riot had symbolized the beginning of the second, more militant stage of the gay movement. For some of the writers included in *The Male Muse*, appearance there was a public coming out. Others had appeared years before in the early homophile publications *One* and *Mattachine Review*, which printed gay verse and published occasional poetry issues and pamphlets. During the late sixties and the seventies, gay liberation journals like *Gay Sunshine* (San Francisco), *Fag Rag* (Boston), *Gay Liberator* (Detroit), and *The Body Politic* (Toronto) included poetry of high quality (though not without opposition from some staff members who regarded art as usually sexist, irrelevant to "the struggle" or even "counterrevolutionary"; fortunately, the antiart forces lost their battle, at least in *Fag Rag* and *Gay Sunshine*, the two most vital of the U.S. gay journals). *Gay Sunshine* has become a kind of cultural organ of American gay lib, and one of the most consistently readable and interesting periodicals in North America.

Little magazines, originating for the most part in California and New York, provided the other outlet for gay poetry in America in the sixties—magazines such as *Evergreen*, Jim Kepner's *Pursuit*, James Mitchell's *Sebastian Quill*, Ed Sanders's *Fuck You: A Magazine of the Arts*, Paul Mariah's and Richard Tagett's *Manroot*, and Harold Norse's *Bastard Angel*. All these helped pave the way for *The Male Muse* and other projects in the seventies such as Andrew Bifrost's *Mouth of the Dragon*, "a poetry journal of male love," and Winston Leyland's *Gay Sunshine*-based anthology, *Angels of the Lyre*. There have also been some serious gay poetry workshops and other groups—Boston's "Good Gay Poets," for example. Lesbian writers have been energetic and successful in books and anthologies, and other small presses, including Panjandrum in San Francisco, Some of Us Press in Washington, D. C., and Catalyst in Toronto, have each published a number of gay works.

Certainly it is possible for gay poets in the seventies to feel part of an artistic community and part of a real community of readers (not just "poetry-lovers") as few other poets in our age do. And a larger audience is beginning to be reached by up-front gay songwriter poets and rock singers like Chris Robinson, Mike Cohen, and Steve Grossman.

In an age when poetry is no longer a "public art" with a large, mass following, gay and lesbian poets with a largely perceptual, personal, existential poetry have begun to remake the connections and shorten the distance between "the poet" and "the public" without compromising their personal vision, and to restore a vital element that poetry has seemed in danger of losing—that of perceptive self-exploration and liberation.

As Charley Shivley put it: "Poets speak with their tongues; they make sex not only with their mouths but with their words as well."

VII
Word Power!

Lesbian Feminist Comedy —
Dyke Humor Out of the Closet

by Sharon McDonald

"In the ninth grade we were making career notebooks. My secret dream was to make a career notebook of being a clown but I was embarrassed, obviously. I mean I was trying to be a hot-shit ninth-grader, so I made it on being a French professor. It's taken me until twenty-eight years old to admit that I want to be a clown and it is so closely intertwined with becoming a lesbian and the whole process of coming out, I don't just mean coming out as a lesbian, but coming OUT, everything that's inside of me coming out."—Bobbi Birleffi, promoter of women's culture and former closet clown.

"You know what made me really want to be funny? I saw Butterflies Are Free *and Goldie Hawn was walking down the street with someone who said something about lesbian, and she said, 'Oh, no, I wouldn't want to be a lesbian, lesbians have no humor.' "*—Sue Fink, music and comedy writer, co-director and co-producer of the All-Women Bicentennial Production.

No humor indeed. Anyone who doubts that lesbian/feminist humor exists should be subjected to the barrage of puns and one-liners I withstood while talking to women about women's and lesbian humor. Though still largely undefined, women's humor is definitely alive and well.

Any old episode of *I Love Lucy* will illustrate the kind of humor that men find lacking in the women's movement. They're right, I can't remember the last time I heard a lesbian say, "Take my wife—please." What I have heard from feminists is a humor that is potentially more piercing and perceptive than any I've yet encountered, and watching the birth of feminist comedy is one of the few rewards of living in the seventies.

Women who have been successful in traditional comedy have had to conform to standards for female behavior that are even stricter than usual. Sue Fink attended a class at UCLA at which Phyllis Diller was a speaker: "She said a beautiful woman cannot be a comedian. You have to be ugly or people won't laugh at you." If women have any tradition in comedy it is as freaks, and freaks whose material must constantly emphasize their shortcomings to remain nonthreatening to a distrustful audience. And so the tremendous creative drive and talent of a woman like Lucille Ball are reduced to the frantic squawking and fluttering we are expected to believe is a style of her own choosing.

There has been no identifiable humor of women as an oppressed group, and the comedy that is emerging from the women's movement now is just starting to explore that need. We have to start from scratch. Dick Gregory's task was to teach white society what black society already knew; feminist humorists still have to educate many women to recognize their own oppression. Joelyn Grippo, music and comedy writer and co-producer of the Bicentennial Production, sees humor as a good way to accomplish this education. "I think humor can get the point across without preaching, without beating them over the head. People don't like lectures."

One example of feminist humor might be the ad for carpentry classes for women that boldly announced, "EXHAUSTIVE RESEARCH suggests that both men and women possess equal number of hands." Or that suggested line for your next run-in with the local exhibitionist, "Why, that looks like a cock. Only smaller, of course." Women's humor is brand new, fluid, and changing, but one characteristic is already obvious. Women are not the brunt of the joke. Beyond that it is difficult to pinpoint, as both forms and content vary. There is Lily Tomlin's highly individual style of characterization, there are the one-liners of Harrison and Tyler, and there are the skits and songs of groups of women like Bread and Roses and the women of the Bicentennial Production, as well as experimentation with clowning and mime.

So now that we don't know what women's humor is, quick, what is lesbian humor? Is it:

A. A man slipping on a banana peel?
B. A satire on beauty contests?
C. A skit about coming out to your mother?
D. A skit about your mother coming out to you? And is lesbian comedy dialogue:

A. "That was no lady, that was my wife."?
B. "That was no lady, that was my sister."?
C. "That was no lady, that was my lover."?
D. "That was no lady, that was my lover's lover."?

Lesbian humor is as difficult to pin down as women's humor, and there is probably much overlap between the two. The boundaries are uncertain, as Bobbi Birleffi points out:

"I think there are lots of issues that lesbians have that lesbians think are different. For example, relationships. Lesbians are trying to build different relationships with no roles, breakdown of roles. However, it has been my experience that in an intimate couple relationship, whether it's heterosexual or homosexual, it still has problems of isolation, jealousy, and possessiveness. In our performance there's going to be a lot of words that will say lesbian and I'm sure it'll really go over with the lesbians but I would love to present it in a mixed—at least 'mixed' meaning straight women—group and see what the response is. Because it may be a very powerful thing, it may be an incredible way to communicate women's culture to a broader audience, a very easy and wonderful way to communicate.

"We don't know what things we can quite laugh at yet about ourselves. It's very tentative, the definition is evolving because we are still in the stage where we are taking ourselves so seriously, we *have* to, that we almost don't trust each other to laugh. I mean if somebody gets up there and comes onstage as a dyke, and if the timing's off or they're not a likable character, women are going to be offended. So here we are doing this comedy workshop about telling your mother you're a lesbian, now to me that's pretty safe for right now, that's basic lesbian humor. But how about when we get into stuff like political meetings, all that bullshit, 'Yes-I-really-hear-you-I-hear-what-you're-saying-I-want-to-validate-what-you-say-but . . .' you know, all the language that we use politically. What happens when we start making fun of that?"

The future of women's humor and lesbian humor is wide open. If the audiences at recent women's shows in Los Angeles are any indication, the women's community is more than ready for comedy. "Starved" might be a better word. The comedy of lesbians and feminists can reach women where formal politics can't, and it can relax, in form, and encourage battle-weary sisters in evenings of solidarity and celebration. Birleffi says, "It's a nourishment, it's a place to get fed, to keep going. It's a watering hole." Whatever women's and lesbian humor evolves into, one thing seems clear: it is at long last a humor for our own amusement, to our own advantage, for our own purposes. And we will have the last laugh.

Mother Wit: Tongue in Cheek

by Julia Penelope Stanley and Susan W. Robbins

In attempting to define and explain the nature and sources of lesbian humor, we found our efforts thwarted initially by the fact that few lesbians appear to be aware that lesbian humor exists. This lack of awareness may be due to two factors. There are as yet very few lesbian "jokes" perpetrated by outsiders, perhaps because of our longstanding invisibility. (Such jokes will undoubtedly increase when we become more visible and more threatening to heterosexist society.) Consequently, although many lesbians report thinking of themselves as extraordinarily "witty," very few can cite specific examples of our humor. Secondly, some jokes exchanged among lesbians bear a superficial resemblance in intent and content to the sexual jokes directed at straight women by straight males. The first of these "problems" can be resolved quite simply, however: A brutal imitation of a lesbian is impossible, since such an imitation would entail assuming "masculine" poses and characteristics, and masculinity is not funny in our culture; men are not helpless or powerless enough to serve as vehicles of such humor. Moreover, as Lenny Bruce has pointed out, men do not make jokes about lesbians, because none of them can be certain that he is not married to one.

The resemblance of lesbian sexual references (including jokes) to straight sexual references cannot be construed as evidence that they are similarly motivated. Much of lesbian humor *is* sexual in content, but it is "in-group" humor based on "in-group" references. While it is difficult to characterize lesbian humor because it is often as fluid as the shifting relationships among the women who participate in it, the jokes which are shared rely on experiences familiar to the women within the group. The joking among them constitutes a kind of bonding process, a communal sharing of similar private experiences.

Sexual references made by straight males, on the other hand, represent at best attempts at male bonding through the exclusion of women, who serve as the butts of sexual jokes, and at worst acts of male aggression directed against women. Freud has labeled male sexual jokes "smut," and argued that they represent imagined sexual assaults which cannot be realized because society inhibits these impulses. Since the sexuality of women-identified women is nonaggressive, lesbian sexual references must also be nonaggressive. Women do not *assault* other women physically, as far as we know; thus, women cannot interpret lesbian sexual humor as an "assault," since the actual *threat* of possible physical violence is not present in the sexual reference, as is the case with heterosexual male humor.

That there exists confusion regarding the *intent* of lesbian sexual references can be seen in a letter printed in *Feminary,* a newsletter published in North Carolina. In it the writer explains that she rejected heterosexuality because she found her relationships with women more emotionally satisfying. She goes on to describe her repulsion when she is around lesbians who behave in ways that she perceives to be the same as male sexual behavior: assessing women in terms of their sexuality and physical attractiveness, flirting, engaging in promiscuous behavior, and making sexual references, jokes, and puns. She argues that if woman-identified women engage in sexual play that she thinks is male-identified, then our behavior is *worse* than that of heterosexual men.

This letter typifies the feelings of women who have just begun to explore their lesbian sexuality. The writer's confusion about lesbian behavior and straight male behavior prompts her to ask, "Isn't this worse than heterosexual men?" Well, no. For the behavior to be "worse," it would also have to be *same* in many respects. That the "sameness" of lesbian and straight male behaviors is an issue in determining what is lesbian humor is revealed by the comments made by our friends. There is a tendency to perceive lesbian humor as a variation of male humor and to condemn it, as such, out of hand. As one woman wrote: "I read that mimeo you sent to me about humor, and must confess total confusion. I'm afraid I didn't find any of it either funny or particularly dykey. Any of those jokes could have been about straight people." This observation reflects the fact that most (if not all) lesbian humor belongs in the category of "you-had-to-be-there" anecdotes. But there may be other factors which cause some women to perceive lesbian humor as identical to straight male humor. A friend from North Carolina offered the following observation: "Women who have recently come out of heterosexual relationships into lesbian relationships don't understand the difference. . . . They accuse lesbians of 'acting like men'—especially when they 'talk trash'—by which I mean most of the things we call humor. The trashy nature of our humor offends some folks—just the way they are—and as long as specifics aren't 'open' then lesbians can maintain the superiority of their choice without being specific." Another friend (from California), also discussing what some women perceive as "straight male" motivations and intentions in lesbian humor, had this to say: "I believe from my experience with faggots that they borrowed from lesbian humor as well as making up their own and that they borrow humor, as lesbians also do, from a heterosexual environment and translate it into homosexual terms. Much of the humor lesbians enjoy may seem to be male humor but in fact we were as much its originators as gay men were."

There are, then, two problems with defining lesbian humor: One is its transience, which all of our friends comment on; the other is perceiving its content and failing to perceive its *function*. Our friend from California had an interesting observation to make on this point: "Because . . . lesbian culture is still not very far away sometimes from heterosexual content and authority, it is hard not to have a humor which protests that in some way. Which leads me to the other point: in lesbian humor I think we're pretty good at making fun of the things we've taken seriously. There are a lot of jokes now about collectivity, political correctness, the goddess, what women do when they engage in separatist activities such as women's dances—and at this point I find an interesting mixture of the old world and the new in our humor."

The content and the intent of straight jokes about lesbi-

301

ans are in stark contrast with lesbian jokes about lesbians. Straight jokes about lesbians are at best condescending, as the following limerick demonstrates:

> A lesbian in old Khartoum,
> Invited a friend to her room,
> And although they tried,
> They couldn't decide,
> Who should do what or to whom.

At their worst, such jokes are vicious. This limerick clearly projects the lesbian sexual experience as confusing, inconclusive, and dissatisfying. Such is straight male humor. "Out-group" jokes about lesbians need not be original; they need only highlight the tired notions straight males have about our sexual inferiority. The differences between their humor and ours derive from the distinctions between "in" and "out" groups, the "in-group" for whom the humor serves as a bonding function, and, finally, the degree of trust that exists among the members of the group. Thus, if a woman has just switched from relationships with males to relationships with women, she's less likely to assess the difference between lesbian sexual references and male sexual references.

Nancy Stockwell, editor of *The Bright Medusa,* has commented that much lesbian humor consists of "playing off" of heterosexist assumptions and institutions, and one must see these subjects as inherently funny or the humor fails. The underpinnings of humor rely on sharing certain assumptions. Bertha Harris, author of several widely acclaimed lesbian novels, has recently provided us with a lesbian one-liner which would scarcely be regarded as humorous by heterosexual men:

> Did you hear about the Polish lesbian? . . .
> Well, it doesn't have to be a Polish lesbian;
> it could be an Italian lesbian, or an Irish lesbian,
> or any other minority group you use as a scapegoat. . . .
> Anyway, did you hear about the Polish lesbian?
> She goes out with men.

This joke obviously relies for its humor on a lesbian's assumption that (contrary to heterosexist assumptions) women naturally prefer women as companions, and implies that only a truly stupid lesbian would seek men out. The reference to an ethnic minority is necessary only to provide the joke work; it is the only way our society provides to indicate stupidity.

Other lesbian humor makes use of explicit references to lesbian sexuality. But such references are not intended to relegate other women in the group to the category of sex objects; they are rather an attempt to facilitate the bonding process through the sharing of laughter. Thus, our humor is often heavily dependent upon context, including the bonds which already exist among the women participating in the joke, which may, as a consequence, be "lost" in the retelling. The following dialogue, in which nearly every lesbian present participated, occurred in an Italian restaurant, to the dismay of the other customers:

L1, cutting hot pizza and shaking the table as she does so. Someone makes a comment about the table shaking.

L2: "You see, some people haven't learned to eat with their fingers."

L1 (explaining seriously and sincerely): "I don't want to burn my tongue." (Uproarious laughter)

L3: "Of course, would a runner wish to damage her knee?" (More uproarious laughter, coupled with pounding on the table)

L4: "Now would you like to open your mouth and put your foot in it further?"

L5: "Or whatever?"

L4: "Or whatever else comes to hand?" (More laughter)

L3 (to L2): "And it would be tactless to point out that she didn't want to burn her fingers, either."

L1: "It's a question of priorities, after all."

L2: "Yes, that would truly be living from hand to mouth, as it were."

One of the finest examples of lesbian humor as bonding process and a means of mocking heterosexist institutions and assumptions is the well-known song by Meg Christian, "Ode to a Gym Teacher," a selection from her album *I Know You Know,* a collection of lesbian ballads. Many of the events Meg mentions are pathetic, but her humor enables us to transcend their pathos. Consider, for example: the phone calls to her gym teacher; hanging up when she found out she was home; the classmates who scramble for front-row seats during the hygiene classes; crawling on her hands and knees to retrieve the broken ruler. It is funny when her classmate snatches the ruler and stuffs it in her purse, funnier when she sells it back to Meg for $1.50, and you fall out when Meg reveals that her classmate could have gotten $5.00 for it. She also parodies heterosexual courting behavior for humor—the unsigned Valentine's Day card, the anonymous phone calls, the love poems by Edna St. Vincent Millay—and her use of heterosexist stereotypes of women athletes, the "butch" dyke stereotype. Her work illustrates the phenomenon mentioned by our California friend: Meg has taken stereotypes from the heterosexual culture and made them a part of lesbian humor. The response of her audience to both the song and her commentary indicates that something was happening among the women who were present in that situation. Meg Christian has clearly struck a responsive chord in her audiences; she has tapped into common experiences of lesbians, events in our lives that we recognize as shared, and that we want to share. For example, two of the points at which she draws enthusiastic audience response are her descriptions of her awareness of her isolation as a lesbian and her comment on lesbianism as "a phase," a common belief about lesbianism. How many

304

lesbians have been told either by parents or other authority figures that they're "just going through a phase"? In essence, Meg Christian has managed one of the supreme transformations of art. She has captured the pain of the adolescent lesbian who is trying to understand herself in a culture that has no "use" for her, that, in fact, denies the validity of her lifestyle and trivializes her feelings, and she made it possible for us to laugh together at shared memories, which is the highest function of humor in our culture. Humor is one of the ways in which human beings disperse pain by sharing laughter.

In trying to define lesbian humor as it occurs among us, perhaps the most significant aspect of it is its "in-group" quality. The existence of such in-group humor among lesbians suggests that it serves a bonding function in specific situations. We would further suggest that some of those lesbians who fail to recognize lesbian humor as such fail to do so because they lack awareness of themselves as a community with shared experiences. We are suggesting that failure to participate in lesbian humor reflects a failure to recognize those distinctive features of the lesbian group that set us apart from other people. It's not what is said that constitutes lesbian humor, it's the function that laughter serves within a group of women. Everyone in the group must be aware of the function and the intent of such humor. If they focus on the content, they wind up misreading the presence of the sexuality and its validity in that context.

In closing this exploratory article on lesbian humor, we would like to quote at length comments on the subject sent to us by Joan Nestle (who lives in the apartment where the Lesbian Herstory Archives are stored, in New York City):

My first thought about lesbian humor was, thank Goddess we don't have the same packaged linguistic labeling that gay men have. I harkened back to my old integration days with gay men and could only remember the stylized linguisitic brutality that passed for humor. Yes, it was based on belittling, but now I realize that it was all joking, camping about power, the wearing of it and the divesting of it. I think the formulated gay male "subculture" is a kind of cultural shorthand where they pick from the power culture what they want to parody or deepen, i.e., leather bars, handkerchief wearing to signify position, the queen humor. I know this is painfully obvious but I feel I have a captive audience (if you haven't already stopped reading and it's going to my head). And it's intoxicating. Anyway, my sense is that lesbian humor is not a packaged response to formulated scenes: we are at once both too removed from the power culture and too sickened by it to have fun throwing its sand around. In the deepest sense of the word, I see lesbian humor as the essence of the playful spirit (in language as well), but play in the most challenging-to-the-cosmos sense. We play with our imagination, with our sexual freedoms, with our clothes (costuming not to represent power parodies like leather, but to laugh at the confines of color and texture, lines), and in our playing we create new worlds because of the deepest sense of the deadliness of this one. *Les Guérillères* is playing at its most powerful, creation of language, names, structures, with joyous energy and warrior strength. I know this sounds philosophical, and it certainly presupposes a feminist awareness, and yet even when I was an old fem I knew there was an amazon world—not by reading or talking but by the strength and adventure I felt in entering the bars, walking the street late at night, stepping out of bounds even if it was to find a closeness that was defined by who did what. The important thing was we did, and we laughed in the faces of the Mafia men. As your examples show to me, our play with language seems to come from the same impulse—to turn around the givens, to reinforce each other's daring and strength in playing above this world. I think our humor, like many other parts of our culture, is celebration—the cheering on of each other to make a new universe in the presence of each other, to drop the sticks of this world at each other's feet and pick up the pieces all mixed up and in doing so to assert our ability to create new worlds. I think our writers have mostly known this; they played with sentence structure and threw their words up in the air—their air—to make them fall into a different way of symbolizing a different life. I better stop. I think we play because this world is not ours and we are self-cherishing enough to know we must live somewhere—and we are connected to each other enough to believe we have the power to create new ones—at this very moment with the words we play with.

A Queer by Any Other Name Would Smell As Sweet

by Michael Riordon

The trouble is, no two people mean exactly the same thing by the same word. The resulting confusion leads directly to high art, adventure, war, and chaos. Clearly a hopeless means of communication, but what are you going to do?

Let's get off to a good start with something we all disagree on. I've heard any number of arguments against the word "gay," most of them from usually unreliable sources, most along the lines of "Gay means cheerful and you people certainly aren't *that*." Yawn. The *Toronto Star* still bans the word, a staff writer told me, I suppose because of its political more than its cheerful implications. My own feeling is, as always, mixed: it's the only name we have that didn't get foisted on us by nasty, ignorant straights, and it's tacitly accepted by a majority of the people who are it and many who aren't. It would be a hell of a job to find or invent, distribute, and sell another. I think what bothers me about it is that it's not exclusively ours and its meaning isn't entirely clear, even to us. A male homosexual trumpeted defiantly: *"I'm* not gay, I'm *queer."* Notable sentiment; trouble is, he was decidedly peculiar, therefore not a good example of creative or rebellious usage. To some people it means simply homosexual (*is* there such a thing?), to others it can only mean *openly* homosexual (dare I say "aggressively"?), a word that's earned by paying a certain kind of dues. Another interesting objection, oddly enough from a straight woman, was that it doesn't *ring* as it should, the way "black" does—she said it's inadequate "because it's a *silly* word." I suppose we'll just have to *build* the ring into it over a period of time, by repetition and tone of voice. I'm glad it's one syllable. . . . On the other hand.

The *Toronto Star*, which continues to be one of the richest sources of reliable rubbish around, had one of its editorial-writing machines (you put in a paycheck and out comes any opinion you want) complain that homosexuals have perverted the word "gay"; you can't use the word in its nice old cheerful context without us looming up unpleasantly behind it, e..g *South Pacific*: 'I'm as corny as Kansas in August/I'm as gay as a baby in May! . . ." Horrors—gay babies? Put 'em out on the hillside! Faced with opinions like that, you want to drill into their witless chambers *our* meaning of the word until it's the only one that matters. Of course, like some stupid giant, *The Star* is at its most outraged when it's most embarrassed.

On the other *other* hand. I heard two fools sharing a joke, the kind that used to be called a faggot joke. Only it began: "Two gays were . . ." And you hear the expression "gay boys" with fully as much venom behind it as behind "fairy," "dyke," etc. Have the more sophisticated goons co-opted our word without, as someone put it, deriving any therapeutic value from it? Really they shouldn't be calling us *anything*: whatever it is, the name diminishes us, distances us, ridicules us, and abuses us. *My Fair Lady*: "Never do I ever want to hear another word/There isn't one I haven't heard. . . ."

Which brings me to "faggot" and "dyke." As far as I know both words have relatively innocent origins, incendiary or hydraulic (faggots/sticks of wood must have been burned to warm soup before they were burned to ignite witches), but both have since been perverted for hate purposes. Both have been dropped more or less from politer liberal conversations (whatever else one says about the poor maligned species, the liberal, it *does* have good manners). Both have been taken up by what seem to be two distinct schools of gay thought: one school is acidly self-deprecating, hoping, I assume, to drown out *their* laughter with ours (immunization: take small nonlethal doses of the venom repeatedly in clinical situations until resistant to the larger doses encountered in the field); the other school makes war cries and banners of "dyke" and "faggot," apparently either to confuse the enemy or to defang the words, to render them absurd and therefore harmless. I wonder if it works. Does it matter what color the venom is? If someone calls me "perfect" with the right tone, I could be dead.

Acceptance of these words seems to depend on context. Let me get it right—am I to laugh when another faggot calls me faggot, or Mary (where did this Mary business come from? I don't know any gay people who could be called virgins in any but the most poetic sense of the word), am I supposed to join in the chorus not to be a wet blanket on the party mood, but bridle and hackle up when some straight creep calls me or another faggot (between you and me) a faggot? If I am a faggot, am I allowed to call a lesbian a dyke? Only to her face or always? Or, like Queen (I think I'm glad that queens are practically an extinct species, though I was concerned when it was an endangered one) Elizabeth, do I have to wait until she says it first? Or then again does it all depend on tone? Can one rendition work and another elicit violence? For me it's simpler this way: I dislike both words, sounds and meanings, theirs and ours, I'm unlikely to answer to either, and would be happy never to hear them again in any context. Same with "queen." It isn't my word.

Have you noticed some words in such common usage that their implications seldom register, consciously at least: "Trick." It means artifice, prank, expedient, mannerism, illusion, a spell of duty or shift. Nice.

Gorgeous word challenges are thrown out all the time by good writers, even in reasonable translation. Genet described one of his lovers as having "mobile buttocks." A ravishing term, I couldn't figure it out, but began earnestly to look for examples. Gradually, with the help of some body insights from a dance class I was taking, it made the prettiest sense: a wonderfully graceful flow of freedom through the back and the legs that makes some men's buttocks—it isn't common by any means—not sloppy, never sloppy, but *mobile*. There's no other way to describe it as well. (Someone accused me of "objectifying" in this little search, but I wasn't, I was "particularizing," which is quite different. What sly tricks you can play with words.)

Speaking of "gay," isn't "straight" a stupid word? You can wring some rude possibilities from it, but generally it implies "correct." As in Molson Diamond lager beer, advertising itself as "straight lager"—if there weren't already ample good reasons for a boycott, surely *there's* one for us. An intriguing alternative to "straight" was offered in a newspaper headline over a milk-marketing story: "Skim subsidizes Homo." If we're the homos and they're the skims, would 2%'s be bisexual? And I guess cream would be on our side, wouldn't it?

Also speaking of "gay," there are a great many public washrooms in the world, and a great many people visit them fairly frequently for one reason or another. So why not more gay graffiti? Not of the "Frank likes hot heavy cocks, call such-and-such a number" variety (though it's probably a reasonable if risky form of communication—or public relations) but higher forms, funny or ringing. I did almost all the washrooms on the New York State Thruway (southbound, at least) last month—nothing classic, just "Gay Rights Now!" Maybe I should have shut up. Will I ever get into the U.S. again? In the men's toilet in the train station, Sudbury, Ontario, not a gracious town: (1) "I love to suck cocks—", there followed a name and address in a small northern town. (2) (with an arrow pointing to 1 above) "Godamn cocksuckers like this one should be shot and used for dog food." (3) (with an arrow to 2 above) "Some psychiatrists say that men who are hostle [sic] to homosexuals are afraid to accept their own homosexuality." The spelling was flawed, the message, under the circumstances, thrilling. Penknife is good if you have the time, spray paint if you have the pockets, either if you have the nerve, magic marker a practical alternative. I'll be looking for you.

Promiscuous/Effeminate/Deviant. What hateful things have been done with and in the name of those words. Stupid people always ask: "Is it true homosexual men are more promiscuous than heterosexual men or lesbians?" Possible answers: "Yes." "No." "Stupid question, no answer required." "We are more flexible in our relationships because, except for a giant umbrella NO, we haven't suffered under the petty restrictions applied to heterosexuals; once we come out from under the NO we can be pretty free in our comings and goings—heterosexuals, by the

311

way, crave this kind of freedom and go to all sorts of bizarre lengths to simulate it."

Then they ask, "What is the basis for the belief that homosexuals are effeminate?" Answer: "The basis is: instead of sensibly recognizing and enjoying a full, lively range of human behavior, the headless have swallowed whole the idea of arbitrary categories, and most of the minority ones have negative connotations. Thus, 'effeminate' men, 'masculine' women—e.g., East German swimmers with broad shoulders are considered in some circles to have lost any legitimate claim to womanhood." How brainless it all is.

Deviant/deviate is another matter; I rather like it. I give it my own proud inflection. Webster says: "an individual who differs considerably from the average." Having no respect for the average, I'm enchanted. And "characterized by or given to considerable departure from the norms of behavior in a given society." Finding the norms of the given society to be by and large a mess, I'm doubly pleased with myself. Of course, there's no denying the word is flung at us like mud, as are "promiscuous" and "effeminate."

Seems the best thing to do is to redefine the words for ourselves and pass on the definitions to as many people as will listen. The others? If they're in a position to harm us, we'll have to silence them. Somehow.

Have you seen the Big Brother (healthy adult male influence for fatherless boys) campaign? "One Boy One Man," it throbs. Well, *here's* a perversion! If *they* say it, it's good works; if we say it, it's preying on defenseless children. Did they have any idea what they were doing? It does have a nice lilt, I must say.

Words say worlds about people, they spring out in bright relief if you watch for them. A man asked me if I would mind terribly if he "sodomized" me. Imagine. That's a very rich word, purple with implications of crime, sin, and hellish perversion. I declined, it sounded to me a very dangerous undertaking. He slipped imperceptibly from "interesting" to "odd" in my ratings.

Why on earth is a "blow-job" called a "blow-job"?

VIII
Young and Gay!

Memoirs of a Lesbian Daughter
by Blynn Garnett

A great deal has been written and said lately about lesbian mothers. At the risk of merely increasing the din rather than clarifying the questions involved, I would like to add my voice to those already raised, but from a somewhat different perspective. I am not a lesbian mother. I am, however, a forty-two-year-old lesbian, but more importantly, a lesbian who was raised in a lesbian household. It is from the standpoint of having been the child rather than the parent in such a home that I would like to look at the question of lesbians raising their children.

My age, I feel, gives me the advantage of distance from the event (and therefore, it is hoped, some objectivity) which most children now being raised by lesbians are still too young to have the abilities to write about. There is a disadvantage to my age as well. When I was being brought up, lesbian mothers and their lovers handled the question of a gay household quite differently from the way they do now; namely, they were very, very quiet about it. The closet door was firmly sealed, and not to be opened by anyone, especially by me. Thus, my perception of the way I was being raised was very different from the perception of children now.

Some family background and autobiographical material would seem to be in order here. Rachael, my mother, was pregnant with me when she met Evelyn, the woman who was to become her lover, and who was to be my "Aunt Evelyn" forever after. It was the middle of the Depression, and so, to save on rent, Evelyn moved in with my mother and ·Larry, my father, a not uncommon arrangement at the time. Rachael and Larry either were married or about to be. Historical facts tend to be a bit fuzzy in my family, in large measure because my mother always found fiction infinitely preferable to fact. I do know that at some point before I was born my parents did get married.

At my birth, Evelyn was eighteen, my mother twenty-seven, and my father thirty-eight. The three of them lived in Greenwich Village, in what would then have been described as a "bohemian" household, with all the Village luminaries of the thirties such as Max Bodenheim, Joe Gould, and the like, friends of theirs.

Around this time the feelings between Rachael and Evelyn began to move in a decidedly sexual direction, though how explicitly I don't know. What I do know is that my father, who disliked both fatherhood and working, did what he could to encourage their relationship so that he could gracefully rid himself of these burdens as soon as Rachael and Evelyn had an ongoing, consummated affair. By the time I was two or three my father was gone, except for visitation rights, which ended when I was four and it was discovered that he had been taking me to bars on his "days." Except for one visit which I initiated when I was about thirty, I never saw him again.

Thus, Evelyn, at the age of twenty-one found herself with a family to support (Rachael was to stay home to take care of me), not an easy thing to do in 1936, but do it she did, and quite happily. It was at this point that we moved from the Village to a more middle-class neighborhood. The stated reason was that the Village was not a healthy place in which to raise a child. I'm sure, however, that the real reason was that everyone Rachael and Evelyn knew in the Village was aware of the nature of their relationship, which made it impossible to keep it a secret from me. Strange as it may sound today, Rachael and Evelyn did decide that I was never, ever to know what was going on between them so that I could have a "normal" upbringing.

Evelyn went to work at a civil service job (yet another reason for secrecy—it was a relatively sensitive job), and Rachael stayed home with me. They told everyone they were sisters, which worked despite the fact that Rachael was very dark, so dark in fact that although she was Jewish many people thought she was black, and Evelyn, also Jewish, was very fair and red-headed, and thought by many to be Irish. However, people usually believe what they're told. I was not told they were sisters. I was told they were "just good friends."

Although there was a good deal of "Mommy-Daddy" role-playing in this arrangement, the role in which my mother found herself did not overly please her. She found staying at home with a young child very boring—I remember her frequently pleading with me to grow up as quickly as possible so that she would have someone to talk to—and she found the other mothers in the neighborhood equally boring with their endless discussions of their children's eating and toilet habits. Finally, perhaps as much from boredom as from political conviction, she joined the Communist Party. Evelyn did not, never being quite as enthralled with the Communists as Rachael, and also fearing that it might endanger her job. They removed themselves as much as possible from gay society, associating almost completely with the families in the neighborhood, the people from Evelyn's job, and, of course, the people from the local Party group.

This, then, was the pattern of my life until I was about fourteen. Evelyn worked, Rachael stayed home, I went to school and, in the summers, starting when I was not quite five, to camp. It was all very middle class, except for the fact that my parents were two women. I never thought of Evelyn as my father, but simply as my other parent. I did find the absence of a father an embarrassment since no one ever got divorced in that neighborhood, at least not the parents of the children I knew. World War II was a godsend to me because I immediately dispatched my father off to the front, and kept him there as long as humanly possible. He'll never know what an immense and prolonged contribution he made to the postwar reconstruction of Japan.

One of the distinguishing features of our home was its intensely political and intellectual atmosphere. By the time I got to kindergarten I knew all the Communist and Wobbly songs, could give you my position on the Spanish Civil War, and generally knew "which side I was on." Would that I possessed such certainty today.

As far as Rachael and Evelyn were concerned, there were three primary virtues: thinking, reading, and speaking well. I learned to read before I was old enough to start school and to this day will be told by Evelyn that "No person can consider herself well educated unless she has read . . . ," whenever I resist reading a book she considers important. And, of course, everything that was read, or thought about, was discussed. My primary memory of my early years is the sound of voices talking, arguing, discoursing, debating. Despite their vehement denials of snobbery, the easiest way to earn my family's contempt was to be unable to speak well.

The relationship between Rachael and Evelyn, at least in terms of my perception of it at that time, is difficult to describe. I understood, without it ever being stated, that they both were my parents, both loved me, both were to be obeyed, and both could and did punish me for my lapses. Although there was always an atmosphere of affection between them, they never showed any physical signs of it in my presence. They did sleep in the same bed, but the supposed reason for this was that we lived in a one-bedroom apartment, and they slept in the living room, having given me the bedroom. You can't, after all, put twin beds in the living room, and everyone knows a growing girl must have her own room—preferably at the other end of the apartment. This was my preference as well as theirs. No matter where we lived I wanted my bedroom as far from everyone else as possible, and always insisted on sleeping with the door firmly shut. Thus, like all my friends, I had two parents, and these two parents slept in the same bed, as did most of my friends' parents, but my parents were both women who obviously were very close, although they never made any demonstration of this when I was around.

In 1948, when I was fourteen, we took a further step into the middle class by moving to Queens, along with millions of others who had made enough money during the war to transfer themselves to the suburbs. I hated Queens from the moment we arrived—which is fairly ironic since the move presumably was for my benefit.

By the time I was sixteen, the difficulties between my mother and me, which had been simmering for some time, erupted into open warfare. I was, as they say, "acting out," primarily by doing very badly in school, and then becoming a chronic truant. In middle-class Jewish families, even middle-class lesbian Jewish families, scholastic failure and truancy are simply not allowed, and so I was sent off, with a good deal of financial hardship for Rachael and Evelyn, to a firmly disciplinarian and scholastically demanding small private school in New England. Here, finally, I did what good Jewish children are supposed to do—I graduated with honors. Also, Rachael was finally able to get out of the house since she had to get a job in order to help pay for my schooling.

Since I always did so well away from home (my summers at camp had always been joyous), it was decided that I should go to a small out-of-town college. This did not work at all as well. For one thing, the college was run by a group of evangelical Christians, and I was a liberal New York Jew. I did not fit.

To complicate matters further, in my junior year I had my first homosexual experience, to which I responded with a singular lack of grace. I alternated between total hysteria, and a Virginia Woolf type of neurasthenia in which I felt so totally sensitive and prone to collapse that I was sure institutionalization was the only answer. I was a bit startled by my reaction since in all school discussions on the subject I had always maintained that the only thing wrong with homosexuality was society's attitude toward it. In 1954 my friends considered this terribly "adult."

What made my extreme reaction even more peculiar is that ostensibly I was prepared for something to happen between Theresa and me. Only a week or so before the occurrence I had told several people, including the young man I was having an affair with, that I was sure Theresa had a sexual interest in me, and probably would make some sort of pass before long. What I was not prepared for was the intensity of my reaction when the overture was made, and my subsequent collapse. In retrospect, it is fairly obvious that I was responding to more than the experience itself. Going to bed with Theresa began to push toward the surface some subconscious recognition of the truth about Rachael and Evelyn which I did not want to acknowledge, since by that time I had as large a stake in their lie as they did.

In any event, I left school, or, more precisely, was asked to leave, before the end of my junior year, which ended what was by then a very messy affair with Theresa, and returned to New York to begin that process known as "finding oneself," a phrase that always makes me think of a dog chasing its own tail.

The next five years were difficult, and, I feel, fairly typical of the way people "came out" in the mid-fifties. To use the word "ambivalence" to describe my feelings about my homosexuality is such an understatement as to be almost absurd. I slept with women, but insisted I was straight. My favorite phrase at that time was "One swallow does not a summer make," a fairly unfortunate choice of words under the circumstances. I slept with men more and more desperately to prove my straightness, counting each of my orgasms as a score for my straight side. The women who were then my friends were all doing exactly the same thing. In fact, we were all sleeping with each other, insisting all the while that these episodes meant absolutely nothing.

I lived at home during all of this, and each time I brought one of these women home, Rachael would immediately spot them as gay (I marveled at her insight), and she and I would have a ferocious battle. She hated them, and made that abundantly clear to them and to me. Periodically she would challenge me to admit I was sleeping with them, which, of course, I would deny. I had learned my lessons well. As time went on, our relationship deteriorated so badly that I spent more and more time away from home, although ostensibly still living there. Evelyn seemed to spend most of her time at work, and was very startled to hear of these battles when I told her about them years later.

After two years of battling I decided to try therapy. I had had brief encounters with therapy before, but this time I stuck with it, choosing not only a woman therapist, but the same doctor one of the women I periodically went to bed with was seeing. I told the doctor that I had these terrible homosexual impulses which I wanted "cured," and

320

she agreed to do what she could to cure them. Getting me to accept them was never considered, but she was a nice lady and didn't mean any harm. I saw her for about three years, during the course of which she occasionally attempted to get me to admit that Rachael and Evelyn were lovers, a proposition I refused to accept. Some of my friends had made similar, equally unsuccessful attempts.

At the end of three years my gay impulses were as strong as ever, and I met Sondra. We began an affair, and finally decided to live together. With this development, the therapist and I parted company, and thus, at the age of twenty-six, I was, at long last, gay.

In June of 1961, three months after I began living with Sondra, my mother died. She was fifty-four and had lived with Evelyn for over twenty-six years. In her overwhelming grief over her loss, Evelyn began to tell me the truth about their life together, initially in the form of poetry and stories she had written to and about Rachael. I don't think she was telling me the truth as the result of any conscious decision to do so as much as she was telling someone—anyone—about the intolerable loss she had suffered. I tried for a while to deny what I was being told, but finally had to admit the truth, and with that admission I stopped playing the game altogether. I no longer made any attempt to conceal my relationship with Sondra from Evelyn, although that had undoubtedly been a vain effort from the start. Evelyn and I, still existing in a parent-child relationship, are now both openly homosexual. In an odd kind of irony, we both came out of the closet at about the same time.

Sondra and I stopped living together after eight years. It should have ended years before, but since Rachael and Evelyn had lived together until Rachael's death, I had a great emotional investment in the idea that you live with only one person until "death do you part." The fact that I could persist in this idea despite seeing all of the gay couples around me constantly break up and then start up again with someone new is, I suppose, proof of how well I had learned to deny the evidence of what I saw.

After living by myself for several years recovering from the strain of this breakup, I found Naomi, and have been

321

living very happily with her for the past couple of years. Her parents have decided to "know," without knowing, and treat me like one of the family, while Evelyn, who never again lived with anyone after my mother's death, knows all and treats Naomi the way all parents treat their daughters- or sons-in-law.

Which brings us up to date and back to square one. I am a forty-two-year-old lesbian who was brought up in a lesbian home. How do I feel about raising children in such an environment? Do I recommend it as a way of life? Do I think I am gay because I was brought up in a gay home?

Dealing with the last question first, yes, I think I am gay because of the way in which I was brought up. I also think I am politically aware, an omnivorous reader, a lover of good music, implacably middle class, incurably in love with the English language as it should be spoken, and opinionated as hell because of the way in which I was raised. In short, the fact that two women who were lovers brought me up is only one of the many influences that shaped my life.

The question becomes more complicated when you think of my childhood being spent with two very strong women, who were able to take care of themselves and me without a man. It never occurred to me that it was necessary for a woman to have a man around in order to function properly or to be "complete." In fact, as far as I was concerned, women were strong and men were weak. Add to that the political environment of my childhood, where it was felt that one must be given the freedom to fulfill oneself to the utmost of one's capacity without any question of gender (I was never told "Girls don't do that" when I was a child, and I was a very active tomboy), and my becoming a lesbian can almost be seen as a feminist inevitability.

Admittedly, my relationship with my mother was difficult, but I am convinced that would have been true had she been straight and her marriage a heterosexual one. Rachael was a complex and neurotic woman, and my birth wrought so many radical changes in her life—many of them unpleasant—that she had to regard my arrival with something less than unalloyed joy. Rachael had often vowed that there were three things she would never be: poor, a mother, or old. My birth destroyed the first two hopes, and, sadly, only by dying at fifty-four did she manage to accomplish any part of her vow.

I dwell on this only because there is a theory, with which, feminism notwithstanding, I agree, which holds that mothers are very often competitive with their daughters, and simultaneously want them to succeed as well as to fail. Consciously, Rachael was extremely anxious for me to be heterosexual, but, without dredging around too much in the murky waters of Freudian theory, I am quite sure that subconsciously she was equally anxious for me to be homosexual, which, in her eyes at least, would represent my failure. In this sense, my mother's homosexuality no doubt contributed to my own, since a heterosexual mother would probably have found another area in which to work out these conflicts.

The question of how I feel about raising children in a gay home brings me to what I feel is the central fact of my life at home—it is not so much that Rachael and Evelyn were lovers, but that they lied to me about it for so long, that is important. For twenty-six years I was told that I was not seeing what I thought I saw, which finally becomes a strange form of brainwashing. If every time you look at a table you are told it is a chair, you are going to have an awfully hard time sorting out the furniture. In its broadest sense, what this kind of lying does is teach you that what you perceive may, or then again may not, be true, and being unable to trust the evidence of your eyes can make you feel almost schizophrenic.

What it did do was make me a chronic liar as a child—Rachael and Evelyn were always very angry when they caught me in a lie, and could never understand why I would do such a thing. It took years of serious effort on my part to learn not to lie when confronted by something unpleasant. More to the point, it also took years for me to trust what I saw rather than what I was told if there was an obvious discrepancy between the two. I believe this is called learning to adjust the concept to the precept, and I was nearly thirty-five years old before I learned that I was to adjust what I thought, *not* what I saw.

When I look back on my childhood now, I don't think of it in terms of being raised by two lesbians, but in terms of being raised in a home where there was a lie which finally became central to everything. I'm sure Rachael and Evelyn thought they had good reasons for concealing the truth, and once the lie had gone on for too long found it impossible to undo, but in the long run lying about their relationship created many more problems, both practical and psychological, than telling me the truth could possibly have done. Since telling children the truth about absolutely everything is now "in," I cannot imagine any lesbian mothers lying to their children today in the way I was lied to, but if any of you gay mothers out there are tempted to lie, take my advice. Don't! Just as there are ways of telling children about sex in a manner appropriate to their age, so are there appropriate ways of telling them the truth about you and your lover.

Finally, as to whether I recommend lesbians raising children as a way of life, the answer must be that I neither recommend nor do I condemn it. I had some good times, and some rotten ones. Almost anyone brought up in a straight home will say the same thing. So, at the risk of using a cliché, lesbian homes are only as good or as bad as the people in them. Two embattled lesbians working out their difficulties on the child in a tension-filled home probably will not do too good a job with the child. The same can be said of a straight home. Two loving women who are concerned for the welfare of the child will probably do a pretty good job. Again, the same applies to a straight home. Those who insist that a lesbian home is the perfect answer to a sexist world are mouthing slogans, not dealing with reality. Those who insist that a lesbian home can do nothing but harm to a child are equally misguided. After all, I was brought up by two people who loved each other for over a quarter of a century, until one of them died. How many children of straight parents can say the same thing?

Growing Up Gay:
Where Were You in '62

by Stuart Byron

Robert J. was not my best friend in high school; there were other guys, straight guys, who were on the same party circuit, with whom I discovered Beethoven or Joyce, to whom I showed the first drafts of my own poor scribblings. Nor was he yet my first lover, that honor belonging to a yahoo with whom I had nothing in common besides the fiery fulminations of adolescent flesh.

But Robert J.—like the others mentioned here, not his real name—was perhaps more important than these. He was my first gay friend, and our friendship, however non-carnal, kept us sane. It was with Robert that I discovered the secret zones of New York, the gay subculture, the bars and baths and parks of the "twilight world." It was with Robert that I could use, on a regular basis, such comforting language as "dish" and "trick" and "my dear." Certainly such was impossible with my lover, like so many teenagers convinced he was really straight and who referred to having sex as "getting completely undressed," and never mind what he did after reaching that naked stage. But Robert and I were mutually supportive, continual reminders that each of us had not, to paraphase Sidney Abbott, "invented homosexuality," ballasts for one another in a world that was straight, strange, hostile—our almost daily telephone conversation reports of doings and discoveries that under no circumstances could be discussed with parents, colleagues, doctors, other friends. It was with Robert, and only Robert, that I shared the news of the first experiments in sex. I don't know how I would have survived those traumatic years without him.

In 1957, we were both seniors, I at a "selective" public high school, he at an exclusive private day school. And like all Jewish middle-class youngsters of that era, there was only one option in our immediate future, and that was college, hopefully the "best" college at which one could be accepted. Robert was bright if not brilliant, studious if not scholarly, imaginative if not creative—in any case, one who, his counselors assured him, would have no trouble being admitted to Oberlin, Dartmouth, or the other schools of like reputation to which he had applied.

But a policeman's flashlight changed all that. One night, as the first winds of winter whispered through the November air, a cop most rudely interrupted Robert as he was taking mutual pleasure with a newfound acquaintance in Central Park. And, naturally enough, a nightmare ensued: the hysterical mother insisting he see a psychiatrist, the proud father cashing in every political chip so that the case was stricken from the books, his private school informed by the police of the matter. Robert was never a very strong-willed person, and it wasn't hard for his parents to force out of him the names of his friends of like sexual persuasion. After one last tearful conversation, he followed their orders and didn't speak to me again.

And then there was his school, which of course "had" to inform the colleges to which Robert had applied of this most scandalous incident. They all rejected him, and he ended up going to Clark, a college to which he had not originally applied. Let me say that Clark is a good school, a fine school, a school of excellent academic standards— but not a school which, other things being equal, one would go to if one could get into Oberlin or Dartmouth. And it was getting into Oberlin or Dartmouth toward which his whole academic career had been steered. Laugh if you will at such a bourgeois goal, but to Robert J. a sociological perspective would have been an impossible suggestion. He had received a blow from which he was never to recover.

I mention this now because the "nostalgic boom" has at last reached *my* era, *my* adolescence, the time of *my* coming of age. In my field, the movies, we have already had *Let the Good Times Roll*, and then George Lucas's *American Graffiti*, the latter undoubtedly *the* smash hit last season, doing for heterosexual high school life in 1962 what *The Last Picture Show* did in terms of the decade before that. And I have no quarrel with its story of girl-

326

chasing, lindy-hopping, and hot rodding on a last night before two of its heroes go off to college in "the east." It is one of the great truths that America's gay history is one of its secret histories, and it is only to be expected that George Lucas can imagine no faggots or lesbians in a small California town in 1962.

But though his intentions are certainly more complex, Lucas's film, like its predecessors, is already drawing forth those references to a "simpler era" when "options were clearer" than they are today. Well, fuck that. The fifties and early sixties were simple all right—simply antigay, simply prejudiced, simply dangerous, simply hell. And sure my option was clear: get in the closet and stay there.

"Where were you in '62?" read the ads. Well, I was where I was for the four years before that (save for a half-year in Europe), and was to be for a year more—at Wesleyan University in Middletown, Connecticut, an all-male pillar of the "little Ivy League," a bastion of Eastern liberalism, a school which could cite chapter and verse (such as college board scores) to prove that it competed successfully with Harvard for the best and the brightest. And it was liberal—as those things go. Freshmen could have liquor in their rooms, could have cars! Liberal—for everyone except gays.

Of course, there were happy moments—some of the happiest of my life, in fact. Friends, teachers, and—though not on campus—occasional lovers. My interest in politics was kindled by the Maryland Freedom Rides of '62, my interest in the cinema by an inspiring professor and an excellent film society. But there was a black diary, too, filled with the incidents which made me and my gay friends always make sure we had dates on party weekends and which convinced us that we would marry one day. Here are the key remembrances.

The Freshman Follies: Tommy E. is one of the few upperclassmen I have come to know well. Curly-haired and clever, dating a girl from Bennington, he is one of the few "independents" on the fraternity-ruled campus, and he tries to convince me to avoid the Greek societies.

One day I notice that I haven't seen him for a week. "Oh, haven't you heard?" says our mutual friend Barry N.

"Tommy was getting serious with this girl, and he felt that to be fair to her he should tell her the truth, which is that he was a homosexual. She got so upset that she told the dean at Bennington. The dean at Bennington told the dean at Wesleyan, and Tommy was kicked out."

Two years later Barry N. discovers his own gayness. They have to pump out his stomach at Middlesex General Hospital.

The Sophomore Slump: Norris C. is from a small border state town; unlike me, he didn't grow up with a newsstand on the corner which sold boy books, nor with gay bars a few subway stops away. The notion of his own homosexuality, therefore, creates an agony and confusion within him which is beyond my own experience: it mortifies him. Somehow we find out about each other and become friends but—totally unattracted to each other— never lovers.

He is shy and sensitive, and a "virgin." I am naïve, unable to comprehend his emotional instability. Like most big-cityites, I have already perfected a campy conversational style, as well as that well-known defense mechanism which dictates that a half-serious (and half-true) attempt be made to brush every straight man a closet queen. So I try to comfort Norris by showing him that he is not alone: in addition to the three or four Wesleyanites I know to be gay, I name a dozen more that I suspect, particularly focusing on one jock after whom I lust ("Oh, her! Look at the way he wears those tight pants! Who's he kidding?").

Norris begins going slightly mad, pursuing this jock day and night—to such an extent that fellow students, and even faculty, begin to notice. Norris hovers menacingly outside the boy's dormitory room. Soon I am approached by Norris's faculty adviser: as his "best friend," what would I recommend? Scared shitless, I reply. "I don't think he can stay in this environment."

A week later a little white Corvair pulls up, containing Norris's father. Norris is placed in an institution, where he is given shock treatments and other forms of aversion therapy.

If there is such a thing as an "end to innocence" in my

328

life, it is this. To integrate the incident, I convince myself that I am totally evil, that I have used the vulnerable Norris to do my own dirty business. For five years thereafter, I lead a radically barren sex life, wracked by guilt.

A decade later, when we are both in the gay liberation movement in New York, Norris tells me that he has felt the same exact guilt toward me—that he had more sexual experience than he had let on, that he had played the *faux naif*, that he had deliberately sought to involve me so as to provide a protective cover for himself. The ultimate oppression is not what straights do to gays, but what straight society forces gays to do to each other.

The Junior Jollies: Harry Y., a class above me, is without question the campus oddball, the only student at Wesleyan who wears jacket and tie morning, noon, and night. The least jocklike of personalities, he is nonetheless a star of the wrestling team—but in a gentleman-athlete, Victorian sort of way. To me there is always a desperation to his sports life: he seems the guy with a "turkey" personality who is trying to prove his "manhood" at all costs. A genius of a scholar, his papers are considered publishable by his English professors.

The son of a military man, Harry gets extremely uptight in the presence of his parents, or when they are brought up in conversation. What thing, what suffering, what conflict is eating away at him? Nobody knows, but while I am in France I receive from him a letter which, while not explicit, is nonetheless the most campy, wittily Oscar Wilde-ish I have ever seen, discussing the Norris affair in a tone whose "vibes" convince me that it is coming from a fellow "pervert." I resolve to have a frank discussion with Harry when I return to campus.

I never have the chance. A few weeks after my return, Harry wins a Wilson Fellowship. Apparently learning once and for all that scholarly accomplishment will not override his inner turmoil, one night he takes his car into the country, places a hose from the gas exhaust to the inside of the car, and dies. His last words, to a dormitory mate, were, "I'm going out for a few minutes."

The Senior Sallies: At a party in New York during Easter vacation I discovered that Mark R., with whom I had been close until he transferred to another school, is gay, and that all those weekends when he was supposedly seeing a girl in New York were actually spent with a dentist he had met in Provincetown. This experience—the knowledge that I had suffered in isolation while some of those around me were doing the same—is to be repeated. After persistent reports that he has been seen in homosexual hangouts, one night a few years ago I ran across Paul A., a Wesleyan roommate, in a New York gay bar. "Well, Paul," I said, "I knew this would happen one day." "What would happen?" he said. "That I would meet you in a place like this." I said. "Oh, it was the only place open around here," he said. This was on one of New York's most crowded bar streets, there being three or four straight establishments within 100 yards of where we were speaking.

I have told this story to various individuals and groups in recent years. Gay people in my generation usually nod sadly, and chime in with stories of their own (one, from Texas, had three friends who became junkies as a consequence of a refusal to accept their homosexuality: two have died from overdoses).

Liberated types sometimes argue that such tales should not be told outside of the family, citing the old rule that we should emphasize the "happy" side of homosexual life and refuse to promulgate the *Boys in the Band* image. This is an argument with which I have never agreed. Gayness has brought me far more happy moments in my life than sad ones—but if the homosexual situation in America was not oppressive there would be little need for gay liberation. It is time that the full force of the "daily violence" against gay people become widely known, with those incidents which have made everyday living for a tenth of a nation a cauldron of fear exposed to journalistic and moral light.

Gay people now in college tend to be stupefied by such details. Could these things have happened only a decade ago, and in such a prestigious place? It seems impossible to them that anyone today could be kicked out of that kind of school simply for being a homosexual; when I visited Wesleyan last year there was a Gay Liberation Front, there was a gay bar in Middletown, and one estimate was that 5 percent of the campus was openly gay. For all the legislative and other failures, it is folly to say that the gay liberation movement hasn't accomplished anything. Indeed, inasmuch as gay liberation was an outgrowth of "the movement" in general, it can be said that something came out of it. Our arms may still be in southeast Asia, we're still boycotting grapes, the poverty statistics haven't changed—but growing up gay in America has become a lot easier. As I contemplate the classes of '77 entering colleges this year, I am glad, very glad, that they aren't "where I was in '62."

I was the Dyke at My High School Reunion

by Loretta Lottman

First notice of Mather High's tenth reunion hits with a shock. I'd cut those years from my mind with an, "Oh, yes, I hated high school, too," and had not allowed myself to remember any of it. Suddenly a fat envelope postmarked West Rogers Park, Illinois, arrived at my New York apartment. My past had caught me. Memories snapped back into focus, etched with fear.

Stephen Tyng Mather High School is a white brick, ostentatiously modern building next to a treeless park in Chicago. It had good teachers, no blacks, no stairs (we were derided as "the country club"), and an almost all-Jewish population. The only anti-Semitism we faced was what we laughingly manufactured for ourselves.

Mather was a state of mind, basic training for life. Boys competed for awards and girls competed for boys. We settled readily into an unspoken hierarchy based on clothes, complexion, and weight. Winners and losers were recognizable at a glance.

I was a loser, but preferred to call myself a nonconformist. Slightly overweight (convinced of obesity), broken out (*knew* it was Chicago's worst acne), the lone tomboy amid training-bra'ed peers, I entered high school planning to survive anonymously. However, schoolmates recognized a good target and would not leave me alone. I was hit with pennies, teased, greeted with sneers and hostility my first semester—because it *was* my first semester and I did not look cool. Class years were a class system.

Alternately ignored and tormented by my peers, I hid in books and morbidly elaborate daydreams. I didn't date for a long time. Boys weren't interested and I didn't consciously think of girls. "Queer" was the ultimate stigma thrown at anyone who dared to be different. I didn't know that queer had sexual connotations, but I recognized a put-down when I heard one. I tried to avoid the label and ignored any outcroppings of sexuality in myself. Mostly, I devoured Ray Bradbury stories with chocolate cake and discussed Albee with my dog. Occasionally, when I could no longer stand it, I would confide my isolation to bits of paper, then hide them in my house for fear that anyone would know my mind.

"These are the best years of your life," the surrounding adults would say—and at fourteen I taped a plastic dry-cleaning bag over my head and waited for the end. "Thank God, it's almost over," I thought, watching black spots converge toward unconsciousness. "Yes, but what *was* it?" my mind thought back. I tore open the bag and never tried again.

Salvation at Mather came in the form of William G. Paulick, our choral director and head of the school show, Ruetama. "Uncle Willie" looked like a beatnik, acted like a madman—and consistently produced one of the best choirs in the city. Other teachers feared his antics, questioned his methods, avoided conversation. Most students couldn't stand him and choir attrition was high.

For those of us who shared only a condition of difference, Paulick was a miracle. He fused supreme respect for art with a passionate drive to create the best we could (ten years later, his protégés would include a Broadway composer an Emmy-winning writer, and an accomplished coloratura in New York). "If you're comfortable, you're not making progress!" he'd shout, eyebrows twitching, mouth skewed to a semi-idiotic grin—and I'd willingly rush to 7:00 A.M. rehearsals. For once my perpetual discomfort with life was treated as something hopeful. To write for Ruetama (an appropriate name for backwards amateurs), I studied Molière and Shakespeare for their structure and language. At fifteen, Paulick perused a scene I'd written, nodded, and said, "Kid, you've got a way with dialogue." I lived off that high for months.

However, I still had to cope with the rest of Mather. Incompetent teachers, teenage cruelty, and a cutthroat competitive environment compounded the regular adolescent problems. My graduation picture still haunts me. That scared virgin didn't learn how sperm and egg met

333

until the second semester of college; kept her virginity three more years; didn't discover and accept her lesbianism for three years after that. The picture, taken after weight loss and Max Factor's Erace, showed my best approximation of a smile. Adults called it a good likeness. I read terror in those eyes.

I had avoided high school as a nightmare I'd barely escaped. Suddenly, a thousand miles and ten years later. Mather caught up. I opened the missive, sent by an obscure classmate named Ruthy (diminutive in the original). It was a questionnaire. "Do you remember . . . ?" It asked.

I did. The history teacher discussing roses and aphids, then tormenting an effeminate boy named Mark by calling him Marsha in front of the class. A shy, intelligent girl we labeled "hermaphrodite" after freshman biology class—and hearing someone call her that on graduation day. A girl in Home Room shouting at me, "You should dress up and take care of yourself. Everyone knows you're a queer." And that word—in my notebooks, on blackboards, whispered behind my back before I knew I had a sexuality.

"Do you remember . . .?" "Yes," I wrote, "the cruelty of those who called me queer before I knew I was one." Under marital status I wrote, "Lesbian." I sent my response with a check. I was committed.

Obsession overtook me. I *had* to remember *every* pertinent detail. I looked at class pictures of some particularly hated classmates, wishing for fat, baldness and too many children. I wanted to see misery. My venom was limitless, fueled by years of untouched rage. I craved revenge.

In Chicago a few days before the reunion, I stayed with a suburban lesbian couple. They could not understand my trip. "Why bother?" they shrugged. Their friends uniformly concurred. Doubt riddled my passion. What was I doing? I didn't really know.

The day before the reunion, I walked through the old neighborhood. While I was buying a pair of Adidas at an old-style department store, the teenage salesperson remarked, "Not many girls buy these." I laughingly asked whether the women's movement had hit town yet. Her jaw dropped. "You're not into *that?!*" she exclaimed. In West

Rogers Park, feminism is still a social disease. I didn't mention homosexuality.

On to Mather. The white monolith had not aged well. It looked dingy, tired. I pressed my nose to the glass doors near the auditorium. It and the choir room were window-less, locked away on the other side of Jerusalem. I tried to visualize that unacoustic hall and Paulick's wedge-shaped domain, but the mind plays tricks and I knew I'd forgotten too much. Deprived, I walked away. A Marine recruiting poster was bolted to the school's chain-link fence. Above the picture, someone had written, "No weirdos or radicals wanted." I scribbled under that, "Thank heavens—at least we're safe," and left.

Reunion day, the temperature hit 100. I moved in slow motion. First, to the family house. With frantic precision I dug out my hidden words. They'd remained, unsuspected, for all those years. They were my heritage, the bare beginnings of my writing. Behind radiators, under rugs, beneath the lining in the bottoms of drawers—I found them all. Words I'd forgotten leaped out at me, hysterical self-denunciations—"automation," "schizophrenic"—as well as bits of poetry and fiction.

Thirty minutes later, I was at a nursing home to pay homage to my Great Aunt Rose. This woman had never married, instead founding the family business, traveling and politicizing in the thirties. She, like Paulick, had been a refuge when I was growing up, explaining Picasso and Guernica, shunting me from *Swan Lake* to the Moiseyev, buying me a piano for my ninth birthday. Now in her senile late eighties, she has not remembered my name for six years, nor much of any language.

Bobbe, a photographer acquaintance, joined me at the "home," and for the first time in two years, I entered Aunt Rose's room. Her back was hunched, shoulders curled in-ward, right hand limp and helpless from a stroke. Her cataractal eyes were almost blind. She looked much worse than the last time.

Rose showed not even vague recognition when I talked to her. Her face was lined and sagging. White walrus hairs had sprouted on her chin. I told her that I loved her. She nodded at my sound. I sang a bit of "our song," "Hava

335

Nagila," and, just once, she hummed back a little snatch of it. Just enough.

Late, with a short stop to change clothes. Bobbe and I left for my tenth high school reunion. As suburbs droned past, I explained my feelings about the night. "I hope you don't walk in there with a chip on your shoulder," she said. I felt Mount Rushmore crushing down, but said nothing.

We arrived. I wasn't ready. I wanted to throw up. Inside the mock-Tudor restaurant, under a blue and white pompom'ed "Welcome Mather" sign, sat five vaguely familiar classmates, the reunion committee. Ruthy exclaimed, "Loretta," and four other women stared at me. Their smiles slipped a bit. They'd read my questionnaire and knew the Dyke had arrived. Andi checked off my name and handed me a name tag, large booklet, and souvenir necklace pen in slim clear plastic box. I joined the crowd and entered my reunion.

Impressions engulfed me. High ceilings. Gold plastic-covered chairs and peach-colored tablecloths. Endless buffet against one wall. Overpopulated bar. And people. Hundreds of people. High-pitched, excited conversations filled the air, punctuated occasionally by squeals as old friends rediscovered each other.

I hit the bar, shakily downed a gin and tonic, ordered another. Around me, cliques reestablished themselves as old cronies exchanged ancient bullshit. I searched in vain for my friends. No luck. Those who'd shared my obsession for Paulick and performance were sensibly absent. I felt deserted.

Finally, I recognized a face. Not a friend; just a face. "Gary!" I squealed, false warmth and alcohol permeating my greeting. "Hi,"—eye dart to name tag—"Loretta!" "What are you doing?" I asked. He listed an occupation. "And you?" I took a deep breath. "Well, I'm living in New York, working as a free-lance writer, a play I helped write was just produced Off-Off Broadway. . . ." He nodded a blankly appreciative grin, "and I've spent three and a half years working in the gay liberation movement." True to our polite upbringing, Gary's smile didn't falter. He did, however, freeze in mid-nod of approval. He fin-

336

ished the nod, losing two beats in the process. "Well,"—he gestured with his drinks—"got to run." And he did.

I next saw Stan, a bass in the choir. Mather's first freak was dressed in a blue polyester suit, white shoes, and belt. We traded pleasantries and labels. At "gay," his smile and eyes jerked wider. He tried to hide his discomfort, but failed. We both split to "see other friends." I later learned he'd had a nervous breakdown in 1972.

Revenge started tasting sour.

The booklet. Lives were cloyingly updated with committee-written descriptions. Women were defined by marriage and offspring; men by their professions and hobbies. "She and hubby . . ." "A natural housewife . . ." "Lady professor . . ." And the ultimate, "She's a women's lib lady." My description was stiffly written but accurate. They even capitalized Gay Liberation Movement.

I remembered people monolithically, whole lives frozen in ten-year-old poses. These were symbols, not human beings. It was déjà vu with age lines.

The first boy I'd ever dated arrived just before dinner. Robert, a tenor, fell comfortably into old conversation patterns. My gayness did not frighten him away. Suddenly, a bumptuous, balding man in mock cowboy shirt abounded at me. "Lori!" he exclaimed, "I never thought you'd show up!" I was showered with hugs and sloppy kisses.

Eye dart. "Hank!" Hank? Our last class together was second grade. We'd not been friends or dates at Mather. He wasn't even in choir. Politely, I offered my formal litany. At "gay" his eyes widened, the smile grew. Was he gay, too?

My hope faded when I realized his eyes were not lodged upon my name tag. As he babbled on and on, he pressed closer to me. I backed away. He advanced. This was a dating bar come-on. I presented my best consciousness to stop the situation.

"You know," he condescended, "you're getting yourself into a trap with all this rhetoric shit." I zapped back Remedial Feminism. He tried to calm me down with a sloppy hug. "Get your hands off me, you prick!" I snapped. He got the hint and walked off for another drink.

Within five minutes, Bobbe stormed over. "You said

you weren't coming here with a chip on your shoulder and that man was genuinely happy to see you, and look what you did to him. I'm disappointed in you." She scowled and rushed off.

And suddenly, it was high school again. I was the nonconformist and the big kids were pointing and making fun of my feelings and telling me I was doing it wrong. All that emotion crystallized into a guilt-edged blow to my gut. My legacy caught up. I felt defeated.

Without knowing why I did it, I joined Hank at the buffet line and apologized. "That's okay," he said, staring at my breasts. Collecting food I didn't want to eat, I subjected myself to more chit-chat. It was truly masochistic.

Enough. Shaken but resolute, I pinned on my most blatant movement button. GAY, its big red capital letters screamed. The knot in my stomach eased. The world was suddenly familiar again; this was just a typical gay-straight consciousness-raising session. That button gave me the power, finally, after all these years, to pay back some of the discomfort I'd endured. I planned to savor every wince.

Walking back from the buffet, I watched people out of the corners of my eyes. Fellow/sister classmates didn't disappoint me. There were vague stirrings as I passed. Fingers pointed. A man whispered nervously to his wife. Once I spotted an elbow jabbed quickly into someone's side.

A woman I'd known since grammar school called me over. "You never told me you were gay," Linda said, smile twitching. "You never asked." She introduced me to her husband. He nervously blurted an explanation of "straightening out" his sexuality after turning thirty and his happiness with his marriage. Standing in the middle of all that suburban pseudo-opulence, I realized with a jolt that Linda had married a "reformed" gay man who was trying to explain to the dyke with the button on why he'd gone straight.

After dinner, Ruthy and the committee did sketches and song parodies about teachers I'd forgotten. Next, they presented class awards—to each other. Finally, a screen was raised, the lights dimmed, and we settled back for the class movie. Barbra Streisand crooned in the background. "Memories . . ."

Scenes flashed by. Neighborhood grammar schools. The bus. Busy intersections.

"Like the corners of my mind . . ."

Mather outside: a vast, beached Moby Dick. Mather inside: desolate. Suddenly, the committee jumped in, full of sound and fury, trying to look sixteen, performing more parodies. My thoughts wandered. All through dinner, people had quietly come up to me and unburdened their own Mather-related gay stories.

"Of the smiles we left behind . . ."

The boy I turned down for the graduation dance ran into the boy I'd gone with, while cruising in a Chicago gay bar.

"Could it be that it was all so simple then . . ."

The girl who'd called me a queer in Home Room committed suicide at age twenty over an unhappy affair with a medical student.

"Or has time rewritten every line . . ."

The "hermaphrodite" tried to talk with me, but when she saw my GAY button, she would not meet my eyes.

"If we had the chance to do it all again . . ."

Mather's best humanities teacher was forced to resign from the faculty amid rumors of homosexuality.

"Tell me, would we? Could we?"

Despite my feminist consciousness, I'd been self-conscious all night that my pants were wrinkled and too short. My hair had frizzed too much. And I tried not to play with the festering pimple on my chin.

"Memories/can be beautiful, and yet . . ."

I looked at my classmates. They were attractive, well dressed, visibly successful. Had we produced no failures?

"What's too painful to remember . . ."

Ah—but only one-third of Mather '66 bothered to show up. High school taught us well the pains inflicted on those who were not winners. Reunions are self-censoring mechanisms. Those who would not fit didn't attend. Only those people who could still play the game were in that room, that night. If I'd not been thin, I wouldn't have come. There are some artificial standards even a political consciousness can't erase.

"We simply choose to forget . . ."

I wondered about those winners, too. Sitting in the darkened room, they all seemed so perfect. Lives, marriages, children couldn't be *that* flawless. But, of course, we all knew the ultimate crime would be to have slipped in that illusive, musty pecking order. We wouldn't risk losing status. So we cheated to make ourselves look better. We exaggerated. Me, too. The play I helped to write turned into "my play" and I lost one "Off" in its relationship to Broadway. Just a little fib. Just one.

And if I left that pimple alone, no one would ever notice.

"So it's the laughter we will remember . . ."

And there, up on the screen, was the Mather auditorium. I felt a surge of nostalgia. That's where I first heard magic as an audience responded to my writing. That's where my soul lived for four years. That was an important stage in my life, in both senses of the word. For the first time that evening, I was deeply grateful I'd returned.

The movie ended, and quickly, quickly, the evening came to a close. Robert refused to dance with me and Hank was drunk, babbling about "My friend Lori the Lesbie." I found a ride back with Harriet, an alto. She is in her second marriage, a refugee of both the New Left and Scientology. Our conversation in the car was the best of my trip.

Twenty-four hours later, I sat alone in my room in New York. With music playing, surrounded by my slightly ordered chaos, I knew the ordeal was over. And then I cried. For the pains of adolescence and the cruel hoax of conformity; for Aunt Rose; for the words I screamed on scraps of paper and the choir room I didn't get to see; for the hate and fear and hurt I'd carried around but ignored for all those years. The mind forgets nothing. A past cannot be left behind; it is always part of one. I tried to amputate years from my life in the flight to forget Mather. Only by facing high school's demons, forcing myself to see

340

and feel and remember, could I put those years to rest.

Numb, but relieved, I toasted Paul Simon's craziness with a glass of wine. Finally, I knew. I had survived. And it would never, never get that bad again.

Gay Youth and the Question of Consent
by Gerald Hannon

It's easy to forget that you're talking about people. The topics can sound pretty academic: age of consent, the sexuality of young people, the concept of consent as it applies to prepubertal children, the idea of innocence . . . they're themes for debate, they can be hotly and variously contested. Psychiatrists used to do the same sort of thing when they talked about gay people. Facts and figures. Examples drawn from case histories reduced to their clinical bones. We don't let them do that anymore. We let them know that when they talk publicly about gay people, when they hold their forums on human sexuality, gay people had better be present. We are not just an interesting variation of human sexuality or whatever which can be debated as if the process did not influence the real lives of the real people with a multitude of joys and problems, needs to fulfill, and gifts to bring.

When we talk about the age-of-consent laws, it's easy to forget that we are debating an issue which crucially affects the lives of millions of people in Canada. People who must lead furtive and dangerous sexual lives until they reach the age of twenty-one. Not a few have six or seven years to go. We want you to meet some of them.

Jim is fourteen. He's taller than most fourteen-year-olds. He's as tall as I am. I am frankly astonished. I try to remember myself at fourteen—I don't think I'd even managed pimples, and I may, just may, have worked up to my first successful jerk-off before I'd reached my fifteenth birthday but I spent most of my early years acting out adventure stories in the woods.

"I've grown up so quickly. . . ." Jim knows it, but he doesn't say it with a sigh for the bittersweet delights of a missed youth—rather the excitement of someone who managed to avoid some of the compulsory silliness of growing up: boy scouts, high school proms, comic books, and the Waltons on TV.

He came out just after his fourteenth birthday. Not, of course, that he hadn't known he was gay for as long as he can remember. So many of the young people I talked to in preparation for this article expressed the same thing—none of them had any doubts about the fact they were gay, and a good three-quarters of them never felt they were anything else. When they were eight, nine, and ten they didn't have a word for it. Now they do. They're gay.

It's crowded in the clubs. And not just the gay ones. There's a glitter "bi" crowd in Toronto, and they make their way to places like David's on Phipps Street. It's packed, and it's noisy, and it's smart, and it's not surprising that a fourteen-year-old might just get separated from his seventeen-year-old sister in the crush and suddenly find himself chatting with an attractive, friendly man of about twenty-four. He touched Jim's hand. That was all that happened that night. They exchanged phone numbers and promised to meet again, and did, and had sex together, but it was the first touch that remains in the memory. The guilt was there—no doubt of that. He couldn't pin down ever being told it was wrong but he *knew* what he was supposed to feel about being a faggot. But as he said: "The urge to do it was stronger."

Jim's mother knows he's gay. So does his sister. But the first person to hear about all this was his Big Brother—not his sibling, of course, but the man from the organization that befriends and helps young boys. That organization has an antigay policy but Jim was lucky. When he was ten years old, he told his Big Brother that he liked guys. There was no rush to enroll him on a hockey team, or buy him a toy rifle, or trot him off to a psychiatrist. He was told that all boys go through a homosexual phase, and that was that. But four years later, Big Brother took him to see the gay movie *A Very Natural Thing*. And went with him to a disco where Jim danced with a man for the first time in his life. He also pressed Jim to tell his mother—"It's about time she should know." So he did. She wasn't broken up, they discussed the whole thing, and she has come to accept him fully as he is. Which has made just about everything a

343

lot easier—from taking many of the tensions out of Jim's life to making it possible to bring his gay friends home, or stay out all night if he wants to.

Jim is blond, with pale, clear skin, vivacious eyes, and a wide, expressive mouth. Pretty, in fact. Which didn't exactly make it easy for him at school, but did make him an instantaneous success as a drag performer at two of the biggest gay clubs in town. He's done three shows, but doesn't think he'll do any more. At first, he found the excitement and attention fabulously rewarding. It was an unadulterated, good old startime thrill to walk into a room and know that everyone there knew who you were. But even after only three shows he found the atmosphere superficial and bitchy and he doesn't think he'll go back.

I reel back a little from this one. He's gone into drag and out again, he's already a little tired of the clubs, and I have to keep reminding myself that this articulate young man with the developing gay consciousness is fourteen years old. Seven years away from being legally able to do anything but masturbate.

There's another side to coming out at fourteen.

"Hey, sweetie, I like your eye shadow!"

"When are we gonna see your new dress?"

It isn't easy, especially if you're the only one in your school who's gay identified. Jim is in grade nine, and he hasn't actually told anyone he's gay, which is probably smart considering the kinds of things that have happened to Anthony and Gary, two fellows who did let the school know, and whose stories we'll hear elsewhere in this article. But a lot of students have guessed about Jim, or maybe it's just the fact that he doesn't like sports, or that he dresses carefully and well—in the sexually turbulent adolescent years it doesn't take much to brand you as a sexual loner, a social pariah.

It's been too much for Jim. He's alone in that school. Not, of course, that there aren't other gay students. And teachers. The fact I find most disturbing about his whole narrative is the reference to two of his teachers. They're gay. And to their (and his) astonishment, he met them in one of the clubs. Neither of them acknowledges his existence now—if they pass him in the halls they stare straight ahead. No greetings, not even eye contact. They're frightened, of course. Theirs is a precarious situation. But they could give Jim support and encouragement, they could try (at least) to cut down on some of the verbal harassment he has to endure from other students. He hasn't gotten that kind of support. So in May of this year he stopped attending classes. He's still in school, but only to the extent that he gets assignments from his teachers and hands the work to them. He wants to go to the university, and says he intends to stick it out in school. He's going to need all the support and encouragement he can get.

For Anthony and Gary the situation seems worse. But at least they've got each other. Even that seems insufficient, sometimes, to the challenge of being openly and admittedly gay at the age of fifteen in a Catholic school for boys.

"I hate Monday mornings."

It's a heartfelt and bitter statement from Anthony, and all the more startling because he's generally so vivacious, good-natured, and optimistic. Or maybe it's a naïveté—both admit to having been a bit naïve, which is a fairly reliable indicator that a certain ingenuousness still lingers. In any case, both of them were popular young men in their school with their ordinary share of friends and acquaintances until Anthony stood up in class and said that he wasn't going to support Premier Davis in the then-upcoming provincial election because "he's against gay liberation." By noon it was all over the school. And since then they've had to endure harassment which has driven them to the edge of despair. No one will dare be seen talking to them on a one-to-one basis. They are taunted ceaselessly. They find obscene things written about them everywhere—on their lockers, on the blackboard when they enter the room, in their books. Gym class is hell. Anthony's gotten into a few fights. And won them. *That* made a difference. As hateful as that use of violence may seem, it also appears to be the only way to earn a bit of respect and freedom from harassment.

Again, there are gay teachers in that school. Anthony and Gary are sure of at least three among the men. But

345

the story's the same. No recognition, and support of any kind is just an unlikely fantasy.

Anthony: "My school life was nothing to turn to as a source of enjoyment. I was an open person and the other kids thought it only natural that I be treated very poorly because of it. Later in the year I and another open gay had extensive talks about being scapegoats, and how this might change if some positiveness was projected by the administration. It never went anywhere, but it might next year because one of the administrators has a gay son and he's in that school and this might give the push that is needed."

How did it happen? What changed the ordinary pattern of adolescence for these two young men so that at fifteen they could stand up in class and say, in effect, "I'm gay"?

They'd already had sex with each other. They'd been friends for years, and the sex just seemed a natural and happy outgrowth of their friendship. Not that there wasn't some guilt—they hadn't grown up cut off from society at large—but it was manageable, it did not kill joy.

What really bothered was the feeling that they were alone. Yes, they had each other. But was there anyone else?

They found *The Body Politic* in a downtown bookstore. Somehow they always knew the answer lay "downtown." Of course, they weren't aware of the existence of the "ghetto," so downtown meant a lot of wandering up, down, and around Yonge Street waiting for something to happen.

They cruised that copy of the paper as they'll probably never cruise another man. Should they pick it up? If so, who should do it? And who should actually *pay* for it? And most troublesome of all, who should take it home?

They bought it. Took it to a restaurant and went from page to page in a state of mounting excitement. They were dazzled, experiencing a feeling that no other minority in the world can know. Heterosexuals never really understand what we mean when we talk of the discovery of our not being alone. They have never been alone, not in that sense anyway. Many, many of us grow up enduring the certainty that there is no one else in the world who feels as we do. The discovery that our cities and towns and villages are bursting with us, that there we are beside you on the bus, and teaching you at school and giving you a parking ticket, and—final surprise—marching past you on the street and calling you to join us; that discovery is one of the great epiphanies of our lives. Soon they had made contact with the gay movement.

Anthony: ". . . I met some gay people which before had been just a day and night fantasy. From here my world changed to one more like that which I had dreamed was possible. I became close to a gay activist who has put new questions and new ideas into my mind. This is helping me create a future that will be of a higher quality and more enjoyable."

Both young men began to cover ground that many of us spent years approaching. They told their parents within a month or two. Unfortunately, they didn't react the way Jim's mother had, and the story of their family confrontations is a combination of the ludicrous and the terrifying.

"If I'd known you'd turn out like this I'd never have had you."

That's Anthony's father talking. The boys were forbidden to see each other, or be out after ten, or use the phone unless Mom and Dad knew who was being called. Gary's father is from Ireland. He began to rant about going back—he was not going to stay in a country that had corrupted his son.

Anthony: "When I told my parents, they became very reactionary. All the freedoms, friendships, and rights guaranteed to all the rest were cut off. That occurred between intervals of my father thinking or praying that his son was straight."

There were fine, crazy moments as well. There was Anthony's mother coming into his bedroom during a thunderstorm and saying: "That's God talking, son. He's saying 'go the other way, go the other way . . .'" There was the pride and relief expressed by both sets of parents when their sons began getting calls from two young women. And when they began dating them, there was no suggestion that they should be home before a certain hour. The parents were completely unaware, of course, that the two "girls" were two young lesbians that the fellows had befriended, and that those downtown dates usually meant the Manatee or a Gate dance for Anthony and Gary, and a romantic outing for the two women.

"Things are better now because I lie to them." Anthony tells his parents what they want to hear. He gains some freedom, the house is relatively calm, and a married couple have pretty much lost their son. The fine irony is that they think they've won him back, that his homosexuality was just a "stage" like all the books said. If it's a stage, it's a stage in the process of disentangling oneself from one's family, and maybe it's finally a good thing that the process has begun.

Anthony and Gary were perhaps less careful than was wise. There were moments of grand and exuberant carelessness. Playing footsy together in full view of everyone while rehearsing with the school orchestra. Or running about like madcaps on the school lawn tossing freshly cut grass at each other while the school machos sat knowingly on the side lines. They earned themselves a lot of hassles trying to be free and open, and until there's some sort of organized gay group operating inside the high schools, it's probably smartest to be careful and discreet. Being out is probably just not worth the agony, most of which has to be endured alone.

*   *   *

Carol and Sarah are lesbians, are lovers. They're older than the men I talked to—Carol is nineteen and Sarah is seventeen—but Sarah has felt that she was gay since she was eleven, and when Carol was six she thought it odd that only men and women should kiss.

Their stories are very different from the men's. Less dramatic certainly, less painful, and much more encouraging. Different stories partly because they were two very political young people (Carol was attending antiwar demonstrations when she was in grade eight), and different because they were surrounded by talk of feminism and sisterhood and in that atmosphere lesbianism as a topic seemed almost respectable. Why even Kate Millett . . .

What struck me in their narrative was the almost complete absence of any sort of guilt. Sarah admitted that for a short time she rather wished she weren't gay, but that was largely because she felt it would separate her from people, that gays were just a tiny minority and she would spend most of her life alone. That misconception vanished rather painlessly after she'd read the special lesbian issue of *Off Our Backs*, an American feminist periodical. It was clear to her then that there were lots and lots of us, but more important than sheer numbers was the fact that there was a strong group of lesbians who were organizing and trying to do something about their second-class status.

There would still be the occasional jarring moment. The time she attended a discussion of lesbianism at a women's center, for example. No one knew she was gay, and it was painful to hear lesbians discussed as "them," never as "we," and to hear women debate whether or not the presence of lesbians would give the center "a bad name." But an incident like that was the exception. Sarah came out almost effortlessly, and I was envious—it was so close to the way things ought to be.

She had her first sexual experience when she was fifteen, and that was with Carol.

Carol got used to being "different" at a very early age. Her family moved around a lot, and she was always the "new girl" in school. She was odd too in that she was always more concerned with American atrocities in Vietnam, or industrial pollution, or a host of other social and political issues than she was with clothes or dates or cheerleading or any of the other traditional outlets for teenage girls.

When she was fifteen she joined the Young Socialists. That was four years ago, and even at that time gay liberation was a topic that the group discussed. She came to lesbianism as a legitimate topic for debate, a controversial issue certainly, but one her political peers felt constrained to come to terms with.

She met her first male and her first female lover through

349

the YS. That too is envy-making because finding one's partners in one's ordinary world is an experience unknown to most gay people. Heterosexuals take it for granted that they can flirt with, date, seduce, befriend, marry, have sex with people chosen from those they meet at work or at school or anywhere else. That has not been our option in the past. We met in the ghetto. And certainly we stayed there. That happens less now. And for Carol and people like her it never happened and that will be one of the things that will distinguish this new generation from ours.

Every person out of the closet makes it easier for someone else to come out, and in people like Carol we glimpse the process of the future.

It is not, of course, the millenium quite yet. One of Carol's close friends simply stopped talking to her when she discovered Carol was a lesbian. And she hasn't told her parents. She's a practical woman. Her parents are supporting her right now, and will continue to do so as long as she's attending school. She doesn't want to jeopardize that support, and since she's uncertain of their reactions to having a lesbian for a daughter she's keeping it quiet, for the moment at least.

Carol is also aware that not everyone's entrance into life will be as easy as hers. She worked on a telephone distress line for a gay group in western Canada and she remembers, week after week, the uncertain voices of young people, thirteen-, fourteen-, fifteen-year-olds, waiting until nightfall, waiting until Mom and Dad were in bed, waiting for the chance to dial out there somewhere and speak, just *speak,* to one other gay person. It hurt. Because there isn't much you can legally tell these people to do. Except wait. "You're fifteen? Well, yes, you can attend meetings . . . but don't get any ideas. You've got six years to go."

* * *

"At least you won't get pregnant."

Sarah's father could only see the positive aspects of lesbianism through heterosexual eyes, and they were inadequate to the task. But he was more ignorant than antagonistic, so was her mother, and both have grown in awareness and understanding since then. Mother told some of her friends, and experienced the shock of having one of them come out to her as a result. Every one "out" makes it easier somehow, somewhere for someone else. . . .

I asked Sarah and Carol if they felt age-of-consent laws should be abolished. They said yes.

During the preparations for this article I talked to dozens of young people ranging in age from eleven to nineteen. They're not difficult to find. They're on the streets, they're in the clubs, they're in existing gay organizations and they're creating their own. Everyone I talked to is enjoying a full sexual life, and that is why none of the names used in this article are the real names of the young people I talked to.

They are all lawbreakers. Every time two fifteen-year-olds, every time two twenty-year-olds go home together after a dance, or a picnic, or an outing on their bikes, they are breaking the law. It does not matter that they know what they're doing, that they have freely chosen their partner, that they may be in love—they are breaking the law. It does not matter that they may be old enough to drink, drive a car, join the army and learn to kill—they are breaking the law. It does not matter that they are being encouraged to make responsible decisions concerning their lives at school or at home or in the community at large—they are breaking the law.

What they do together is called gross indecency. Think about that for a minute. Gross indecency. It means two young bodies lovingly entwined.

"Everything's changed for the good for me." We are seated in a circle in a brightly painted room at the Church Street Community Centre in Toronto. This is a meeting of the Gay Youth Group. It is early evening on a Tuesday, light (and a lot of street noise) pour through the large half-open windows, someone has just gone out for Cokes.

The speaker, Bob, is letting us know how his life has changed in the last six weeks, in the time he's been out of the closet. It's a relaxed, casual atmosphere, and Bob finds it easy to be open, easy to tell us about how not so long ago he'd been a "regular guy" with a girlfriend and the

351

feeling that he ought to think of getting married some-day. . . .

Meeting Edward, one of the organizers of the group, changed all that. He's gay now, realizes he always was, has let his straight roommates know. He's having a good time. Things look pretty bright to Bob.

There were five of us meeting that night, all but one un-der twenty and all male. The group would like to attract young lesbians, but they don't know how to go about it. It's much easier to advertise to young gay men, and they're getting their first leaflets ready to distribute at David's, at the Manatee, and the other clubs and bars in Toronto's gay ghetto.

I sit off to the side, observing, taking notes. As a meeting it is less formal, less structured than I am used to, than I have come to learn expedites and simplifies the business of keeping a group moving. And I have to resist an impulse to step in and say no, no, do it this way, select these priorities, put Edward in the chair and ask Bob to be secretary and you'll find that meetings become much more efficient. Perhaps at some point that sort of input from an older gay would be appreciated, but not tonight. Perhaps not for a while because certainly one of the articulated aims of the organization is to provide a sympathetic, warm, and supportive atmosphere for young gays coming out of the closet. That, rather than being very "political" and goal-oriented.

I think it works. One of them was there that night. John is seventeen, shy, and tells us that we are the first open gay people that he's ever spoken to. It's a "coming out" for John, and the others chat lightly with him, gently drawing him out, finding out what he's interested in, where he goes to school, what aspects of the group he might like to participate in.

They have an ambitious program. Eventually they'll be a group consisting of smaller committees which will under-take the main work of the organization—a political committee to lobby for things like the abolition of age-of-consent laws, a discussion committee to help young gays new to the scene talk out their feelings, a social committee to plan dances and other social events. . . .

352

How did all this start? I asked Edward and Donald, the two organizers, how it all began.

They met in the sexuality group organized by Huntley Youth Services, a Toronto organization (formerly Big Sisters) that works with troubled young people in the city. There were about eight young men in the sexuality group, all were gay and having trouble coming to terms with it, but had the advantage of meeting under the guidance of George Hislop, president of the Community Homophile Association of Toronto, and a sympathetic but straight female social worker.

During their discussion it occurred to Donald that this sort of thing was needed on a larger scale than could be provided by Huntley, and it was the sort of thing that young people could and should do themselves. He talked it over with Edward, who agreed that it was a good idea, and sometime around the end of March the group held its first meeting. They met in Edward's apartment, and continued to do so until a month ago when they applied for, and got, permission to meet at the Church Street Community Centre.

It was not easy to get. They had to obtain letters of endorsement from at least a half dozen agencies and individuals. Liberal Member of Parliament Margaret Campbell spoke on their behalf. So did Toronto alderperson Dan Heap. And Allan Sparrow, another city alderperson. Even with that prestigious support the vote was close: seven for, six against with one abstention.

It was certainly a victory of sorts: gay people winning the right to use community facilities as any other legitimate group could. But there were drawbacks. The Centre insisted that the lower age limit for membership had to be sixteen. That cuts out a lot of young people. It cuts out Anthony, Gary, Jim, and many like them. But the group has decided to live with it for the time being. After all, some board members wanted a psychiatrist and a social worker present at all Gay Youth Group meetings! At least they avoided having to put up with that.

Before I left that evening. I asked them what they felt about age-of-consent laws. Two were uncertain, but certainly felt the age of consent for gay sex should be at

353

least lowered to equal that for straights. Three of the five promptly said "abolish them."

It surprised me somewhat that not all of these young men would advocate the complete abolition of such archaic legislation. Then I realized that's why the group is there, and that's why it is important.

Simply being young does not endow you with a perspective on social change. That has to be learned. Consciousness-raising is crucial. Together, among your peers, in the heat of debate—that's one of the ways it happens. And if the Gay Youth Group isn't prepared quite yet to demand an abolition to age-of-consent laws, that's all right. But it's one of the things they're preparing for.

I have tried not to sentimentalize these young people and their plight. It would be easy, it would be very much in the tradition of our attitudes to the young, and it would cheapen and demean their struggle. If we see these people as puppies, clumsily—ableit charmingly—playing at life and liberation, if we see their passions as ephemeral, or ignorant, or tedious, if we see their convictions as misplaced or their struggles as idealistic but vain, we become part of the vast conspiracy against them.

There is perhaps nothing quite so destructive of one's self-esteem and one's convictions as not being taken seriously. And that is the final effect of the sentimental view of young people. It protects us from having to deal with the raw and real emotions and aspirations of people who are not just preparing for life, but who are living, living now. It protects us and deadens them—deadens them because all their urgent sound, all their lived and living fury signifies precisely nothing to us. At least, nothing more than a rather inept but charming imitation of what grown-ups carry off so much more successfully.

If I have learned any one thing from these young people, it is the breadth of their disenfranchisement, and their bitter awareness of it. Theirs are lives circumscribed by the restrictions of home and church and state. One of the most deeply felt, and certainly the most resented, is the restriction placed upon their right to full use of their bodies.

Nothing can persuade me that these young people I

talked to, these thirteen-, fourteen-, and fifteen-year-olds, should not be having sex with one another. They want to. And they are. Furtively, when they can steal the time, when they can find the place, when they can forget they are breaking the law and putting themselves and their partners in danger.

They know their love harms neither themselves nor society, and they have only contempt for the laws and attitudes which would try to prevent them.

The age-of-consent law. It is a law we must fight to abolish. That we must be *seen* to fight to abolish. A fight that must involve the energies and talents of young people themselves. They know it. And they're telling us. As Anthony puts it, "This past year has been a different one from years past, but it has given me new goals and shown me what gayness means in an antigay society. It has also shown me how much work is really necessary to change the destiny of gay people and society."

* * *

Why is childhood necessary? That seems an odd question. It seems odd to question a fact—like asking why four is necessarily the sum of two and two. Four is the *definition* of the sum of two groups of two, childhood is the *definition* of a particular period in human life history and that is that. Nothing simpler. Childhood is a word which describes what we all see, describes real and significant stages in the development of a human being. We have a lot of other words, in fact, which appear to describe equally verifiable and significant stages in the development of a human being. We have a lot of other words, in fact, which appear to describe equally verifiable and significant steps in all our lives: infant, child, preteen, youngster, adolescent, teenager, mid-teen. . . . Again that seems to make sense—we can all remember being a child, it was different from being a newly pubescent early teen, which was different again from being a full-fledged teenager. We were expected to behave differently at each of these stages, and certainly *we* felt that our needs and expectations varied considerably from age group to age group. We even insisted on dressing differently in order to mark the change from one significant age level to another. When I was growing up, a teenager would rather have developed terminal acne than have been seen wearing braces instead of a belt to hold up his pants.

That was not always the case. It is not the case everywhere today. Some years ago I spent a considerable amount of time living with an isolated group of Mexican peasant farmers. It was a small village of some 200 people, and life revolved totally around agriculture—the simple necessity of growing enough food to eat. I worked in the community, became very much part of it, and at first imagined that I saw the groupings of my own society mirrored there—after all, I saw infants and children and teenagers, young adults, mature individuals, and so on. But I soon ran into problems trying to refer to those distinctions in conversation, and I realized they didn't make the rigid distinctions found in our society. They didn't need to.

I have been glancing through Philippe Aries' book, *Centuries of Childhood,* and discover that in European society as well the idea of childhood had no particular impact or reality until the fourteenth century or so. And even then it took a few hundred years more before it developed the lineaments which we recognize today: the innocence, the graceful, helpless, or picturesque qualities. Medieval artists potrtrayed children as miniature men or women, and it seems they did that because children were either little men or women or they were nothing. They wore the same clothing as adults did, they mingled freely with them in every aspect of their lives, they did the same work to the extent that they were physically capable, and they did amounts of work which we would assume today would be beyond the capabilities of a mere child. I was continually astonished, for example, at the difficult, backbreaking tasks which my Mexican village expected its children to perform.

Why is childhood necessary? It is a more comprehensible question now. It wasn't always necessary. And even today, the many subdivisions of preadulthood do not correspond to any social reality in the sierras of Mexico, and very likely in other peasant societies as well.

The categories of childhood—and by that I mean infancy, childhood itself, adolescence, and so on—seem necessary as a result of the technological sophistication of a society, and of its economic organization.

We live in a technologically advanced, capitalist society. A capitalist society which produces and partly trains its future workers in social units which we call families. It seems to me that a technologically sophisticated society requires a protracted youth. There is no way a young man of thirteen or fourteen could amass the knowledge necessary to work as an aerospace engineer. (But he *could* work as a janitor. And we have ways of shuttling some young people out of adolescence and into early adulthood because our society needs a certain number of janitors, clerks, garbagemen, etc.) It also seems to me that a capitalist society profits from a protracted youth. One of the dazzling things about capitalism is the way in which it isolates groups of people for the purpose of marketing items to them which appeal to characteristics of that group which other groups are presumed not to have. There are a number of different clothing styles which are appropriate only during very specific times periods—no sixteen-year-old would wear what a thirteen-year-old would wear who would be appalled at the suggestion that he wear what his ten-year-old brother is wearing. There are games and toys which are to be used only by specific age groups. Books are graded. Even certain foods are deemed the province of one or another distinct age bracket. It is all very profitable, but it seems to be our economic system taking advantage, in its marvellous little way, of a time period which our society finds necessary for other reasons. (I would speculate that a society even more technologically refined than ours would no longer need childhood. If machines do most of the work, including running and reproducing themselves, an extended childhood would seem unnecessary. We might yet duplicate the medieval mingling of all the ages.)

Is all this really necessary? We seem to have strayed a long way from Anthony and Gary and Carol and the pungent realities of their lives. Yet in a discussion of age of consent, and whether it should be eighteen or fourteen or there at all, or whether children or teens or preteens should have sex, it is important to realize that we are being forced to deal with categories that are largely artificial, a result of the way our society is organized. It seems to clarify the issue if we insist on seeing childhood as a *process*, a learning process basically, and one that intersects as frequently as possible with adult lives, rather than a series of plateaus which, once overcome, leave one stranded in adulthood. In effect, I am saying that childhood is a concept with which we should refuse to deal. It is *their* concept, really, and is generated by an organization of society which is not organized in our best interests, nor in the best interests of most people. It is difficult to change our way of looking at people who are not adults, because the various categories into which they now fit seem so natural and right. But I think we must. It helps to clarify why it seems as foolish to deny to a young individual something it both wants and can cope with as it is to deny to an adult the right to play hopscotch.

* * *

Why is sexual childhood necessary? By that I mean why is it necessary to maintain the myth that children are not sexual beings? It is maintained, after all, in the face of rather massive evidence to the contrary. Infants in their cribs have orgasms—Kinsey documented them in babies less than a year old. Six-year-olds masturbate, and most "liberal" Spock books are even saying it's all right. We have our own memories, the testimony of our friends, and if we interact with children at all we have but to use our eyes—children are sexual beings. I think their sexual lives have a different value to them than ours do to us—they do not seem as linked to the debilitating passions of the heart—but the outlines are sufficiently similar so that we can recognize what is going on. In spite of all that, most people would rather believe that children have no sexual desires, and if they are brought face to face with the evidence they feel that it's all happening too soon, that the kid ought to be into more "wholesome" things like camping or basketball, something that will work up a very nonverbal sweat.

On the surface, it would seem that these attitudes are the result of two archaic concepts which still linger in our society—the idea of the innocence of children, and the idea of the potential harmfulness of sex. Sex is seen to be so linked to the most explosive human passions, so likely to bring out the worst in human venality and duplicity that a mere child is considered simply incapable of surviving such a situation. It is too innocent—it will be taken in. It is too defenseless—it will be harmed. Better, therefore, to wait until it is wise in the ways of the world before it is allowed to grapple with so muscled an opponent.

If that were the case, if society were merely laboring under certain misconceptions, then the solution would seem to be to simply correct these misconceptions. One would likely go about doing that in the traditional way—through the dissemination of correct information.

The fact that that doesn't seem to work suggests to me that there are other basic reasons for the maintenance of the myth of sexual childhood. Let me give you an example of how the "misinformation" theory breaks down. I have read a number of popular sexual advice magazines, and from time to time they deal with the question of how parents should deal with the situation of discovering their child has been "molested." Now by "molested" they do not mean the child has been raped or theatened or psychologically coerced—they mean the child has been discovered in some sexual relationship or other with an older individual. The advice to parents usually starts off rather well: don't panic, your child has not been harmed; don't call the police unless you really want to punish the adult because it's likely to traumatize the child far more than the sexual incident; don't punish the child; the child is very likely to have initiated the event and may even want to continue it. The article usually finishes by suggesting ways of preventing this sort of thing from happening in the future. That is astonishing. It requires a dismembering of the logical process. The evidence cited—the harmlessness of the activity, the fact that the child may well have initiated the scene and was certainly instrumental in perpetuating it—would tend to lead one to the conclusion that if the child's explorations were not to be actively encouraged, they should at least be tolerated. The advice, however, is to stop it, and ways of doing so are suggested.

It seems to me that the author of such advice has digested the facts that children are not "innocent," and that sex is not intrinsically harmful. If that is the case, there must be some reason why he is avoiding the implications of those certainties, or why he is refusing to promulgate them.

I think the myth of sexual childhood is maintained because of the way our society is organized, and because it is in the interests of certain groups to keep it organized that way.

I mentioned earlier that we live in a capitalist society which produces and partly trains its future workers in social units called families. I hate to use words like "capitalist" and "family"—they are buzz words that turn off just about everybody because they usually signal a flight into rather boring theoretical domains. But they're still useful—I want people to note at this point that we live in a society which produces primarily for profit (the profit of a relatively small number of people) and not for use, and the social unit which makes capitalism easy is the family. The family provides the unpaid labor of one person—the woman—to guarantee the continuance of the underpaid labor of another—the man. Children learn the naturalness and inevitability of this arrangement. Whereas in reality it is a limited view of the broad possibilities of human relationships, it is seen as safe, correct, "natural."

It is my contention that sex is a disruptive element within this particular arrangement. Sex is a centrifugal force which leads one outward into the community. It is exploration oriented. It can lead to the discovery that there is no particular need to relate to *one* individual on a lifelong basis, that one can relate to many individuals, that there might be a variety of satisfying, loving ways for people to group themselves together. Happiness could be something other than living with one other person of the opposite sex for the rest of one's life. The earlier you begin sexual exploration, the sooner you discover the possibility of more broadly based human relationships, the sooner you discover that your family is not necessarily the only locus of human warmth and affection.

This society must see sex as a centripetal force, one which binds the family together rather than contributes to its dissolution. Sex, therefore, must be seen as legitimate only within the confines of the family. That is a tall order. I think sex is a very strong centrifugal force—given its own way it spins people wildly out and into the community. That is not to be discovered or admitted, and the frightful problem of persuading people that sex is a binding, cohesive force requires the grotesque solution of preventing people from having sex during that period when they are likely to discover the opposite is true. That is why sexual childhood is necessary. Biting into the sexual apple will lead them right out of the familial Eden. The age-of-consent laws are there to keep the apples out of reach. To a large extent they work. And when they don't, and young people make their forays into sexual territory, they become so crippled by guilt that the expedition becomes not so much a voyage of discovery as an accidental holiday. One returns from holidays, and what one returns to is the family.

More and more gay people are opposed to the continuance of the family as it is presently constituted. We are always babbling on about how it distorts human relationships, how it exploits women, how it has no room for gays. I wonder sometimes if that disturbs people, people who see us attacking what appears to be one of the few remaining centers of human warmth in a society grown increasingly cold and uncaring. I think we ought to be clearer than we are in explaining that an attack on the family is *not* an attack on loving ways of relating, it is *not* a plea for a society organized solely around considerations of the equitable distribution of wealth. It is a statement that there are a number of ways of relating in a loving manner that cannot exist in the confines of the family as it is. It is because we say those loving ways of relating are more important than the family that we feel the family has to go. I sometimes feel we have *some* warm memories of family life only because the human capacity for loving has exceeded the family's capacity to strangle it.

I have wanted people to think about two things in this article: that the problem of children and sex is something of an artificial one because the very concept of childhood is somewhat of a fabrication, and that childhood must be seen as a nonsexual time because it is dangerous to the way society is presently constituted to see it otherwise. I believe that means we have to behave in a certain way vis-à-vis young people. I believe that means we have to proselytize.

Such a dirty word. Proselytize. It's what they're always afraid we're going to do if too much freedom is extended to us, it's the horrifying probability if an openly gay person ever becomes a teacher, or a counselor, or a Big Brother. We're gonna turn all the kids into little fruits. We're sexual vampires—we aim lower than the jugular but the result is the same—our victims join the world of the giving head, the twilight world of the homosexual.

It is not true. It is one of the great disappointments of life that one cannot produce a homosexual by simply pawing a heterosexual, no matter what its age. By proselytize, of course, I mean reaching young gay people with the message that gay is good, that they are not diseased or sinful, that they should get out of their families as soon as they can, that they should organize with other gay people, that it's all right to be having sex. If we don't proselytize with our message *they're* going to with theirs and we will have further generations of gay people who wait until their twenties before they start to live. Gay people, and gay people in gay movements, have not seen proselytization as a priority, partly because the concept has such bad P.R., and partly because other aspects of the gay struggle have seemed—and rightly so, I think—to be of more immediate importance. The situation is changing though. I think it's time to reconsider.

During the recent gay conference in Toronto, the matter of age-of-consent laws surfaced for reconsideration. Their abolition is one of the demands of the National Gay Rights Coalition (NGRC), but there were forces at the conference who wanted to see that demand removed, and replaced with the demand that age-of-consent laws be the same for heterosexuals and homosexuals. The interesting thing was that this proposal was not moved by a conservative group—it was urged on us by Gays of Ottawa, one of the most progressive, action-oriented gay organizers in the country.

Their concern was quite understandable. As the group in the nation's capital, theirs was the responsibility of making the policies of the gay organizations of Canada clear to Members of Parliament and various official organizations located in Ottawa. Their experience tended to be that the whole program of the Canadian gay movement was discredited by the inclusion of that *one* demand: the abolition of age of consent. They discovered that as soon as someone noticed that one phrase rationality went out the window, and they were forced into the position of spending all of their time defending one demand while the others, equally important others, received no attention at all. They have been the butts of insult and derision as a result. It is easy to understand their disillusion. It would seem a simple matter of smart political tactics to water down one demand so that the other nine in your program will gain a fair hearing. It would be tempting to put all that boorishness and bigotry behind you by simply tinkering a little and *still* ending up, after all, with a reasonably progressive program.

It isn't reasonably progressive, though, to ask for something reactionary in its effect. And it isn't reasonably progressive to exclude from the gay movement (by saying, in effect, that we are not interested in their rights) the hundreds of thousands of gay people in this country who happen to be under twenty-one. But one is still left with the strategic question of how to publicly handle this very explosive proposition.

The answer is to proselytize. Aggressively so. We must try to ensure that young people are attracted to the gay movement in large numbers. It won't be an easy task, considering the social barriers that are erected between gay people and the young. And there may even be legal problems surrounding the too active solicitation of the underaged. But certainly one thing that could be done is that every public pronouncement of the gay movement, every poster and handbill, every speech should make it clear that young people are wanted and needed, that they have a crucial part to play in the struggle for gay rights in this country. We should not shrink from interacting with young people on a one-to-one basis—that is what makes people feel welcome.

In the final analysis, the demand for the abolition of age-of-consent laws must come from young people themselves. When *we* demand it, it can be dismissed as the self-serving craziness of a group that simply wants to get its hands on a lot of hot, young bodies. The demand must be taken seriously when the voices demanding it are those of the young people of this country. The next time the NGRC brings its demands before the legislature, its contingent should contain a few teenagers, and part of the formalities of introduction should be a mention of one's age. The next time *any* gay group in Canada interacts with *any* official or public body, there ought to be fourteen-, fifteen- and sixteen-year-olds present. And again, introduction ought to include a declaration of one's age.

The question is where to get them. The answer, again, is to proselytize. At present, we do not have organizations that are chock-a-block full of young people. As far as I am aware, Toronto is the only city in Canada that has a gay youth group. To attract young people to the gay movement in large numbers should be the challenge to the next phase of the movement. It is a challenge we have set ourselves simply by placing the abolition of age-of-consent laws among the demands of our national coalition. I do not think we realized what we did when we were very properly added that demand to the list, but we had better start realizing its implications because a failure to do so might result in a bitterly divided national movement.

We must work together. Yet it will only be because young people are seen as a distinct entity within gay groups that we will have much success in our attempts to abolish repressive, ageist legislation. To alter the aphorism: the abolition of age-of-consent laws can only be the work of young people.

364

IX
Challenging Macho Norms

The Boys in the Barracks

by Andrew Kopkind

Love and death are both military moods. The armed force that creates a culture of killing also produces passions more profound than inhabit any civilian community. Romance in the trenches, brotherhood in the barracks, and intimacy in the cockpits of combat are as much a part of military life as the lessons of war. But the affections that might seem the most natural—of soldier for soldier—are also the most unacceptable; and until now, the American armed forces have reacted to homosexuality with fear and loathing that is excessive even by the puritan standards off base. Long after there were publicly gay priests and politicians, there are no openly gay PFCs—at least none who are not under some kind of prosecution.

Suddenly, but not so surprisingly, an army of gay lovers is gearing up for battle with the Army of straight soldiers. Or perhaps the formation is on the order of a platoon against a division. It's not always easy to see the lines, or the action, but it is clear that a decade's liberation movements, countercultural styles, and political activism have penetrated deep into the reaches of the most regimented and restrictive establishment in America. Soldiers, seamen, airmen; women and men; officers, enlistees, and reservists are challenging the military's strictures against homosexuality—where even an unexpressed "tendency," according to the rules, is enough to warrant a dishonorable discharge, or worse.

The opening gun, or at least the biggest blast, in that fight so far, was fired by Technical Sergeant Leonard Matlovich, who decided last March [1975] that twelve years in the Air Force closet was too long, and in the style of thousands of homosexuals in the past few years, "came out" to his employer, co-workers, parents, and friends. Unlike those other hundreds of servicemen and women who are mustered out of their units and less-than-honorably

367

discharged each year for loving against Government Issue, Matt Matlovich was not under suspicion, investigation, or prosecution. He was not caught *in flagrante delicto*, but trapped in the schizoid world of hidden homosexuals.

"I was tired of hiding from myself and everyone else," Matlovich said recently as we talked above the air-conditioner hum in his bungalow in Hampton, Virginia, near his post at Langley Air Force Base. He was going about his business in these steamy summer weeks before the authorities responded to his simple disclosure. Not much had changed on the surface of his life. He dressed in Air Force blue each morning, traveled the few miles to his office on post, did his paperwork, chatted amiably with the others in his office. Throughout the day he would meet other gay NCOs in the cafeteria, the parking lot, or by the water cooler down the hall from his desk. They talked furtively, quickly, about developments in Matlovich's "case," or about news of the local community of homosexuals. Then they parted without much of a fond goodbye.

"My boss told me to stay away from Matt," Sergeant Pat Walters, another gay airman who works in a nearby office, said when I met him with Matlovich at the water cooler. The two sergeants chuckled: "So I got to go now," Walters said, already on the run. ("Walters," like others in this account who have not made public their homosexuality, are referred to by pseudonyms. Perhaps it may not be necessary much longer to be so guarded in such reports.)

No one else among the hundreds—perhaps thousands —of homosexuals at Langley and the surrounding military posts had joined Matlovich in coming out, unasked. But although it was his own solitary choice to reveal his sexual orientation to his superiors—and thereby provoke discharge proceedings against him—Matlovich was in some sense not alone. He stands at a peculiar juncture of cultural history, between conflicting systems of values about sexuality, masculinity, privacy, and self-identity. The military system has the force of tradition behind it, but it has lost its forward drive. Younger homosexual servicepeople never forget the regulations, but cannot resist expressing those aspects of gay culture that are tolerated—even chic—in civilian life. They live as lovers, travel to gay resorts, dance at the bars, and socialize within the gay sets on every military post. They tell their straight friends about their lives and loves—and hope they won't be reported. They rarely are. Change is evident everywhere at the lowest echelons of the military order, but it has not yet gained the top. Matlovich is a victim as well as an agent of change, and it is his dangerous mission to draw fire to the system, as a point man on patrol presents himself as a target.

By coincidence—but not without some historical logic—a band of other servicepeople have joined Matlovich this summer at that cultural crossroads where he took his exposed position. Two WAC lesbians—PFC Barbara Randolph and Private Debbie Watson—are contesting their less-than-honorable discharges from the service; they had gone to the authorities at Fort Devens, Massachusetts, for help in sorting out their difficulties as Army lovers, and the Army responded by giving them the boot. At Dover Air Force Base in Delaware, Sergeant Skip Keith declared his homosexuality to a roomful of fellow students in his "race relations" class; he thought his double oppression as a black homosexual might be relevant to the class's discussion of discrimination. He is now awaiting formal discharge hearings. Navy nurses and Army reservists are at various stages of appeals from administrative discharge boards.

None of them knew—or knew much—of the other challenges, but they all express an idea of resistance whose time has come. The pace is sometimes slow, but private and public institutions—from A. T. & T. to the U.S. Civil Service Commission—have relaxed or abandoned their restrictions against homosexual employees. Twelve states have stricken their sodomy laws and twenty-two cities have enacted various sexual freedom and antidiscrimination laws. At last, as the movement for sexual civil rights reaches the most inflexible, intolerant institution of all, the military is closing ranks against the acceptance of homosexuality. Lest current trends of sexual tolerance cause reluctance at the local level to search out and destroy illicit love, the secretary of defense issued orders in June for the "prompt separation" of homosexuals and the preclusion of their service in the armed forces "in any capacity."

"Sooner or later, one of these cases will produce a court decision declaring discrimination against homosexuals unconstitutional," said ACLU lawyer Jerry Cohen, the man who defended the two Fort Devens women. "It's likely to happen in the armed services because their intolerance is so blatant, and it has the force of law. The military is the key institution. Just as the racial integration of the military in the late forties set the stage for a national social policy of integration, the critical sexual battles are going to be fought here."

It is not as if the handful of homosexuals now putting up a fight, or even those others cashiered every year in semisecret shame, constitute the entire gay population in the services. Careful research is hard to come by, and the Pentagon's figures are skewed, but two Kinsey Institute scholars estimated in 1971 that the percentage of homosexuals in the military hardly differ from the number in civilian society. The various defense lawyers and experts in the current cases use a standard estimate of "10 percent gay," in and out of uniform, although Alfred Kinsey believed that "the active incidence of the homosexual in the . . . U.S. population among men of Army and Navy age is nearly 30 percent." One gay sergeant I met thought even that larger figure was low: "If all the gay people in the military were laid end to end . . ." he began, and laughed instead of ending the gag.

The evidence of one's eyes and ears is more telling than the statistics. In the days I spent around Langley Air Force Base, I traveled easily in the gay subculture, and watched as it collided with and accommodated the dominant military culture. Gay people know each other—or know about each other—in every office and barracks. Everyone knows stories about homosexual generals and colonels. A former commanding general of the Air Force in Europe is widely reported to have been gay. One young airman told of his relationship with an Air Force general in the Far East that included weekend "R and R" holidays to romantic places aboard military planes. I mentioned to one sergeant at Langley that I had just talked with the

370

(straight) wing information officer, and that he seemed uptight about the gay issue. "Well, you should have seen the guy who had his job a while back—he was a real queen!" the sergeant reported with a mocking flick of the wrist—a ghetto joke that he would not have made among straights.

Homosexuals have a hundred ways of "signaling" their identity to each other: a movement of the eyes, a motion of a hand, a certain walk. Rarely do those mannerisms conform to the broad stereotypes of gay behavior—male and female—that fill gay ghetto humor as well as straight cruel comedy. They are simply subtle and sometimes subliminal expressions of a different culture. That "difference" is crucial. Gay people learn to act out the apartness they feel either in broad parody or careful imitation of straight styles. Nongays invariably seize on the parodies. Hollywood's version of a homosexual soldier is either a mincing transvestite or a vicious, suicidal "butch" psychotic like Rod Steiger's caricature in *The Sergeant*. The gay men I met at Langley had nothing to do with either image. They could spot each other, perhaps, but they were necessarily invisible to the rest of the military world.

Beyond the signals, gays meet in one another's off-base apartments, or at beaches, or in the "cruising" areas that serve as pickup points for the kind of encounters that straight people find it possible to achieve in better-lighted environments. Not the least irony of the military's confrontation with homosexual life is the gays' use of the Iwo Jima Memorial atop a hill in Arlington, Virginia, as a nighttime cruising ground. Lovers can meet, or make out, with a breathtaking view of the Pentagon, the Capitol, and the Washington Monument, for whatever symbolic value any of those edifices may carry.

Gay bars are still the favorite meeting place, and there is probably one or more within shooting distance of every major military post in the country. The custom spreads rapidly, as well, to the outposts of empire. Skip Keith recalled that there were at least two exclusively gay bars on Tu Do Street in old Saigon, and the USO "service clubs" at the big Air Force bases—Cam Ranh Bay, Bien Hoa, and Danang—were "very cruisy."

"The best place to cruise was the military swimming pool just by Tan Son Nhut Airport," Keith said. "It was subtle, of course, but people cruised there left and right."

In Norfolk the place to go these days is the Cue Club, a large warehouse of a building on a back street of town. What makes it popular is that it stands virtually in the center of the largest concentration of military manpower in the country.

At midnight on a weekday night the bar was crowded. The disco-soul music was loud, the dance floor was active with male and female couples bumping and jerking just as they do in New York and San Francisco. A sailor from the aircraft carrier *Nimitz* walked in and Matt Matlovich gave him a big hug and kiss. "We once had a brief 'thing,' " an Air Force major standing next to me said as the sailor walked away, "but I got sent to Indochina, and when I got back he'd found somebody else." The major chuckled and shrugged his shoulders.

Other servicemen in civvies came over to greet Matlovich, who is already something of a gay hero in Virginia Tidewater military lore. There were seamen from their ships, soldiers from Fort Eustis and Fort Monroe, Air Force officers from T.A.C. headquarters at Langley, Marines, medical corpsmen, WAFs, WACs, and WAVEs—and civilian gays who work on all the bases. Almost everyone I spoke with was in the service, and Matlovich estimated that the crowd is 75 to 80 percent military on an average night. No one seems to worry about raids. "Once in a while there's an Intelligence agent in here, but he's usually working on a specific case," Matlovich said. "The military could bust 10 percent of its personnel in this area just by rounding up the people who come here, but it's the last thing they want to do."

The coexistence of gay and military communities presents scores of such paradoxes, and none of them is easy to explain. The harsh regulations against the admission or retention of gays in the service are enforced only selectively—but then with accompanying flights of rhetorical contempt. At the "hearing" for Barbara Randolph at Fort Devens—it was more like a trial or, at times, a medieval inquisition—the prosecuting (male) Army captain railed against "this insidious, sinister thing," whispered "psychosis" and warned, "Don't let this spread." And yet more and more accused homosexuals are retained in the service each year, or given honorable or general discharges, instead of dishonorable ones, as was once the case. And the gay communities around the bases continue to grow.

"Everywhere I've been in eight years in the services I've found a gay social life," Steve Lockhart, an Air Force captain, said. He and his lover—a civilian hairdresser—sat around the living room in the house of a gay retired Air Force major and talked with a half dozen other gay servicemen about the homosexual military subculture.

"I joined the Air Force hoping it would make me straight," Lockhart said. "That's how much I knew. I was stationed at Nellis Air Force Base [in Nevada] and everyone would come into the gay bar in Las Vegas, and pretty soon I was in the gay community. As long as I'm careful I don't think I'll have any trouble. At this point, I hope to stay in for twenty years."

Gary Jones and Tim Vasquez are both sergeants. They've just become lovers and are sharing their first apartment. Jones came along to the major's house and waited for Vasquez, who was working late at his office. There was a bad thunderstorm outside, and Jones was nervous about driving conditions. At length, the door burst open and Vasquez ran in, soaking wet. He hugged Jones, who was much relieved, and the two joined the conversation.

"I enlisted to *forget* I was gay," Jones said. "I guess for some people it's like joining a monastery or a nunnery. It's another way you can find security and a kind of family, without being married and living in the suburbs with the wife and the kids."

"Gay people are never satisfied," Lockhart joked. "They either want to get in or they want to get out. A lot of people enlisted as medics or some special service to get out of the draft. Then they said they were gay and wanted a discharge."

"The thing is, they don't know what it's going to be

like," Jones added, lifting his eyes and shaking his head, and everyone agreed.

"I tried it for four years," another sergeant said finally, "but the military is no place for gays."

But not everyone agrees with that. Skip Keith likes the Air Force so much—at least he likes maintaining C-5 transports—that he re-upped after briefly trying out civilian life between periods of service. Barbara Randolph and Debbie Watson fought hard to stay in the Army. They were enthusiastic about their schoolwork at the Army Security Agency at Fort Devens. They were eager to do whatever electronic surveillance analysis they were supposed to be trained for, and they were proud not to be able to tell me about it. They valued their top-secret clearance.

But the Army's way is to take away what its members prize, and give them exactly what they do not want. Randolph and Watson were relieved of their school assignment and their clearance. Worse, they were drummed out of the honor drill team, where they had spent some of their happiest hours marching together. Still, they maintained an almost inexhaustible affection for the Army. "It's not the military or the people," Watson said, "it's the regulations." Despite everything—at least for a while—the military is an available and secure source of authority for many homosexuals as well as heterosexuals who need it.

Many gays I met—Matlovich and Randolph, for two—were "Air Force brats"; that is, their fathers had been career airmen. In some ways, the military became a surrogate for their fathers in later life. But for some, "coming out" has been accompanied by a rejection of military regimentation and the authoritarian values they once found attractive. Matlovich, for instance, is hardly the "flag-waving, right-wing racist," he says, with horror, he once was.

The very process of self-disclosure and the inevitable conflict it produces can easily bring gay service people to make connections between forms of oppression and discrimination throughout the social structure. They can feel an affinity, if not an identity, with blacks, the poor, women, and (in the case of Vietnam) the "enemy." Liberation is hard to contain in only one area of consciousness.

Civilian political activists find it contradictory to support gay enlisted men and women who want to stay in the service, and they often seem impatient about the process of consciousness-raising. At an antimilitarism demonstration at Fort Devens that was supposed to—but did not—include support for the lesbians' rights, I encountered almost as much hostility to the women's pro-Army position as to their gay oppression. "We can't get excited about their fight to stay in the Army and to do all that surveillance stuff," a demonstrator said huffily.

But oppression is where you find it, and for gays in the military it is never farther away than the anxious heterosexual in the next office—or the next bunk. Paranoia runs deep, and fears of discovery—and self-discovery—keep many homosexual servicepeople locked tightly in their closets, entirely coloring the lives of those who have to any degree "come out." Self-disclosure may be liberating, but the military authorities see it as a confession of crime. Fellow servicepeople may see it as an admission of sin—or a threat of contamination. Skip Keith's roommate moved out the day after Keith came out. "He said he just couldn't handle it," Keith said. Matlovich once told a roommate of his that he was attracted to him; the man moved "in five minutes."

Homosexuals in the military are bound by a stifling series of catches—more so than in civilian life, where there are at least possible avenues of escape. In the service, regulations define gays as mentally unstable and a threat to good order. Straight or presumably straight servicemen are reinforced in their fears and prejudices against homosexuality. A system of anxiety and hostility is developed in which good order *is* undone and mental stability *is* often impaired. The military's prophecies are thus fulfilled and the gays are discharged.

At Barbara Randolph's hearing, expert witness Frank Kameny, the Washington, D.C., gay activist, tried to explain that triple bind to the panel of colonels and captain with an analogy to the military's experience with racial integration:

"When you had problems with racism, you didn't throw

375

out the blacks," Kameny argued. "You threw out the recalcitrant racists."

Randolph had been the "soldier of the month" in March, as a shakedown of sexual habits in the WAC barracks began. But prosecution witnesses said that her lesbianism had made her a "bad soldier" (in the same way, Matlovich's overall efficiency rating was automatically dropped from a "9"—the highest—to an "0" when he came out to his superiors). "It affects the girls," Randolph's WAC company executive officer said on the stand.

"Could it be that the 'bigotry' of straight women and the Army's enforced intolerance created the tensions in the barracks?" the defense asked. No, the captain said primly, "that's an individual matter. The Army is not responsible for bigotry." In other words, sexuality is private when it suits the military's terms, but political when it does not.

The politics of sexuality in the armed services are not qualitatively different for heteros or homos, but the effects are widely disparate. Straights get lessons in avoiding heterosexual V.D. They are encouraged by the macho military culture to "sow their wild oats," put up pinups of big-breasted women, pick up dates at singles bars, frequent brothels in places where they exist. There is a voluminous literature of wife-swapping among the officer class, and many military posts have "key clubs" where group sex is not only tolerated, but institutionalized. Straight men have the regulation version of the fantasies of fighting in the day and fucking at night, and straight women in the service have the correct-gender expectations of finding true love in the olive drab.

But gay fantasies are determined by the authorities to impair morale and order. It's hardly surprising that gay servicepeople half believe that their expectations of love— and the infrequent expressions of it that they are allowed—are somehow perverse, if not exactly pathological. With friends, they are eager to tell their stories, as if they were tales of combat and danger:

"I was once in love with my co-pilot," an Air Force navigator with fourteen years of service began. "He was straight, and when he figured out what was happening, he wouldn't talk to me for two weeks. Finally, we discussed it in the Officers' Club one night, and everything was okay after that.

"But I would get very depressed, and I couldn't tell anyone what was bothering me. About ten years ago I was going through a very bad time and my roommate, my closest friend, tried to get me to say what it was, but I was afraid to let it out. One night in Tokyo we had a few drinks and he looked at me and said, 'What you need is to go to bed with a man.' Well, we started a relationship, and it would have gone on but he was killed a little later in Vietnam. Also, he was married and he had two kids."

Most gay men in the service have stories like that. Fred Seligman, a medical corpsman in Vietnam, was deeply attracted to his Marine sergeant:

"I guess I was in love with him. He was a kind of substitute father for me, the top man in the platoon, a real tough guy who knew his shit. One day we were out on patrol near An Wa. We were walking along a river when I heard an explosion and everyone started screaming. I ran back and looked down. His body was by the side of a crater. I tripped over his foot, which was strewn further on down the path. His guts were over everything. I took my poncho out and put him in it and went back and put his foot in the poncho, too. His bones were poking through the plastic. I carried him half a mile back to camp. It's taken me six years to be able to cry about it."

Seligman (who is now a civilian physician in the South) thinks of his love for the sergeant as "ethereal, pure—and unconsummated." Death was part of it, too: the military drenches everything with death and danger, and then uses the banal bureaucracy to keep the hearts and minds of its members off the subject. Repression merely feeds the fantasies.

"This may be a kind of sadomasochistic trip, you know," Will Gerzon, an Air Force buck sergeant, said mischievously as we talked near the jukebox at the Cue Club in Norfolk. "Everything in the military is 'yes, sir'—with boots on!" Uniforms as drag, weapons as gear, military manners as bondage and discipline: life in the Army, for straights no less than gays, is porn by other means. "It's like being a diabetic in a candy shop,"

Seligman, the former corpsman, joked. "You can look, but you can't touch."

Matt Matlovich hears it all the time. His house is filled with boxes of letters from gay servicepeople around the country who believe that at last they have found someone who understands.

"I left a small town to join the service," an Air Force staff sergeant in the upper Midwest wrote Matlovich. "I knew what I was when I enlisted. I did so to be around guys, even if I couldn't touch. At least I could look and wonder what it would be like. I've met guys in the Air Force who make it quite obvious what they are after, but I never mess with anybody. I couldn't afford it. Like so many other gay military men and women, I too walk on eggshells, but for now I've learned to live my life of loneliness and pain behind a mask of smiles."

It was that loneliness, in fact, that led Matlovich to his own startling act of defiance:

"I just adored the military. I joined the Air Force when we were stationed in England. I wanted to go to Vietnam to 'kill a Commie for Mommy,' the whole patriotic thing. I rang doorbells for Goldwater in California until they told me it was against Air Force regulations and threatened to court-martial me. I was continuously volunteering for Vietnam. I guess I wanted to prove myself as a man. Being gay, you hear all the stereotypes and you want to prove them wrong."

Matlovich did three tours in Vietnam. On his second, he nearly blew himself to bits on a land mine—an American-made antipersonnel cluster grenade that had not detonated when it was dropped in a bomb. Vietnamese guerillas replanted it as a booby trap, and Matlovich touched it off digging with his shovel. He got the Purple Heart, then tried to go back to the 'Nam. "Maybe it was a death wish, I don't know," he says now.

But whatever else it was, combat in Indochina was a way for him to avoid the reality of his emotional life. For almost ten years he was on the run, alighting for only a few months at bases at home or abroad. Then, two summers ago, he settled in at Elgin Air Force Base in Florida. His job was instructing airmen in race relations. Something had turned him from the "right-wing racist" to a civil rights advocate. Maybe the same thing—a psychological awakening at a critical historical moment—was propelling him into the struggle for his own sexual liberation. In that certain summer he met other gay people for the first time.

"I never found any other homosexuals in the Air Force," Matlovich continued. "I thought the whole gay world was dirty bookstores and fuck books. I'd never heard of gay liberation, I didn't know there were gay bars. One day I went to a dirty bookstore in Pensacola, hoping to meet someone—anyone—and I saw five airmen from my base. I overheard their conversation and I could tell they were gay. Later I saw one of them on base and I got my nerve up and walked up to him and said, 'Listen, can you help me?' He said he'd introduce me to a civilian friend of his who worked on the base. The two of us went to the friend's house; I looked around and it dawned on me that there were three gay people in the room! I wasn't the only faggot in the world!"

With additional increments of nerve, Matlovich made it to the gay bar in Pensacola, where he saw hundreds of military homosexuals—men and women—dancing, touching, feeling fine together. "I was thirty and I not only was still a virgin, I had never held another person in my arms, never kissed another person since I was a child."

Matlovich sensed but did not articulate that he was moving with the gay liberation campaign. Like so many others, he was already on board that train and there was no getting off. Magazine articles appeared with stories about "coming out"; he somehow had missed them before. Friends started to talk about gay life; he had never heard such conversations. A special issue of *Family*, a weekly magazine published by *Army/Navy/Air Force Times*, was devoted to "Homosexuals in Uniform," and while an introductory editorial included an obligatory judgment that homosexuals should be kept out of the service, the article itself was always sensitive and positive about gay experiences in the military. It all had its effect on Matlovich.

Soon he was flying to Washington to talk with gay activist Kameny and a civil liberties lawyer, David Addlestone. The two of them were looking for the "perfect case" to test the constitutionality of the military's regulations against gays. Matlovich, obviously, was it.

It took him nine months to summon up the guts to do what he knew on that first night in the bar in Pensacola he had to do. He composed, revised, and rewrote his coming-out letter. On stationery from Addlestone's Lawyers Military Defense Committee he informed his commanding officers:

"After some years of uncertainty, I have arrived at the conclusion that my sexual preferences are homosexual. . . . I have also concluded that my sexual preferences will in no way interfere with my Air Force duties. . . ."

He held the letter for two weeks more, then one day in March stopped his boss, a black captain who runs Matlovich's section of the race relations instruction office.

"I have something to give you, but you'd better sit down," Matlovich told the captain. The officer remained standing. Behind him, over his desk, was a poster declaring: "I Don't Discriminate—I Hate Everybody."

"I mean it. You'd better sit down." The captain did not oblige. Matlovich handed him the letter.

"What is this?" the captain asked incredulously, after a quick read. He read it once again.

"What the hell does this mean?"

"It means," Matlovich said, staring straight ahead, "*Brown v. Board of Education.*" The captain sat down.

Matlovich v. Schlesinger (if it ever comes to that) may or may not be a landmark case in civil rights law. It is barely possible that Matlovich will be reinstated in the Air Force before his case makes it to the end of the judicial line. Even if he isn't, lawyer Addlestone is far from convinced that the Supreme Court could ever find a majority to vote against the Defense Department, should the case go before the justices. As likely as not, the job of forbidding discrimination against sexual minorities may have to be left to Congress—or to a military command that finally catches up with the newer values it now despises.

But at bottom, the contest between gay soldiers and the military is not simply a civil rights issue. If being gay were merely a matter of sexual preference, then it would be easy enough to establish a principle of official tolerance and be done with it. Mere sexual orientation is the way the cases must be framed, but both the military and gay people know that the "problem" of homosexuals in the service is not primarily a question of sex. Being a homosexual means being part of a special culture, with its specific manners, perspectives, and values. That culture and all its attributes didn't "just grow" out of the blue, but has been formed from the special experiences of gay people. It is defensive, ghettoized, and xenophobic. It has its own language and mores, as do the subcultures of all minorities forced by law or circumstance out of the mainstreams of life.

In that, the gay subculture is remarkably analogous to the black community or the new "counterculture" as they both exist within the military environment. The services have had an enormously difficult time adjusting to those alien units in the regular armies. Black consciousness was a real and present danger to the morale and good order of the military's mission in Indochina; in fact, the appearance of a black "movement" in the services that related to the politics of American black and Third World liberation in the 1960s was a factor in the defeat of that imperial mission.

From the very start, the existence of a minority subculture means that those who partake are more comfortable in the company of their fellows. It is true for gays no less than blacks or counterculture "freaks." The straight world is somehow tame, or lame, or irrelevant to their concerns and their style. Contemporary gay culture essentially denies the validity of much in the military order. Stripped of those attributes imposed by social discrimination and self-hate, gay consciousness disdains military machismo, downgrades regimentation, deplores insensitivity. And for its part, the military invalidates the specific cultural identity of every homosexual in its ranks.

"If we were gay, we wouldn't be in the Army, and we're in the Army, so we're not gay," a lesbian WAC said at Fort Devens. "The Army ignores us, or degrades us, or

381

throws us out. They say we don't exist until they find us out, and then they don't *allow* us to exist."

The armed forces have in some ways accommodated the disruptive presence of blacks and freaks who would not adjust to the white, straight (in the older sense) military command. From the late forties on, the services have committed themselves to a policy of racial desegregation that is still incomplete, but has gone farther than any other major public or private institution in the country to equalize the participation of blacks and whites within the ranks. Lately, policies to make service life more comfortable for the turned-on generations of the sixties and seventies, and make the male-dominant military more accepting of women, have changed the character of the forces—and the minds of the troops.

The Defense Department's rules against homosexuals grow out of its unwillingness to accommodate another conflicting community. There are specific rationalizations, of course: at various times, the Pentagon claimed that homosexuality is "infectious," that it implies acts forbidden in the criminal codes of many jurisdictions, that it poses threats to security because of the possibility of blackmail, that it is sinful or pathological or just plain unnatural. Yet there is little to support such fears. Every psychosexual study shows that homosexuality cannot be "caught" like the mumps, and the American Psychiatric Association's declassification of homosexuality as a mental disorder removes a major cause for exclusion. The criminal codes are changing. Churchmen and other moral arbiters are revising their restrictions. And blackmail is a problem only if the military makes it so.

What's left is the real fear that the services would have to change if they accommodated gays, as they have changed to accommodate straight women, blacks, and longhairs. Whether from basic instinct or the insights gained in coming out, gay servicepeople are more inclined than straights to question the necessity of the most authoritarian aspects of the military. Homosexuals can, of course, be just as hell-for-leather as any straight macho Marine, but many gays in the service find that coming out dulls the hard edge of the killer instinct.

382

That is not to say that homosexuals have not, or cannot, make successful careers in the armed service. Ancient military history, of course, is practically a gay chronicle. Greek armies were collections of homosexual comrades: "The reason why, before the battle of Thebes, the Spartans offered sacrifice to Eros," the historian Athenaeus wrote, "was that they were convinced that in the comradeship of a pair of friends, fighting side by side, lay safety and victory."

Eros was the god of sexual love; "friends" in that context were anything but Platonic. More romantic gay military lore can be found in the novels of Mary Renault, who has built an impressive library of books (*The Persian Boy, The Charioteer*, etc.) about homosexual affections in archaic armies and imperial courts. No one in the Macedonian military seemed scandalized by the great Alexander's gay affairs.

The Greek ideal seems to have been abandoned over the centuries, but the practice certainly continued. There's a famous story in gay academic circles of the regiment of homosexuals the Germans formed in World War I. The soldiers had taken the option of hazardous duty rather than be discharged for their sexual preferences. The German High Command put them in the front line in the battle of the Marne, and they very nearly whipped the Allies, while the straight German divisions fell back in disarray.

What would it have been like if they had not had to *prove* that they were good soldiers? In the documentary film *The Sorrow and the Pity,* a British officer who completed all sorts of daring exploits behind enemy lines in France during World War II tells the interviewer that he did his derring-do because he was a ho-mo-sex-u-al (he enunciates the syllables carefully) and thought to be less than "a man." Perhaps feelings like his motivate many gay men and women to join the armed forces. But the Army is not yet ready to let them prove their worth, nor will it encourage the idea that it may not be necessary for them to prove themselves according to the old strict standards of "manliness."

Under order from Congress or the courts, or under pressure from gays within its ranks and activists outside, the military will sooner or later decide that it must deviate from its straight and narrow policy of exclusion of homosexuals, and that it can no longer ignore the large gay population in its barracks. The size and importance of the military institution make that a crucial event in social history. And the special role of the services as a repository for values that are antithetical to sexual liberation means that the conflict will be sharp and the eventual changes far-reaching. The new action Army that emerges from that battle will not be an army of lovers, but it will not despise love in the way it does today.

Sports and the Macho Male

by John Mitzel

I have always loathed compulsory sports, no matter what the sport and no matter what form the coercion took. Whether it was the daily after-dinner game of "catch" my older brother prodded me into as a youth, or the required courses in "physical education" through high school (and amazingly at many universities), to the obsessed chatter of my fellow adult men about professional sports, I have held them all in extreme contempt and done my best to avoid inclusion—even to the point of suffering harsh consequences.

Initially, I assumed my dislike of organized team sports and the fanaticism sparked by athletic competitions was merely a matter of personal taste. I *did* wonder at the extent to which sports commanded such a huge and intense following among other men. It seemed a trifle odd that my personal preference would be in such a tiny minority.

I noticed this obsession with sports crossed all age and class lines, as well as occupational and racial ones. In earlier years, it rarely crossed sex lines (though lately "jocky" women have become a pet of the media—and "women in sports" has become a "social issue," the one aspect of the women's movement which is most willingly accommodated). Were all men this way? Had I missed out on something? There appeared to be no escape from this ubiquitous kowtowing to the sports obsession. One was just as likely to be bombarded with sports trivia in a lower-class workingman's tavern as one would be in an elite club or college fraternity house, just as likely to be asked about the big game on the assembly line as in a posh corporation board room. Most surprising of all to me was the admission by members of the intelligentsia that they harbored an enthusiasm for professional sports. (Can you really trust a writer who admits he stops writing to watch a football game?)

385

At some point in my life it became clear to me that an interest in sports and the incorporation of as many men as possible into some contact with the system of values promoted by the sports—either as player, coach, "booster" in the stands, or TV viewing fan at home—was deliberate and calculated policy for recruiting and maintaining males in a sexually repressed, ego-fragmented, homophobic macho manner of living.

This grip that sports holds over our male population is staggering. It permeates every social gathering; it complements every militaristic or industrial structure; it's foisted on us constantly by the agents of control to transmit the values and behavior which most benefit *them*. This system called "sports" in our society is methodical in its enlistment of males and rigorous in its maintenance of a code of behavior among them. At our institutions of "higher learning," for example, one could more successfully suggest the curtailment of library services, or even their elimination than if one were to suggest the same for the football team. In the fall of 1975, when the city of San Francisco's public school system faced a money shortage, "sports" (football, particularly) were slated to be eliminated from the curricula. The outroar was heard across the nation. And through private subscription and other means, Saturday afternoon gridiron savagery was rescheduled and "education" was returned to normalcy.

Competitive term athletics are used by macho straight men to concentrate, stereotype, and enforce their superficial heterosexuality, their *actual* state of sexual repression, and their power-obsessed interpretation of masculinity. Sports are important instruments which daily rekindle the repression and competitive drive a macho man needs to fend off fears about the kind of masculinity he has so tightly adopted for himself. Sports remain the socially approved pattern of the vestigial need of men to form into assaultive gangs—Lionel Tiger's turf.*

The kind of behavior most highly valued among macho straight men is found in clear, uncomplicated form in

* See *Men in Groups,* by Lionel Tiger, Vintage Books, 1970—Eds.

team, competitive sports. Sports are a projection of the collective image of how straight macho men *wish to see themselves*—a kind of fantasy in other words. By examining the attitudes and values which support professional sports in particular, those which fire the macho man's sports obsession, we will get a better understanding of why men behave as they do in our society, and *misbehave* to the extent they do and are certain they can get away with such thuggery.

Sports become a symbol for all those aspects of macho masculinity that American men seek to embody or at least identify themselves with. Since most men are unable, either through sloth, physical ineptitude, or consumed with the frantic pursuit of the elusive dollar, to make it a full-time job possessing these macho masculine qualities in a flashy, developed form, they settle for displaying an aggressive *attraction* to these characteristics as they are embodied by "professional men" and I mean *professional men*, guys who are paid to represent society's ideal of masculinity to other men. These "stars" are the actual carriers of machismo and sexual repression which they are paid to offer up as a desirable lifestyle to the masses, and they are paid handsomely for it, this meat, and curiously even allowed, as part of their reward, some exemptions from the rigidity of the role they promulgate.

Before proceeding too far, I'd like to define or at least narrow down the use of some of the terms employed in this discussion.

By "sports" I will be referring to the system of team competitions and all it involves. This includes the values and process used in selection and elimination of those who get to play (how many maudlin American household dramas have unfolded to tearful conclusions just because Sonny didn't make the team?), the training used to mold individuals to fit expectations, the discipline and subservience required of the individual to form a part of a collective obedient unit, and the promotion and exploitation and manipulation of men, women, and children to make them into "fans" (e.g., pep rallies).

In this discussion I have in mind college and "professional" sports like football, hockey, baseball, basketball, those sports in which the greatest number of people "involved" are merely spectators. I also include the vast network of neighborhood leagues, Catholic sports programs, tot team competitions, all those activities which model themselves on big-time teams and which boldly proffer behavior which is expected to form the core of a life.

But I direct most of this criticism at the most visible and potent of the sports agents: professional teams, those men who are "owned" by corporations and whose lives are used to bend and shape and exploit social attitudes for private monetary gain. The macho attitude of the fans—already extant by their being "fans"—are pandered to by professional sports; their visions of themselves as tough guy upholders of macho straightness are reinforced and exaggerated if they are willing to pay the price of admission and make the psychological commitment, which of course they are, no matter how personally bumbling and ungraceful they themselves may be. *Identification with the gang is sufficient.*

But as exploitative team sports become increasingly established as *the* ideal enactment of macho projections, lesser levels of group activity mimic them: minor leagues, schoolboy sports and little leagues, picking up the corruptions even the name "professional sports" denotes to a person who realizes what physical exercise and expression might otherwise be all about. To quote a review of some sports book which appeared in the Sunday New York *Times* book section January 7, 1973: "At a Midget League football game I watched recently, I saw a man berate a little lineman for missing a block until the boy wept. Like too many American men these days, that parent took the game much too seriously." All too true, sadly. The guy probably screamed at the kid even more once they got home, for crying in public.

I will not include a criticism of voluntary, participatory sports here, that is, those physical activities organized and held in the right spirit and not simply enacted as one more manifestation of compulsory aggressive competitiveness to assert a sexually repressed form of masculinity. (How could I *dare* say anything nasty when the newest gay

388

group in Boston is the Gay Recreational Activities Committee—GRAC—which organizes gay men and women for soccer, bowling, handball, swimming, volleyball, etc. In fact, the leaders of GRAC carried a volleyball net as their "sign" in the 1975 Gay Day Parade!)

I believe in physical culture and the necessity of regular exercise. I admire a well-disciplined body and an elegant and exercised physique. But exercise need not be "sports," and it need not be competitive. Athletic activity shouldn't be streamlined to serve the needs of social repression, political reaction, and become a feeder system for profit-making concerns which exploit their players for vast profits. Against the background of present-day American culture, professional sports cultivate and excite attitudes and behavior among the masses which would better be left unstirred.

So when I attack the sports obsession and the sports-fan mentality, I am not automatically demeaning the Tuesday night bowling league, or the group that convenes on Saturday morning for a few rounds of golf. Though, having worked as a bowling alley manager in the depths of South Boston, I observed firsthand how "bowling leagues" were almost always organized out of churches, industrial plants, or offices as part of the church's or company's policy to use recreation to keep church control and to keep production high on the assembly line.

I also exempt "individualist sports," like golf, tennis, boxing, swimming, etc., from this discussion. Even though some of these contests have large followings and may see the award of great amounts of cash, it seems to me that these sports are in a period of general eclipse as the mass audience spectator sports continue their ascendancy. Also, there is a level of abstraction that makes a considerable difference between identifying oneself with a specific man or woman of achievement in an individualist sport and identifying *with a team*. Individuals grow old, retire, lose their competence, display human characteristics; a team endures all by replacing its members with an occasional overhaul, just like in industrial production. In addition, a successful athlete in an individualist sport has no protection from the fans turning on him; his can be more

389

like a tragic condition—something for which there is no place in modern, mass-marketed, standardized society. Take Big Bill Tilden, world tennis champ in the 1940s. His arrest and conviction for having sex with teenaged boys not only ruined his career and his life, but it added to the stigma that tennis was a "sissy-boy" sport, a reputation it has only lately begun to shake. This room for tragedy is why Patricia Nell Warren, in her two-hankie weeper *The Front Runner,* chose to make her gay, doomed athlete of the individualist stripe and not, say, a hockey goalie or football liner. The youth's isolation and fate seem greater since he's standing Out There Alone Against the Prejudice of the World and does not try to mitigate his condition through a teamful of buddies.

In a certain way, Dave Kopay, the ex-football star who came out in late 1975 and is now author of a best-selling autobiography—fits this pattern: square-jawed, All-American athlete setting himself outside and challenging to the expectations of the sports world. Though I respect his coming out, what is curious is the media brouhaha surrounding/exploiting him. Kopay would likely have not come out if a recent change in public attitudes had not made it possible (indeed, in his case, financially profitable) to do so. And having benefited by the *new* conditions created by the grass-roots gay liberationists. Kopay has been transformed by the popular media (including much of the gay press) into gay star, authoritative spokesperson, expert, positive role model, etc. Though what he did is valuable and to be commended, his transformation is a *more* valuable lesson in co-optation than is the iniquitous function of the established media vis-à-vis a growing movement for radical social change.

My targets are, then, to list them in concentric circles starting at the center and moving out: the professional team itself, its players, coaches, managers, owners, and all they aim to exploit in our society; the dedicated "fanatics" who attach great importance to everything that happens to the team and who adopt their own system of coercion to get others to follow their model; the system which establishes macho straightness as the only acceptable form of masculine identity and then exploits the demand that *all* men associate themselves with this system; the network of popular press, educationalists, politicians, and churchmen who support and celebrate the values promoted by competitive team sports (a network which often adopts the terminology of sports to win support for their own manipulative policies).

By "straight" and/or "straightist" I do not refer to the incidental fact that someone is heterosexually oriented in his social/sexual behavior. (This fact, by the way, is more often an effect of his being a straightist.) The words "gay" and "straight" are not exactly interchangeable with "homosexual" and "heterosexual" respectively, despite the common incorrect usage to the contrary. To label someone straight in this context takes into consideration other aspects of a man's social attitudes and behavior beyond publicly acknowledged sexual orientation and activity. (And God knows, there's plenty of homosexualists around today—I've been meeting lots in the leather and denim bars—who could hardly be tagged as gay.)

I offer the idea that there exists a social imperative which sets very strict parameters on all male behavior; one's socially admitted sexual behavior is only one function of that imperative. As *actual* sexual performance is not so important to the macho straight man, so is it not to us in labeling him. He is more concerned with gaining power for himself through whatever means are available to him.

His being straight means that he has done little honest and independent thinking about his sexual nature and what he should do with his Eros energy beyond the pap he has accepted as handouts of the institutions of the society. Sexual tension, to the extent he is free to exercise it, is used as a tool for maximizing his power over others of both sexes. The macho straight man is not acquainted with the extensive outlets for erotic energy in his life. He is profoundly embarrassed by open displays of sensuality. To the straightist, sex is only one more battlefield on which he must be sure he triumphs. And he is angered, threatened, and thoroughly challenged by any greater competence in sexual technique, either in men or women, especially in a peer situation.

What makes a straightist is his unquestioning adhesion to a standard of conformity which keeps him uninformed (or detesting) of his natural capacities. After all, the straightist spends so much of his time following the minutiae of sports—feeling he maintains an elevated masculine status by doing so—he just doesn't have a great deal of time to concern himself with some of the more real forces in his life, e.g., his condition of repressed sexuality, his economic exploitation, his sexist attitudes. Life is short enough as it is; to spend it becoming a compendium of locker-room statistics seems a pathetic way to speed it along.

The straightist is repressed often without even knowing it, antisexual, antisensuous, antiexpressive, preferring rather to see destructive behavior flourish than permit "deviant" and unharmful expression unfold. Not only is he repressed, he lives in dread of lifting his repression. He sees far too much to lose vis-à-vis his macho masculinity. He bought a flashy but shoddy lot of goods, and his pride is so mixed up in it by the time he realizes what he got stuck with that he refuses to relinquish what he possesses. This is also an accurate characterization of the militarist, and that these two types of gent overlap is no coincidence.

What are some of the specifics so appealing about the way sports depict macho masculinity to their susceptible audiences?

First and foremost, professional sports glorify the team. The team has always been the traditional authoritarian technique for abnegating the responsibilities of the adult ego and feeling into childlike irresponsible collectivity. The team is the place where one's individuality is subsumed to the welfare of the whole, which in turn acts as the instrument of some other collectivity's will. Every team obeys a tight pecking order of authority. There are rookies, veterans, captains, and co-captains; there is always the coach, the figure of the higher authority, usually an older man to whom "the boys" are subservient, and behind him are the cigar-chomping, nickel-counting owners and front men.

Competitive sports mimick the military in this regard among others. And why not? Good athletes make good soldiers. Both are conditioned "properly" to serve the powers that be, in our case, to the glory of an expanding empire and its imperial male heroes.

The boys on the team wear uniforms, whereas the coach is not required to. The coach rarely gets dirty, engaged, or actively involved. He is the father figure on the sidelines, representing a patriarchy and its values in the process of perpetuating itself, symbolically sending his sons into combat to defend the "honor" of the school, the city, the region, etc. This, I suggest, is the classic pattern of how males must relate to the other males in a culture of repressed homosexuality. If you succeed in knocking the opposition's teeth out, your buddy may let you pat him on the ass. The "boys" may share the homosexually inspired camaraderie in their role as subservients but not that of equals in pursuit of it for its own sake.

To digress for a minute, it's refreshing that that horrible phrase "latent homosexuality" has all but vanished from common usage. It was largely a body raised in the 1950s, that decade of revered psychoanalysts and perceived threats, political and psychological, from within. "Latent homosexuality" was some scary demon one had to fear might be lurking within oneself without knowing *for certain* if it was really there! *Repressed* homosexuality, on the other hand, has a certain measure of dignity and personal control involved in it; it acknowledges the possibility of homosexuality, but puts one on top of it and at the reins, and the macho straightist can be proud of keeping it under control. Writing in *One* magazine in the 1950s, Norman Mailer stated that any man who has successfully repressed his homosexuality has earned the right not to be called a homosexual. In other words, close the hatch, man, and welcome to the club; now let's choose up sides for the game! What I like in this current view is the implication that any and every man, given opportunity and instruction, is potentially a successful homoerotic.

The main reason for two teams to be meeting on the field or court is so that one may beat the other. *To beat one's opponent* is the culmination of all ambitions of macho straightists, a clear establishment of power. Hence the importance of "standings." In our macho-obsessed society, in which males enforce a hierarchical concept of the *thoroughness* of one's masculinity, "standings" are very important. To be *too low* in the standings suggests a defect in a man's or team's collective virility.

The early years of the New York Mets baseball team raised this problem: they were constant losers. But the team managed to slip into the role of deliberate buffoons and by this ruse temporarily increased their popularity. Failing at being tough guy conquerors, they became stunt men and clowns. Fortunately for them, they ultimately vindicated themselves by asserting their potency and winning the so-called World Series.

(This "World Series" business is often quite visibly a case of not only biting off more than one can chew but attempting to swallow it as well and winding up barfing up the whole mess. The World Series of Little Leagues at one time actually encouraged international competitions. Alas, the Taiwanese team kept winning the title year after year, which finally provoked the American sponsors to *forbid* any foreign teams from entering "World Series" contests, thereby assuring that the winner would *always* be an American team. Late in 1975, no doubt on account of the turning of the historical tide in Southeast Asia, the Americans relented and allowed the world back into the event named after it!)

The playing field, then, is a battlefield manqué. It is kept under stricter supervision. Where the battlefield is the real thing in being indiscriminate in its allowing for destruction as the test of masculine superiority through violence, the playing field is more selective and ritualistic. (If Eton and Waterloo share a metaphor, let's throw fear of the bedroom in there too.)

"Manliness" through the force of power and conquest, and the constant threat of these, is what macho is all about. It's the outcome of the game that's important to macho straightists. Calling what occurs between the two big-league teams a "sport" is like calling ITT a "business"; it's not totally incorrect, but it's wildly misleading; it leaves the truth of the matter undetailed.

The game is essentially one of power. The professional clubs may have begun with what was once an amusement for participants and their friends, but they have perverted this purpose and offered what they do as a litmus paper test for affiliation with macho straightness.

Apropos of this, one little-publicized fact about the visit of the American Ping-Pong team to the People's Republic of China in the spring of 1971 was that the printed accounts of the games themselves did not boast of the final scores, Team A "slamming" Team B (though, of course, the Americans lost). The Chinese press mentioned the good-natured spirit of the games and the enthusiasm of the spectators. But the scores and the victories were not triumphed. This would be unthinkable in popular American competitions.

On the same note, in May of 1975 an American track and field team wound up two weeks of competitions in the P.R.C. and at a final dinner, hosted by the highest-ranking Chinese "sports dignitaries," men on the American team got drunk on mai tais and started beating on tables, screaming, and clapping during the speeches. According to the New York *Times*, "One American was particularly unruly. Finally, three U.S. weightmen picked him up and carried him to the team bus . . . Bruce Cummings, a hurdler from Philadelphia, described this display as 'terrible,' adding: 'I was embarrassed at the way some of our men acted. I thought it was discourteous to the Chinese.'" Why the dummies freeloading on the payroll at the U.S. Department of State *imagine* that sports teams can well represent U.S. citizenry perplexes me. Anyone who's seen male teams from the outside *or* inside knows one thing for certain: you can count on them being unruly, violent, drunk, and thuggish. Teams like this sent abroad might *typically* present U.S. behavior, but certainly not diplomatically put a best foot forward.

Professional team sports are short-order, comparatively neat, highly stylized forms of organized violence. *As* violence, they again mimic the military. In this active physical encounter, whether restrained by brawling, those patterns of behavior most adored by macho straightist poseurs come to the fore.

The Politics of Dress

by David Holland

It's not easy to arouse reactions in anyone today. On some levels we have been so desensitized that hardly any action raises an eyebrow. But mention the word "drag." I suspect more hysteria results from a bearded man in drag than a contingent of nudes.

I had the pleasure of mentioning the word "drag" in several gay bars in Boston lately in order to write this article. I'm still alive and hardly bruised.

"Those nelly queens!" a man, bedecked in denim, noted with no subtle calm. "They should stay with their own fucking kind!"

"What kind are you?" I asked, ducking slightly. Responses about men in drag ranged from passive uncaring to tempered reactionary dislike. Perhaps some of the stronger reactions might have turned from verbal to physical had I waited longer.

One couple I questioned voiced the general attitude I found prevelant in the majority of bars. "Drag queens?" They questioned. "No," I replied. "Men in drag, men in women's clothes."

"Oh, I don't know," the woman interjected. "They certaily add color. I'm not particularly offended by them, but I've never really talked to them either."

Another time, another place.

"Ah, they don't bother me. They just don't belong here."

"Where do they belong?" I asked.

"In their own places. In their own bars."

"Which ones are those?" I asked again, but got no reply other than, "I dunno."

During these interviews, the tables were turned more than once. I become the one interviewed.

"I don't know if they really bother me. I just want to know what they do it for. I mean, what are they into?"

Since man adopted a biped stance and his new position commanded a larger view, he has learned the significance of appearance. Even from the earliest, copper, iron, and glass were used as ornaments before they became technological tools. Lewis Mumford has pointed out that "As with language and ritual, body decoration was an effort to establish a human identity."

People wear clothes to identify themselves as part of their social group, but clothing also provides a means by which to make a unique statement about oneself. William James coined the expression the "material me" in identifying clothes as the extension of the body and self.

Clothing's primary function is providing people with visual clues to the social identity of the person they see. They also choose clothes to make them a unique personality within that group.

It is important to look at the historical significance of dress before we can truly understand its importance in today's context and within the gay culture.

Clothing has been used throughout the ages as a symbol of social standing and prestige. As early as the fourteenth century, outrageous attire was employed to denote social status. The chopine, equivalent to today's platforms, reached heights of twenty inches or more. The wearers, obviously of the "leisure class," needed servants to assist their lofty ambulations. Pointed toes arrived shortly thereafter. Their lengths became so pointedly perilous that a decree was issued: only upper-class people could wear shoe toes of twenty inches while the middle class was limited to six to twelve.

The social status of clothes and adornments became so significant that in 1651 the General Court of Massachusetts legislated this act:

> We declare our utter detestation and dislike that men and women of meane condition should take upon themselves the garb of gentlemen by wearing gold or silver lace or buttons or points at their knees or to walk in bootes or women of the same rancke to weare silke or tiffany horlles or scarfes, which though allowable to persons of greater estates or more liberal

education, yet we cannot but judge it intollerable in persons of such like condition.

Actually it was Americans' love of sport, rather than love of democracy, that loosened dress codes. When swimming became a respectable activity, beachwear became the first clothing designed for comfort rather than to denote status. For both sexes the bathing suit was singularly most important in the development of less rigidity in dress. For women, acceptance of the sport of bicycling gave them the right to wear pants. Pants (bloomers) were designed for safety in cycling. These two styles were the first signs that Americans would move toward a more unisex look in clothing.

It seems that historically clothing styles followed life-styles. A quick glance around will show that that is still true today. The more women enter the traditional male world, the more acceptable male clothing becomes for women. Today, a woman in pants would not be considered a cross-gender dresser.

Cross-gender dressing reaches as far back as the French Revolution when women adopted men's clothes in the spirit of egalitarianism. Women's reform in America in the 1850s affected free-love colonies such as the one in Modern Times, Long Island, where the people indicated their freedom by dressing for comfort and practicality. However, as fashion dictators picked up on the commercial aspects of this burgeoning liberation, they added lace, ribbons, and feminine fabrics until the costume was no longer male identified.

Men's tradition-breaking began much later. Not until the sarong wraparound beachwear of the 1950s did the thought of a skirted male emerge. Although Jacques Esterel's spring collection of 1967 included a plaid skirted men's suit, the fashion obviously never reached prominence.

Designers since then have tried to balance the two. Rudi Gernreich predicted the unisex look for the seventies. He felt that like dressing would "enhance their bodily difference." But this idea and the adopting and acceptance of like dressing or "cross" dressing has not attained popularity because we live in a patriarchal society. In matriarchal societies, clothes worn by both sexes are more similar.

In the paternal distastes of this society lies the oppression of dress. While women in men's clothing are perfectly acceptable today, men in traditional women's clothing are still objects of ridicule. Within present society, it is only some members of the gay community who have attempted to purge the sexist perception of dress by cross-dressing. Yet within our own small enclave the oppression and stereotyping continues. I suspect that a skirt is not de rigueur in any gay men's bar but a work shirt and jeans, long the machismo emblem, are as revolutionary as the light bulb not only in lesbian circles but in straight society. It is important to ask the question why and to reassess whether we are following, within our own culture, the dictates of our oppressors.

The issue of dress surfaced recently in Boston when a radical grouping of gay men, the Fort Hill Faggots for Freedom, paraded with their plumage into Sporters, a bar nationally famous for its discreet masculine image (a bar where drag queens have been distinctly unwelcome). The Fort Hill Faggots invaded Sporters with one specific intention—to make the community look more closely at the sexist way we still view types of clothing. It seems unfortunate, though, that the dazzle of drag easily clouds any political issue, and certainly the interests of the group were political ones. Also, given the basis of their dissatisfaction, they could easily have chosen any bar. So we must look at what issue the demonstration has raised. We must strip away the personalities that were involved on both sides, for if we don't we will surely miss the issue.

John Cummings, in an article appearing in the *Gay Community News*, addressed the ideals of "political drag":

Gender-fucking [cross-dressing] may be thought of as any condition which aspires to being a violation of societally prescribed gender roles. Gender-fucking is why we are feared and despised by most of society. It allows us to be vividly enlightened to the ugliness, sickness, and hyprocrisy of so much of straight society. Being an explosion in the midst of gender prison, drag creates a profound statement of love. Very simply, it says, "I love being gay, I love my sisters and brothers, and I reject the system of values which seeks to oppress me."

Yet, in a rebuttal article in the same publication, Darius Dappletree replies,

Drag-queens by their very appearance are a challenge to the patriarchal definition of maleness; but on the other hand, they are doing this by identifying with the most oppressive aspects of femininity; that of being nothing but bubble-headed sex objects, helpless, overemotional and playing up to their opposite—real (butch) men. Drag queens are men who identify totally with the patriarchal definition of femininity, thereby in reality supporting patriarchal values . . . thus increasing the polarization of masculine and feminine roles.

Dappletree's argument, it appears, best illustrates lesbian and feminist viewpoints on the matter. Karen Lindsay, an outspoken and respected feminist, says about drag in an article in the feminist publication *Sojourner* that "Drag is a blatant mockery of women, as genuine a manifestation of misogyny as the straight male practice of sexual harassment. Many gay men display their hostility most overtly by sexual mockery. (And if there is an element of self-hate, or gay self-hate in this as well, that too can be traced to misogyny—the mockery of the 'female' component in themselves.)"

True enough, men in drag do not appear as the smartly attired or fashionable Bonwit's customer but as the most outrageous females of the past twenty years. The emphasis is on exaggeration—layers of chiffon, taffeta, black silk, rhinestones, and other gaudy adornments. It is an image one might expect to find on the tawdry side of New Orleans, certainly not a good view of women as a whole.

However, people who use "political" drag are not what one considers drag "queens." A drag queen is someone who cross-dresses to attain a stereotypical feminine appearance. Those who are making other statements have no desire to make that kind of appearance. Their role is more clearly "gender-fuck." They wear fabrics stitched into dresses and jewelry of glitter and clunk the same as the women wearing jeans. If the jeans are to be categorized as male apparel, and similarly, if women intend to smash that image by wearing them, so, conversely, men must attempt to kill the same sacred cow of dress. This is the focus of drag statements today.

If women dress so that they create an image that society decrees to be a male one in order to equate themselves with men, it is a shallow attempt. At that point they sacrifice the unique qualities that make them women. If, on the other hand, the reason for dressing in "men's" clothes is to begin to liberate dress roles, it is a far better stance. Drag here is intended for that purpose. It is not, as it is so usually misunderstood, to be to equate oneself with women.

In questioning people in the bars on their reaction to drag, I found that oppositions were born clearly from a misunderstanding of its meaning. Most negative comments tend to underscore a confusion. Men in drag do not try to be women or even pretend to be women, but simply want to help release the Victorian corsets of image dressing that lurk around every pair of jeans, that is imprinted on every Chemise LaCoste shirt, and that is in the treads of every boot. The mere presence of a drag may serve to remind others that their dress may protect them from ridicule, but allows them few choices of style, fabric, and adornments.

Of course, there is, for some, the simple fact that going in drag is pleasurable. "It's fun," said Merrill Frady, a pantomime singer with Sylvia Sidney's show at Together, a Boston gay bar. "I just like to look good, and to me a drama makes me look good. I can't look good in a tux. . . . I've always adored evening gowns. When I was fourteen, I used to sit in school and doodle and draw pictures of evening gowns. I thought I was going to grow up to be a dress designer."

Since there is a design of dress that this society indicates for men and women, there is also a design of fabrics and ornamentation. Silks, taffetas, and chiffons have generally been exclusively in the woman's closet. Rhinestones and precious gems similarly remain in women's jewelry boxes. The men, as expressed by the Fort Hill group, pick these up like the shunned toys of the seventies. No longer having to tiptoe to Grandma's attic, they can fling wide the doors of feminists' closets and be adorned with the sensuous materials from a bygone era. They can enjoy the mere costuming of drag and draping themselves in layers of heretofore untouchable fabrics. It's a steak dinner after years of starvation. I suspect that like children at Christmas they have a hard time deciding what to unwrap and try on first.

The fun side is wonderful silliness and a drunkenness of fabric, but the serious side has no humor intended. The primary stigma of drag is just that giddy silliness. The assumption that a man in woman's clothing must be dizzy is another sexist attitude that political drag hopes to smash.

Drag may open our eyes, but it can only open the eyes of those who wish to see. Political drag is this reminder: men are society's constant, whether gay or straight. Most of us appear neither to strive for nor ask for any deviation from our role. Perhaps some, if not many, of us do not wish to change, but similarly we give no room to those who do. The more men lock themselves into their self-defined supremacist stance, the more difficult it becomes to explore any new definition of ourselves. The feminist movement has helped women make their role choice. Hopefully the "drag movement," in the end, will help us make ours.

X
Rites of Passage

Letter to M

by Andrea Dworkin

> Whence come I and on what wings that it should
> take me so long, humiliated and exiled, to accept
> that I am myself?
>
> Colette, *The Vagabond*

Dear M,

I wouldnt have the courage to try to write this letter after all these years if I didnt need to more than I need not
to. Suddenly Im aware that for years Ive needed not to. I
could have tried to call you on the phone. I know the
name you use now. Probably we live in the same city. Or
I could have called yr mother, I know where she lives. Im
not brave like that.

I dont know where to begin. I hadnt thought about you
in years—the proof that memory is political. Then, about
two years ago, I went to the country to visit Barbara Dem-
ing. We had a talk, painful and intense, which brought me
right to the thought of you.

Barbara and I first met 12 years ago on the David
Susskind Show. We were there to talk about jails. I had
spent 4 days in the Womens House of Detention in New
York City. Barbara had been in jail several times on civil
rights and peace marches. We had much in common. We
were both pacifists, both women, both committed to civil
disobedience as a serious political tactic and moral act.
Barbara had written a book called *Prison Notes*, which is
the story of how she and others were arrested on a peace
walk in Albany, Ga. They were arrested because they
walked down a street, black and white together. They were
arrested, jailed, in jail they fasted, they were released, they
walked down a street again black and white together, they
were arrested again, jailed again, fasted again, and finally
released again to walk down that street again, black and
white together. That unjust law crumbled before the

strength of their conviction and the courage of their acts. They did walk down that street.

Barbara and I met on that television show, and I admired her as I had rarely admired another woman. She was, for me, heroic—strong, brave, authentic, honest. We met as sisters, though we did not use the word then, in the same struggle. We wanted, both of us, to tell with clarity what jail is so that those who sustain jails, build them, pay for them, staff them, advocate them, would know what it is that happens inside them. We talked, each of us, of what it was.

For me, those 4 days had been a devastating nightmare. Two doctors had brutalized me during an internal examination. I was 18 years old, ignorant of so much. For the first time, I was forced to lay on an examining table, feet in stirrups, no sheet to cover me or give me the illusion of safety. They stuck steel in me, cold steel, hurting me all over with their hands and their instruments. The pain had been agonizing and mysterious. I did not know what they were doing or why. As one doctor kept manipulating the cold steel, the other sat watching me and taunting me. With their hands, they pummelled my abdomen until I cried out in pain. When they were finished and I was returned to my cell, I found that I was bleeding. I tried to cry but couldnt. I bled for 15 days, telling myself that it was my period or syphilis. When I did finally go to a doctor (and by then I was terrified of doctors), he said that I had been bruised and injured internally. It was a nightmare, one I still live with and through 12 years later.

On the television show, Barbara described jail and I described jail. I told how my vagina was entered over and over again by rude hands searching for dope or disease. I told how I had been raped by the hands of those doctors, by their instruments.

We told what we knew about who the other women prisoners were—black and poor women, mostly prostitutes and junkies. We described the filth, and the dreadful slop that passed for food.

Then I spoke in a way that I have deeply regretted since. I said that lesbianism in the jail was "rampant," brutal, aggressive, terrifying. And it was, to me it was. The threat of sexual assault was always present. The dykes were "like men"—macho, brutish, threatening. I had come out of that jail terrified of *women*—wanting never to be touched by one again. In jail, one of the women I had been arrested with had been held down by a group of women, and again, her legs spread open, her vagina entered. I was sickened and confused and horribly afraid.

As I sat in Barbaras home, 10 years after the events I have described, she told me what it had been like for her to sit there, a lesbian, unable to speak, maligned, anguished. She told me what it had been like to sit there, a lesbian, silent, not able to address me directly and authentically. She said to me then, 10 years later: "Of course we couldnt talk. Those men were between us. Their world stood between us."

I must tell you what this meant to me. First, I understood, for the first time in my life, the anguish of lesbians who are unable to live fully and openly in the world, robbed of pride and selfhood, robbed of a sexual identity which is nourished by visibility and dialogue. I felt what it must have been like to be silenced by that kind of fear. I had some idea of the kind of fear it was because Barbara is a woman who is heroically strong and brave. She walked in the South and risked her life. She went to jail and risked her life. She acts according to her conscience at the risk of her life. I have seen and known this to be true consistently over a period of many years. Whatever fear she felt when she walked down those southern streets, still she walked. Fear of revealing her lesbian identity silenced her. Imagine fear like that.

Second, I saw vividly how my own life would have been different if women had spoken the truth to women as I was growing up. All of the years of childhood and not one true word about women loving women. Growing up, in school, reading books for every scrap of information about life, every ray of light that might show how to live bravely and tenderly—and nothing about what would have mattered to me most. This seems silly to say, it is so obvious—yet sometimes I can see how the whole shape of my life would be different if those silences had not existed. No one taught us our herstory or anything at all about our

407

lives as women. It seems perhaps silly for me to mourn it now. Except that sometimes I feel it in the saddest way.

But the first time I met Barbara, when I was 18, I was in a specific desperation. My life did depend on knowing the truth. I had been horrified by my 4 days in jail. I was in terror. My skin crawled afterwards when a woman touched me in the most casual way. I had made love with women before, but those had been tender meetings. Now, in jail, something different had happened, and I did not recognize that the one kind of erotic intimacy that I knew with women had anything at all to do with that other forced, terrifying, threatening intimacy. I did not connect my own personal erotic relations with women with anything I experienced in that jail. I had never named myself a lesbian, so I thought, *they* are lesbians and *that* is lesbianism. I connected nothing. I was frightened and mystified.

These last years would have been very different for me if Barbara and I had been able to speak together when we met. I needed her so very much. I am saying, of course— if only things werent as they were. The fact is that in 1965 women did not speak to women at all, and lesbians did not speak at all. There was no womens movement. There was no consciousness raising, or understanding of dominance and submission, or forthright talk of homoerotic love. There was no deep thought or dialogue on male-female sex roles, how we act them out, what they mean. I didnt know why the women in jail were "like men"—boyfriend and girlfriend, rapist and victim. I could find no way out of my terror and Barbara could find no way out of her silence. We were locked into isolation from each other.

As I talked with Barbara, 10 years later, I thought about you. I remembered you, I remembered us. As I sat with Barbara, I remembered us and understood all at once how the same system of masculinist values, male dominance, sexual repression derived from the oppression of women, had come between us, taken us from each other and from ourselves. I thought, where is M, and why have we not yet found a way to talk about who we really are, what we were to each other, what happened between us.

The silence between women has kept us locked in isolation from each other for so long.

You and I were best friends. Remember how that was. We did everything together, went everywhere together, then called each other on the telephone as soon as we parted to discuss every detail of every event that had happened when we were together. You were a painter, brilliant, forceful, disliked by teachers and parents because you were outspoken, immodest, ambitious. Yr very posture and bearing refuted their authority. I was a writer, and we always talked together of how we would be artists one day. During science class we both worked on our novels. Yrs was about a woman named Belle who was horribly poor, lived above a saloon, and was going to law school against all odds. I dont remember mine. At yr house we would take yr pastels and draw. You painted. You worked mostly in oils, sometimes water colors, and you had an astonishing talent.

We loved each other as two girls often do, and when that love exploded into touching and kissing and passion, when that eroticism suffused our bodies and brought us to each other, and all night long, neither of us knowing anything conceptual or verbal about what was happening between us, we made love, all consuming, passionate, tender, lusty love, over and over, neither of us knew what had happened or why or what to call it or what to do about the next day or the day after. And so, in the morning we went to school, the 8th grade I think, and continued to act with each other as we always had. Only we were driven to crushes on the boys with new resolve. We didnt sleep together again.

Then we both fell in love with another girl. I think now that we probably still wanted each other but didnt know that so we loved her. Whatever the truth of that, we fought over our new friend. I was maddened by it, enraged, betrayed. I set out to win her and I did. Then she was my friend and you werent. Then yr mother took you out of school and sent you away. You had some sort of nervous breakdown. I wonder, did you tell yr mother what had happened? I wonder, did you know? I didnt. Everything just happened, there were no names, no shame or guilt, almost no memory. After you left I was lonely, I felt remorse, even grief. But I didnt know why.

Within months, by the time you were 15, you were fucking a 35 year old painter with assorted exwives and children and models who tried to kill themselves when he left them. You were insanely in love with him. You never finished high school. You stayed with that painter for many years. You navigated through his exwives and suicidal mistresses and held on ruthlessly. You had yr nose fixed and yr hair bleached and curled. You wore ruffles. Are you with him still? I saw you once in New York when we were 18. I was going to Bennington, you were a cocktail waitress. You were a beautiful woman whose presence in the world was entirely circumscribed by the costume you wore (tarty and demeaning) and the bastard whose mistress you were. All that I know about you since then is that you changed yr name and stopped painting.

When we saw each other that time, the love was still between us, the eroticism, our old camaraderie. So many shared hours and days, so many shared dreams and ideals. And yet we didnt speak one honest word to each other. We babbled about men as I remember it. I didnt say then, because I didnt know then, you were my first love, my first lover, I loved you then and I love you still. It wasnt until I talked with Barbara that I saw the silence between us as atrocity—cruel, damaging, not of our making as the world is not of our making.

For me this means now to end the silence wherever I find it, to give the love a name, a way of being in the world, so that young girls who love each other as we did can live that love fully and joyously. We had a right to love each other and that right was taken from us before we were born. We should have lived in a time and place where that love could have grown as we grew, so that we would not have been deprived of each other as sisters, lovers, and friends over all these years. It is too late for us to reclaim our childhoods but we can imagine a world in which we could have known each other fully. I believe that we have to create that world.

I have this fearful picture of you now—as wreckage, scar tissue, a painted empty shell, yr boyfriends aging refuse. I hope it isnt true. Its too late maybe for it to matter that now I know something about the wounds inside you from that time when we were 14. I wish it had been different. I wish I had some kind of magic that could take the hurt out of you. I wish we could have been best friends forever, or at least until we grew up. I wish we were best friends now. I wish I could hold you in my arms and kiss the hurt away.

I hope that this movement of women, this ocean of womens love and feeling and new presence in the world, has reached you as it has reached me. If it has, then along with the pain, along with the full recognition of our loss, has come some measure of healing. I hope that sisterhood sustains you, and that through it we can find each other again. At this moment I would give my life to be with you again.

Im so sorry, so grieved over what you went through—

A.

Neither Profit nor Salvation

by Barbara Grier

In the last several months while I've worked on this article, I've often thought—talking to myself in the bathroom mirror, riding back and forth to work—how extremely arrogant it is for anyone to pretend to be able to discuss in a few pages the subject of Lesbians and Lesbianism.

I'm 43 years old. I've spent virtually my entire life from age 14 studying the subject. (If I have 5 more lifetimes ahead of me, I'll barely begin to scratch the surface, even though I've specialized primarily in one tiny aspect of the panorama of our existence, the Lesbian in literature, because, after all, there are millions of Lesbians.) There are millions of Lesbians in the United States. Not thousands nor hundreds of thousands, but millions of women who are Lesbians. We have many things in common, but we have many more things not in common with one another. What is true for one of us may not be true for hundreds or thousands of us in different personal circumstances.

Probably the Lesbians reading this have a little higher sense of what we call "consciousness" but maybe that's not true, because I'll bet there are some closeted Lesbians reading this too. In fact, there will probably be quite a few secret Lesbians reading this book. And as you read, you're beginning to shake inside or squirm a little. There's bound to be some of you out there. There are always some of you in every room where there are a few women, always. Every time you ride a bus and there are a handful of women on the bus, someone on that bus is probably a closet Lesbian, maybe several someones on that bus. In fact, the closet, that ridiculous place, may be just exactly the only other thing we have in common besides the basic one, that we are Lesbians.

I'm not even sure that I want to try to define the word *Lesbian* for you. Those of you out there who know what

412

the word means don't need any explanation, and those of you who do not will when you've finished this book. But the closet, we all know about closets. We hang our coats, shirts, pants, shoes, lives in the closets. Some of us live all of our lives in closets. In fact, not just some of us, not just a few of us, not half of us, or three quarters but more like 95% of us live our lives in closets.

Now, even the closet folk have differing levels of "closetism" . . . I guess I'll coin that word. Some of us live in closets part of the time, some of us live in closets, say, 75% of the time and 25% we're out of the closet. We have select people to be out of the closet with. We're out of the closet with all of our gay friends, for example, and five select heterosexual individuals that we've chosen throughout our lives to decide to confer the great honor on them of telling them that we're Lesbians, and holding very still for a few moments and looking into their eyes for fear they'll flinch, back up, turn away, reject us outright, as if it mattered. As if it mattered a damn bit. It is the closet that is our sin and shame.

There's been a lot of talk since the late 1960s about coming out of the closet. There've been marches and speeches. There'll be many more speeches, at least, if not so many marches since marching doesn't seem to be this year's thing. There'll be some slogans:

"2, 4, 6, 8, gay is just as good as straight"
"3, 5, 7, 9, Lesbians are mighty fine."

The first slogan is an insult, the second slogan is silly.

There will be speeches and more slogans. There will be another tiny percentile point rise at the end of the year in the number of visible Lesbians. This or that artist, this or that writer, this or that composer, this or that politician, this or that priest, this or that minister. A few more of us will come out of the closet. Come out, come out, wherever you are. That will be very good for them and that will be very good for the handful of people whose lives they touch and it will probably even be somewhat beneficial for the Lesbians who have access to their public derring-do and take some comfort and courage from their acts.

But coming out of the closet is getting to be less and less of an option and more and more of an obligation. It is not a matter of "you ought to be because it's healthier to live like an open free person" or "you ought to because it's easier" because deception is difficult at best . . . you have to carry it forward and it keeps you busy looking over your shoulder on both sides. And you ought to because being in the closet is not necessary any longer. It's a moral obligation. It's not a matter of coming out of the closet because it's good for you. It's not a matter of coming out of the closet because it's good for your lover, because you're going to feel better, because it'll eventually loosen up your relationship with your family or loosen up your relationships with your neighbors or help at work. It's nothing to do with that. You need to come out of the closet because *you know* you're a Lesbian and every one of you who stays in the closet makes it harder for the woman down the street to come out of the closet. We help oppress each other, we are our own oppression. There are even a few women who are ashamed of being Lesbians. That's hard to imagine, I know, but it's true. There are still Lesbians in the world who are ashamed of being Lesbians. Incomprehensible, illogical, of course, but it exists. Now, there are a few people who remain in the closet and enjoy being uncomfortable about being Lesbians, and I'm not sure if anything they read is going to have any effect on them. But there are some weird people everywhere, there are even some weird Lesbians, so if you're weird in this way, fine, stay in the closet, I'm not talking to you. I'm talking to the run-of-the-mill Lesbians out there, the women who do not belong in the closet, are not comfortable in the closet, don't really want to be in the closet, but think for some real or imagined reason—and imagined reasons are every bit as good as real reasons—that they must remain there because if they don't stay in the closet, if they come out, they're going to lose their jobs or no one will love them or people will point at them on the street and laugh or their co-workers will have nothing to do with them, or well, make up your own reasons. I'm sure there are as many reasons as there are closet cases out there.

But it's not a matter of choice any longer. I'm not really asking you to come out of the closet, I'm telling you. You have to come out of the closet, you have to come out. Not

414

only do you have to, the time has come where those of us who are out of the closet need to put pressure on those who are in. And I do not mean unkind pressure but real pressure. We need to talk to the women we know who know that they are gay and that we know they're gay and that they know we know they're gay but who for one reason or another still remain in the closet. If there is a crusade in the future, the crusade is to strengthen our numbers publicly. I mean make those women who are Lesbians and know they are Lesbians stand up and be counted. It is time to do so. Once again, I am not advocating that you run around with sandwich boards, I am not saying you need to go out on the street and chalk it in front of your house. I am saying that you need to start acting like you really are. Don't lie, don't pretend. Behave as you are, you're a Lesbian, act like a Lesbian, be glad you're a Lesbian, tell the world you're a Lesbian, subtly, of course. But make sure that every thinking, intelligent person anywhere around you, that has any relationship with you, however casual, is aware or likely to be aware of your orientation. It's the least you can do for the cause, it's the least you can do for your own people. We have a terrible disadvantage—we aren't marked in some clear-cut way. We can't be seen, we aren't visible. As others have suggested, I too wish we'd all wake up lavender some morning and solve that part of the problem. We cannot be seen and because we can't be seen, we can pretend, and in years past, perhaps there were reasons for it. Perhaps it was better, perhaps it was easier to pretend. But it's not good anymore, it's not healthy, it doesn't feel good, it's not good for you, and it's very bad for the movement. It's very bad for the future. It's extremely bad for the young Lesbians now, the 10-year-olds, the 15-year-olds, the ones who are 20 and looking to us as examples. Why not make this world a little easier for everyone who comes after us? It's really not too much to ask. Don't we owe the world that? Shouldn't our passage through it enrich it? Shouldn't our having lived mean something good for those who come after us? And what about our own lives? There are an awful lot of young people in this world. Why should we reinforce in them fear for the safety of any job? Why should you for a minute imagine that you have to fear for your job? One of the reasons that women are having touble in universities and in businesses on a professional level is the closet. Many women who would be active in the women's movement, women who have the knowledge and the wherewithal to do wonders, are cautious in many cases because they fear that if they rock the boat about feminism, someone will come out with the fact that they're closet Lesbians and rock their boat back a little. I've heard that argument offered up so many times, I can't count it. The way to combat it is to come out first.

What it boils down to is this: when you start counting the women who have succeeded on an historical level, you find that virtually all famous women were Lesbians. Not all, but virtually all. Such enormous quantitites of them, such a proportion far out of reasonable belief that you're forced to come up with one of two conclusions. Either almost every woman must be a Lesbian given the choice to be, which happens to be my personal opinion, or, if you can't accept that you must at least accept that those women who step out in the world and do something important in it are Lesbians. It is unrealistic to believe that some social body is going to turn upon all of the successful and creative women in the world and put them out of commission by some kind of mass genocide. I rather doubt that that's going to happen. For one thing, there are far too many women for it to happen. If all the Lesbians come out of the closet, think how many famous women that's going to concern. Think for a minute in your head about every entertainer you can name who is gay, every movie star that you know is a Lesbian. Think about that for a few minutes. Then let's talk about all the women we learned about in school in literature. Let's take one relatively small group—American women poets. Let's name the famous American women poets that we now have reasonable proof were Lesbians. There's Amy Lowell, and Emily Dickinson, Edna St. Vincent Millay, Elinor Wylie, and Sara Teasdale. Get the point? Did you ever hear of any of those women? Could you get through school without having heard of any of them? We can go on, there's quite a list more. Let's see, who's the latest one to come out publicly? Adrienne Rich was the winner of the National Book Award a couple of years back. She's just come out and Olga Broumas has established her reputation on her Lesbian poetry. In fact, I have trouble finding heterosexual women poets. Marianne Moore as far as I know is the only famous American one, but I'm sure there are some others. There just aren't very many, for some reason, there just aren't very many. So when all these women come out, including all the women who work in factories and work on switchboards and run elevators and work for Macy's Department Store as I do, when all these women come out, how is it going to change the world? Well, for one thing, it's going to make it easier for all of us to live in the world. It's going to make it impossible for people to be fired for being Lesbians because it is going to be extremely difficult to fire all the Lesbians and still run all the businesses, and all the schools, and all the universities, and all the churches because you cannot get rid of all your talent and keep everything moving forward properly. And an awful lot of talent would have to go. But I'm not really asking or cajoling or convincing, I'm trying to tell you in as kind a way as I can that it's time to come out of the closet and it's time to make sure everyone around you comes out of the closet too.

I'd like to tell you about my sister. My sister is 5 years younger than I am. Her name is Diane. She lives less than an eighth of a mile away from me in a valley in Missouri, 40 miles east of Kansas City, Mo. She lives with another woman. They consider themselves married. They have a number of closeted gay friends like themselves, both male couples and Lesbian couples. They're very open with them or at least as open as they are able to be open with anybody or anything. They've both worked at the same company for more than 10 years and it's a company with a hundred or so employees. They've been together all of those years and in that length of time owned two pieces of property together. They still think, and will tell you, that none of the people they work with know they're a Lesbian couple. I don't think all the people they work with are that stupid myself, but maybe they are. But when you ask them why they don't let the people they work with know, for sure, they say they don't fear for their jobs at all and they wouldn't mind if their bosses knew, but they'd hate for their co-workers to know they are Lesbians. Have you ever thought for a minute what people think of you if they don't think you're Lesbians? Think about that. Do you really want to be thought heterosexual? I personally do not. Think about it, just think about it.

I'd like to tell you about Donna, the woman I'm married to. She is head of several departments at the Kansas City (Missouri) Public Library. When we started living together over 5 years ago, I had been a patron of that library for 15 years or so. Needless to say, every librarian in the system had heard about the notorious Barbara Grier who collects thooooose books, so there would have been no possible way that Donna could have remained in the closet in any sense. It's been a rich and rewarding experience for her in every way.

I think I can demonstrate, using her as an example, how seriously it can disadvantage you to be known as a Lesbian. When we began living together, she was an assistant in a department in the library, a professional librarian, simply one of many in a department. She's now head of several departments and she's doubled her salary, and she's very well thought of by everyone she works with, very well liked, and they know that she's a Lesbian. They know that we're a couple. They don't make a big point of it, they don't run around discussing it at great length, at least, not with Donna. But if it's caused her any inconvenience, she hasn't noticed it.

But there's another comparison between my sister Diane and her life and the life Donna and I enjoy, and it's probably the most important one. There are young Lesbians in the library in various positions who are open, increasingly open, and they are using as their example the obvious, unstated but present-presence of Donna in their lives. It's okay to be open in the library. Not flamboyant, not troublesome, not obnoxious, but open, casual, obvious. After all, why not?

I don't know how the young Lesbians at Diane's company feel about her ludicrous behavior but I can guess.

418

And if there are any shy and timid ones I hope they are not hurt by her bad example.

Now, coming out despite everything you ever heard or feared is not difficult. I came out when I was 12 years old. I have been out ever since and I have been out with all the people I've ever been around. And I'm not a special and not a privileged person. I worked in a non-professional position in a public library. I worked for a mutual fund called Hamilton Funds. I've worked in a whole bunch of miscellaneous offices, the Singer Sewing Machine Co., Pyramid Life Insurance, Macy's Department Store where I now have a quasi-clerical job, but it's a perfectly ordinary punch-a-timeclock kind of job, but every person in Macy's knows who I am and what I do. There was an article about my life in *Christopher Street* magazine in October, 1976. There's a dog-eared, tattered copy of *Christopher Street* that went all over my department. Everybody in the place read it and everyone came and talked to me. My boss, who is a stereotyped male-chauvinist-pig oppressive person who dislikes everything that he doesn't particularly share an intimate acquaintance with, the kind of person who has a bumper sticker that reads "Take your boy hunting and you won't go hunting for your boy," even my boss finds somehow an obscure pride in my openness.

But I'm not asking you, I'm telling you you have to come out of the closet, we have to, we all have to be out, we have to because there's nowhere else to go. We've done all we can do as a small, isolated, spotlighted public movement. It's not enough that every year a few thousand kids come out of high school and decide, boy, oh boy, I'm going to break with the enemy, my family, I'm going out and I'm going to live my life. That's one kind of coming out. They've got a long way to go. They're going to walk out of society and walk back into it, and walk out of it and into it and go through a lot of changes, a lot of education processes, a lot of jobs, a lot of things. Right now, I want all of those women who have made their "place" in the world, I want all of those women over 25 or 50 who have jobs and responsibilities and obligations and functions to perform and a life of their own and don't-bother-me, I'll-call-you, and I don't-see-why-I-should-do-that-because-I-did-it-all-myself, let-them-drag-themselves-up-by-their-boot-straps. I did it all myself, let them drag themselves up by their bootstraps, I don't owe them anything. But you do. You owe them plenty. You owe them your wit and wisdom. You owe them all the suffering you went through or passed by, the right not to have to go through it all just like you did. It's not that it wouldn't make them stronger, perhaps, but it's just not necessary anymore. What is necessary is coming out. Coming out every day in every way. Neither for profit nor salvation, but because *this* is the time to come out.

Grandmothers

by Jane Rule

I suppose even a six-year-old could write about being
"an aging lesbian," might even feel the need if she'd suffered already a couple of years at the hands of a
heterosexual nurse, been reprimanded by a mother for
picking forget-me-nots for the lady next door, and been
told in kindergarten to stop drawing the same picture over
and over again: a stick figure at the top of a pointed
mountain. At forty-six I may find it harder because by
now the catalogue of mortal blows and pleasures is far too
long and complex for a short entertainment.

I think it's probably a "masculine trait" to practice dying from a very young age. Anyway, it's always the boy
children I invent who shoot themselves with their own bow
ties, grab their arrow-pierced stomachs and fall to the
ground, and most of the real hypochondriacs I've known
have been men who at the first twinge of headache are
convinced of spinal meningitis, at the gentlest fart terminal
cancer. I also have a hunch that fatherhood is a way men
practice dying. Women don't seem as often to need to invent melodramatic premonitions of death, the house of the
body so much a way station for other life that even those
of us who do not give birth acknowledge the wasted blood,
the monthly murder of some new soul for the sake of our
own lives. Our bodies seem to practice dying for us without aid of our imaginations. It is only when women have
imposed on them men's fear of dying that they are caught
up in the vanity of pretending not to age, contemplate
suicide at my age for a lost womb, a second chin, bifocals.

I love all my grandparents, but I loved the *bodies* of my
grandmothers, both of whom suffered from arthritis as I
do now. They were fragile and deliberate in the way they
moved, and from the time I was tall and sturdy enough to
be some aid, they used my body as brace or hoist. They
taught me early how to touch pain and to comfort because

421

they were at the candid mercy of my love. From them, far more than from my marvelously ample-bodied and competent mother, I learned the close intimacy of flesh. When, as an adolescent, I was physically shy with my mother, I always had sweet excuse to touch my grandmothers, to brush their hair, to help them dress, to choose among the rings which would still traverse the swollen joints of what were to me their beautiful hands, accurate still with needle and thread, with cards, with flowers, accurate with requests. I found their faces lovelier than any others of my childhood because they were *made*, could be understood as the bland faces of other children could not, as even those of my parents could not since they did not yet know themselves and masked their ignorance as best they could. My mother has that wondrous face now.

When I was twenty-three, I fell permanently in love with a woman who was not much younger than I am now, whose face had already begun to be defined by time, and who has stayed there fifteen years ahead of me for twenty-three years, half my life. At sixty she is more distinguished, more readable, more beautiful than she was when I first met her. The gap between our ages finally begins to close with the premature aging of my disease. In fact, it is I who teach her how to touch pain and to comfort. She sometimes has a moment of surprise even at a child's heedless running across a field. I do not like some of the irritating limitations of an ailing spine. Not to be able to lift a child is a deprivation, but young Kate down the road will soon be tall and sturdy enough to offer me a steadying shoulder. The natural imbalance of our erotic energies which has plagued, amused, and taught us patience with each other is not as pronounced as it used to be. As the erotic fuses with the simply physical, we return together to a place which shares with childhood long moments in the present, no future hope of accomplishment as commanding as the sight of eagles in the high air or a sudden colony of mushrooms in the daffodil bed.

To become an old woman has always been my ambition, and it may be that my life span is to be short enough to make a speeding up of the process necessary. I have had a long apprenticeship as lover, and, in the way I can,

I will still carry out those patterns of courtship, but I am coming into a time when I must be the beloved of children and the young, who will measure their confidence in terms of my growing needs. As my grandmothers taught me the real lessons of erotic love with their beautifully requiring flesh and speaking faces, so I would wish to teach the children I love that they are capable of tenderness and of strength, capable of knowledge because of what they can see in my face, clear in pain and wonder, intent on practicing life as long as it lasts.

Aging is a State of Mind

by Julie Lee

"No one grows old.
You are old when you stop growing."
Anonymous

Aging is a state of mind! Because the condition of our bodies influences our minds, and our minds influence our bodies, aging is a combination of how we think and how our bodies function. Negative thinking and ill health can make the aging process a negative experience. Positive thinking and a healthy body can make growing older a pleasure rather than a threat.

I have enjoyed adding years to my life, because I feel that they add experience, knowledge, and a wider horizon to my existence. I love looking back with Jinny—my life partner for the past twenty-seven years—and comparing how it was then to how it is now; to share things we have learned, and the good—and bad—times we have seen. Nothing is more reassuring to me than to be with a friend of many years standing. Somehow the years that have passed are comforting, a promise that the years ahead will also be worthwhile. Hardly a day passes in my life without a new learning experience—sometimes important, at other times less so—but all helpful for constantly updating my views and opinions. As long as I change, I feel that I cannot really get old—mentally, emotionally, or physically.

All this is only possible, of course, if the body is in reasonaby good shape. There are many factors that influence our health, not the least of which is, as I mentioned before, a positive attitude. There are also lifelong habits, both good and bad; there is heredity; and there is some luck. Those of us who had good nutrition as children have a head start toward a longer and healthier life. I personally consider nutrition *the* key to good health and vigor in middle age.

While I was never afraid of aging as such, I was always concerned about preparing for my later years. This included financial preparation, but even more so I was aware that bad habits and a poor diet in my early years would influence my physical well-being in later life. I was never able to laugh off the effects of bad habits by saying, as some of my friends did, that I did not expect to live past age forty. I not only hoped to live longer than that, but I was also determined to live as long as possible inside a healthy and vigorous body. So, even in my twenties, I avoided certain chemicals and tried to "eat right." I was already aware that cellular damage, once done, cannot be undone later on. Since my mid-thirties I have been a stickler for a slim body, a healthy diet and food supplements, and I feel that it has been worthwhile in my own life. At present I live on a modified high-protein diet, which I supplement with large doses of natural vitamins. I avoid refined foods, especially sugar and white flour. I eat nuts, seeds, fresh fruits and vegetables, and I avoid artificial substances of all types as much as possible.

I have always shied away from medications, and do so more than ever now. This does not mean that I do not occasionally take an aspirin, but I refuse to take medications over an extended period of time. I have found that many physical "discords" respond to natural (nutritional) means. I let both physicians and friends laugh at me while I swallow my garlic perles, liver powder, Dolomite, bone meal, and the many vitamins and stress capsules that I take every day. My opinion is that I have nothing to lose, and everything to gain.

Because I feel and look well most of the time, I live my life today much as I did thirty years ago. I was never an athlete, so do not compete in sports; but I find that I can climb stairs and walk as well as the next person, years younger than I, and most importantly, I enjoy life and living as much—or more—than I did when I was in my twenties.

There are certain changes that occur in almost everyone's body that are supposed to be the inevitable result of aging. However, some authorities now attribute many of these changes to misuse of the body and stress. (It has been found, for instance, that people in comas do not seem to age.) These changes include a tendency to deposit calcium in the joints, a loss of elasticity of the skin, loss of muscle flexibility, including the muscles controlling eyesight, and—in women—the onset of menopause. The first three can, in my opinion, be greatly delayed, or even reversed, once they have started. Joint and muscle problems can be reversed with yoga and similar exercises, and skin can be kept youthful-looking by avoiding cosmetics and using natural lubricants. Menopause, however, apparently cannot be indefinitely postponed, and it does present a crisis time in a woman's life. While some women experience a minimum of discomfort—a few mild hot flashes—others, including myself, can have a rough time of it. For more than five years now I have experienced hot flashes as often as ten an hour, and it seems that none of the natural means I have tried have made a measurable difference. I know that estrogen "replacement" therapy eliminates hot flashes, but then, given the choice between the flashes and the dangerous side effects of artificial estrogen, I have little hesitation in choosing the flashes. Some women experience other unpleasant symptoms such as depression, fatigue, numbness in arms and legs, fluid retention—the list is endless. Except for some fluid retention (a tendency which I have had all of my life) I personally have been quite free of all such symptoms. Here again the emotional component of such complaints as depression and fatigue is a strong one, and greatly influenced by a woman's attitude toward aging. And while menopause is classified as an aging phenomenon, it really isn't, since the age of onset ranges from the mid-thirties to the late fifties, and this too seems to be influenced by nutrition, the well-nourished woman apparently experiencing a later onset generally.

Yes, of course, I too have my "aches and pains" occasionally. My left arm has developed a "tennis elbow" (although I do not play the game!)—a condition caused by a lessening elasticity of the tendons. I sometimes feel stiff when I wake up in the morning. But I make it a point to ignore these minor discomforts as much as possible, and most go away when ignored. All of us, if we pay attention to it, have little twitches and discomforts a good deal of the time at any age, and—for instance—the headaches I used to have from age ten on are getting less as I get older, and I have not had a disabling one for years, while in my twenties and thirties they would often be a real problem to me.

The only symptom that bothers me on a continual basis is that I can no longer read or see small things at close range without glasses. Here again, experts differ. Some specialists feel that everyone who has normal eyesight during their earlier years will develop far-sightedness after their forties. Others insist that this condition, which is caused by the weakening of certain eye muscles and loss of elasticity of the lenses, can be avoided, and even reversed, through proper exercises. I have tried these exercises half-heartedly from time to time, but I cannot honestly say that I have given them a fair chance. I am a tense person, which aggravates the condition, and I can't see spending an hour or more a day on these complicated exercises. I know that when I spend more time out of doors, and let my eyes look into the distance more, my sight improves, but I am an indoor person—so here again, the "aging" factor is questionable.

Some research is finally being done on the phenomenon of aging—starting with the cell, and going on from there. Some recent researchers claim to have found evidence that five factors help in staying youthful into middle age. They are: yogurt, vitamin E, honey, exercise, and red wine (the grape skins seem to have some special antiaging properties). Since we have followed the first four of these for some time, we recently decided to add red wine to our evening meal, and while it might not help to keep us young, it certainly adds pleasure to the meals!

Somehow the fear of old age seems to scare gay men and lesbians even more than it does straights in our culture. This has always puzzled me, especially among lesbian feminists, where the cultural values of "youth above all" and outward physical beauty do not hold. There is no reason for a woman to lose her attractiveness, which is spiritual as well as physical. There certainly is no reason to give up on love and relationships just because a woman passes her fortieth birthday—or even her fiftieth or sixtieth.

I had a most beautiful and exciting new love relationship at age fifty, and it could not have been more meaningful or romantic had I been twenty-five.

I value permanence in my own life, and I believe that the constant presence of a lover has not only added to my enjoyment of life, but I definitely believe that the years of happiness we have had together have given both of us a better chance for good health today. Having someone care for and about me has given me the incentive to take care of myself. I have always kept in the back of my mind the desire to be both attractive and in good health for my life companion.

Being in the movement has constantly kept me in touch with women much younger than myself, and it has helped me keep "up to date" in my thinking and acting. It prevents me from looking back too much, and encourages me to look ahead each day. I am sure that without the help of my much younger sisters in the movement I would not feel as youthful as I do.

Because there is ageism in our society, there tends to be ageism in all of us. I fully realize that ageism goes both ways—that sometimes those older and with more experience do not value those younger with less experience. I can truthfully say that much of the consciousness-raising I have experienced in the feminist movement, especially in the early days, has come from women half my age, and I remember this with gratitude. Years of living give me an edge in some ways over younger sisters, but a freshness of approach often makes up for lack of years in younger women. We need both to succeed.

As for me personally—I love being fifty-five. I feel that my life has been full and fascinating, if not always easy. I have loved and been loved by two beautiful women. I have shared many years with one, and a shorter time with the other. By being conscious of the fact that what I do/eat/think today will affect what I will be tomorrow, I have managed to keep my body in reasonably good shape. I feel that my more than ten years in the movement have given me a fabulous background which hopefully will be useful to women just starting out. I have been able to help women in trouble through my twenty-seven years' experience as a happy lesbian by being a living proof that this is a viable lifestyle.

I love my white hair and other physical signs of middle age. I encourage my body to give me the best possible service by supplying it with what I consider optimal nourishment—physical, emotional, and spiritual—and by avoiding as much as possible the poisons all around us—physical, emotional, and spiritual.

And maybe most of all, because I love myself and have respect for the physical, emotional, and spiritual *me*, I continue to look forward without fear to the years ahead. I don't know how many years I will have, but those that I do I expect to live fully, together with those I have loved and hope to continue to love—in the circle of beautiful sisters of all ages. And I certainly do not fear the years as they come and go.

And neither need you!

XI
Changes and Visions

Learning from Lesbian Separatism

by Charlotte Bunch

It was December when I first slept with a woman: I was married, it was snowing outside, and my days were filled with the unceasing events of women's liberation. Six months later, my four-year-old marriage was finished, my life with women was entire, and the sweltering summer heat of Washington, D.C., had replaced the snow. I sat on a mattress in a back room with eleven other women planning what to do now: we had just declared ourselves *lesbian-feminist separatists* and had disassociated ourselves from all women's movement activities. It was 1971. We realized, as similar groups did in other cities during that early fast-moving spread of lesbianism through the women's movement, that we had to figure out what had happened to us, and why. A few members of our group had been lesbians for years, some had previous experience in the gay liberation movement; but the majority of us— for a variety of reasons—had come out within the context of feminism. The movement had been our family—our mother and our child. When we began to proclaim our love for one another in ways that went beyond the boundaries of "familial love," most of us did not realize how savagely we would be disinherited by our "sisters."

We had to ask the difficult question: why? Why was a movement devoted to women's freedom of choice so afraid of women who chose to love women—instead of men? We could tell ourselves that such organizations as the National Organization for Women were frightened of losing their acceptance in the male world, but that didn't seem enough of an answer. Furthermore, most of our own experience had not been in reformist structures like NOW, but in the radical feminist movement: that loose network of consciousness-raising, theoretical and activist groups talking about a deep and revolutionary change in every part of society, not just reforms that left basic patriarchy

433

intact. Yet our experiences as lesbians in radical feminist groups had been no less painful than those of other lesbians in NOW.

Coletta Reid was a feminist who had also recently left her husband, found her identity as a lesbian, and then chosen a lesbian-separatist stance. In an article called "Coming out in the Women's Movement" (*Lesbianism and the Women's Movement*, Diana Press, 1975), she describes an incident that helps to explain why we became separatists:

> The full range of attitudes and prejudices came out in the course of a meeting of a day-care center I had helped found and worked in for nine months. One woman expressed misgivings about me or my friends being around her daughter since I had become a lesbian. She evidently thought I would molest her little precious; she had no similar qualms about my being around her son when I was heterosexual. Nor had she any qualms about the heterosexual men being around her daughter, which is strange since 100 percent of the child molestation cases reported in the District of Columbia last year were committed by men. Another woman said she thought lesbians were too hostile, angry, and man-hating to be around children who needed love and good vibes. . . . Some of the men at the day-care center were outrageously piggy toward the children, but they were never called on the carpet at a meeting or put in the position of having to defend themselves as I was.

The lesbians who had been gay prior to the existence of the feminist movement were less surprised by our rejection than those of us newly gay and full of enthusiasm for our recent self-discoveries. The "older" lesbians knew something that we had just begun to learn: lesbianism is not only a threat to men, but also to many heterosexual women. It suggests that women do not inevitably have to love men, or to love them at any cost.

Of course, challenging heterosexuality in any form is seen as threatening by some women. We are sometimes accused by "straight" feminists of guilt-tripping them about their personal lives; of implying that sexual dependence on men made them somehow less feminist. In fact, we were less concerned about an individual woman's personal choice than about the institution of heterosexuality; less concerned with sex roles than with sex power. Furthermore, challenging almost any issue impacting women— marriage, motherhood, and so on—necessarily raises questions about women's lives. We cannot abandon our insights into these institutions of male supremacy in order to avoid making each other uncomfortable.

As separatists, we stopped trying to justify our lives to straight society and instead concentrated on ourselves. We began to analyze our experiences and our perceptions of the world in the relative isolation of a collective of twelve white lesbians from varying class backgrounds. In January of 1972, we began a newspaper, *The Furies,* dedicated to lesbian-feminist political analysis and ideology.

For the first time in our lives, our reality was the dominant one, and we were able to begin to understand how it differed from the heterosexual reality that dominated everywhere else. We had become separatists for many reasons, but one was to learn about ourselves as a people—and learn we did. We discovered the strengths of women who have to live on their own. Heterosexuality, in providing some of us with a buffer zone in a man's world, had stunted our growth. We also encountered acute class and race conflict in our own midst, made all the more clear by the absence of men and male influence. We experienced the pain and the exhilaration of developing relationships where society gave us no models; relationships among equals, not based on preset male and female roles. Most of all we saw that lesbians are indeed a people, similar to other women, but also different: our uniqueness provided us with a perspective on feminism which we began to develop into a politics, called lesbian-feminism.

Separatism was the only way we saw to create lesbian-feminist politics and build a community of our own in the hostile environment of the early seventies. Many lesbians chose a separatist strategy in order to build our own pride, strength, and unity as a people, to develop an analysis of our particular oppression, and to create a political ideology and strategy that would both force the movement's recognition of us and lead to the end of male supremacy.

Thanks in part to this time of separatism by lesbian groups in many cities, lesbian communities can now exist openly and proudly throughout the nation as the backbone of many feminist political, cultural, and economic activities. Most women's groups now recognize the "legitimacy" of lesbians' civil rights in society, as well as our right to exist openly in their midst.

Lesbian-feminism, however. is far more than civil rights for queers or lesbian communities and culture. It is a political perspective on a crucial aspect of male supremacy—heterosexism, the ideological and institutional domination of heterosexuality. The development of this political perspective was one of the most important results of lesbian separatism.

The first public statement of lesbian-feminist politics can be dated, at least symbolically, from a paper called "The Woman-Identified Woman," issued by Radicalesbians in New York City on May 1, 1970. It begins:

> What is a lesbian? A lesbian is the rage of all women condensed to the point of explosion. She is the woman who, often beginning at an extremely early age, acts in accordance with her inner compulsion to be a more complete and freer human being than her society—perhaps then, but certainly later—cares to allow her. . . . On some level she has not been able to accept the limitations and oppressions laid on her by the most basic role of her society—the female role.

The paper went on to analyze the nascent political power and consciousness in the power and consciousness in the personal act of being a lesbian in a male-supremacist society; of putting women first in defiance of a culture that has structured the female life around the male. It discussed how the word, the label, "lesbian," has been used to keep women divided:

When a woman hears this word tossed her way, she knows she is stepping out of line . . . for a woman to be independent means she *can't be* a woman—she must be a dyke. . . . As long as the label "dyke" can be used to frighten women into a less militant stand, keep her separate from her sisters, keep her from giving primacy to anything other than men and family—then to that extent she is controlled by the male culture.

The statement expanded the definition of lesbianism by developing the idea of women-identification as an act of self-affirmation and love for all women; primary identification with women that gives energy through a positive sense of self, developed with reference to ourselves, and not in relation to men. As Rita Mae Brown, one of the founders of both Radicalesbians and *The Furies,* explained in "The Shape of Things to Come":

Women who love women are lesbians. Men, because they can only think of women in sexual terms, define lesbian as sex between women. However, lesbians know that it is far more than that, it is a different way of life. It is a life determined by a woman for her own benefit and the benefit of other women. It is a life that draws its strength, support, and direction from women. . . . You refuse to limit yourself by the male definitions of women. You free yourself from male concepts of "feminine" behavior.

Since all traditionally defined lesbians were not women-identified in their heads and hearts, this definition might not apply to some of them. Yet potentially, any woman could become woman-identified. The original paper concluded with a call for woman-identification and suggested that this was the central importance of lesbianism to the women's movement.

The heart of the woman-identified-woman statement and of all lesbian-feminist politics is the recognition that, in a male-supremacist society, heterosexuality is a political institution. Both lesbianism and heterosexuality are therefore political forces as well as personal lifestyles. At first, we saw this insight as a natural outgrowth of feminism and expected it to be incorporated into the theory and action of the women's movement. However, as many feminists shied away from the political significance of lesbianism, most of that politics was developed by separatists, outside the formal confines of the movement.

Recognition of the political significance of lesbianism led us to an analysis of exactly how heterosexuality functions to support male supremacy. Every insitution that feminists have shown to be oppressive to women—the workplace, schools, the family, the media, organized religion—is also based on heterosexism on the assumption that every woman either is or wishes to be bonded to a man both economically and emotionally. In order to effectively challenge our oppression in those institutions, we must also challenge the ideology of heterosexism.

Granted, this challenge must seem initially difficult for women whose sexual life is bound up with men; but less difficult as we understand that heterosexuality is more than sex. In our society, heterosexuality goes hand in hand with the sexist assumption that each woman exists for a man— her body, her children, and her services are his property. If a woman does not accept that definition of heterosexuality and of herself, she is queer—no matter who she sleeps with. Heterosexism depends on the idea that heterosexuality is both the only natural and the superior form of human sexuality, thus providing ideological support to male supermacy. Heterosexism is basic to women's oppression in the family and to discrimination against single or other women who live outside the nuclear family.

Heterosexism also supports male supremacy in the workplace. Women are defined and exploited as secondary and marginal workers on the assumption that work is not our primary vocation; even if we work all our lives, we are assumed to be primarily committed to home and to have a second (major) breadwinner supporting us. No matter how false this is for most women, especially gay, black, and lower-class women, the ideology of heterosexuality continues to justify the mythology, and thus the discrimination against women at work.

One of the things that keeps heterosexual domination going is heterosexual privilege; those actual or promised benefits for a woman who stays in line: legitimacy, economic security, social acceptance, legal and physical protection. Through these privileges, a woman is given a stake in behaving properly and in maintaining her own oppression. She works against her own self-interest by becoming dependent on a man and on male privileges and undermines her self-respect. She also separates herself from her sisters—in particular her lesbian sisters—who have no such privileges. Unless a woman, no matter what personal connection to men, realizes that her own survival is tied more to that of all women than it is to one man, the "privileges" she receives are not lasting benefits but links in the chain of oppression.

Feminists, whatever their sexual orientation, have to understand that heterosexual privilege is a small and short-term bribe in return for giving up lasting self-discovery and collective power. I have seen countless instances when women gave up their long-term interests and power in exchange for such a "benefit." For example, one woman actively involved in a fight against female job discrimination at a university deserted her position when the battle closed in on her man's job privileges and thus indirectly on her heterosexual privileges.

Straight feminists sometimes ask me how they can fight heterosexism if they do not choose to live a lesbian lifestyle. This is a crucial question in bridging the gay-straight gap. Heterosexual women can, for example, challenge the assumptions and privileges of heterosexuality as they encounter them daily, in every area from the denial of spousal benefits for lesbians in various health, life insurance, and pension policies to social attitudes about correct behavior at a party. (For example, why must people come in pairs, or be seated alternately "boy-girl" no matter what their interests?)

One of the ways to understand better what I am saying—and what anyone can do—is to "think queer," no matter what your sexuality. By "think queer," I mean imagine life as a lesbian for a week. Announce to everyone—family, roommate, on the job, everywhere you go—

that you are a lesbian. Walk in the street and go out only with women, especially at night. Imagine your life, economically and emotionally, with women instead of men. For a whole week, experience life as if you were a lesbian, and you will learn quickly what heterosexual privileges and assumptions are, and how they function to keep male supremacy working.

You will also see, as lesbians have learned, that it is *not* okay to be a lesbian in America. And it is not okay for a reason that goes beyond individual attitudes or bigotry. It is not okay -because self-loving and independent women are a challenge to the idea that men are superior, an idea that social institutions strengthen and enshrine. Most men know that, even though women have often been slow to realize it. The more any woman steps outside of society's assumptions, the more "lesbian" she becomes and the more clearly she sees exactly how those heterosexist assumptions confine her as an individual and women as a group.

One week of pretending will show you why the life of a lesbian is not the same as that of a straight woman. This does not necessarily make lesbians better or worse feminists; but it does make our perspective on male society different. That difference, like differences of race and class, can be the basis of division among women or it can be an opportunity for broader feminist analysis and action. To deny these differences is to deny both our particular oppression and our particular strength. True unity is grounded not on a false notion of sameness, but on understanding and utilizing diversity to gain the greatest possible scope and power.

A lesbian's reality and perspective is also not the same as that of a gay man. This was one of the first and hardest lessons that we learned in the gay liberation movement. Gay men, because they frequently seem to challenge sex role stereotypes, are punished in this society: to seem like a "woman" when one can be a "man" is to betray male supremacy. But gay men are still men. And they rarely challenge male prerogatives and power directly. In fact those gay men who want to share equally with straight men in male privileges are no less our oppressors than their heterosexual counterparts. For this reason, many les-

440

bian-feminists have been no more comfortable in the gay movement than in the women's movement.

Nevertheless, our experiences in both the gay and the feminist movements and as separatists have shown us the close relationship between male supremacy and heterosexual domination: homophobia and gay oppression are based in sexism and the institutional power of male supremacy. While gay men have some male privileges, particularly when they remain closeted or out-woman-hate heterosexual men, they will be scorned as long as women are scorned and as long as "real" men must fuck and fuck over "real" women. Their long-term interests lie not in attempting to gain straight acceptance as "real" men but in challenging sexism along with heterosexism. Gay men face a choice similar to that of straight women: they can accept society's offers of short-term benefits (male privilege for one and heterosexual privilege for the other) or they can reject the patriarchal basis of those privileges and work for a long-term elimination of the entire system of sexual oppression.

In the past couple of years, many lesbian-feminist separatists have begun to work again with straight feminists and with gay men. My own move away from complete separatism began in 1973. I had learned, changed, and grown during those years as a separatist, but I felt that I was becoming too isolated. Since the core of a lesbian-feminist politics and community had been developed, it seemed important that we become involved with other feminist projects and analytical developments. (In reporting my own experiences, I do not mean to imply that separatism is dead. In some places it is still performing that first task of uniting lesbians. Separatism is a dynamic strategy to be moved in and out of whenever a minority feels that its interests are being overlooked by the majority, or that its insights need more space to be developed.)

Lucia Valeska, a lesbian-feminist from Albuquerque, New Mexico, analyzed the separatist situation concisely in an article for *Quest: A Feminist Quarterly* entitled "The Future of Female Separatism," where she wrote: "Whatever your opinion of it, female separatism has just as long and viable a future as male supremacy." So, too, lesbian-feminist separation will no doubt continue in some forms as long as there is heterosexual domination. And, as Valeska concluded: "In the meantime, regardless of the strategical success of feminism, individual women will continue to find a perpetual well-spring of freedom, affirmation, strength, and joy in lesbianism. That is, reduced to its smallest conceivable contribution, lesbianism remains a powerful political force."

While I am as glad as any woman that the most painful days of separatism seem to be behind us, we must not lose sight of why they happened in the first place. Separatism happened for a reason. It happened because straight feminists were unable to allow lesbians space to grow—to develop our personal lives and our political insights. And unless lesbian-feminist politics is incorporated into feminist analysis and action, we will reexperience the old and destructive gay–straight split. Furthermore, we will ultimately lose the battle against male supremacy, for no woman is truly free to be anything until she is also free to be a lesbian.

Lesbian-feminist separatism, whether chosen or enforced, has produced not only a political analysis vital to all women, but structural innovations as well. After all, lesbians must create new institutions for survival, particularly once we have come out publicly, because we do not fit anywhere, whether it's the family or church, schools or nightclubs. Of necessity, we must challenge those structures to change or create alternatives.

Lesbians have played a leading role in the creation of women's art, media, and other cultural institutions, as well as in feminist economic ventures such as credit unions, bookstores, and restaurants. In the final issue of *The Furies*, Lee Schwing and Helaine Harris discussed this move toward the building of feminist institutions:

> We believe that our next step is to create such institutions. They have tremendous potential in terms of providing economic security for women. We will no longer be wasting our time at shit jobs we don't care about. We will be in control of our time, products we

442

produce, and the learning of new skills. Those institutions will kindle our energies and give up space to research, talk, and have insights into developing our ideology and strategy. This should help create another step towards a feminist society.

Our enforced economic independence has led to a growing class-consciousness and an emphasis on the economic problems of women. When lesbians come out and actively pursue the meaning of woman-identification, survival questions must immediately be faced. Like all single women, we are solely responsible for our lives—all of our lifetime. We face survival issues without heterosexual cushions and come closer to the reality of lower-class and black women: we must provide for ourselves, our children, and each other—economically, emotionally, and politically. Lesbians have not waited for others to grant us money, time, and space—we have begun to make it for ourselves. We have taken care of ourselves, and in so doing have been addressing many of the needs of the women's movement as a whole.

If I return to the women whose story started this article—for instance, the women who formed *The Furies* collective—the life force of lesbian feminism becomes very clear. Most of the women in that group have continued to be involved in the development of feminist theory, communications, economic and cultural strategies. *The Furies* ceased publication in 1973. (There are three books of articles from *The Furies: Women Remembered, Class and Feminism,* and *Lesbianism and the Women's Movement,* edited by Nancy Myron and myself and published by Diana Press), but many of us went on to found and sustain a variety of projects, all national in scope. Rita Mae Brown and I became part of the group that started *Quest: A Feminist Quarterly;* Colette Reid and Nancy Myron helped develop and expand Diana Press into one of the major feminist presses; Joan Biren is one of the founders of Moonforce Media, a national women's film company. Several other *Furies* members helped to conceive and develop Olivia Records, a women's recording company, and later, Women in Distribution (WIND), a national distribution service for women's media.

Our time as lesbian-feminist separatists, like that of lesbians in other cities, was less a period of being "out" of the women's movement than of being profoundly "in" the heart of its matter. It was a time that allowed us to develop both political insights and concrete projects that now aid women's survival and strength. We learned that change is a process. And in that process, becoming woman-indetified women may be the only way that women, whatever our sexual identity, can begin to see our potential for change.

A Question of Culture: Mirror Without Image
by Rose Jordan

Culture: "an organized body of rules concerning ways in which individuals in a population should communicate with one another, think about themselves and their environments, and behave toward one another and toward objects in their environments." [from *Culture, Behavior and Personality*, Robert A. LeVine, (London: Hutchinson & Co., 1973)]

Before the riot at the Stonewall (a bar on Christopher Street in New York City), lesbians and gay men evaluated themselves according to society's definition that they were perverts, sexual deviates, criminals, neurotics incapable of maturity, or, at the very least, disturbed, tortured individuals in need of a cure for a malady that eroded their characters and distorted their identities. Religionists, who not only justified this programming but created the circuits through which it could travel, and psychiatrists, who institutionalized their interpretations, were directly responsible for the oppressive laws (and actions subsequently initiated in their name) that attempted to legislate a morality that restricted the private sexual and emotional rights of approximately ten to twenty million adults. (Of course, this figure depends to a large extent on who is doing the estimating since no one, to my knowledge, has concerned themselves with taking a "homosexual" census; and, even if they did, there would be no way to count those who stubbornly remain in the "closet.") To circumvent the contempt and hostility directed toward homosexuals, it became imperative to evolve an elaborate "body of rules" (most of which were negative since they dictated extreme caution concerning our true identities and forced us to live double lives) and create an "environment" that could shield us from a violent world that was bent on our destruction. An underground network was slowly constructed over the years that we assumed would afford us some measure of security so we could be ourselves without fear of discovery. We codified a language and a manner that superficially could be labeled "ethnic"—we used words that would identify certain types among us like: drag queen, butch, diesel dyke, Mary, etc. But our best achievement was the creation of the "gay bar" as the focal point of our social activities. While straight society fundamentally used church socials, weddings, formal introductions, etc., as a means of enlarging their circle of friends and family, we went in search of ourselves in the only places where we could partake of a small degree of anonymity while enlarging *our* world in what we believed to be comparative safety. In these gay bars, our friendships and potential lovers were discovered and cultivated while, in the process, our individualistic life styles evolved. We "cruised," danced, drank abundant amounts of alcohol, and became, in our estimation, quite sophisticated—about *that* life, at least. We were like somnambulists who walked in a dreamland where all our wishes would be gratified and emotional needs fulfilled. The rude awakening came as soon as we stepped out of this ambience back into the harsh reality of the other world that played such an important part in our "double life"—the place where we felt like unwelcome visitors who would be forcibly ejected if we were discovered to be frauds.

Convinced that because we had a different lifestyle from straight society we also had constructed a different "culture" that was uniquely gay, we proceeded to act out our existence, unknowingly integrating the prejudices and values we learned from our families (society) into our new lifestyle. We embraced the philosophy concerning a productive life; we philosophized about love and sharing using the identical, one-faceted viewpoint of our society, which included stereotypical attitudes about the feminine and masculine roles; we eulogized the importance (or nonimportance) of status, money, power, and class. In short, we abosrbed all of the myths, values, and goals of our basic culture and transported them intact into our other world. We created a *sub*culture which had at its core only *one* difference from the rest of society—that was our emotional/sexual orientation toward members of our own gender. Although there are as many discrepancies of attitude and behavior within the heterosexual community as there are within the gay community, gays behaved within theirs in the same manner as the larger society does within the framework of its social structures or class groups; because, as Robert A. LeVine expressed it in the above-mentioned book, "Acquiring the situationally appropriate overt behavior of another culture does not eliminate the emotional response patterns acquired early in life from one's own culture." In other words, because we matured within our society's social structures and were conditioned to believe and accept its basic value systems (more or less), we unwittingly interwove them into the fabric of our lifestyle. We used those systems when we proselytized the "correct" image to be cultivated in order to blend favorably with our chosen gay group. In most of these "sophisticated" circles, a transvestite (of either gender) was totally unacceptable and, therefore, unwelcome—just as an open (or "obvious") gay might be ostracized from a straight group. We, too, had a class structure, a youth cult, an ageist attitude, a "beautiful people" ideal. As hard as we scoffed at "straights" for being provincial, we imitated them down to the minutest detail. The raunchiest of us did not escape the emulation—if we examine our society carefully, we can easily recognize a "straight" counterpart in every lifestyle, in every attitude of every group. Every facet of the society we feared and hated because we felt abandoned by it became our model in our effort to survive it. We merely succeeded in fashioning a subterranean world that included all of its unglorious ideology. What we assumed to be a "gay culture" was, instead, a life*style;* there was nothing else possible since we had not altered our "emotional responses" but only substituted our own gender to apply them to. There was no way to accurately measure our uniqueness—if we possessed any outside of our humanness or emotional sexual preferences. Our methodology may have been different, but our viewpoints about what we expected out of life could be matched with the identical feelings shared by the rest of society; the only disagreement we had was who our partners would be. Therefore,

447

we tricked ourselves into believing that our "body of rules" and "environment" were the evolutionary process toward a "gay" culture when all they accomplished was to keep us hidden from our enemies in places where we felt their hostility couldn't reach us. In the long run, however, this was not really true since the bars we thought would be a haven became instead a trap that we would escape easily—society allowed their existence so we could be separated and kept out of their social domain.

Then, gay liberation intruded itself upon the status quo. Its birth pains were the Stonewall riot that occurred one warm night in June of 1969 when an angry group of lesbians, transvestites, and gay men decided they had enough harassment and bullying by the police. An in-depth analysis of this historical event can be found in such books as *Sappho Was a Right-On Woman*, by Sidney Abbott and Barbara Love, and *Dancing the Gay Lib Blues*, by Arthur Bell—to mention just two. As a direct result of the Stonewall riot, gay liberation fronts were established all over the country. We, as gays, gravitated toward each other for a totally different purpose now—in self-exploration in order to redefine our attitudes about ourselves and our interrelationship with our society as an open homosexual community. The early groups created our political theory, while the later ones actively exposed this theory to the world. "Gay Is Good" became our slogan; the consciousness-raising that evolved from that one statement was monumental. Finally, gays were saying: it's all right to be gay; my preference for my own gender as people whom I can love is just as normal a choice as the heterosexual preference for members of the opposite gender. Many gays "came out" practically en masse with a self-pride and determination to be themselves no matter what the price. Unfortunately, there were many homosexuals who were horrified at the bright light shining into their closets, and they vociferously attacked us as "wild-eyed fanatics" who couldn't leave well enough alone. But, in spite of this resistance to change that is always popular with reactionaries, gay liberation was here to stay! Once a minority realizes what oppression has done to them, and once they also recognize their complicity in it, there's no going back to the old ways—a taste of honey is too sweet. Our insistence that we be treated as real human beings instead of some mythical creatures from an alien world made the rest of society sit up and take note. Originally, we had been a problem to be "dealt with," and severely at times, utilizing all the negative propaganda at their disposal. Now we were turning the tables on them by also using propaganda, but a positive one. And it was working! We were no longer as fearful; and we certainly were not separated from each other as a group. Now it was important for society to acquiesce to some of our demands since we were obviously becoming a large voting bloc—even those remaining in the closet would be likely to cast their ballot with us. Celebrities spoke in our behalf, and politicians courted us shamelessly and assured us our demands for equality, under the law, were reasonable ones and would certainly be met. As of this writing, however, only eighteen states have removed sodomy laws from their statutes; and thirty-nine municipalities and four counties, nationally, have existing gay rights protection of various types.

Now, where does all of the foregoing leave us on the question concerning the existence of a "gay" culture? Unfortunately, or not (as the case may be), the conclusion appears to be negative. Although we have struggled against adverse societal conditions and are still involved in this struggle; and although we have succeeded in changing some of society's attitudes and behavior to some degree in certain areas of the country; and in spite of the fact that our efforts to influence public opinion through street demonstrations, TV and radio interviews and discussions, and although public debates with members of the church and psychiatric profession have resulted in the American Psychiatric Association's actual removal of the label "sickness" from its *Diagnostic and Statistical Manual of Mental Disorders* (the "bible" of insurance companies, social agencies, and hospital clinics) when referring to homosexuality, we have *not*—regardless of all this willingness on the part of our societal institutions to present a more liberal "face" toward us—succeeded in creating a different "body of rules" or "environment" or "thinking about one another" that would reflect, in this writer's opinion, a new culture that is "gay." Admittedly, there are lesbian and gay men's groups that are examining their sexism, racism, classism, ageism (and any other rhetorical "isms") toward each other and are investigating certain ways to interrelate that might be an alteration of their behavior style. But since there are no signposts on this road to change, their efforts sometimes end in confusing and conflicting ideologies and they come full circle back to where they started.

As a case in point: on the one hand, it is quite evident that the "new" lesbian and gay man have finally reached the understanding that role-playing in which one person is dominant and the other subservient is damaging to each individual involved, and as evident in the butch/femme phenomenon which emulates the man/woman relationship. Despite the awareness concerning the destructive effects of heterosexual coupling and the sincere efforts on behalf of certain groups (and individuals) to correct this behavior within the gay community, there has been an upsurge in the institutionalizing of sadomasochism as a viable lifestyle for lesbians and gay men. Apparently these cultists are not cognizant of (or dismiss as irrelevant) the fact that sadomasochism is a blatant expression, translated to physical terms at times, of the old butch/femme (man/woman), dominant versus passive lifestyle. In fact, some of the people who support feminism and/or gay liberation are themselves avid proponents of and/or participants in the sadomasochistic ideology. In other words, they are again absorbing behavior patterns from our larger society and incorporating into their own lives everything that gay liberationists have attempted to discard as damaging to the human psyche.

Except for the minority-within-a-minority who are genuinely grappling with this problem of behavioral change away from the traditional heterosexual concepts of personal relationships, gays and gay groups are basically pursuing their fulfillment as people much in the same manner as our larger society. Setting aside for a moment our emotional/sexual orientation, we can notice a marked resemblance gays have to our society as a whole. For example, we also define a "people" as men and their women. Putting the word "gay" in front does not alter the similarity between how women in our society are put in secondary positions to men and how (gay) women are also in secondary positions (in attitude, if not in fact) to (gay) men. Everyone seems to be dancing to the same tune in pursuit of happiness even though the steps appear to be different.

So, despite these uplifting victories we have experienced recently for which we all can be grateful, we have become *more* a part of our original culture than we ever were because in seeking tolerance and acceptance from a group of anything we are really stating our desire to become one with that group. When any minority fights for recognition, the next logical step is absorption into the mainstream of that group—not a reconstruction of a new culture. Of course, absorption is only desirable if in its accomplishment those absorbed can continue to effect a change in the social structure. This is not usually the case. Corruption of purpose usually takes place since none of the rules have been altered, only the acceptance of "new" people to abide by them. Until we can honestly realize that we must dispense with the unrewarding values of a particular culture and not join it to reinforce its status quo—only then will we be able to transcend that society and create a new culture based upon the values we claim will make it a uniquely "gay" culture.

A Journey to the End of Meetings

by Karla Jay

Since it would be impossible or unfair for me to write about what has happened to the lesbian movement since the Stonewall uprising, I have decided to write about myself. After all, the lesbian movement is not a cohesive group; and although the first post-Stonewall lesbian action happened in May 1970 at the Second Congress to Unite Women in New York City, many lesbian groups did not start until much later. In addition, different groups have different priorities and focuses centering around their needs (which are not necessarily mine). Finally, having spent the past eight years on the East and West Coasts, I certainly cannot speak for my sisters in the middle of the continent. Therefore, while straight people and even gay men might view lesbians as one unit, I perceive us as a magnificent rainbow, so diverse in shadings that any definition or description would necessarily limit and fail to recreate the original.

It seems almost equally impossible to capsulize for general readership consumption the myriad changes that I have personally gone through since the beginning of the post-Stonewall lesbian movement in 1970, for I must first relate how I got to that movement in the first place. Perhaps that tale goes far back to my early childhood, when, at age four, I had my first "love affair" with a female counselor at summer camp. Or perhaps I should start with the conflicting images I grew up with—my positive relations with girls in high school, while at the same time my relatives and my family's neighbors insinuated that I would "outgrow *it*." (I actually thought that when I reached a certain physical height, 5'5", my life would change, but I only grew to a final height of 5'4"!) But maybe my journey to the lesbian movement actually started later in college when I first developed negative feelings toward my own lesbian impulses and toward the

452

lesbians I met in the oppressive bar scene. During this period, I made a futile (thank the Goddess) attempt to "go straight," which might also be a crucial starting point for where I am today.

It seems that my quest for lesbian identity and my voyage through the movement has no beginning, as I know that my quest for identity will have no end, but perhaps I can start with my entrance into the feminist movement, since that can be tied to an irrevocable and positive change in my attitude toward lesbians and therefore toward myself. In late 1969, I believe, I entered Redstockings, a Marxist-oriented feminist group which developed a class analysis of the plight of women and which brought consciousness-raising to this country. In my consciousness-raising group and in the feminist movement in general, I met lesbians whom I liked and who I felt were like me. Unlike the lesbians I had met until then in the smoky, greasy Mafia-run bars, they were not into butch/femme roles so prevalent in the fifties and early sixties—roles which had turned me off to the only lesbian scene I could find (and which had totally confused me, since I could never figure out whether I was butch or femme, a question invariably asked in the bars).

And so Redstockings helped me to develop a positive image of lesbians and of myself as a lesbian and led to a "second coming out." But the feminist movement, including Redstockings, refused to deal with the lesbian they had helped me to discover in myself. The straight women were not interested in what they called "my private sex life," although all they discussed were men, including their own sex lives with men (and in a group supposedly devoted to the topic of *women*). For all the political overtones and class-oriented conclusions, the consciousness-raising group was often not very different from college lunches where most of my Barnard friends discussed only the boys across the street at Columbia.

If Redstockings were in general not very supportive (although some individual straight women were genuinely warm, friendly, interested, and unbiased), the feminist movement reached a peak of hostility in late 1969 and early 1970. Few will have forgotten that Betty Friedan, in an apparent fit of paranoia, called us a "lavender menace," while Susan Brownmiller in an article in *The New York Times Magazine* attempted to dismiss us as a "lavender herring" (that is, something misleading and irrelevant, like a "red herring," except queer). Therefore, it was not surprising that I ran (did not walk) to the Gay Liberation Front soon after it started in 1969 and shortly thereafter became the chairwoman of the group. And just as it was briefly euphoric to find women who gave me such a positive self-image of myself as a woman when I joined Redstockings, it was a real "high" to suddenly discover brothers and sisters who supported me as a lesbian. I also agreed with the early ideology of the gay movement, part of which stressed that homosexuality is just a sexual label and that we are complete people of whom sexuality is just one facet (albeit an important one). This philosophy totally rejected the idea of straight society (including some of my feminist sisters) that we were merely sexual beings, period. The early gay movement also seemed to embrace what I considered the most important part of feminism—a revolution against sex roles and sex role stereotyping plus a recognition of and willingness to ally ourselves with other oppressed groups. (This latter idea has been almost totally dropped by most post-Gay Liberation Front groups, which work only around gay civil rights.)

However, the gay liberation movement was in reality only a weak alliance of many disparate groups, including transvestites, transsexuals, and Third World people, and we were dealing with each other's needs on only the most superficial level. We even often related to people as the labels we sought to combat. For example, someone might stress that we needed a black lesbian, a transvestite, etc., on certain committees or panels. In addition, while many men mouthed slogans against all oppressors, they harbored deeply inlaid antiwoman feelings. At best, some of them did not comprehend my oppression as a woman; at worst, they were more oppressive than any straight man I had known. (Some gay men seemed to be gay because they found women to be "too inferior" to love.)

It was not long before the lesbians, including myself, split into separate groups in 1970, the first of which we called (to Friedan's horror, I suppose) the Lavender Menace. We went through an endless series of names (such as Radicalesbians and even later Radical Radishes) and an almost equally endless series of political structures until finally the political groups slowly dissolved and only consciousness-raising groups remained. (The reason for the dissolution of the political structures is too complex to analyze here and not necessary to explain my own evolution.)

During the period from my move to the Gay Liberation Front to after the dissolution of Radicalesbians, I became a full-time worker for the gay liberation movement, although I did not entirely drop my feminist activities (and certainly my feminist consciousness is a permanent fixture!). It seemed that I attended endless meetings eight nights a week, chipped ice to cool the beer at dances, and swept the floors of endless meeting rooms and dance halls. I became the ultimate in "lesbian visibility"; in fact, I was the first "lesbian poster lady" in California in 1970, and my face seemed to be plastered on every gay bar wall out there to advertise a gay festival. My entire life was spent organizing gay people and lecturing to straights and gays to tell them "who we are and what we want." In addition to speaking and organizing, I began to write (something which had disappeared when I suppressed my lesbianism after high school) and also began to collect material for my first anthology, which I eventually co-edited with Allen Young.

But while I had become a professional lesbian, I felt I had lost something along the way. I suppose it was inevitable, and I can explain the process best by analogy. It was like being a baby and learning a language. Babies can babble in every language, but in learning and perfecting English certain sounds are reinforced and others are suppressed and finally lost. I felt that somewhere in becoming a "professional dyke," I had lost part of my human identity, and that I had filtered out parts of my life which had been valid as well as valuable for me. For example, my movement activities slowed down my doctorate, since I had so little time for classes and papers that I had to drop out for a while. (I also had two gay roommates

455

who were in my department at graduate school, and they also dropped out due to movement involvement and never returned.)

I realized that I had been labeled and limited. I was now little more than a "dyke," and everything not connected with my lesbianism had been almost totally destroyed. I was the person I had accused straights of trying to stereotype me as. Oh, yes, straights still saw me only as a lesbian, but these straights also included and include "liberated" leftist presses who only wanted me to review lesbian books or discuss lesbian ideas. But the labelers also included many of my gay brothers and sisters who only wanted to hear what I had to say when I spoke of gay liberation. If I wanted to talk about a movie, for example, they wanted to know how that related to gay oppression. If it didn't, they showed no interest, nor was I ever encouraged to develop myself or spend any energy in nongay areas, such as my doctorate or the peace movement. Lastly, I allowed the oppression to happen to me and was indeed a willing victim, as I continued to devote my life to the "movement" and sacrifice anything I could not directly relate to that movement. Ironically, I (as well as other people) became the very image we had set out to destroy.

Don't think that I want to "lose my lesbianism." My lesbian consciousness, my lesbian friends, and my devotion to the lesbian liberation movement are still primary in my life. But I still regret part of what I lost in the process of "perfecting" my lesbianism. This feeling of regret became particularly acute after the publication of my first anthology in 1973 when lesbian demands on my time increased and what little privacy I had left was destroyed. Since then, I have made a conscious effort to somehow limit my involvement in the lesbian movement and to take my lesbian perspective and identity with me into other areas. Therefore, this new identity means that I can no longer be a "full-time" lesbian. I no longer go to meetings, not even consciousness-raising groups. I rarely speak in public. I have given up chipping ice and sweeping floors. Although I greatly admire people who have the energy to do all these things and know they must be done by someone, I now limit my involvement in the movement to writing, primarily for lesbian newspapers and magazines. Also, I am now willing to relate to nongay as well as gay people in nongay vocabularies around nongay events and issues (such as vegetarianism, for example).

And while I have since completed co-editing two more anthologies and am working on a sex and lifestyles book, I have also finished my graduate course work and am currently writing my dissertation on American lesbians who settled in Paris from 1900–1940. In addition, I teach (with great enjoyment) English to speakers of other languages. I hope to continue writing as well as teaching and I also hope to write on nonlesbian subjects, subjects which express my wholeness as a human being.

And so, while I await and work for a peaceful revolution based on the feminist and gay principles of role destruction and the removal of phallic hierarchies, I am also working at bringing a more complete person into that struggle and into that new society which shall arise from such struggle.

Blacks and Gay Liberation

by Jon L. Clayborne

It is unfortunate that oppression is not a very good instructor; all too often the victims of oppression resort, themselves, to intolerance and persecution in dealing with others who are different and whom they do not understand. While prejudice and irrational assumptions are obviously the basis for racism, they are less readily conceived as the basis for society's condemnation and harassment of homosexually oriented men and women. Therefore antigay sentiment among blacks seems all the more appalling, not only because of the historical experience of blacks in the United States, but also because of the parallels which can be drawn between the oppression of blacks and society's hostility toward homosexuals.

False stereotypes have been fostered to create the impression that blacks and gays are inferior beings; they are induced to accept the majority's standards as their salvation from discrimination, yet both blacks and gays are continually rebuffed by a large segment of the American society; for years school textbooks mentioned few, if any, black contributions to the betterment of society, while the homosexual orientation of creative Americans is still laundered out of their biographies. Yet despite the similarities in their plight, blacks seem just as compelled to debase and caricature homosexuals as the majority of whites in our heterosexual-dominated society.

Harassment of "faggots" and the misconceptions regarding homosexuality did not originate within the black community. Whether the fate of homosexuals in ancient Africa was comparable to that of homosexuals who were executed in medieval Britain and burned at the stake on the Continent has, so far, gone uninvestigated; yet, just as the fashion and foods of the majority culture were assimilated by black Americans, so also much of the European attitude toward life became ingrained in black thought.

Conditioned to deny their own worth as human beings, blacks unquestioningly accepted the puritanical denunciation of homosexuality. Society declared that homosexuals considered themselves to be members of their opposite sex and behaved accordingly; that homosexuals were intent on seducing heterosexuals, particularly children; and that the disapprobation of homosexuality was divined by God. The homosexual stereotypes, based on fear and alleged inferiority (as black stereotypes have been), gained credence through constant repetition, exaggeration, and the behavior of many homosexuals themselves, who adopted at least some traits of the stereotypes as a result of the self-fulfilling prophecy (i.e., human beings can be conditioned by other humans to react in the manner repeatedly suggested by the others).

Another cause of antigay sentiment among blacks is the Christian church. Deep involvement with the church has been a significant characteristic of the black tradition in the United States, and blacks have long depended on their faith for sustenance in difficult times and guidance in their day-to-day existence. The church's influence in the black community remains considerable, regardless of the decline in religious fervor evident since the late sixties. Perhaps the popular interpretation of the destruction of Sodom and Gomorrah and the pronouncement in Leviticus 20:13 condemning sexual relationships among males are more familiar to older blacks; nonetheless the Bible has provided a religious basis for black abhorrence of homosexuality which transverses age groups.

Most blacks, like most people in general, have no realistic conception of how many homosexuals surround them; mistakenly, they think they can readily identify a homosexual by his or her attire or mannerisms. During the question-and-answer session of a panel discussion on homosexuality, a black male in the audience asked me why all the black homosexuals in his local bar wore female garb. In response, I pointed out that it was a misconception that homosexual males conceived of themselves as women and that there were probably more homosexuals present in the bar whom he did not recognize as such, because they wore the usual male-identifying clothes. The highly visible drag queen and bull dyke comprise only a small percentage of the homosexual population and cannot be considered representative of homosexuals in general.

No fewer lies, no fewer distortions have been employed to malign the nature of homosexuality than have been used to malign blacks; however, blacks have not only accepted heterosexist propaganda without expressing doubt, but even many enlightened blacks have viewed gay liberation as a threat. Black attempts to attain the benefits and enjoy the opportunities extended to white citizens have persisted for well over three centuries; the guarantee of black civil rights, often the paramount issue confronting the American society, has never been displaced from the nation's conscience since the mid-nineteenth century. In recent years, however, white backlash under the guise of "law and order," as well as the issues of the Vietnam War, ecology, the women's movement, etc., have all risen to seemingly compete with blacks for society's attention; therefore, any social objective not directly associated with the plight of black people has tended to be viewed with reserve or hostility by blacks. The feminist movement has most notably had to contend with a lack of enthusiasm from black males and females alike. The black males' reaction was anticipated; of course, they would feel that the women's struggle for equality would jeopardize male dominance. The certainty that black sisters would eagerly join ranks with their white sisters to secure essential goals like equal job opportunities and wages proved premature. Most blacks, regardless of sexual gender, consider racism, not sexism, the source of their difficulties in achieving n equal footing in society. Similarly, gay liberation is dismissed as irrelevant to the black struggle.

Additional factors contribute to the black community's virtual uninterest in gay liberation. While women's rights proponents have initially not been persuasive in presenting their arguments to blacks, they have recently managed to arouse wide attention. Compared to the news reports accorded to the feminist movement, mass media coverage of the gay liberation movement, however, has been negligible and the result is obvious. Although many black politicians in public office have supported gay rights, most blacks think gay rights are a joke and have no conception of the philosophy sustaining gay liberationists. Even among black homosexuals, one usually encounters uninformed comments regarding the gay liberation movement (one black homosexual declared to me that he had been in the gay movement for years, obviously and unconsciously equating the homosexual subculture with the gay liberation movement) or even indignation with what appears to many blacks to be another white-dominated endeavor. The few blacks active in the gay liberation movement have yet to overcome the obstacles arising from dual (black and gay) and triple (black, gay, and female) minority status and have been unable to facilitate an understanding of gay liberation among the majority of black homosexuals.

Unjustifiably, the homosexual stereotypes have contributed to black contempt for homosexuals and the misconceptions about gay rights. Add to this the strong sense of sex role-playing in the black community, and the situation appears dismal. Centuries of oppression in a male-dominated society, during which time the black male has been subjected to severely demoralizing abuse, has intensified black dependence on the superficial delineations between males and females. The dogma that the male leads and the female follows, which is being uprooted in the general society, is still largely observed in the black community. Acquainted with only those homosexuals who cross-dress, heterosexually oriented blacks assume that role-playing is also an essential part of the homosexual experience. Some blacks also assume that homosexuals merely have their genders confused: a male homosexual can have masculinity beaten into him, and all a lesbian needs is the service of a good man. It is permissible to ridicule and victimize homosexuals. Subconsciously, some blacks who react vehemently to homosexuals may even appreciate their existence, thinking that, since blacks have had to look up to whites, homosexuals have to look up to them.

The political rhetoric of the black militants in the late sixties was often employed to further alienate blacks from homosexuals. Opposition to the ideology and trappings of a capitalist society did not prevent black radical activists from adopting that same society's unjust attitude toward homosexuals. All the traditional stereotypes used to deny homosexuals their humanity endured among the new, socially conscious thinkers, who let nothing aside from skin color determine their thoughts. There were few within the radical black liberation movement who challenged the unrealistic outlook regarding homosexuality; just as the homosexual civil rights worker had concealed his or her identity a decade earlier, so the black militant who found his or her sexual orientation under attack did not dare speak out. The homophobia among black militants was generally hidden from view until it was revealed by concerned gay activists.

During 1969 and 1970, the Panthers' ideological sympathizers in the Gay Liberation Front in New York were willing to overlook the Panthers' sexist prejudice, openly expressed by Eldridge Cleaver, for example, in the widely read *Soul on Ice*. They were hopeful that the blacks would eventually overcome their conditioned hostility to homosexuals; other members of the gay organization felt it was totally inequitable to denounce right-wing oppressors, while not only refraining from opposing, but actually boosting left-wing sexists. A message to the Gay Liberation Front from Jean Genet urged the membership to be patient with the Panthers, but did not soothe those who objected to giving gay support and even money to the Panthers. Some gay radicals continued to support the Panthers as the most visible method of opposing racism and police brutality against blacks. They were delighted when Huey Newton released a policy statement declaring that a homosexual could be as devoted and effective a revolutionary as any other individual, but it is doubtful whether Newton's statement left any impression other than on paper. Within the past several years I have heard a few blacks who profess to socialistic and nationalistic ideologies accuse black homosexuals of committing genocide, an update of the "downfall of Greece" indictment.

Whereas I once perceived the genocide theory as indicative of the black approach to homosexuality, I have now come to sense a diverse reaction to homosexuality in the black community. Very few blacks accept the idea of homosexuality, some tolerate it, many oppose it, and some rabidly condemn it. Most homosexuals have accustomed themselves to provoking negative sentiment from the remainder of society, and usually attempt to conceal their sexuality from all except similarly oriented friends and associates. Passing as "straight" is a long-practiced game that homosexuals have become adept at playing, particularly since one of the rules seems to be that even if you do not fool anyone, as long as you keep trying then you are "passing." A homosexual can easily condition him- or herself to be careful not to sit a certain way or talk a certain way or substitute the appropriate pronouns to cover up a same-sex date, but occasionally the homosexual becomes aware that "passing" is really a device society allows homosexuals to use to depreciate their lifestyle.

Thousands of white homosexuals have renounced the idea of pretending to be heterosexual and risked the loss of jobs, homes, families, and friends. A comparably small number of black homosexuals have come out publicly as well; but most black homosexuals could no more publicly declare their homosexuality than they could change color. I have heard several excuses offered by black homosexuals to explain their refusal to become involved in the gay liberation movement, but evident throughout the explanations is the fear that being black and homosexual involves obstacles twice as difficult to surmount. There is nothing the black homosexual can do to hide his or her dark complexion, but sexuality need not be revealed.

Corresponding to the desire to avoid additional oppression where unnecessary is the belief among some black homosexuals that once laws securing gay rights are legislated, blacks will still have to contend with racism while white homosexuals will be free of any oppression. Of course, gay rights will probably be guaranteed slowly and sporadically throughout the United States and laws do not assure the eradication of prejudice, but the existence of racism within the homosexual subculture and the perception of the gay liberation movement as white dominated have justified a distrust of all whites, regardless of sexual orientation, by many black homosexuals.

While most black homosexuals, whether deliberately or

otherwise, remain unfamiliar with the political aspect of homosexuality, there are a few blacks who are actively involved in the gay liberation movement. During the early years of the movement, the enthusiasm that arose from defying society's taboo against revealing one's homosexuality was sufficient to commit gays to the cause. The implications of gay liberation, however, exceed combatting the New York Tactical Police Force in Sheridan Square and zapping public officials at Lincoln Center. As the gay liberation movement developed, activists became cognizant of the other areas of concern, initially unrealized. Pressing for the abolition of sodomy and solicitation statutes used to convict male homosexuals was an obvious goal of the movement, but lesbian activists had to force the movement's mostly male leadership to acknowledge that child custody guarantees for lesbian mothers and other gay women's issues were also urgent concerns for the gay liberation movement. Black gay activists have yet to create interest within the movement concerning problems pertaining to their dual minority status. Attempts to establish black (or Third World) caucuses within major gay liberation organizations have frequently been stifled by a lack of enthusiasm from both the organizations' leadership and the membership on the whole. The few black gay liberation organizations in existence have never had a substantial impact on the movement. While Third World workshops have been scheduled at gay conferences in the past, the workshops usually attracted few participants and/or were disorganized and lacking in focus.

Refusing to tolerate sexism in the black community and incensed by racism among homosexuals, black gay activists have sought a personal concurrence between their black and gay consciousness. Once they have seriously dealt with being black and gay in their own minds and are able to verbalize their thoughts to each other, perhaps then blacks involved in the gay liberation movement will develop specific issues with which they can instill a black consciousness in the movement, and subsequently facilitate greater gay involvement by black homosexuals.

The black experience encompasses various economic levels, social environments, academic and vocational aspirations, creative accomplishments, etc.; for the black community to exclude homosexuality as a component of the black experience is self-deceptive. The many blacks who dismiss gay liberation as a frivolous diversion for whites are forfeiting the welfare of hundreds of thousands of homosexually oriented blacks whose existence, at best, is denied. Despite the cultural and emotional factors prompting one's commitment to black liberation, it is psychologically debilitating for a black homosexual to espouse equality while simultaneously accepting his or her denigration. Beyond jeopardizing the healthy development of black homosexuals, the black community inhibits its own maturation toward liberation by perpetuating homophobic stereotypes and disdaining gay liberation.

Three for the Price of One:
Notes from a Gay Black Feminist

by Anita Cornwell

For quite some time now, I have been wondering what kind of life I would have led if I had not become a lesbian. Of course, at this late date, I am firmly convinced that all lesbians are born, not made, but due to our rigid heterosexual conditioning, more womyn* are seldom fortunate enough to discover the joys of being a womin-identified womin.*

Which is not to say that lesbians do not face problems in this society. We do. By and large, however, many of our difficulties would disappear if America would somehow overcome its archaic homophobic tendencies. Obviously though, even if it did, the gay womin would still be left with all the problems confronting womyn in a nation that—to quote one "expert"—worships the male.

Finally, if the seemingly well-nigh impossible should ever occur and we are freed from the bondage of sexism and homophobia, the nonwhite lesbian would still be subjected to racism, that endemic virus that has plagued the nation since its inception. Dealing with any one of these demons takes quite a bit of doing; having to endure all three is worse than living in the crater of a volcano.

Fortunately, my mother brought me up to be an independent womin. She had to if she wanted me to survive, because for any black female born in America before the aftermath of civil rights movement to assure some measure of dignity and justice for the black American, she had to know how to shift for herself—otherwise she would surely have perished. It was as simple and as perilous as that. Perilous because any independent female in a patriarchal society is a marked womin.

---

* I am, of course, using the variant spelling. Many sisters feel that womyn (plural) and womin (singular) are preferable to the old forms. See *Dyke, A Quarterly*, No. 3, Fall, 1976.

Consequently, inasmuch as I was brought up to be an independent womin, I could never quite get the hang of the game that so many straight womyn had to play if they wanted to land a man. And believe me, she who did not want a man back in those days of *togetherness* in the early fifties was in for a world of trouble. So trouble dogged my footsteps for many a year.

During those years, before I had even heard of the word *gay*, I spent an inordinate amount of time fielding such questions as "When are you going to get married, Neet?" I never came up with a good answer, not even after I had had my first relationship with a womin. I was aware that it wasn't good politics to tell people I didn't want to get married. In fact, I knew it would have bordered on the disastrous.

Besides, although I was positive that I did not want a traditional type of marriage (which was the only kind one heard of in those years when the *Feminine Mystique* was ravaging the land), I was not at all certain what kind of alternative lifestyle I would be able to have. That one lesbian relationship (with a married womin at that) did very little to help resolve my dilemma. I knew only her, and if she knew other gay women, she kept them rather well hidden from me.

As was the case with many incipient lesbians of that period, I had read *The Well of Loneliness*, but that was even less promising than my elusive lover. Those characters seemed to exist in a kind of world that I had never seen and one that had vanished as completely as the dinosaur and the dodo bird.

Perhaps if I had not been so badly scarred from having been born black, poor, and female in the Deep South at a time when all blacks were invisible (and, of course, even today, being poor or female in affluent, male-oriented America is about on a par with having leprosy in India), I might have been more enterprising. Perhaps if I hadn't had to cope with all those battles, fears, phobias, and anxieties continually raging within me, I might have gone to live in Greenwich Village, or Paris, or Los Angeles, or any place except conservative Philadelphia, where we had settled while I was still in high school.

It wasn't until after I had had my fourth lesbian relationship—sometime during the early sixties—that I decided that, for better or worse, I was irrevocably gay. And from that time onward I began to withdraw as much as possible from the heterosexual world. I found most straight men too sexist, and I was tired of listening to straight womyn complain about the problems they were eternally having with their men.

Not that I didn't sympathize with my straight sisters and their oppression, but I was having a devil of a time trying to keep my own canoe from capsizing. Besides, even then I was baffled as to why so many heterosexual womyn continued to let men use and abuse them in the same manner that their mothers, grandmothers, and even their great-grandmothers, dating back to the rise of the patriarchy, had done.

Not the least of the many problems that the black lesbian has to contend with is the extreme conservatism that prevails in the black community—a conservatism that most white people are totally unaware of. For some reason that has always amazed me, many white people seem to consider black people "liberal" because of our insistence on racial equality. That is not liberalism but is simply a healthy instinct for self-preservation.

I suppose another factor contributing to this misconception is that living together "without benefit of clergy" was rather common in some black circles at one time. But the truth is that most of this was done because of the extreme shortage of funds that has always been the lot of far too many Afro-Americans.

"No matter how radical most black men may be, when it comes time to dealing with womyn, they get their ideas straight out of *The Ladies Home Journal*," a disgusted black sister once complained. And black men aren't the only ones afflicted with ancient ideas and precepts about womyn. Even unto this very day, all too many black womyn are still so hung up on Jesus Christ and the Bible, they may as well be living in the time of Moses and the Burning Bush.

During the time of our greatest oppression in America, the Bible was about the only source of comfort for most black womyn. They made it such a deep part of their lives it became rooted in their bones—so much so that in time it apparently became the only framework that sustained them. And if there is any document anywhere that is more antifemale and pro-male than the Bible, I simply do not want to hear about it.

In retrospect, I believe that's why many black lesbians feel so guilty about being gay. I now think that factor was the most important one that made some of my lesbian relationships with black womyn such harrowing experiences. And probably the reason it did not occur to me at the time of the turmoil is that I simply was unaware of the terrible hold that religious beliefs often have on many people.

By some miracle or other I escaped that curse. And since none of my lovers ever directly said anything such as "This is a sin. The Bible says thus and so, . . ." I never made any connection between the two—in spite of the fact that one lover was a devout Catholic (or at least she seemed to spend half of her life going to mass), while another one would turn those Sunday-morning, down-home church services up so loud they were most likely heard by Jesus Christ up yonder swinging on them Pearly Gates.

If black conservatism is one ogre that keeps the black lesbian forever wading in troubled waters, then white racism is the second demon waiting at the other end of the tunnel. For most of my life, I had always been reluctant to socialize with white people because I felt most of them really did not want to associate with black people on a socially equal basis.

Yet, oddly enough, by the time I finally entered the womyn's movement, I had somehow convinced myself that the color of my skin would have little or no bearing on how movement womyn would accept me. Although I am now hard-pressed to understand where I got the notion from, I felt the fact that I was gay would count against me more than the fact that I was black.

Perhaps my long distrust of the mass media prevented me from accepting the value judgment implied by the press when it repeatedly declared that most movement womyn were white, middle-class, and under thirty. I also knew that the lesbian issue had had unpleasant repercussions in other cities.

After I became an active part of the struggle, however, it was a pleasant surprise to find that gay was considered good, by some womyn at least. Consequently, since I thought black was beautiful, I felt I had at last found my place under the sun. And so anxious was I to hold to that illusion, many months passed before I finally faced the truth—racism did exist in the movement.

The first major unsettling incident occurred at a weekend conference about two months after I entered the movement. At this fairly large gathering, two white womyn began a formal discussion program by relating the actions of several black womyn who had not in the least seemed displeased when foreign womyn had made several unflattering remarks about America.

"Of course, I can understand why they feel the way they do," one of the white womyn added when she evidently caught me staring intently at her. There seemed to be a frightened, or guilty, look on her face when she looked at me, and it suddenly struck me that she had absolutely no comprehension whatsoever why those black sisters were not ardent flag-wavers.

The second thing happened a week after the conference and disturbed me even more at the time. I was in the process of moving from one section of the city to another and needed someone with an automobile to help with this expensive undertaking. But none of the white movement womyn with cars, and whom I had been thinking of as sisters, offered to transport one single item.

It is, of course, always more difficult to deal with subtle racisms than the more blatant variety. You're apt to think, "Oh, I'm just being too sensitive." And perhaps I was. But, in the meanwhile, I couldn't help but notice that so-and-so was given a going-away party and invitations were issued all around me, *but not to me.*

Likewise, I often thought, "Well, I'm older than most of them, that's why they're a bit standoffish at times." But then I noticed that another black womin in her early twenties who had wandered into the group wasn't exactly being overwhelmed with the welcome mat either.

Yet, I am not saying that I met racism every step of the way in the womyn's movement. I did not. It was there, however, and is still there. I must also point out that during the time that I was having my most excruciating experience with racism in the movement, a white sister was of the greatest comfort to me. "Don't keep on at the Womyn's Center unless you really think you're getting something worthwhile out of the experience," she suggested to me at one point.

Although I wasn't sure at that moment whether I was getting anything of lasting value from the movement, I shall always be grateful for that sister's understanding. Because if I had withdrawn then, I might have become embittered and never trusted another white womin again.

And, sadly enough, fear of encountering racism seems to be one of the main reasons that so many black womyn refuse to join the womyn's movement. This is especially unfortunate for the black lesbians because unless they have come across feminist ideas from somewhere, they are apt to remain in the old rut of sexual role-playing that apparently affects all traditional lesbian circles.

When I first became acquainted with more than one lesbian at a time, these womyn immediately assumed that I was a femme, although I didn't know the word as it existed in that context. Then, as I grew older—and heavier—other sisters automatically assumed that I was a "stud," a term that really made my hair stand on end when I first heard it directly applied to me.

One day when Dee and I were up in her apartment rapping, I finally suggested that we go down to my place for a few cocktails. We were almost out the door when her telephone rang.

Impatiently, she yanked at the receiver, her face screwed in deep frowns. The frowns quickly evaporated, however, when she recognized the voice of a recent lover. "Hi. I was just getting ready to go to Neet's place . . ."

Then, after a long pause, she declared, "Oh, no! Neet's a stud!"

I hadn't tried to overhear Dee's conversation, and after hearing it I certainly wished I had not. And, to make matters worse, Dee, who also called herself a "stud," thought

471

she had done me a favor by "elevating" me to her level. There actually had been a note of pride in her vóice when she said I was a *stud*.

It was such a frustrating business, because if she had been trying to insult me, I could have felt justified in getting pissed off and acting accordingly. At any rate, I later tried to point out that I was a womin, and as far as I could recall a *stud* was a male horse. But whether or no, *a stud was not me!*

I wasted my breath, of course, which I found out a few days later when I was up to hér apartment along with several other friends. Sometime during the evening, while I was fixing myself a drink, she gave me a scornful look and declared, "You're the most *feminine stud* I have ever seen!"

Presumably, she said that because I was mixing my booze while she was drinking hers on the rocks. But she would seldom explain where she was coming from. And sometimes she seemed to come from rather far out, such as the time she told me, "You don't talk the way you look."

When I asked her how I should talk, she merely smiled and shook her head. Finally, really alarmed, I asked, "Then how should I look?"

Still she refused to comment, but as much as I could surmise, I think she believed that since I wore slacks most of the time, I should swagger around and boast about how great I was the way she occasionally did.

One of Dee's problems seemed to be the same that affects so many men—she could not readily relate to womyn except on a sexual basis, unless they were "studs." Consequently, most of her friends were gay men. And she was forever urging me to "Come up and meet the fellows, Neet."

I never did get around to doing that, however, and perhaps that's why she told me one evening, "You are *not* like the fellows."

"That's because I'm *not* a fellow," I replied logically, but it didn't seem to make much impression on her.

Of course, most black lesbians that I have known do not fall into the kind of pattern that Dee was into. Still, I do

472

believe that most white people simply do not realize what a devastating effect racism has on black people in general and on black womyn in particular. And, obviously, the black lesbian is usually the most victimized of all.

Perhaps one reason that white womyn do not realize just how crippling racism is, is that most black womyn seem so strong to them. Frankly, until I entered the womyn's movement and came into contact with far more white womyn than I had ever known before on a fairly close basis, I had assumed that white womyn were more self-sufficient and/or independent than black womyn. I assumed that because, after all, white womyn have more affluence and influence than most black womyn have ever even heard of. Or so it appeared to me from afar.

And in the beginning, whenever I heard a young white movement womin saying such things as, "Mary Jones is such a strong black womin," I would mentally conjure up a big, hefty weight lifter or some such creature. Only gradually did it occur to me that they were speaking of a different kind of strength. Then, as I got to know those young white sisters better, I could well understand why black womyn seemed so strong to them.

Yet it is simply a matter of the survival of the fittest, so to speak. Most black sisters still do not have influential fathers or husbands or white law enforcement institutions to lean on in some form or fashion. Most black womyn learn very early in life that there is very little insulation between them and "the school of hard knocks," as my mother is so fond of calling life in the raw.

It is not my contention that womyn of any race should be exposed to the brutal experience that black womyn have endured in America so they may be "strong and self-sufficient." But why isn't there some middle ground? Why should womyn either be strong and independent because of societal brutalization or dependent and indecisive because of excessive sheltering or other restrictive influences?

As incredible as it may seem to most feminists, however, the often declared goal of many black people is to achieve the life led by the typical white, middle-class suburban family of the fifties, wherein Mother is buried at

473

home all day with two and a half kids, one dog, and perhaps a small swimming pool near the newly erected two-car garage, while Papa struts around with his attaché case, sporting his gray flannels and button-down blue pin-striped Van Heusen shirt—that or much worse.

"We want *our* womyn spoiled rotten," a well-known young black actor once confessed to a news reporter. What he had in mind, of course, was his ideal female: the slender, beautiful, fluffily dressed young womin with nary a brain in her head who is mainly concerned with clothes, men, and beauty tips. Then, when *her man* gets tired of her or she loses her looks, out she goes, the same as any other disposable commodity.

During the height of the civil rights struggle in the mid-sixties, I shall never forget the stirring anguish that resounded in one leader's voice when he declared, "We are tired of our womyn having to slave in the white man's kitchen. We want them home, taking care of our children *and waiting on us!*"

I also recall a little story I once read about how a certain organization to save humanity came into being out in Chicago. "A group of us black ministers began meeting on Saturday mornings and discussing the many problems facing our people in the city. As time went on, the group grew larger, and some of the ministers began to bring their wives. *Then the wives started bringing lunch. . . .*"

Around the same time there was a little story in a well-known black magazine obviously written by a young dude who had had it up to here with racism in America. The story, a fantasy set in the year 2500 A.D., concerned another young dude about the same age as the author who leaned back in his chair enjoying the serenity that is his in an America that is no longer infected with racism.

Inevitably, of course, our hero's mind finally begins to reflect on twentieth-century America and the horrors that black folk endured then. All ends well, however, because he is soon brought back to the present tranquility of the year 2500 A.D., *when his wife begins to serve his breakfast!*

The ideas that most black men have regarding black womyn are indeed fascinating to behold. A couple of years ago when I was a member of a colloquium held at a

474

large, nearly all-white eastern university by the school of social work, I found myself, as a majority of one almost, having to point out in a firm (but not hostile) manner that black men were just as sexist as other men. Then I eventually realized that most of the vocal members in the room were holding fast to the idea that black womyn only had one of two choices: either they had to join the womyn's liberation movement and be led by white womyn, or become part of the civil rights movement and be led by black men.

Finally, I put my question to this young black dude who seemed even more insistent than the others—although they all seemed to have definite ideas about the black womin's place, etc.—"You seem to be saying that I have to be led either by white womyn or by black men. Why can't I lead myself?"

He hemmed and hawed but never came out with any clear-cut reply. After all, what could he say? Certainly not what was on his mind. Or perhaps he wasn't entirely aware of what his deepest feelings on the subject were. But it was painfully obvious to me that he simply could not endure the thought that black womyn are capable of running their own lives.

Then, after the young man stopped sputtering, another caseworker-student, a black womin, said to me, "Many black womyn in my caseload tell me they would love to be able to stop working and stay home and just be a plain old housewife."

"Yes, that may be what they're thinking now," I pointed out. "But once the marriage begins to go wrong and she gets knocked around once or twice for burning the toast or some other such business, she'll probably begin to see things in a different light."

The caseworker simply stared at me, as most of the others in the room seemed to be doing. Not that everyone seemed to think I was from outer space, but there were a great many perplexed expressions around the room. The group was about one-fourth to one-third black (a rather large percentage for that university, but after all, social work is one of our greatest domains), and for the most part I appeared to be the only black in the room in favor of the womyn's movement, which seemed to surprise about 95 percent of everybody present.

I don't know where all this "Back-to-the-Doll-House-Movement" is going to end for the middle-class straight black womin, but it is certainly a disastrous voyage she is about to embark on, because in a patriarchal society, the middle-aged womin is about as relevant as the square-earth theory, and even more ridiculed.

So, what would my life have been like if I had not become a gay womin? I don't exactly know, but I am damn sure glad I will never have to find out.

Practical Economics for a Women's Community

by Nancy Groschwitz

What do dykes want? While there are undoubtedly as many answers to this as there are women to ask, a start might be to say: they want jobs that pay their rent without sacrificing their self-respect. They want to be able to support businesses which share their values and their political consciousness. They want to withdraw their support from the patriarchal/capitalistic system which oppresses them. They want to enjoy the experience of women's music and women's art. And, often, they simply want to spend as much of their time as possible with other women, and as little time as possible with men.

In short, they want their own community, a women's community. Some women are striving to achieve such a community by physically withdrawing from urban life and setting up land collectives in rural areas. Those of us, however, who are tied to the cities for reasons of employment, school, political commitment, or a basic preference for city living are faced with the task of establishing an economically viable network of services and businesses separate from, and in spite of, the larger society.

Ideally this community would offer an ever widening range of services, everything from health clinics and food co-ops for the body, books and music and meeting places for the spirit, and skilled mechanics to fix plumbing, cars, or whatever we own that occasionally breaks down.

As an example, a partial list of what's available here in San Diego would include a number of women's cultural productions: local musicians and singers, guerrilla theatre group, two feminist newspapers, a film (Jan Oxenberg's *A Comedy in Six Unnatural Acts*) and a book (Helen McKenna's *The Toilet Book*) funded by the feminist credit union, and frequent visits by musicians from other parts of California. We also have the coffee house, Las Hermanas, a woman-only space where many of these events occur. We have several health clinics, businesses (everything from a bookstore to a printing press to a dog-grooming business), the Feminist Free University, the Feminist Federal Credit Union, an assortment of women's centers, the Gay Center, and the inevitable set of women's bars.

There are still a lot of gaps. Recently I heard several women bemoaning the lack of a women's movie theatre, and then speculating on whether there would be enough feminist films around to keep such a place in operation. For anyone trying to avoid dealing with men as much as possible, the gaps are especially evident. When my car breaks down, it still has to go to The Man. (Any of you auto mechanics out there want to relocate to San Diego?) The last time I moved, I looked in vain for a woman with a truck, and ended up renting a trailer from Avis. I'm still hoping to find a woman to fix the stereo. It goes without saying that my veterinarian, gas-station attendant, salesperson at the hardware store are all men.

While most people will readily concede the political impact of, say, a feminist newspaper, they might wonder about the importance of a feminist auto mechanic. Isn't one business pretty much like another, irrespective of who runs it? I would argue that there are at least three reasons why it's preferable for me to go to another feminist. First of all, it's more pleasant for me since I know that I won't walk in the door and be tagged as a dumb broad and an easy mark. Second, I'll be helping to give a job to a woman who needs a job, possibly in a field she would have trouble getting into in the straight world and hopefully in a more positive working environment. The chances are good that we will both come away from the interaction with our feelings of competence and intelligence strengthened. Third, since this woman is far more likely than is my local Exxon dealer to buy a book at the Women's Store or some coffee at Las Hermanas, more of my money is kept circulating within the community.

What keeps all these worthy projects and businesses from getting started? The womanpower is available: women with straight jobs who long to work with and for other dykes, women who have no job at all and need one, women with spare time and energy that they want to contribute to other women. The ideas are available; listen to any conversation between a group of women and you're sure to hear at least one sentence that begins "Wouldn't it be nice if we could start a ... ?"

What's often lacking, most simply, is money. It takes money to build a community. Money is needed to publish books, produce albums, run clinics, buy land, pay the rent on meeting places, buy tools, make films, or hold music festivals. Money is needed, but single self-supporting women are traditionally the poorest and most underpaid members of this society, and any dyke who can't or won't clean up her act and play straight for the sake of a job is going to be in the worst shape of all. The jobs which are traditionally women's jobs (secretary, waitress, bank teller, sales clerk) usually require "feminine" attire, a docile demeanor, and friendly subservience to a male boss and/or male customers, all of which the political lesbian finds particularly offensive. The better paid, less demeaning, and usually more interesting skilled trades have begun to employ a few women, but nowhere near the number who need and want such jobs.

Given that most of us are poor, where are we going to find the money to build ourselves a community? One answer comes from the fact that there are a lot of us. Individually we may be poor but collectively we are not. This idea has led to the formation of feminist credit unions. A credit union consists of a group of women who get together and pool their savings, make low-interest loans to each other, and collectively share in the income. Women who have money to save know that it is being used to help other women, rather than being put in a bank which invests in corporations which oppress women (and people in general); women who would never qualify for a loan from a bank can get money, avoid the bank's high interest rates, and establish credit for themselves. At the California Feminist Federal Credit Union, the average account is about $200, which doesn't sound like much, but the total assets are currently over $300,000, most of which is being loaned out to the women's community. In its political statement, CFFCU has promised to give priority to loans to feminists and feminist projects.

Although the credit union is doing well and filling a real need, many women have pointed out that women who have money to save are still collecting profits (in the form of interest on their savings) from women who have less money and who need loans. In addition, there are limits on what kinds of loans the credit union can make, in part because of federal rules and regulations and in part because of a need to remain financially stable and to avoid high-risk loans.

A Feminist Community Fund is now being organized by members of the credit union. This fund is intended to initiate a system of true profit sharing, by making money available for interest-free loans to feminist groups and projects. Women with savings accounts at the credit union will be able to have all or part of the interest on their savings transferred into the FCF account, thus putting the profit made on their money directly back into the community.

Four percent of $300,000 is $12,000 yearly. While none of us is idealistic enough to believe that all credit union members will choose to participate in the fund, even a substantial fraction of $12,000 would be enough to produce significant changes in the women's community of San Diego. In addition, we are exploring ways of making what money we have go even farther. We are attempting to expand the concept of a "loan" to include other forms of resource sharing; for example, women who are unable to repay their loan with money might donate their skills and energies to some other feminist project for a specified period.

Women are trying to create a community of a sort which has never been created before, and that necessarily involves risks, and mistakes, and many false starts. Traditional financial institutions are not prepared to deal with such a process; therefore, we must create our own institutions. While we expect that the fund will have difficulties, because of our own inexperience, we intend to learn from our mistakes, and we will be able to advise other women at other credit unions how to do better, and that too is part of the process.

But even the credit union and Feminist Community Fund cannot fund the entire women's community. They can give a valuable start to many projects, but they can't indefinitely support such projects, nor provide jobs to all women who need employment. If we want to create a community, we need to start thinking of ourselves as a group, and having some awareness of what helps the financial state of the whole group. One way to start would be through an analysis of where our money is going. If we were to conceive of ourselves for a moment as a separate country, we would quickly see that our balance of payments is in terrible shape. In other words, there's a serious money drain. Women are spending money for needed services that the group does not yet provide. For example, the chances are good that the single biggest item in your monthly budget is rent. The chances are also good that your landlady/lord is not a feminist, does not save at your local credit union, and doesn't advocate the end of capitalism and the patriarchy. Yet every month you support this person through your rent. What can be done about this? One possibility is the organization of women's housing co-ops. If a group of women could get together the down payment on a house or apartment building, and then rent it to other women (or live in it themselves) instead of the rent going into the pocket of some landlord, it would be going to pay off the mortgage of a space which would eventually be owned by, and available to, local women (or which could continue to be rented, with the income going to the community).

We need to identify other areas of money drain, and to develop creative solutions to the problem of keeping our money circulating among women. What about woman-run secondhand stores and/or trading places? What about a centralized place to borrow or rent tools? (Why should every women's household in a city have to afford its own tune-up kit, plumber's tools, lawn mower, socket wrenches, vacuum cleaner, etc.?) Where does your money go? Think about it.

Attacking the problem from the opposite direction, we

481

might also work on bringing money into the community, in addition to keeping what money we have circulating among ourselves. Radical lesbians, especially those who have worked in the male left/socialist movements, sometimes take a negative view of money and of money-making businesses. We need to remember, however, that money is not the same thing as capitalism. Capitalism means making money for its own sake, which leads to a system in which there are always a few rich people and a lot of poor people. But money itself isn't inherently bad or evil; what matters is what you do with it. Until somebody comes up with a more efficient barter system, our hopes of having a rape crisis center (or coffee house, printing press, or whatever) will only be realized when we have the necessary fistful of dollars to pay for it.

One method of adding money to the community is through income sharing. There are at least a few women who have creative, interesting, useful jobs which are also very well paid. In some cases, these women have come to realize the unusually privileged position they are in and are using their resources to help support other women who are doing valuable, but unpaid, political work. Sisters, if you've got it, spread it around! One possibility: find an organization whose goals you support and offer to pay a salary to a full- or part-time worker.

On a more impoverished level, Rita Mae Brown has suggested that committed feminists ought to be willing to tithe 10 percent of their income to the movement. Probably all but the very poorest of us could manage such a tithe.

Another method of bringing money into the community is to establish a business which reaches out to women who might not normally consider themselves feminists. These women might be apolitical lesbians or women who are still relating to men. A business which reaches these women will have the advantage of a larger (and less impoverished) clientele and may at the same time serve as a link between the community and these potential members. One example of such a business is Los Angeles–based Olivia Records. Olivia is a national women's recording company. Besides nontraditional and nonoppressive jobs for women in technical fields, Olivia provides music which speaks to all women and which is surely the finest propaganda the women's community could produce. Other examples of businesses which generate money for the community are feminist-run restaurants and women's concerts.

So far I have frequently, and intentionally, glossed over the distinction between feminist-run alternative versions of standard services (e.g., carpentry) and truly radical services—that is, services which help women change their image of themselves as human beings or which give them space to find their own ways of living. Examples of these truly radical services might be: self-help clinics, shelters for battered wives, cultural productions and women's music, self-defense classes, and living collectives/land collectives.

The reason I have chosen to give equal emphasis to both is that both are vital to a functioning community. If we had such a community, we would see that fixing a roof to keep the rain off someone's head is as useful and worthy an activity as the more radical services mentioned above. In our present system, however, what we do to make a living is frequently irrelevant or even counterproductive to our feminist aims.

Hopefully, we will soon be able to integrate the pieces of our lives and stop this schizophrenic existence of a straight job by day and radical political work at night. It keeps us in a state of permanent culture shock and drains our energy. With the space that the feminist community will provide, we will be able to collect our strength and focus our energies on the work to be done.

Second Five-Year Plan

by the Fag Rag Collective

The spirit of Stonewall lives. Despite rumors to the contrary, the butterflies of '69 are still alive and not about to be pinned down on some millionaire's drying board. *Fag Rag* has struggled in our first five years to keep alive that spirit of rage, revolt, and resistance that began on Christopher Street. In 1976, as in 1971, we look forward, not back. We will not mourn an alleged death of the sixties.

Susan Saxe, in a statement issued from jail, speaks to and for us when she says:

> . . . We have failed to do enough talking about what was right. We have swallowed the myths created by the government and the media that the 60s are dead, that our political protest was just some form of adolescent trauma, a psychological reaction to our parents, like swallowing goldfish or cramming phone booths. . . . To believe this myth is to cheat ourselves out of our past, and worse, to cheat ourselves out of our future.

Despite errors, despite contradictions, despite failures—we were doing the right thing at the right time.

Our first five years have been largely taken up in attacking oppressive institutions with emphasis on zaps, marches, demonstrations, conferences, manifestos, and interminable meetings. Our most common experience has been the consciousness-raising groups out of which a generation of activists is emerging. All these devices have been valuable and will find uses in the future, but we cannot simply repeat good things we have done in the past. That would be as great an error as those who call the Stonewall Revolt distasteful or unnecessary.

* * *

484

The *Fag Rag* collective has come up with a platform, a sort of Second Five-Year Plan of struggle, for keeping alive the spirit of '69.

1) We must build more networks of support and action linking antiestablishment communities and groups in all parts of the world. For instance, we should receive guidance and inspiration from revolutionary gay Portuguese groups no less than San Francisco's Angels of Light. To do this, we must have ready-made communication and relationship channels. Such a network is already beginning to be built among North American rural gay people; urban radicals also need support.

We need these networks *now* so that faggots, lesbians, and allied radicals can become more conscious of themselves as a growing, worldwide force. These networks can provide the nexus for discussion and action groups, manifestations of our radical consciousness, and planned attacks on the straight hierarchy, its anticulture and its prerogatives.

The word *network* indicates a *linkage* between widely scattered local groups that is needed to overcome our feelings of isolation and powerlessness. Such networks can also better tackle our common needs for support as faggots living in an alien straight world. The networks could provide meeting places and contacts for faggots and others with radical consciousness. Many emerging "gay institutions" have failed to provide such a network for those of us who challenge the straight world. They foster a boring, pacified ghetto, more and more mirroring the somewhat liberalized but all the more deadening mass Kultur.

Our own networks would have to be noncommercial. They would deal directly with alienation through action and by building our own authentic culture, free of "professional" or "tasteful" norms. At the same time, they could address the ageism and sexism that remain among us, supporting firmly teenage and old-age faggots and creating alternatives to "lovers," "gay marriage," and bar-cruising.

2) We are opposed to breeding for its own sake and to any emphasis on procreation and human reproduction as a measure of human value. People are valuable in them-

485

selves for themselves, and not because they contain semen or eggs. Our purpose is to *be*, not to reproduce.

3) We favor the continuing development of sexuality, sensuality, and body pleasure. As Will Hollis wrote in the now defunct Detroit periodical *Gay Liberator*, "The enemies of gay liberation are not heterosexuals as a group, but those people—heterosexuals *and homosexuals*—who think sex is bad, dirty, immoral, shameful, nasty." And we might add, who think it should conform to current fads, trends, and norms.

4) We are still creating a gay culture, a value system, an ideology: our essays, music, poetry, letters, nursing, listening, kissing, loving, painting, photographs, newspapers, meetings, learning, teaching, sewing, and other activities help bring into being a new counterculture. Like the fabulous phoenix, we are arising out of the ashes of a dying civilization. Our culture is precious to us, and we will not sell it to the highest advertising market to be packaged and pacified.

5) We vigorously oppose movements toward integration into the existing patriarchal and capitalist institutions. We do not want a slice of the pie; the pie is rotten. We support those who would segregate themselves: yet at the same time most of us will move and act in every place, organization, and situation that will further our own consciousness or spread the influence of our liberation. Some of us will relate to the straight male world, planting our seed of consciousness in their heads and hearts, bringing out the faggot in them. It is in this sense that we say, "Proselytize!"

Some of us have been exhausted after the effect of our own liberation and our initial thrust to liberate others. We were surprised, though we should not have been, by the resurgence of respectability, normalization, and good taste even among faggots. Caught off balance by such attitudes, we may have stepped back from levels of activism that would shock or frighten others. In so doing we may have abrogated leadership among faggots. In any case, the resulting lukewarmness of the "gay community" has been so unchallenging to most faggots that they are abandoning that false community even before it is built. The truly radical consciousness of countless isolated and unorganized faggots can be seen by reading the letters to the editors of the "gay press." It is time to join with them in reassessing both our distinctive separateness and our all-inclusiveness.

* * *

This platform will bring up severe opposition. Some of the most virulently antigay institutions—our oppressors for millennia—now have nabobs attempting to bring gay people into the folds of the state, phychiatry, academia, and religion. And some of the so-called gay institutions have taken on all the forms of straight oppressiveness.

Law reform, political candidates, and general appeals to the state have always been dead-end streets. As a tactic to educate people and rally them, political programs sometimes offer a first step. Such efforts, however, often tend in the opposite direction: to pacify people. As with the women's movement, the gay liberation movement has been overrun by pro-state strategies. The needs of those working with the state suppress those working against the state. Advocates of bills before various governmental bodies, demand "respectability" from their community even if it has to be *imposed*.

The Vietnamese say that electing candidates gives them wings to fly away, never to be seen again. The elected official takes an oath to serve not the gay community but the county, city, state, federal government, or some part of the patriarchy. Their role within our community is one of pacification and suppression. Thus money is taken from the people to elect the candidate; the candidate is then put in the pay of the state (if elected) and learns the meaning of self-service.

This is not a matter of individual morality—one particular person being a scoundrel (or even a whole administration). It is a standard part of the corrupting process of politics, where the purpose of the government is to enrich the rich and powerful and impoverish and disempower everyone else. Many groups have experienced this betrayal: the Irish, Greeks, Italians, blacks, Wasps, women and anyone else foolish or weak enough to trust politicians. We might vote for gay candidates, but must remember they serve themselves first, their government second, and us last.

The psycho workers are not far behind (if not ahead of) the government in subverting gay liberation. The most prosperous gay organizations are now those giving so-called "therapy" to faggots and lesbians. Big funds come in for these programs meant to fix us up. And the more conservative the ideas behind the program, the more money received. Those assuming the individual coming to them has failed and needs to be patched up in order to get back into the competitive economy—these programs line up first for funding. And some of the programs take their money directly from the gay community itself. One clinic is set up on an unashamedly profit-making basis: $35 per hour per client. If you can't pay, tough. All these programs operate on the false assumption that the "therapist" is a superior, wiser, more able person than the patient, client, or whatever they call us. If you accept that, you're already in trouble.

Much ado has been made of the American Psychiatric Association's removing us from the crippled list as though it were an honor to be severed from schizophrenics and others who have suffered from the doctors making many times the salaries of most of their patients. If we are not "sick," what about the rest? In our battle with the shrinks, too many have been willing to let them off by negotiating special favors with the doctors: if they hurt us less, they can concentrate on those less organized and at the moment less able to defend themselves. Quite frankly, no one has ever shown that a person cannot help him or herself just as well without psycho-psychiatric intervention. Every one of us may sometime or other in some crisis need a gay friend to talk with; or we may need a place to retreat to for a time. Or we may need a group in which to be mutually open and honest. (That is what a "support network" could provide.) But none of us ever needs any of the existing "therapies."

488

Another area of recolonization is academia. One of the implicit functions of the "academic" groups has been not to serve but to exclude all but a conservative minority of the gay community. By defining themselves narrowly as university-affiliated people, they automatically exclude everyone not at some university. The academy is a bastion of middle-class values: it is the paid mind-guardian of the patriarchy/fund of the republic/capitalism. It excludes women, blacks, poor people, communists, and even sloppy dressers. If we need a Gay Academic Union, we need one that would fight (not get into) the club. Gay academia must denounce false consciousness as intellectuals to help break the monopoly of academic/technological power.

And then there is religion. Frankly, we can't believe it: after years of persecution and destruction, so many gay people are willing just to forget it all! So, we must address this disgusting subject. Almost every church now has its pet gay caucus, its very own gay minister. And we have several exclusively or not-so-exclusively "gay" churches. Much of their energies go into fighting old theological battles: Jews, Protestants, Catholics, fundamentalists, Unitarians continue to spar with each other—as though their antiquated battles had anything whatever to do with us. One would think the gory business of the Reformation had been safely consigned to history, yet here are gay people still slugging it out.

Religion represents everything that is evil in humans; more than an opiate, it is an absolute poison. We see sexual repression as inherent in all the so-called "major" religions and practically every popular "minor" one we can imagine. We need not add to the centuries-long literature about the deficiencies of the church and of "God" as well. But we should describe what religion is doing within gay circles. It gobbles up inordinate amounts of money (after the psychos, MCC must be the best-financed gay group in the U.S.). Then it perpetuates the patriarchy with its male ministry. It encourages "marriage," "prayer," and other noxious habits so infused with straight meaning as to be incapable of liberation. Every outward symbol or form lends itself to some meaning, some consciousness, some interest. The symbols of religion long ago were bought off by power and oppression and straight male dominance. This goes, by the way, for the trappings of various "rational religions" as well, like formal Humanism, Transcendental Meditation, or Unitarianism.

* * *

Enough about the trials and tribulations of the struggle! Let us also congratulate ourselves for years of advance and a consolidation of our forces and successes. Faggots are popping up everywhere and faggot influence has penetrated society from rock 'n' roll to Monty Python, from modes of dress and hair to everyday language and style. We are not foolish enough to accept these as face-value triumphs. These are attempts to co-opt our revolution by the straight world, but they are desperate, last-ditch, compromises to stem the tide. Meanwhile, more positively, gay liberation periodicals like *Gay Sunshine, Gay Alternative,* and *Fag Rag* have been exploring the meaning and phenomenon of gay culture. Such literature is "the morning star of revolution."

We have had to struggle through dogmatism, "final answers," authoritarianism, didacticism, and other such pretensions that emerge again and again at every level of our understanding of ourselves. Literature has come to mean so much to all of us working on *Fag Rag* not because we have renounced politics, but because we suspect its oversimplification and seduction. Likewise, we have seemed to some to renounce literature itself and "literary values," when we merely have suspected the reactionary content of all such "standards," and necessarily have had to find our *own* literature and values—modestly, somewhat hesitantly, but with affirmation and confidence.

Some have asked radicals, "What are you doing?" This is what we're doing: we are not giving up on the gay consciousness we found after 1969. Using it as an inspiration, we are seeking new ways, implications, strategies, possibilities for its realization. Some of us are even Marxists and anarchists—in the spirit of Bertolt Brecht, who said the party needed fewer answers—people were tired of hearing know-it-alls—Brecht wanted ten questions no one could answer. Actions based on questions are the basis of our platform.

Permissions

"No Longer the Court Jesters" by Allen Young is from manuscript. It is partially based on "What Is Gay Culture," published in the *Gay Liberator* (Detroit), No. 40, Sept.–Oct. 1974. It is printed by permission of the author. Copyright © 1978 by Allen Young.

"No Man's Land" by Karla Jay is from manuscript and is printed by permission of the author. Copyright © 1978 by Karla Jay.

"Queen for a Day: A Stranger in Paradise" by Rita Mae Brown was published as "Queen for a Day" in the *Real Paper* (Cambridge, Mass.), Oct. 8, 1975, and is reprinted by permission of the author and the *Real Paper*. Copyright © 1975 by the Real Paper, Inc.

"The Bath Life Gets Respectability" by Arthur Bell was published in the *Village Voice,* Sept. 27, 1976, and is reprinted by permission of the author and the *Village Voice.* Copyright © 1976 by The Village Voice, Inc.

"Forum on Sadomasochism" is from manuscript and is printed by permission of Ian Young, John Stoltenberg, Lyn Rosen, Rose Jordan, Karla Jay, and Allen Young. Portions by Ian Young copyright © 1979 by Ian Young. Portions by John Stoltenberg copyright © 1979 by John Stoltenberg. Portions by Lyn Rosen copyright © 1979 by Lyn Rosen. Portions by Rose Jordan copyright © 1979 by Rose Jordan. Acknowledgment is made to Harper & Row for permission to reprint from *Our Blood: Prophecies and Discourses on Sexual Politics* by Andrea Dworkin, copyright © 1976 by Andrea Dworkin, and to Doubleday & Company, Inc., for permission to reprint from *Sexual Politics,* by Kate Millett, copyright © 1969 by Kate Millett.

"Phantasy Revolution" by Charley Shively was published in *Fag Rag,* No. 15, Spring 1976, and is reprinted by permission of the author and *Fag Rag.* Copyright © 1976 by *Fag Rag.*

"Sexual Anarchy" by Brandon Judell was published in

slightly different form in *Blueboy* (Miami), Aug.–Sept. 1977, and is printed by permission of the author and *Blueboy*. Copyright © 1977 by *Blueboy*.

"Why I'm Not Dancing" by Felice Newman was excerpted in the *Allegheny Feminist* (Pittsburgh) in 1977 and is reprinted by permission of the author. Copyright © 1979 by Felice Newman.

"The Cleveland Bar Scene in the Forties" by John Kelsey was published as "Cleveland Bar Scene: 30 Years Ago" by Codger in *High Gear* (Cleveland), March 1977, and is printed, with slight revisions, by permission of the author and *High Gear*. Copyright © 1977 by *High Gear*.

"Missing the Ports o Call" by Jim Jackman was published as "Ports O Call" in *Fag Rag* (Boston), No. 19, Spring 1977, and is reprinted by permission of the author and *Fag Rag*. Copyright © 1977 by *Fag Rag*.

"Toeing the Line: In Search of the Gay Male Image in Contemporary Classical Ballet" by Graham Jackson was published in the *Body Politic* (Toronto), No. 25, August 1976, and is reprinted by permission of the author and the *Body Politic*. Copyright © 1976 by The Body Politic.

"Dance Liberation" by Rob Dobson was published in *RFD* (Wolf Creek, Oregon), No. 4, Summer 1975, and is reprinted by permission of the author of *RFD*. Copyright © 1975 by *RFD*.

"Images of Gays in Rock Music" by Tommi Avicolli is from manuscript and is printed by permission of the author. Copyright © 1979 by Tommi Avicolli. Acknowledgment is made to United Artists Music Co., Inc. for permission to reprint lyrics from "Michael, Michael" by Dory Previn, copyright © 1970 by Mediarts Music Inc./Bouquet Music, and from "Midget's Lament" by Dory Previn, copyright © 1972 by Mediarts Music, Inc./Bouquet Music.

"The Growing Business Behind Women's Music" by Lynne D. Shapiro is from manuscript and is printed by permission of the author. Copyright © 1978 by Lynne D. Shapiro.

"Judy Garland and Others: Notes on Idolization and Derision" by Michael Bronski is based on an article entitled "Eighth Row Center: Where the Boys Are" in *Gay Commu-*

494